# FRESH LIPSTICK

# FRESH LIPSTICK

## Redressing Fashion and Feminism

LINDA M. SCOTT



palgrave macmillan

Pictures of ducks on page 111: From *Homes* by Sian Tucker, first published in the UK by Orchard Books, a division of The Watts Publishing Group Limited, 96 Leonard St., London EC2A 4XD.

From *Quack!* By Alan Snow, published by Doubleday. Reprinted by permission of The Random House Group, Ltd.



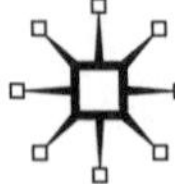



First published 2005 by
PALGRAVE MACMILLAN™
175 Fifth Avenue, New York, N.Y. 10010 and
Houndmills, Basingstoke, Hampshire, England RG21 6XS.
Companies and representatives throughout the world.

PALGRAVE MACMILLAN is the global academic imprint of the Palgrave Macmillan division of St. Martin's Press, LLC and of Palgrave Macmillan Ltd. Macmillan® is a registered trademark in the United States, United Kingdom and other countries. Palgrave is a registered trademark in the European Union and other countries.

ISBN 1-4039-6686-9

**Library of Congress Cataloging-in-Publication Data**
Scott, Linda M.
Fresh lipstick : redressing fashion and feminism / Linda M. Scott.
p. cm.
Includes bibliographical references.
ISBN 1-4039-6686-9
1. Women's clothing. 2. Clothing and dress—Psychological aspects. 3. Clothing and dress—Political aspects. 4. Fashion—Psychological aspects. 5. Feminist theory. I. Title.

GT1720.S36 2005
391'.2—dc22

2004053388

A catalogue record for this book is available from the British Library.

Design by Letra Libre, Inc.

First edition: January 2005
10 9 8 7 6 5 4 3 2 1
Printed in the United States of America.

# CONTENTS

# ACKNOWLEDGMENTS

AN ENORMOUS AMOUNT OF BACKGROUND RESEARCH WENT INTO THIS BOOK. BECAUSE I wanted it to be accessible to a wide variety of readers—in terms of length, price, density of text, and number of notes—the full documentation available does not appear here in printed form. Instead, I have posted additional documentation—not only citations but images, charts, bibliographic essays, and related links—on a website for that purpose: freshlipstick.com. I invite readers to visit and learn more about the topics covered here.

The level of data collected would not have been possible had it not been for the team of graduate students who worked with me at the University of Illinois. Their patience, perseverance, resourcefulness, and impressive work ethic made this book possible. They were sent off to the library with assignments to:

- Find all the articles about the women's movement in the *Ladies' Home Journal* and the *Woman's Home Companion* between 1910 and 1919.
- Photocopy every advertisement that refers to the women's wartime effort appearing in *Vogue* between 1941 and 1945.
- Run down every article on "women's lib" listed in the *Reader's Guide to Periodical Literature* between 1969 and 1973.
- Look at every full-page ad in each of four magazines from 1935 to 1985 and count how many models have dark hair and how many have light hair.

These are just a few of the time-counsuming but ultimately very enlightening projects that these young people accomplished. The depth of understanding that this material brought to the task of writing was substantial, so I want to thank them first: Claudia Campeanu, Catherine Coleman, Elizabeth Dailing, Nishant Dass, Bora Esenler, Amber Kramme, Arathi Kysalam, Gary LaPage, Barlow Levold, Terry Mertens, Jessica Ni, Shelley Novick, Kimberly Paul, Seema Ramalingam, Katherine Sredl, Natasha Tolstikova, Andrea Winters, and Meaka Zalkin.

Michael Schudson has been actively in support of this book since it was only a five-page proposal. I am not sure I would ever have finished all this without his encouragement. Once the book was done, James and Mary Twitchell's enthusiasm really pushed me to find a publisher. Tom O'Guinn read the entire first draft—which was

1,000 pages long—and gave wonderful comments and criticism. I am grateful to all four of these people beyond what they can ever know.

Some people say that authors write books to discover things about themselves. I thought that was silly until I wrote this book. In the process, I did learn a lot about myself, especially how important the women in my family have been in forming my sense of dress as art, as play, and as a form of self-expression. I want to thank, especially, my mother for this gift.

I am grateful to Cinda Robbins-Cornstubble and Janette Bradley Wright for having made much of the work possible. John Fleckner and his staff at the National Museum of American History and Ellen Gartrell and her staff in the Special Collections at Duke University were all of invaluable assistance. Last, I wish to thank Amanda Johson, my editor, for having been just the right audience.

INTRODUCTION

# TOSSING DOWN THE GLOVE

> All I say is examine; enquire. Look into the nature of things. Search out the ground of your opinions, the *for* and the *against.* Know why you believe, understand what you believe, and possess a reason for the faith that is in you.
>
> —*Fanny Wright*

AMERICAN FEMINISM TAKES A DIM VIEW OF BEAUTY. ACROSS THE SPECTRUM OF ACADEMIC and popular literature, feminist writers have consistently argued that a woman's attempt to cultivate her appearance makes her a dupe of fashion, the plaything of men, and thus a collaborator in her own oppression. Although this wisdom has seldom been open to question as a matter of principle, it has always produced discord at the level of practice. Even among the earliest activists, internal disputes over self-presentation were a source of divisiveness. The "founding feminists" of the nineteenth century sniped at each other for being too fashionable or too ascetic, too sexy or too prim, too vain or too careless. The suffrage organizers of the 1910s disapproved of the fashions and flirtations among the working women of their fragile coalition. Mainstream feminist leaders of the 1920s, a decidedly conservative group, cast a cold eye on the young "flappers" of their day—even though the grooming, dress, and behavior of these girls challenged gender roles at every turn. Fifty years later Second Wave feminists insisted "liberated women" stop wearing makeup and shaving their legs, a demand that polarized recruits and alienated many from the movement. The internal animosity continues to this day. The contemporary press has thoroughly noted the fault line between young women of today and feminists of the 1970s: It breaks on the topics of sex and personal appearance. Fewer have noticed that feminism alienated many mature women on these questions long ago.

My objective in this book is to demonstrate that established feminist theorists and leaders, not the ranks of the Third Wave nor the ladies at the corner beauty parlor, need to experience a change in consciousness with regard to the politics of personal appearance. By the end of my argument, I hope to convince readers that feminism's antibeauty ideology serves the interests of the few at the expense of the many. The social superiority of feminist dress reformers on dimensions of class, education, and ethnicity is recurrent: In every generation, the women with more education, more leisure, and more connections to institutions of power—from the church, to the press, to the university—have been the ones who tried to tell other women what they must wear in order to be liberated. I argue further that the received view stands on ideas about self-presentation, sexuality, consumption, power, and images that are specific to certain ethnic and class groups—and therefore needs to be reexamined if the feminist movement is to be genuinely representative of all women. I recognize that for many women, it is inconceivable that a commitment to feminism could ever be reconciled with an interest in fashion. That's because this ideology has been with us so long, is so closely linked to other cultural beliefs we now take for granted, and has been so thoroughly integrated into the histories we read that we no longer can see where it comes from.

Whether you consult popular works that press history into the service of a fashion critique—such as those written by Susan Faludi or Naomi Wolf—or more scholarly tracts—such as those by Lois Banner or Susan Bordo—the narrative is the same.[1] From the time of the industrial revolution, it is written, American women have struggled under the patriarchal power of the fashion business. The opening tableau of the antifashion narrative is invariably the steel engraving of the early fashion press. These "fashion plates" announced the ideal all were to pursue by showing tiny-waisted ladies with huge skirts and pointed toes. According to the prevailing story, women of the early 1800s obediently squeezed themselves into corsets, burdened themselves with yards of fabric, and forced their feet into miniscule slippers. Thus deprived of breath and mobility, they became the passive pawns of male capitalists.

Within a few decades, we learn, an enlightened cadre of feminists rose up to save their sisters from this plight. Somehow able to resist the powers that held all other American women in thrall, a small group of New England Protestants—among them Susan B. Anthony and Elizabeth Cady Stanton—challenged the patriarchy by refusing to conform to fashion. Although their success was limited at the time, these women inspired feminists for generations to come. As the fashion industry became ever more cunning, critics intone, the challenge to feminism was always a growing menace. The more success women had in grabbing privileges away from men, prominent authors have argued, the more fashion was retooled to keep them down.

By reinstating important omissions from this story, I plan to reveal the interests that lie behind the way it has been told. I begin with the circumstances surrounding the original dress reform movement of the mid-nineteenth century. The feminists led by Anthony and Stanton belonged to the most aggressive and powerful cultural subgroup in industrializing America: the Yankee Protestant descendants of the pre-Revolutionary aristocracy. As I explain, this early effort at "dress reform" was only one of several social initiatives in which the founding feminists joined with males of their own class to enforce dominant norms. In a nation then spinning in the power vacuum of a newly created democracy, bursting with the energy of a different kind of economy, and already teeming with hordes of immigrants who were neither Anglo nor Protestant, such "reform" efforts had implications going well beyond gender politics.

The neo-Puritan tenets of the feminist critique appear like universal truths to us now because Yankee Protestants continued to dominate American society. Thus, their views became "naturalized," as they say in cultural criticism. Other cultures and religions, including some present in America at the outset, have had markedly different attitudes toward self-decoration and considerably less discomfort with images. Indeed, the sectarian origins of American feminism are perhaps most blatantly visible in its critique of pictures. With all the fervor of Calvinists attacking Catholics, contemporary feminists have attributed magical properties to the images of commercial capitalism.

The first fashion plates appeared in the mid-1800s, but the image reproduction technology of the last quarter of the nineteenth century produced an explosion of picturing unlike anything that had gone before. The sudden availability of multiple images, consistently reproduced, created a discourse of icons that rivaled that of the printed word. It was also a time in which images of "pretty girls" held tremendous attraction for American viewers. One of the most popular, the Gibson Girl, has drawn attention from feminist writers. Therefore, I address the iconophobia of feminism in the context of the Gibson Girl, giving us an opportunity to come into close contact with the arguments about images.

The prevailing narrative consistently characterizes the new industrial economy as an all male development. And, after all, most of us grew up thinking of the "industrial revolution" as a phenomenon of heavy industry (steel, railroads, etc.), so the characterization makes intuitive sense to us. In truth, America's first industry—the business that propelled the young nation into the modern economy and put it on the map of world markets—was fashion. Textile mills, followed rapidly by factories producing shoes, hats, jewelry, and notions, produced an explosion of prosperity that had profound effects on both labor and consumption. The "mass media," also born at this time, found its most stable success in the early fashion magazines. At every level of this broadscale economic change, women were implicated: as laborers and consumers, but also as designers, writers, editors, artists, and manufacturers.

Characterizing the beauty and fashion industry as a patriarchy has therefore never been accurate or fair. Cosmetics, in particular, have been dominated by women. My readers, if they will take a moment, probably can list some of the names right off the tops of their heads: Estée Lauder, Elizabeth Arden, Helena Rubinstein, Hazel Bishop,

Dorothy Gray, Germaine Monteil, Mary Kay. These were all real people, although we know very little about most of them. In history, there are still others whose names are now unknown to most people—Ellen Demorest and Harriet Hubbard Ayer, for example—but who were once undisputed leaders of the industry. Furthermore, writing beauty ads has historically been considered "women's work" by the male managers of advertising agencies. For this reason, many of the ads feminists have dismissed as missives from manhood are actually women's texts: messages written by women, for women, about women, to women.

The changes wrought by the new economy were broad in scope and mixed in value. One thing that was clear from the start, however, was that the new economy and its products—stylish, but affordable clothing—represented a serious threat to the dominance of America's agrarian aristocracy. Employment opportunities drew people away from the farms and into the cities, put cash in their hands, and made clothing previously allowed only to aristocrats widely available. The rhetoric against fashion in the 1800s, therefore, attacked the industry that was quickly displacing the land-owning ruling class by draining away their labor force, creating new sources of wealth and forms of power, and blurring the lines between social classes through the consumption of its manufactures.

The fashion economy forever changed the class relations among women. Just as was the case before the Revolution, the broadest, deepest divide in nineteenth century America was between all who worked and those of the leisure class. An important factor in the new mix was the relative wealth and social mobility now claimed by some groups of working women. As actresses, businesswomen, and members of the women's press began to command respect previously accorded only to the nobility, alternative role models emerged. These new ideals implied different aesthetics of dress and often directly contradicted the ways "beauty," "fashion," and even "virtue" were modeled by ruling class women. Of special importance to us is that the working women's side of the culture, unlike the aristocrats', was also able to provide a plausibly attainable model of economic autonomy, something that was quite attractive to the greater population of women. Therefore, as some women began to experience success in the new industrial economy, females who had led the old society by virtue of their "noble birth" began to lose hold over the imagination of the populace. A good bit of defensive mythologizing occurred as a result. I retell one very prominent story—the tale of the bloomer costume—in a way that illuminates the lines drawn between the women of the landed aristocracy and those of the modern economy.

The "modern women" of the industrial order had their own brand of feminism, one that I argue was not only more economically oriented, but was also more tolerant and ecumenical. During the past 150 years, this more secular group has supported major feminist initiatives through its market and media activities—and, in many cases, has made a profound difference in the success of those efforts. So, although it has become commonplace for feminists to assert the fundamental incompatibility between feminism and the market, the historical record is considerably less clear-cut than we might think.

The association of feminism with intellectual women emerged in force during the suffrage campaign of the 1910s. The most radical leaders of the suffrage initiative were employed by universities, usually women's colleges. Even today, fewer than 30 percent of Americans have finished college, and only in the past ten years have women equaled men in their attendance. So the college-educated woman is still a minority among the total population of females. Imagine, then, how far removed from the average woman these early twentieth-century academics were. Known in their time as scholastic suffragists, these women dressed in austere uniforms and lived alone or with other women. They were noticeably different from the fabulously wealthy women who supported them with money and connections, *and* from the genteel middle-class women who marched and petitioned, *and* from the working women who put their considerable numbers behind the cause. But the scholastic suffragists considered themselves superior to *all* the women they led, based on their greater education. To them, other women's desires for creature comforts, pretty clothes, affection, and family were merely the private weaknesses of the less committed. Here arrives full-blown a philosophical split that could already be seen faintly in the Anthony-Stanton years—that between the "heroine of the mind" and the "heroine of the body." First articulated in the 1910s, this privileging of the mind over the body continues to this day in feminist works.[2] Such critics have come to view "intellectual" and "feminist" as synonyms, thus giving educated women automatic superiority over those who had fewer opportunities or other talents.

Today's scholastic feminists take the same liberties their forebears did. For instance, Sherna Berger Gluck, a feminist sociologist, opens her book by unabashedly describing her own first-day-of-class assessments of students; she quickly pegged those who wore "symbols of oppression" (e.g., high heels) as complacent backsliders who had no clue about the sacrifices made for them by her own generation. As recent books, articles, and surveys have made evident, young women are keenly aware of the snap judgments made of them by the older generation of feminists. Perhaps younger readers will take some comfort in learning that dress has been a point of conflict whenever the power of one generation of feminists had to be handed to next. For instance, when Stanton and Anthony were deposed by the second generation, they deeply resented the way the new leader tried to get them to act and dress "like ladies" at public appearances. Stanton and Anthony, so certain of their own vision, felt the younger group took the gains women had won for granted and saw this attention to dress and manners as a mark of *their* complacency.[3]

This generational conflict has been repeated, often at subtle levels and other times rising to a crisis. In the schism of the Roaring Twenties, for example, feminist leaders failed to come to terms with the "private desires" of younger women for beauty, pleasure, affection, and family. Their close-mindedness resulted in a significant loss of steam for the movement—one that was not really recovered until the Second Wave of the 1970s. I highlight the uncanny similarities between the intergenerational conflict of our own times and the destructive struggle that occurred between the "Old Feminists" of the suffrage movement and the "New Feminists" of the Jazz Age. For those of us "old feminists" who would rather leave behind a living legacy than a politically-correct graveyard, it is a lesson of history to be taken humbly to the heart.

Moving through the Great Depression and war years, I document the steady rise of businesswomen as role models in both public life and fashion. Late-twentieth-century feminists have written as if working women first appeared in the 1970s and as if American culture has always found them masculine and unappealing. Therefore, I expect readers will be surprised to learn that businesswomen were popular heroines and fashion leaders through most of the century, often deemed the most desirable of women by men.

Of course, the function of dress to attract men is at the center of the issue. Feminist writers, in an extreme bias, consistently cast personal appearance in terms of sexual provocation. Explaining the appearance of *any* woman in *any* society requires assembling a mass of detail about the natural environment, the historical moment, the social hierarchy, the rituals and metaphors of the culture, as well as her own character, politics, skills, resources, and hopes. Yet feminist theory doggedly reduces self-presentation to sexual allure—and does so in a way that condemns desire as a matter of principle.

Feminism is caricatured today as a haven for man-hating, asexual women, of whom the epitome is the butch lesbian. Yet the problem with American feminism's sexualizing of dress is *nowhere* more painfully evident than in the way it has treated the lesbian community. I suspect that another surprise awaiting readers is that the lesbian subculture has so often been at odds with mainstream feminism in matters of personal presentation.

In the post–World War II period, the old Puritan precepts about fashion, images, and sex remained largely intact, but were dressed anew in theories that held currency with feminists through the last half of the twentieth century. The Cold War brought fear of control by unseen forces to a high pitch among the American populace. Many of the theories that emerged in this context—such as subliminal control through images—were incorporated into the feminist critique, allowing the old Calvinism to seem once again fresh. Despite the authors' critical approach to Freud, it was Simone de Beauvoir's *The Second Sex* (1953) and Betty Friedan's *The Feminine Mystique* (1963) that first made Freudian analysis a major tool in the feminist critique of fashion, advertising, and consumer culture.[4] In the chapter on the 1950s, I look closely at Beauvoir's and Friedan's foundational texts for their special relationship to the fears of their times.

The major theoretical influence on late-twentieth-century feminists, however, was Marxism. Having grown up in the material comfort of Cold War capitalism's households, the Baby Boomers flaunted their parents' ideological Satan in service to agendas that would have been as shocking to Marx as they were to Mom and Dad. The free love, theatrical dress, body painting, and "let-it-all-hang-out" sensuality of the 1960s counterculture were no more consistent with socialist ideology than with capitalist militarism. The "disconnect" became only too clear as Second Wave feminism rolled forward. Dress became a point of contention when militant refugees from campus groups took over the movement from the professional women who founded the National Organization for Women (NOW). Thereafter, Second Wave factions often were caught up in their own political pettiness—and their borders were marked in terms of appearance. I document the Second Wave's rather nasty internal discourse over dress as a symptom of competing groups struggling for preeminence within the movement itself.

The influence of Marxism solidified in the 1980s, when many campus radicals ended up on university faculties. Pointedly overlooking the female oppression universally manifest in traditional cultures and communist states, these radical academics also unwittingly furthered views that went back to the Puritan aristocrats. A large body of literature was produced that involved, primarily, a critique of capitalism through an attack on pictures and self-decoration. The result was an ideology that dealt with significant social problems by blaming them on the images of fashion. Child abuse became the fault of cosmetic advertisers, and rape could be blamed on the manufacturers of bedsheets. Campus feminist groups developing under this influence used dress as an instrument of exclusion. One 1990s graduate reported that, though she was converted to feminism upon her arrival at college, took classes in women's studies, and joined the women's coalition, her lipstick habit drew fire from her new friends: "I was different and, therefore, a threat to their neat, closed, secret, homogeneous community."[5]

"Celebrity feminism" developed in concert with academic feminism: Journalists and academics both wrote books or produced videos centered on beauty as oppression. This very lucrative development for the publishing industry produced a number of works, such as Naomi Wolf's *The Beauty Myth,* that have been marketed to the next generation with resounding success. Much of that literature, of which Mary Pipher's *Reviving Ophelia* is the most prominent example, focused on eating disorders. Today those young women who do identify themselves as feminists define their mission in terms of their own body image, with particular emphasis on questions of weight. Elsewhere, however, feminist offshoots like the Girlies differentiate themselves from their mothers' feminism by embracing the pleasures of dress and the powers of sexuality—and are promptly discredited and dismissed by older feminists. By far the most common response to feminism among young women today, however, is to embrace women's rights but deny the label "feminist"—a development that seems to be closely linked to the lingering Second Wave politics of appearance.[6]

Working women have fought different battles since the 1970s, chalking up a staggering number of "firsts" in one generation. Feminist professors, however, uniformly hostile to anything market-oriented, categorically dismissed the claims of corporate women to membership in the movement, although the books they write consistently count the recent gains of professionals among the fruits of feminism. Thus, once more a rift between feminist academics and women's rights–oriented professionals can be observed on the American scene, punctuated as always by a difference in dress.

My hope is that the framework provided by this book will allow readers to see within today's debate traces of previous battles, former jealousies, and long-standing prejudices. By learning the history of the antibeauty ideology, we can come to understand why conflicts now occur between, on one side, feminists with ties to universities and, on the other side, any one of many subgroups: young women, women in business, lesbians, women of color, women in the arts, and women of the working class. What I hope will also become clear is that academic feminists have a vested interest in perpetuating the antibeauty ideology. Ultimately, therefore, I wish to convince readers that the stance of today's "Old Feminists" originated in the cultural control efforts of an aristocratic, sectarian group, but evolved over the next fifteen decades as a way of maintaining the leadership of academics against the rising power of more secular women.

The history of feminism as most Americans know it—the story of the women's movement as it appears in textbooks, introductory books, and surveys—invariably focuses on the Stanton–Anthony dynasty as the origin and progression of the movement.[7] Thus, for most folks, this *is* the story of feminism. The women recognized as the founders of the movement belonged to a class that valued education for both genders; as a result, they themselves were literate and articulate. And, although they challenged institutional power over women, they themselves were well connected to the institutions that held sway over early industrial America. As women of the leisure class, they used their free time, their education, and their good connections to publish articles and books. Their writings have since comprised the bulk of the documentary evidence from which feminist history is written.

Yet there were other women actively involved in the movement, and some did leave behind a record. I introduce several of these women—Elizabeth Oakes Smith, Sarah Josepha Hale, Jane Cunningham Croly, for instance—in the story I am about to tell. These women differed from the mainstream feminist ideology of their day in that they valued economic empowerment over legal solutions, believed that dress was important, and thought that affectionate relations with men were crucial. All of them were employed by the fashion industry or its media. And all of them have been either ignored or discredited by feminist historians, despite their clear, active, and important contributions to women's rights. Still others, such as Fanny Wright, Victoria Woodhull, and Emma Goldman, were social activists who argued passionately for the rights of women to have beauty and pleasure, especially in sexual expression. These three are *easily* among the most radical women in feminist history, not only for their thoughts but for their actions. When today's feminists argue that sex, beauty, and pleasure make us weak or turn us into "objects," the voices of these brave forebears are simply blocked out. By helping readers hear those who have been forgotten or unfairly dismissed, I hope to show them that viable choices are there to be made.

At the base of the antibeauty prejudice is a compulsion to enforce homogeneity. Put differently, what we are dealing with here is the *intolerance of difference.* Feminist criticism glosses over this issue by insisting upon our sameness. Whatever other inequalities may exist among us, they say, we are equally enjoined to push up our breasts, redden our lips, or arrange our hair. Drawing as always on the narrative of the Steel-Engraving Lady, historian Lois Banner blatantly asserts that it has always been such: "It was women who curled their hair and dyed it, who painted their faces and fingernails, who tight-laced their corsets and wore tiny shoes that pinched their toes, who tried in a variety of ways to be beautiful. In doing so, they participated in rituals as central to women's separate experience of life as childbirth or the domestic chores on which historians have usually focused. And of all the elements that have defined women's separate culture, the pursuit of beauty, then as now, transcended class and racial barriers."[8]

While self-decoration is a behavior that transcends all human groupings (and not just the females), access to the means of decoration, the social circumstances of dress, the local aesthetics of grooming, and the morality of self-presentation vary a great deal. Thus, all women in American history have *not* experienced the beauty issue in the uniform way Banner asserts. Because of the wide variation involved, the general rules and universal principles feminists have claimed for their view do not bear up under critical examination. In the next chapter, I take a look at some nineteenth-century female groups that didn't match the demographic profile of the early dress reformers—and see how their situations cause us to question the "natural" ideal of the Puritan feminists.

CHAPTER 1

# THE NATURAL FALLACY

WHETHER SKIRTS WERE UP OR DOWN, HAIR CURLY OR STRAIGHT, MAKE-UP "IN" OR "out," feminists have criticized whatever the prevailing fashion found attractive, advocating instead a more "natural" look. Exactly *what* counted as natural was only defined in negative terms: "natural" is what we would look like if we did *not* wear corsets, hoop skirts, lipstick, push-up bras, or whatever the latest bugaboo happened to be. The alternative was presumed to be self-evident. "Natural" is what we would look like if we weren't forced to spend so many hours and use so many products making ourselves look presentable. "Natural" is the absence of artifice.

If we try to define "natural" in positive terms, however—what *is* permissible, rather than what is not—we run into a little difficulty. Let's imagine a woman as she would be found "in nature," without "man-made" intervention. Under this requirement, any tool or substance not occurring in the natural environment would be an artifice. There would be no scissors for haircuts, razors for shaving, soaps for cleaning. No toothbrushes or combs. All naturally occurring processes would be allowed to run their course: nails growing, hair matting, teeth rotting. A human being totally free of artifice would be unkempt, unclean, unshaven, and probably uncomfortable and unhealthy.

But wait. I can anticipate readers protesting that I am taking the argument to an unintended extreme. Perhaps we really just want to imagine a woman as she would be without the trappings of modernity, before the corruption of industrialization—the precapitalist, advertising-free woman. Suppose we were to go in search of this woman, into the rainforests or across the deserts to anyplace as yet untouched by "civilization"; what would we find?

Around the globe and throughout historical time, we would find human beings grooming and decorating themselves. We would find that even our ideas about what is "basic" grooming (and therefore natural and permissible) are peculiar to our times. Indeed, guidelines and practices, such as how to keep your teeth clean and what to wash with, vary a great deal over time and across cultures. Furthermore, people in preindustrial societies display a wealth of purely decorative practices, such as braiding or beading the hair and painting the skin. Many groups use techniques that permanently alter the body and employ practices our society views has traditionally viewed as harmful: tattooing, scarification, piercing. In short, humans demonstrate a consistent propensity to alter their appearance, often in dramatic ways. From a cross-cultural perspective, the feminist notion of "natural" grooming is a perverse fiction. What is natural for human beings is artifice.[1]

Grooming, in fact, is part of the essence of being human, the mark of a creature who is inescapably social and inextricably enmeshed in the use of symbols. Our manner of self-presentation is central to both individual identity and group membership. This is one reason why prisons, concentration camps, and other institutions of incarceration shave the heads of inmates, issue uniforms, and restrict access to mirrors or grooming aids. Being barred from grooming tends to obliterate a sense of self, while severing the felt connection to the community. When we refer to such policies as "dehumanizing," we mean exactly what we say. Is it any wonder, then, that telling women they must stop grooming themselves—or that they must groom themselves in some prespecified way—meets with resistance?

As a visible expression of the social order, grooming practices mark a society's members by rank, gender, occupation, and age, and also communicate identity, affinity, or aspiration. Failure or refusal to groom communicates resistance, carelessness, or incapacity. Thus, it is never possible simply to "opt out" of the discourse of dress. No one can dress in a way that signifies nothing.

Nor can we generalize on the basis of effort, coverage, or encumbrance in the way that feminists writing about the oppression that inheres in hair curling, cosmetics, or high heels often do. It is not true that the amount of decoration—or its permanence or painfulness—is always greater for those of lesser status. On the contrary, the right to alter one's appearance is often an earned privilege. Neither theatricality nor sensual display, furthermore, are the exclusive domain of the female and powerless. In many societies, it is the man who paints his face and struts his stuff while the woman remains modestly adorned or wrapped in secrecy.

What gives dress significance is the social and historical setting. Innovations and alternatives become infused with meanings associated with the times or the group adopting them: Bobby sox, peace beads, and leisure suits all point to a period in time as well as a social subgroup. Even these are subject to reinterpretation when adopted by a different group or reinvented in a new time. A Mohawk, for example, is not just for Mohawks anymore. No single practice or manner always suggests either power or oppression. Instead, like any other set of symbols, the signs of grooming must always be read in context.

In a complex society such as our own, the variation in self-presentation is enormous. The explosion in material culture has also created an endless stream of vehicles for expression through dress. Amid all this finely differentiated grooming activity, we should be suspicious of any *one* group that lays claim to a "natural" manner of self-presentation. Asserting the power to define what is "natural" is a characteristic of ideology—and therefore a symptom of dominant class interests struggling to maintain control.

The idea that feminism's antibeauty stance is a gesture of dominance seems counterintuitive at first. How can an oppressed group (women) be trying to maintain a control they have never had? Herein lies the reason it has been so important to universalize this argument. As long as we ignore the fact that all women belong *also* to other groups—different classes, races, religions—we can turn a blind eye to the reality that some women have advantages over others and have, in the past, acted alongside the men of their own group to ensure the continuation of their privileges. By asserting that women must all dress the same way—conform to the same "ideal"—we make a space where we can overlook their unequal access to the goods used in grooming and dress, as well as the ethnic differences that cause each group to view particular items or colors or methods as acceptable, beautiful, or immoral.

The suggestion that feminism's natural standard is a form of ideology also seems counterintuitive because "basic" grooming practices—bathing, brushing the teeth—are seldom attacked. Instead, the focus is on "superficial" practices, such as the use of makeup. We assume that makeup is a modern phenomenon, imposed by capitalism on humans who otherwise would not paint, while it seems obvious to us that any natural appearance would also be a washed and brushed one. As we shall see, however, the habits underpinning what we take to be a natural appearance actually constitute an aesthetic with identifiable—and recent—historical origins. Bathing with soap, washing the hair, brushing the teeth, and manicuring the nails have been made practicable by the products of industrialization—with no little assistance from advertising. These practices, in fact, are newer and more peculiar to our culture than face and body painting, which have long been found in societies around the planet.

The imperial powers of seventeenth- and eighteenth-century Europe attempted to rout the practice of body painting in conquered nations on every continent. The conquerors found such practices immoral, reading sexual provocation into whatever "primitive" grooming they found, regardless of the meaning for the native group. Further, the amount of time indigenous people spent on self-decoration seemed inordinate to the new rulers—not surprising, since most conquered people were harnessed to labor for the Europeans. Thus, the insistence that indigenous groups stop painting themselves was symptomatic of the enforcement of the conquerors' values and instrumental in carrying out their agendas. This attempt appears in the American experience as the Europeans broke both the Natives they found and the Africans they brought.

Keep in mind that, like the Africans and Indians, the Europeans were not themselves a completely homogeneous group. The French, certainly, had very different ideas about self-presentation than did the British. Even among the British subjects who emigrated to the New World, Puritans and Anglicans were viciously at odds about the morality of soap. As the many tribes of indigenous peoples, the transported clans of Africa, and the migrants from Europe intermingled, their dress and grooming habits also intermixed. For this reason, the local cultures across the continent at the opening of the nineteenth century had widely varying practices and attitudes.

Nevertheless, the dress reform movement that originated at the same time and place as American feminism pretended to a clear-cut choice between "nature" and "artifice." As was so typical of the Yankee Protestant culture, the risks of "artifice" were cast in moral and magical terms—sex or sorcery was never far behind a fashionable look. Of course, the Puritan tradition is familiar to most of us. In fact, it's the only American tradition many of us know much about, because our mythology (the landing of the *Mayflower,* the first Thanksgiving, the Salem witch trials) leads us to think of the New England Puritans as our national forebears. In point of fact, however, most of us hail from one or more of the *other* ethnic groups that lived in America in the 1800s.

## SITUATING THE SUBCULTURE

When we look at the peoples who occupied the entire geographic area that would eventually become the forty-eight contiguous states, we can see that cultural diversity is not a new thing in America. At the time of the Revolution, about half of the colonists claimed British descent, but that group was concentrated in New England. Elsewhere on the East Coast, English immigrants mingled with Dutch, German, French, and other European strains. African descendants accounted for about 17 percent of the population; most were in the South. Up until the 1830s, large numbers of Creek, Cherokee, Choctaw, Chickasaw, and Seminole still lived in Georgia, Mississippi, Alabama, and the Carolinas. When Louisiana joined the young United States, New Orleans immediately became the fourth largest city in America and there was very little that was Anglo-Protestant about it. By midcentury, Salt Lake City had a population of 148, all of them Mormons, and many people in St. Louis still spoke French. The population in many areas of the West was predominantly Spanish and, therefore, Catholic.[2]

Beginning in the mid-1840s—at exactly the time the early feminists began organizing—the ethnic makeup of the former British colonies underwent a sweeping change. Prior to 1840, fewer than 10,000 persons a year had emigrated to the United States. Then, in 1842, over 100,000 immigrants arrived in America, rising to more than 200,000 five years later, and reaching nearly 500,000 a year by the mid-1850s. Up until the 1880s, most immigrants (about 85 percent) were from countries in northern or western Europe, such as Ireland, Germany, and France. By the turn of the century, fully 80 percent were from southern and eastern Europe, primarily Italy,

Poland, and Russia. Notably, throughout the period of increased immigration, the newcomers were mostly Catholic or Jewish, not Protestant.

If we keep in mind that the entire population of the colonies was only about 6 million at the beginning of this period, we can better appreciate how invasive this influx of foreigners must have felt to American citizens. By 1850, in fact, nearly half of the Boston population was either foreign-born or of foreign parentage; within thirty years, the Yankee Protestants had become a minority. By 1900 three-quarters or more of Boston, New York, Chicago, and Detroit were "of foreign stock." And by that time, Anglo Protestants were an ethnic minority in most cities of the Northeast. The notion that American culture is identical to Anglo-Protestant culture, therefore, has always had a certain purposeful myopia about it. That group, although large, was nevertheless a limited and identifiable ethnic subculture.

America's early feminists—such as Susan B. Anthony, Lucretia Mott, and Elizabeth Cady Stanton—were passionately loyal to this Anglo-Protestant group. Their attitudes toward dress were also clearly rooted in the Puritan tradition. The founding feminists, for instance, showed a strong preference for simple black dresses with white collars. And, although they did indeed complain of the discomfort of corsets and the nuisance of long, heavy skirts, these women made fashion a moral issue, not just a practical one. Among them, the simplest adornment—a single flower in a bonnet, for example—could bring charges of vanity, false values, social aspiration, and wastefulness. In their calls for simplicity of dress, the founding feminists were echoing years of conservative tradition in their own community rather than making a groundbreaking critique, as is often claimed.[3]

Histories usually omit the sectarian subtext of the early feminists' dress attitudes, even though it was clearly a motivating factor in their efforts to "reform" the dress of other women. Instead, we are told only that the founding mothers wished to cast off the shackles of fashion so they could dress in a "natural" manner that was less sexy or confining than women of their times were forced to wear. Critics of the period (as well as those writing today) focused rhetorically on the evils of the corset. Corsets, by squeezing internal organs and restricting breathing, are supposed to actually have brought about the fragile passivity of the women who wore them. Horror stories of tight-laced, tiny waists suggest the entire female population of the nineteenth century struggled for breath. Like the bound feet of her Chinese sister, the American female's bound body was said to be the visible chain of her enslavement. Freedom of movement, after all, was symptomatic of the legal and economic liberty enjoyed by men.

Feminist historians, ignoring the subcultural struggles over dress in mid-nineteenth-century America, argue that a single ideal—the Steel-Engraving Lady—was imposed uniformly on all females. Dress reformers then and now have argued that, if freed from the pressures of fashion, women would embrace a more natural aesthetic.

They would move freely, dress modestly, and refrain from artifices. Their minds would be liberated, and they would speak out against oppression. They would eat right, exercise, and sleep well. They would not try to look attractive to men, nor yearn for other pleasures of the flesh, but would focus on developing the spirit.

To fully grasp how important it is to situate this argument in the class and ethnic origins of the early feminists, it helps to consider groups of women who, although they lived in America at the same time, had a different relationship to the Steel-Engraving ideal. So, let's take a look at some women who inhabited the same continent when the feminists first gathered together in Seneca Falls, New York, in 1848.

## COUNTEREXAMPLES TO THE COMMON WISDOM

In the same year as the Seneca Falls meeting, but beside a lake about five hundred miles to the west, a group of white missionaries was trying to enforce its own dress reform movement. The Great Lakes Indians—Ojibwa, Cree, and Algonquin—had been hunter-gatherer societies before the arrival of French Jesuits in the early seventeenth century. For nearly two hundred years, the women of the native tribes had foiled the "reform" efforts first of Catholic, then Lutheran, Methodist, and Presbyterian missionaries by refusing to wear western dress, convert to Christianity, or send their daughters to the mission school. In the traditional culture of the Great Lakes tribes, the native men and women both openly expressed sexual desire, freely choosing and changing mates. The effort to subjugate these women involved setting severe restrictions on their previous sexual freedom. The European missionaries found the Great Lakes women dirty, licentious, and generally brazen. The tenacity with which these "savage" women held to traditional religious beliefs and rituals only reinforced the Europeans' contempt. But by the end of the 1840s, the missionaries were still at a stalemate.[4]

Efforts to impose western dress were typical of the European culture's attempts to "civilize" the Native Americans. The missionaries saw the clothing of the Great Lakes tribes, although probably more comfortable and practical than any they were trying to impose, as symptomatic of cultural differences in sexual behavior (the perceived licentiousness) and religious practices (the "heathenism" or "idolatry") of the native spirituality. Thus, the directive to wear western dress was not a request to wear objectively more "moral" clothing; rather it was the concrete articulation of the missionaries' disdain for the native culture itself.

Due south of Seneca Falls lived still more women whose experience with "fashion" was radically different. Seldom given access to grooming materials and almost never allowed to bathe, slave women wore their clothes, usually issued to them once a year with little regard to size or gender, until they were rags. These African women were routinely made to do "men's work" and were forced to wear breeches while they did it. Slaveowners purposely blurred sex distinctions through clothing as a tactic to destroy the slaves' individual identities in part by denying their gender. Wearing trousers certainly allowed the freedom of movement to work, but the unrestricted movement the slaves had in their dress was symptomatic of subordination, not dominance. Withholding grooming tools also dehumanized black women in order that they could be traded as commodities and owned as property—masters often groomed their slaves for market using the same tools they used on animals. Thus these women were "natural" as a direct consequence of their utter powerlessness and chattel status. To talk of free white women being "forced" to wear corsets by magical fashion icons, thereby becoming "slaves to fashion," seems an insensitive exaggeration in light of the physical and institutional force articulated in the black female slave's "natural" look.[5]

In the backwoods of the South, poor whites intermarried with Seminole and Cherokee, mingling blood, custom, and property until, in the early 1800s, the Indians were betrayed by the national government and marched west to reservations. Experience with the duplicity of educated Anglos made poor white women wary of outsiders. Because of their isolation and their previous interchange with Natives, they dressed more like their indigenous sisters than like Yankee feminists. The young ones, in fact, displayed their bodies in a way that would have incensed the reformers. An itinerant preacher once described them: "The Young Women have a most uncommon Practise, which I cannot break them off. They draw their Shift as tight as possible to the Body, and pin it close, to shew the roundness of their breasts, and slender Waists (for they are generally finely shaped) and draw their Petticoat close to their Hips to shew the fineness of their limbs—so that they might as well be in Puri Naturalibus—Indeed Nakedness is not censurable or indecent here, and they expose themselves often quite Naked, without Cermony [*sic*]—Rubbing themselves and their Hair with Bears Oil and tying it up behind them in a Bunch like the Indians." The women of the remote hills of the South were uniformly illiterate. They lived in a world peopled by spirits and demons, where God spoke directly and conjuring was a prestige occupation. Potions and spells were the expected accompaniments to beauty aids. The "natural" state of these women, although they were sheltered from the fashion magazines and artifices of commercial culture, was not what the dress reformer would expect. Here, far removed from the ire of moralists, women dabbled in magic and mated without benefit of contract or sacrament, "more irregularly and unchastely than the Indians." Yet these women were hardly fragile sex toys. They knew danger and hardship in a way none of the Seneca Falls women could have imagined.[6]

❧

Another group of women moving westward across the prairies in the late 1840s held on desperately to the accoutrements of their civilization. Mature pioneer women often resisted abandoning families, friends, and culture to plunge into the wilderness toward some unknown end. Many died on the trip West. Others went mad. Some retained their sense of connectedness by holding on to objects and practices of the culture they had left behind.[7]

Women smuggled velvet or lace dresses in wagons their men had dedicated to "necessities." In the wilderness, the gowns were lovingly mended and patched, sometimes with pieces of cotton or homespun, until they must have looked outrageous. The physical conditions on the frontier—dust, dirty water—also precluded the maintenance of Eastern standards of grooming. And, in any case, the need for labor was so great that time for grooming or pleasure was scarce. Because homesteads were often at long distances from each other, there were few social gatherings, creating among settlers an often overwhelming sense of social isolation. The rare occasion for wearing pretty clothes provided a badly needed break from the drudgery everyday life became. "Dressing up" reasserted both personhood and cultural identity. Ridiculous as they may have looked in their patched and outdated clothes, occasionally these women could use their dress to remind the community (and themselves) that they were not merely work animals. Among the women who moved west, a "natural" appearance often bespoke isolation and anomie, not superior spirituality or feminist awareness.

Those who moved to the West as young girls, however, often reveled in the freedom of the frontier, gladly dropping the restrictions of the "civilized" culture, eager to exchange fine manners for six-shooters and corsets for saddles. This difference in response was often played out in generational conflict. Adrietta Applegate Hixon, for instance, remembered that her mother made her wear a sunbonnet across the entire Overland Trail: "While traveling, mother was particular about Louvinia and me wearing our sunbonnets and long mitts in order to protect our complexions, hair and hands. Much of the time I should like to have gone without that long bonnet poking out over my face, but mother pointed out to me some girls who did not wear bonnets and as I did not want to look as they did, I stuck to my bonnet, finally growing used to it. . . . In the evening our bonnets were hung up to the ridge pole above the wagon, and mother had some sort of cream lotion for our hands and faces that we occasionally used when her eye was upon us." The pains taken by Mrs. Hixon was a poignant expression of hope, since it articulated the presumption that the daughters would survive to the end of the journey, an outcome that was by no means assured. Imposing sunbonnets further asserted the hope that at the other end of their travels would be a culture not unlike the one they had left behind, with women in bonnets, acceptable men, and a sympathetic community. Given the deprivation that probably lay ahead for Mrs. Hixon and her daughters, the story of the sunbonnets seems more heartbreaking than frivolous.[8]

Historians have called the glorified story of the brave pioneer mothers "the sunbonnet myth." To the first daughters of the West, however, the sunbonnet symbolized the sad legacy of displacement. The next generation, therefore, claimed new modes of dress—whether fancy, fashionable, or aggressively masculine—as the rights of daughters whose mothers had so little and struggled so much. By the end of the nineteenth century, the unconventional and theatrical styles characteristic of "western girls" were viewed contemptuously by moralists in the East. Popular interest, however, fueled sensational novels and Wild West shows—complete with heroines who provided an attractive alternative ideal to the Steel-Engraving Lady. Many women on the Atlantic seaboard emulated western celebrities such as Annie Oakley, a fact that casts doubt on feminist assertions that only one model was available and that nineteenth-century women were so duped they could not make choices.[9]

At the time of the first women's rights convention, a community of two hundred shacks stood on the edge of a cold bay about 2,600 miles due west of Seneca Falls. Although the government of the United States had just annexed the area, San Francisco was not—nor would it ever be—very similar to the New England Puritan culture that arrogantly declared itself to be "American." Within a year the discovery of gold brought thousands into northern California. Many came across the Overland Trail from the former British colonies, but other immigrants came by sea, pouring into the area without ever passing through Boston, New York, or Philadelphia.

Some of the fastest growth was in the Chinese population. Only 325 Chinese came to California in 1849; by 1851, 20,000 were arriving every year. Chinese males outnumbered females twenty to one. Most men left wives or fiancées at home, expecting to return to married life. Because of unanticipated hardships and severe immigration restrictions, many never went home and most were unable to bring families to America. So the Chinese population was a community of bachelors—with a huge demand for prostitutes.

An enormous smuggling operation brought thousands of Chinese girls into the country as sex slaves. Most actually were children—ranging in age from six to nineteen—and most were brought by force or deception. Many were sold to slave traders by their own parents. Because they were peasants, none of these girls had the bound feet American culture associates with Chinese women. Instead, these captives wore traditional Chinese peasant dress: sturdy sandals, cotton tunics, and trousers. Although their clothing should have given them freedom of movement and self-determination—at least according to feminist theory—these young girls were kept like caged animals from the moment they left China. Some were smuggled into the country packed in crates. A few gained a modicum of freedom by dressing in fancy clothes and becoming "high-class prostitutes," but most were kept in "cribs," four-by-six-foot compartments with heavily barred doors. They were forced to have sex with hundreds of men; if they refused or even failed to please any of their customers, they were beaten with sticks or starved to death.[10]

In time, American Protestant missionary women began a rescue effort. As visible representatives of the eastern U.S. culture, these women could stride boldly into the Chinatowns of California and release the crib girls. Chinese men were afraid to interfere in public with a woman whose appearance announced her alliance with white Protestantism. The juxtaposition of the (relatively) powerful white woman in her corset and long skirts against the utter degradation of the Chinese child in trousers is an instructive contradiction to the current feminist ideology on dress.

In the nineteenth century, stories occasionally surfaced of women posing as husband and wife. Often some unforeseen tragedy caused their discovery: an arrest, an illness, a death. In a few cases, the couple had been living in a community for years and the revelation was met with shock. Thus there were women, however few, who dressed and lived as men for most of their lives. They had the rights and privileges that men were given, as long as the community believed they were male. Were these women free? Were they powerful? Did their male dress liberate them from the bondage of sex?[11]

It hardly seems reasonable to say that women who had to live their lives posing as what they were not were actually more free than privileged Victorian women in their corsets and petticoats. Although these cross-dressers may have been more physically comfortable, the emotional discomfort of living as a sexual being for which the culture had, as yet, no words must have been painful in the extreme. And what of the "wives"? Even though they dressed to be feminine in the conventional way, these women could scarcely be dismissed as dupes of the patriarchy, since they lived in perilous defiance of sexual norms every day of their lives.

Native Americans, slave women, frontier women, poor whites, Chinese, and lesbians seem to have had quite a different experience with fashion than that which was described by nineteenth-century dress reformers or by historians of feminism. It seems that the Steel-Engraving Lady ideal, far from being uniformly imposed on all women, was peculiar to a specific historical subgroup. Further, these counterexamples, each in its own way, disprove principles of dress first articulated in the nineteenth century and taken for granted today. We cannot assume that "natural" is an easy thing to define or that a natural state is always good or rational. We certainly cannot assume that powerlessness is universally expressed in restrictive, sexually provocative dress. The notion that a natural appearance would be any less sexual than an "artificial" one is definitely not indicated. These counterexamples, therefore, suggest that something is fundamentally false about an argument we have accepted these 150 years.

And what of the relationship between such counterexemplars and the culture's ideas of beauty? It is axiomatic in feminist criticism that our culture offers only one ideal at a time and that disempowered groups are explicitly excluded from the acceptable range of what is beautiful—thus, the women admired in American popular culture are always of Anglo ethnicity. But the historical record suggests that many images of women were attractive to our forebears, reflecting the diversity that has always characterized American culture. Although Europeans consistently declared Indian women ugly, dirty, and subhuman, the idea of a beautiful "Indian princess" is present in the earliest myths and pictures of North America. During the nineteenth century, at the very moment when the Native Americans were being extinguished, an extraordinary number of Indian heroines appeared in plays, poems, novels, and pictures. Sarah Winnemucca and Bright Eyes La Flesche used the idea of the Indian Princess quite effectively to appeal to eastern Americans in their efforts to save their own tribes.[12] Chinese immigrants were despised with a vicious rancor, but images of Chinese women still appeared in advertisements for silks and fragrances from "the Orient." The first traders from the United States to go through New Mexico, Arizona, and California were struck by "the young women of Spanish ancestry," who deliberately made themselves attractive to men, wore considerably less clothing than women in the East, and yet were just as "respectable." Relations between Anglos and Hispanics in the Southwest were bloody in the nineteenth century, but the Spanish ideal of beauty remained.

While Latina, Asian, and Native American women do appear in the popular imagery, pictures of beautiful black women are absent until the 1960s. Yet American history provides many stories of black women mating with white men—sometimes for life. The racism emerging in the United States after the Civil War masked the reality that the races were intimately co-mingled, even in the South.[13] The difficulty of determining who was black and who was white created the "one drop" rule of racial identity, in which any black blood in a person's ancestry made the person black in the eyes of the law and the community. Laws against intermarriage between whites and blacks remained on the books of most states until the 1950s. None of this would have been necessary if whites did not sometimes find blacks attractive.

Some black women even used beauty in unorthodox ways to gain power over whites. For instance, in nineteenth-century New Orleans, beautiful voodoo queen Marie Laveau commanded fear and respect from both black and white communities by dressing in a provocative way and orchestrating sensual theater that evoked danger and the underworld. San Francisco's Mary Ellen Pleasant produced the same effect.[14] Underneath the stereotypical "Mammy" images of the white press, therefore, is a subtext of racial anxiety over the attractiveness of real black women.

In contrast to the conventional feminist wisdom, therefore, I maintain that there has never been only one female ideal in the American cultural discourse, or even only two, but always many. Throughout this book, I identify images drawn around particular cultural subtypes. Some of these, like the Indian princess, are rooted in racial differences; others, like the Gibson Girl and the flapper, derive from age cohorts. Still others, like the California Girl, are geographic types, while the Modern Woman and the New Woman speak to politics and lifestyle. The multiplicity of ideals is a symptom of the ongoing discourse through which women create themselves (and defend their groups). In all these cases, identifiable images showed a high degree of plasticity and were used in the give-and-take of life, rather than being rigid archetypes, dropped from the sky and blindly followed. As long as feminism deems only one way of presenting the self as "natural" (and therefore "authentic," "moral," or "feminist"), then the movement is itself trying to impose a single ideal—and thereby to restrict the self-actualization of others who are different.

We are not, most of us, descended from the Puritans. Instead, most Americans hail from a probably-forgotten mix of ethnic forebears who struggled to survive in a city or a wilderness. And, though we are living testimony to the substantial interbreeding that occurred among diverse groups, we should remember, when evaluating historical narratives, that our ancestors were engaged in intercultural disputes that sometimes led to serious abuses, dangerous social unrest, and even mass killings. Our forebears fought with each other over a range of issues, some momentous, such as slavery, and some trivial, such as clothing. Each case, however, was a test of values in which one group stood to gain power over the others. To lose many of these tests, even the small ones, was to risk extinction; to win offered the power to control what was considered moral, proper, beautiful, and even "natural." It was in this context that the feminist initiative against fashion first appeared.

# CHAPTER 2

# DRESS REFORM AND DOMINATION

ELIZABETH OAKES SMITH AND PAULINA WRIGHT DAVIS WORE MATCHING DRESSES TO the 1852 Women's Convention. The dresses were white and, in the latest fashion of the day, low-cut and sleeveless. The frocks were distinguished from each other only by the overblouse, or "sacque." One friend's sacque was pink, the other blue.

These two beautiful, sophisticated friends were veterans of the "woman movement," as it was called in the nineteenth century, having demonstrated their early commitment by their activism and their willingness to withstand controversy. Davis had signed the Declaration of Sentiments at Seneca Falls in 1848. She had also been the prime mover in organizing the first national convention and was an early activist in the effort to secure passage of the New York Married Woman's Property Act of 1848. Smith had written a series of women's rights articles for Horace Greeley's *New York Tribune.* These articles provoked a national controversy and were reprinted in 1851 as a twenty-five-cent pamphlet, "A Woman and Her Needs." The author had been deluged with sympathetic and moving letters from women in all walks of life and from around the country. Smith was a speaker on the popular lecture circuit, a forum she used to speak for women's rights. Both women were connected to the movement by friendships with Lucretia Mott and Elizabeth Cady Stanton. In sum, both of these women could be accurately described as pioneer feminists.[1]

Davis, who was on the nominating committee for the convention leadership, wanted Smith to serve as its president. Lucretia Mott's husband, James, made the nomination, which was met with unexpected resistance. A Quaker woman unknown to most of the group argued strenuously against Smith. The stranger, who had never been to a women's rights meeting before, stated outright that "nobody who dressed as [Smith] did could represent the earnest, solid, hardworking women of the country for whom they were making the demand for equal rights." Mott, himself a Quaker, responded gently that not all women could be expected to dress as plainly as the Friends.

The women around the room were silent, however, and they acquiesced to the stranger's wishes, nominating instead her preferred candidate.[2]

The Quaker who objected, Susan B. Anthony, became a feminist leader, as well as one of Smith's admirers. Biographers offer explanations for Anthony's behavior in this meeting ranging from her superior judgment to her characteristic prudishness. What is of interest here, however, is not Anthony's motivation in stopping Smith's nomination. I wish to focus instead on explaining why this group allowed an unknown woman to attack an exemplary member on such a trivial issue and then deny the nomination to a respected feminist who had already demonstrated both her commitment and her ability to appeal to "earnest, solid, hardworking women." I want to discuss how it came to be that Elizabeth Oakes Smith's manner of dress would be more important than ability, reputation, dedication, and friendship in deciding this matter.

## THE FOUNDATION

The first-generation feminists were the immediate descendants of two groups whose ideas about dress formed their beliefs and influenced their reform activities: the Puritan-Quakers of New England and the aristocrats of colonial America. These two traditions were melded together in the rhetoric they adopted, affecting not only what they believed was appropriate in dress, but which groups they chose to reform, and why.[3]

Most Americans know that the Puritan tradition valued plain dress and minimal grooming; however, they probably are unaware of the selective way in which these expectations were enforced and of the consistent resistance against them. While plain dress was held as a spiritual ideal and any enhancement of appearance was considered sinful by the church, only the common folk among the early Puritan communities were actually expected to refrain from the use of cosmetics or from wearing pretty clothes. Sumptuary laws—that is, laws regulating consumption—on the books of the Massachusetts Bay Colony from 1634 stipulated a long list of forbidden clothing, but if defendants could prove that he or she had a personal fortune of at least 200 pounds, they were exempt from the rule. The forbidden items—lace, silver or gold thread, cutwork or embroidery, hatbands, belts, ruffs, beaver hats, double ruffles, capes, gold or silver buttons—could apply to either male or female dress. The crime of "excessive dress," therefore, was gender neutral but class specific.

As the New England community began to enjoy prosperity, men and women both openly defied the laws against "wicked apparell" in ever larger numbers and in an increasingly insolent manner. In 1659, for instance, thirty-eight women were brought, all at once, before the court at Northampton, accused of excessive dress. One of them, a sixteen-year-old named Hannah Lyman, appeared in the very dress she had been arrested for owning. The court was shocked at this act of open rebellion, as it noted in its record of her conviction. But within six years the law had become so unpopular that the court stopped prosecuting. Custom and clergy, nevertheless, continued to enforce class restrictions on dress until the Revolution. Such customs and laws had always been pointedly enforced against women who challenged the social hierarchy—whether by dressing up or by running a successful business. The protofeminists among the Puritans were those who defied this system, not the obedient and simply dressed.[4]

Puritans were quite intolerant of outsiders and their ways, believing as they did that they were expressly favored by God. Well before the Revolution, Puritan attempts at dominating other ethnic groups in the colonies produced regional tensions. During the colonial period, settlers from New England had moved down the Atlantic seaboard, where they agitated for the exclusion of Catholics. Because of these intolerant religious attitudes, Catholicism had been essentially outlawed throughout the colonies by the time of the Revolution. At the opening of the nineteenth century, in the new United States Catholics accounted for less than 1 percent of the population, so most Americans had little experience with Catholics in the flesh. New England Protestants, however, had maintained their hatred for two hundred years through sermons, folktales, laws, and even schoolbooks. Thus, the figure of the "Romish believer" had become like the bogeyman, something fearsome but never seen.[5]

The early feminists shared their forebears' horror of Catholics, but, unlike previous generations, they were living through a huge influx of the dreaded "papists" because of the immigration sweeping their shores. As the ethnic mix of the entire North American population began its dramatic change, many "real Americans," particularly in New England and upstate New York, where feminism was born, began to feel that Anglo-Protestant supremacy needed defending. The early woman movement, because its leaders were part of this general surge of "Nativism" among Yankee Protestants, was consistently anti-Catholic and xenophobic.

The second group from whence the first feminists came, the aristocrats of the colonial period, were small in number, but wealth and power had been securely concentrated in their hands. Hierarchy was rigidly proscribed by family ties: The closer people's bloodline put them to the British throne, the higher they were in rank. Family ties, rather than merit or popular support, gave them the right to rule as well as access to a network of privilege and favors. Elaborate inbreeding protected both concentrated wealth and the ancestral power structure by creating an immense biological barrier separating gentry from common folk. The American aristocracy actually claimed to represent a higher order of being, genetically more beautiful, chaste, and honorable than ordinary people. With their gene pool sealed off, the ruling class could (and did) make claims that desirable personal traits were the result of "good breeding." Aristocrats saw commoners as inherently ugly, promiscuous, and deceitful—fundamentally unfit either for self-governance or mingling socially with the elites. In keeping with their aristocratic backgrounds, the early feminists consistently assumed that the morals, values, and prejudices of their own sort were intrinsically more virtuous than those of the lower classes, lending them a sense of superiority and a horror of mingling with "low company." In their writings they frequently expressed consciousness of their privileged status, including their pride in belonging to the "noblest class of men and women."[6]

The American aristocracy was, quite literally, a leisure class—a group whose privilege was expressed primarily in its exemption from work. As large landowners, they lived off the rents from tenant farmers as well as from investments. They were the only Americans of the preindustrial period who might be said to be economically self-sufficient, having their own shops, laundries, foundries, and the like on their estates, as well as numerous servants, land, and livestock.

In contrast, most Americans produced what they could for their own needs and then traded either surplus or services for the things they could not make. The need to participate in market exchange in order to meet everyday needs was, therefore, an index of class. For this reason, the ruling stratum considered both manual labor and engaging in trade demeaning. The terms "commerce," "commercial," and "trade" were pejoratives that described the way ordinary people made their living.[7]

Because most of the population was "common," trade was an important part of daily life. Currency was scarce, so trade was conducted on a barter basis—or, as they say in anthropology, the economy was a "gift system." Young girls, for instance, were usually hired out as servants in exchange for goods their families needed. These girls were not paid in cash, but in material produce that went to their families. Exchange arrangements such as these often stretched out over time; indeed, even one-time trades were often months or years apart. The delay between trades resulted in an understood indebtedness among many different people for a variety of goods. This network of obligation was like a great web that held the community together.

While commoners struggled to produce or acquire the means to live, gentry devoted themselves to leisure. The definition of "leisure" was broader than we allow today, referring to parties and sports but also to other pastimes considered appropriate to gentlefolk, such as study and charitable work. "Leisure" also encompassed a number of activities we now consider "work," such as government service and the practice of law, the ministry, academics, and medicine. The post-Revolutionary ladies who began the movement were gentlewomen in the full sense. Virtually none had jobs, and nearly all had servants. More tellingly, *none of their men worked for a living*—except at "leisure" occupations such as ministry and law.

In the colonial period, manners, dress, and grooming had been a primary way of making class differences visible, thus enforcing the separation between common and noble. Gentry wore smooth, brightly colored fabrics in styles that used great quantities of expensive cloth. Commoners were expected to wear rough cloth colored only by earth-toned natural dyes. Ordinary people were not allowed to wear large amounts of material, ornaments, or revealing clothing; men and women of the upper ranks were allowed buckles, ruffles, wigs, and makeup. These sartorial stipulations were enforced by sumptuary laws that were enacted by all of the colonies.

Even if law and custom did not keep commoners from dressing up, technology and economics usually did. More than two-thirds of America's clothing was made in the home—by women, as it had been around the world for thousands of years. Before industrialization, women raised sheep and grew flax, then did the shearing, carding, harvesting, soaking, pounding, and combing to produce fibers for spinning. On their spinning wheels, they drew out the fibers, twisting them into thread. On looms, they then wove the yarn into fabric before cutting and sewing garments. This whole process was seldom done by one family from beginning to end, however. Estate records and other documents indicate that it was unusual for a single household to own all the implements of production, as well as the land and livestock, to fully make their own clothing. So most women worked only part of the process, trading with others for the raw materials or the finished products they needed. Consequently, for women, making materials for clothing was a significant part of their production, but it was *also* a primary point of contact with the marketplace.

Despite shared production, providing clothing for a family was an enormous, never-ending task. Because making it was so labor-intensive, clothing was scarce and simple. Most people wore the same clothes year after year and so did not even attempt to keep up with fluctuations in style. Indeed, wills often show ordinary items of clothing being passed from one generation to the next.

Accessories were practically nonexistent. Although we're told that American women of the past had their feet pinched by tiny shoes, the truth is that few Americans owned any shoes until after factory footwear was available. In rural, preindustrial America, nearly everyone spent the summer barefoot, just as people in preindustrial nations often do today. In winter, crude, handmade moccasins might be worn, but in many families only the men had boots. Decorative items—hats, fans, jewelry, and gloves—were simply unavailable to the majority of our forebears.

Common people thought underclothing too expensive to buy, too difficult to make, and just generally unnecessary. Even among the gentry, the habit of wearing pantaloons under the skirt was adopted only in the nineteenth century—and only with reluctance. Pantaloons were worn by the French and thus were associated with immorality, especially prostitution. Corsets, or "stays," however, had been worn by both men and women of the upper class since the sixteenth century.[8]

The hated corset has its origins in the different postures that marked rank. Common folk were expected to show deference for their superiors through their manner and posture. By slumping their shoulders, ducking their heads, and averting their eyes in the presence of an aristocrat, commoners acknowledged their inferior status and communicated their willingness to serve. In contrast, gentry had to maintain perfect posture at all times—the slightest slouch signified the servility required of commonfolk. Aristocratic clothing was designed to help nobles keep their bodies upright and in place. A lady's midriff was held up by bone stays; for men, the same end was accomplished through coats cut to pull the shoulders down and push them back, as well as snug waistcoats underneath (and a corset if needed).

Aristocratic clothing also had to remain buttoned up so as not to suggest the free movement needed by a working person: "A coatless man with a free-flowing shirt and an unbuttoned vest would be instantly identified as a tradesman or laborer, never a gentleman. The flowing shirt or smock freed the arms to reach, lift, and swing, as was necessary for the work of commoners but unnecessary and unsuitable for gentry." Thus, the freedom of movement to work that feminists admire in what they assume is "masculine" clothing was originally a mark of class rather than sex.[9]

Because free movement suggested the indignity of common labor, genteel motion was to be graceful, controlled, close to the body. Books such as George Washington's *Rules of Civility and Decent Behaviour In Company and Conversation* contained elaborate descriptions of proper deportment: how to enter a room, put on a hat, walk, and bow. Not only were singing, whistling, lounging, loud laughter, and putting your feet on the furniture disallowed, but the rules explicitly required that you must cover your mouth when you yawned, that you must not talk with your mouth full or spit into the fire, and that you must close your mouth while walking. A genteel person should not let the tongue hang out of the mouth or allow the jaw to go slack. Maintaining this level of bodily control was a task of constant concentration even for the aristocrat. Thus, what seems like basic comportment to us now is really a list of learned habits whose origins can be historically identified and used to differentiate our sense of the "natural" from that of other cultures.

A gentleperson's appearance was the outward sign of inward grace, while the dirtiness of the common folk was an index of their moral slovenliness. The aristocratic body was kept perfectly clean, nails trimmed, hair combed, teeth washed. But bathing was virtually unknown among common folk because frequent baths were practical only for those who had servants to lug water. Soap was a rarity, so most people just rubbed the dirt off their skin with a coarse towel. It was not uncommon for ordinary folks to be infested with lice and ticks. If teeth were brushed at all, it was with a chewed twig and some table salt. Men and women who worked with their hands usually had dirty or discolored nails—before the invention of modern manicure products, there wasn't much to be done about it.

Among aristocrats, clean skin was to be set off by perfectly white linen at the neck and wrists. Noble homes often had both a laundress and a room specifically for doing laundry, but in ordinary households laundering was done infrequently because of the inordinate amount of labor it required. This was true even though most people only had one set of clothes (the more prosperous commoners might have a second set for Sundays). Not only did people wear the same things day in and day out; they bathed so very seldom that clean clothes usually went on over a body smelling of sweat and covered with filth. Since there were no deodorants or antiperspirants before the late nineteenth century, most shirts and bodices had permanent perspiration stains. Few people had closets or more than a peg on the wall to hang their clothes when they weren't being worn, so clothing was perpetually wrinkled, stained, and foul smelling.

Genteel clothing, grooming, and manners were difficult for commoners to imitate, yet the most insurmountable barrier was education. An aristocrat of either sex was expected to be able to converse well on a thousand topics suitable for "small talk," which might range from horticulture to philosophy. Both sexes, therefore, were carefully educated. Reading, in fact, was so central to the cult of gentility that some argued being well read could, by itself, win a young woman a good husband. The education of gentlewomen was not seen as preparation for a career, certainly, but since neither the men nor the women of this class had careers in the modern sense, this distinction was not as meaningful as it is today.

The education of gentlepersons was intended to produce a specific set of aristocratic "virtues," such as delicacy, sensibility, and taste. Historian Richard Bushman explains that "ideally all were cheerful, sweet, modest, and cautious never to give offense." "Delicacy" was "aversion to every form of coarse behavior or thought, and even the suggestion of erotic passion." "Sensibility" described a genteel person's responsiveness to experience, often manifest in spontaneous weeping or swooning. Such sensitivity to feelings was also thought to engender fine aesthetic judgment, or "taste."[10]

One of the explicit prerogatives of the gentry was to consume the kinds of luxuries that made such fine taste observable. The rightful responsibility of the commoner was to produce, not consume, while the gentlefolk consumed, but did not produce. The needs of gentry and common were held to be different—a gentleman's needs were a common man's indulgences. Common persons consuming genteel objects—such as a fashionable hat—were criticized for consuming beyond their rank; the same hat on a gentleperson would be displaying his or her own superior grace. The world of objects was divided into things that were "genteel" and those that were "common": There were genteel wigs, genteel saddles, genteel furniture, as well as their "vulgar" counterparts. "Fashionable" and "unfashionable" were alternatives for "genteel" and "common" in categories ranging from clubs to carriages.

The genteel aesthetic was, essentially, a basis for including some people and excluding others, whether from clubs, government, social occasions, or matrimony. The ability of the select few to exhibit appropriate taste and manners was the visible evidence of the "good breeding" that gave them a rightful place in the ancestral elite. Failure to meet the standards could result in exclusion, which meant far worse than a sudden absence of party invitations. Ostracization was a judgment of one's moral, intellectual, and even genetic weakness, so excommunicated souls would find themselves refused marriage partners and barred from the economic system.

Conforming well to the genteel aesthetic was synonymous with "conforming to fashion." Being up-to-date on the latest styles was part of the aesthetic, but the term "fashionable" did not refer merely to a stylish appearance. Instead, "fashion" specified the whole complex set of behaviors required for inclusion in what came to be known as Society. The system of rules was stable in many respects, but changed enough from year to year that a man or woman who wanted to stay in the good opinion of the elite community had to be alert to sudden swings in expectations. Thus, the attention that this group paid to the vagaries of "fashion" was based on considerations far more weighty than mere personal vanity.

Given this context of strict standards and constant surveillance, we can easily see the influence of class behind the alleged pressure to imitate the engraved steel plates of the fashion press. According to feminist writers, however, the image of the Steel-Engraving Lady was the pictorial manifestation of the Victorian ideology of femininity, often called "the Cult of True Womanhood."[11] In the True Womanhood ideal, they say, all females were presumed to be purer and nobler than men, but more delicate. A disturbing topic of conversation, a loud noise, a rude remark, or an unpleasant sight could cause the sensibilities of True Womanhood to break down, resulting in a swoon or worse. The ideal woman had to maintain the demure manner indicative of such a spirit: Her gestures were few, graceful, and close to her body; her voice was soft, low, and measured; her facial expression placid, but luminous. Similarly, her grooming and dress reflected this "feminine" temperament. Her toilet was meticulous, her creamy white skin setting off an elaborately contrived hairdo. Her shoes were tiny and pointed—just as in the pictures that, according to feminist orthodoxy, also gave her a name.

Notice, however, the striking similarities between the symptoms of True Womanhood and the expectations of the ideal eighteenth-century aristocrat of *either sex.* Please consider also that the objects and practices marking the Steel-Engraving ideal—baths, laundries, shoes—had been practically, legally, and economically out of common reach. The Steel-Engraving Lady ideal, therefore, clearly had antecedents in class structure and was not, in its moment of origination, exclusively (or even primarily) a gender distinction. Both the corsets and bulky skirts of which the founding feminists complained were vestiges of the genteel aesthetic, in which stays and huge skirts were the tangible signs of rank. When today's feminists generalize about their great-grandmothers being forced to wear tight corsets and multiple petticoats, or to keep their skin out of the sun and speak in a soft voice, they are overlooking the experience of the greater majority (upward of 80 percent of all women) who were not as carefully cultivated, who had no choice but to work in the sun, and who actually had been restricted from wearing the same clothing feminists criticize.

If most women were forbidden to wear fancy clothes and too poor to have good grooming habits, why did the feminists organize to change the dress of ordinary females? And how did it happen that the Steel-Engraving Lady, originally a symbol of class, was reinterpreted into a sign read as "feminine" rather than "aristocratic"? The answers to these questions lie in the changes wrought by two apocalyptic forces: the social instability produced by sudden democracy and the new material culture brought by industrialization.

## THE CHALLENGE

The American Revolution destroyed the infrastructure of this social hierarchy by removing its anchor point, the British monarchy. Thus, at the end of the eighteenth century the ancestral aristocracy abruptly lost its hegemony over American life. And, though the Revolution had been instigated and led by gentry, the leaders did not anticipate that commoners would take all the rhetoric about being created equal quite as literally as they evidently did. Therefore, the first fifty years after the Revolution saw a struggle between gentry and commoners for control of the government, as well as many related challenges to the cultural authority of the elites. The founding feminists were the daughters or granddaughters of these disempowered aristocrats, and the sense of unjust loss was still intensely felt. Some of the ruling clans, such as Elizabeth Cady Stanton's family, had survived as wealthy aristocrats. Other feminists, such as Lucy Stone, came from families who could trace their ancestry to the original Massachusetts Bay Colony, but had suffered severe economic losses in the interim. Regardless of their financial position, however, the former gentry had endured a substantial loss of community influence.[12]

Trying to recapture the loyalties of the new electorate, gentlemen began wearing clothing more like the common folk and at least feigned the appearance of work. (Lawyering was redefined as "work" practically overnight.) Aristocratic men stopped wearing breeches, broad-tailed coats, and cocked hats, taking up instead trousers, shorter coats, and tall ("stove-pipe") hats. They switched from bright colors in showy fabrics to browns, blacks, and grays in muted textures. They stopped wearing wigs and makeup. Buckled shoes gave way to stout boots. The craze to look "republican" also affected gentlewomen's dress, but only very briefly. Women dropped heavy clothing in favor of light, high-waisted dresses with kid slippers. They stopped wearing wigs, corsets, and makeup. Within only a decade, however, women's big heavy dresses were back, along with elaborate hats and hairpieces (but not makeup). According to feminist theorists, nineteenth-century men made women wear heavy clothing to keep them out of the workforce. Remember, however, that this transition occurred at a time when working had not been considered a social, political, or even economic asset. On the contrary, leisure was a privilege and a sign of spiritual worthiness. The gentle*men* who went to work did so out of political expediency; gentle*women* held on to the right to remain above labor and to wear the clothing of privilege. Instead of changing their own clothing to fit the new times, as the men did, aristocratic women concentrated on keeping common women dressed *down.*

Democracy removed the formal structure of the class distinctions governing consumption, so ordinary people suddenly had the freedom to dress as they pleased. However, such freedom would have been pointless without the second event, the opening of the first factories in the 1810s. Mass-produced shoes, hats, notions, fabrics, and accessories suddenly put clothing items formerly available only to the aristocracy within nearly anyone's reach. A wider variety of goods at low prices, higher disposable incomes, fewer social restrictions, and a greater supply of currency resulted in skyrocketing consumption of the textiles and dry goods manufactured by the new economy.

The first factories hired mostly young women, who sent a portion of their wages—now paid in currency—home and kept the rest for living expenses. With whatever was left, they did what young women have done with extra spending money ever since: They dressed up. The horrified response of the Puritan aristocracy to teenagers in fancy clothes was just the first symptom of shifts in the basic social structure. By 1850, the sight of a working-class woman wearing "fashionable" clothing was a frequent occurrence. Such behavior was not only an affront to the early feminists' Puritan sensibilities but a challenge to their social superiority—a posture of sartorial impertinence. Amelia Bloomer, writing in her temperance paper, *The Lily,* complained that women *of all classes* and *in all regions* were now trying to wear fashionable clothing—as if the lack of class restriction was as much a concern as the clothing itself. Abba Gould Woolson, a prominent dress reformer, wrote, "There are few lines of dress demarcation here to distinguish mistress from maid; and while the one enjoys a large share of favor, based, it may be, wholly upon externals, is it any wonder that the other apes her, even though it prove a hard-earned folly?" Constant dismay expressed that *even* the servant girls are carrying parasols or *even* the "Negro women" are wearing satin dresses cries out for political contextualization. But feminist historians just write off the servants and blacks as vain, foolish, and corrupt.[13]

Industrial towns sprang up overnight and cities, especially the seaports, mushroomed. As large landowners, the former gentry identified strongly with the agrarian life that was passing away as the population, economy, and culture shifted to urban areas. Their suspicion of the cities and wistfulness for the farmland gave rise to what Richard Hofstadter called "the agrarian myth." This view of America romanticized rural life and placed the blame for vice in all forms on urban commerce. As an extension of this myth, the genteel fiction, poetry, and images of the nineteenth century idealized the innocent dress of the country girl as a contrast to the corrupt fashionability of the city girl. But the actual appearance of ordinary rural citizens, as you might imagine, was not particularly pleasing. Thus two images of the country girl emerged in American culture, the genteel innocent of the agrarian myth and the crudely dressed, often dirty, bumpkin. Still observable in twentieth-century imagery was the gingham-and-lace country girl romanticized in fashion, while the cruder version appears in caricatures from Moonbeam MacSwine to Ellie May Clampett.[14]

A competing ideology, often called "the rise of the common man," directly opposed the values of the old aristocracy. This group admired frontier or urban virtues, such as courage, physical strength, risk taking, and the ability to hold one's liquor. In their view, the true destiny of a republican society was to offer opportunity to all, including access to "luxury" goods. This group, too, had its feminine ideal. In popular literature and theater, the young working girl making her way in the city represented the resourcefulness, independence, and good humor that the "common man" ideology valued—and thus became one of this culture's most lasting heroines. In the imagery of the gentry, however, the city girl was either a corrupt little slut who tempted heroes with the ways of the world or a pathetic creature doomed to didactic demise.

Adding further to the rural elite's dismay, the growing fashion industry created a nouveau riche class. The colorful attire and elaborate grooming of the newly rich class were called "decadent," "vulgar," and even inappropriately "aristocratic." The new urban elite built palatial homes and spent money in lavish style. Members of the old order took moral offense at the "excesses" of the intruders, but continued to defend their own luxurious consumption as a civilizing force that "encouraged refinement, developed taste, and restrained the most vulgar tendencies of new wealth." Contemporary social critics sympathetic to the old elites scorned the "coarse faces, loud voices, bad English, and vulgar manners" of the new pretenders and loved to draw comparisons between the dress of nouveau riche women and that of prostitutes. Puritan ministers criticized the newcomers for their conspicuous consumption and their social climbing activities, helping to give snobbery a moral ground.[15]

The old elite became alarmed that the emerging society defined itself on commercial ties rather than those of kin, and had begun to equate power with wealth, rather than with inborn rights to rule. Aristocrats attempted to protect their preeminence in business, society, and politics by exclusive social behavior. In cities across America, "old money" and the nouveau riche lived in uneasy proximity. Different neighborhoods, parallel clubs, and separate parties served to maintain the distinctions between the two groups, as each tried to upstage the other in their dress, homes, and carriages.

The two elites might have gone on forever in this parallel fashion, but the biological barrier protecting the aristocracy's gene pool sprang a leak. The daughters of the new order were just as pretty as those of the old, but often they were more independent and vivacious than the old genteel aesthetic prescribed. Their appearance and attitude appealed to young men, including those of established families. Marriages between the sons of the old order and the daughters of the new took place. With intruders reducing the available pool of suitable matches, the security of gentlewomen was seriously threatened. Aristocrats worried that they could no longer rest on their position in the social network to win a mate. In self-defense, the superior morals, breeding, and education of aristocratic women were pushed forward as greater prizes than the "mere externals" of beauty or charm. In an exchange of money for status, marriages between the daughters of the old order and the sons of the new also occurred. The posturing of the old gentry to acquire the cash of the new wealth was as calculated as the efforts of new money to buy the ancestry of the aristocrats.

In the end, the old aristocracy was transformed by the infusion of common genes. In place of the old ethic of arranged unions within an exclusive group emerged the belief that mutual affection should be the basis for marriage. Of course, the conservative elite saw a direct link between "romantic" ideas and the new democratic ones. For instance, the editor of the leading New York "Society" magazine, commented disapprovingly: "So long as the ability to read was confined to a comparatively small number in any community, and so long also as woman was uneducated and dependent, the theory that the attraction that two young people feel for one another was to know no law had few adherents, but when universal education and individualism came into favor, and the din of woman's rights, children's rights, working-men's rights, began to deafen and startle a conservative public, the 'right to love' began also to challenge attention."[16]

The early feminists espoused an antiromance view of courtship and matrimony, in which "true marriage" could occur only between two persons who had known each other since birth, had attended the same church and schools, had known the same people, and therefore shared the same values, a position that confined marriage within homogeneous groups—an outcome that worked to their own class advantage.[17] In contrast, the democratic strength of the romantic ethic was the value it placed on surmounting social barriers. Over time, the romantic idea of marriage won out, with far-reaching effects on class structure, resulting in marriages not only between new elites and old, but eventually between wealthy and poor.

In the old order, commonfolk meekly accepted their station; the new "moderns," male and female, actively sought access to power and wealth by luck, talent, intrigue, looks, or love. Such worldly ambitions were described as "the go-ahead attitude." Success was usually more modest than industrial fortunes or aristocratic marriages, but nevertheless go-ahead efforts brought about another important social change: the rise of a middle class. As they accumulated wealth, the "middling sort" consumed "beyond their station" in clothing and home decoration. They also sought the respectability that had formerly come only from leisure class status. So, in addition to building parlors and buying furniture, middle-class parents carefully taught their children to stand straight, keep their hands clean, and speak politely.

The old aristocrats criticized middle-class women, finding fault with their manners and claiming their tastes ran to gaudy colors and excessive decoration. By the 1870s, new women's magazines had stepped into the breach. The texts of these magazines are transparent on the intentions of their instruction: to help the reader acquire an appearance and manner like those of the "better sort." Their pages display the exquisite attention to details that characterized the etiquette books of Washington's generation. A regular feature of the *Delineator*, for example, described "The Delsarte System of Physical Culture," a "system" of instruction in manners and health. One installment taught readers facial expressions, hand movements, and head positions: "Turn the eyes with the subjective gaze, and the head normally, toward the individual or object, with the lips in the attitude of approval; the expression will then signify simple, interested attention with approval or satisfaction." The same article then runs through twenty-nine expressions, including respect, dissatisfaction, exaltation, determination, joyous anticipation, dejection, stupor, perplexity, and contentment, all complete with detailed instructions and illustrations (see figure 2.1). The emphasis on the posture of the torso also remains: a slumping posture shown in illustration continues to carry the stigma of lower-class membership, signifying "indolence, fatigue, prostration or imbecility." Another slumping figure is described: "Drawing the chest inward and thrusting the abdomen forward will produce an attitude expressive of sensuality, the animal nature of vulgarity, and an added aggressiveness of the shoulders is significant of thorough baseness, as expressed in the meaner passions." Importantly, by instructing their readers to avoid the attitudes of the "meaner passions," these magazines were explicitly instructing them *not* to cultivate themselves as seductresses. Such a goal would run in the opposite direction from what was required for gentility.[18]

People who acquired the genteel way came to look "with condescension, pity, or scorn on the vulgar common people existing on the other side of the spiritual divide."[19] In time, the erstwhile requisites of gentility formed the base level of acceptability in an American's appearance: "simple" cleanliness, trimmed hair and nails, a composed facial expression (no tongue hanging out, no mouth open), and an erect

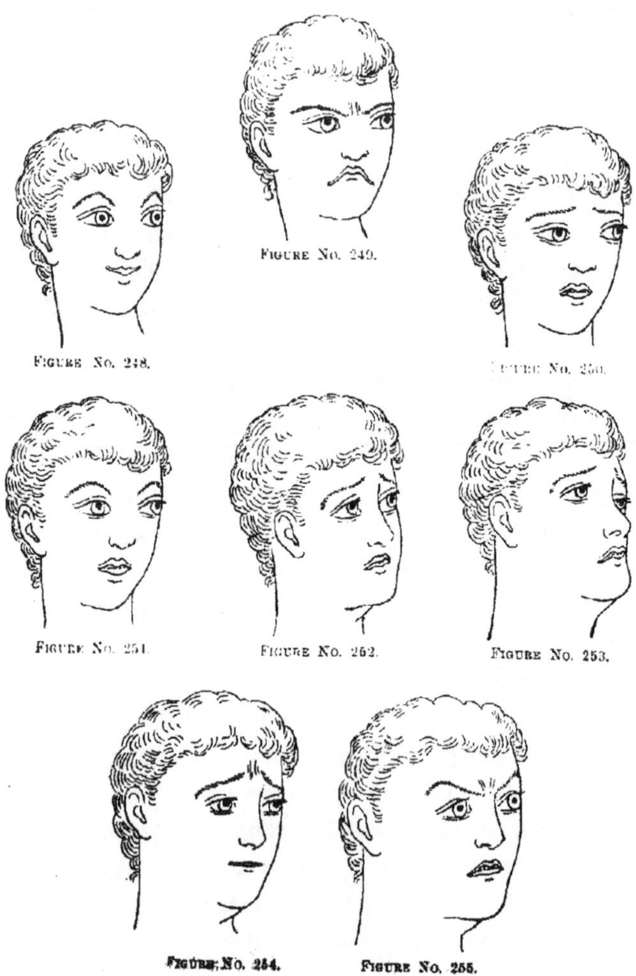


Figure 2.1. The Delsarte System of Physical Culture

posture. Today we expect these basic civilities of everyone. When we don't see them (e.g., as in the case of the homeless or the mad), we look for causes. In other words, the genteel way is now the standard that feminists call "natural."

With this manner of self-presentation becoming identified with good character, respectable status, and acceptable morality, it is no wonder that achieving the manners, dress, grooming, and speech of the Steel-Engraving Lady became an important goal for nineteenth-century women. However, as the "common man" dress became universal among males, the attributes of the Steel-Engraving Lady became increasingly identified as "feminine" rather than "upper class."

For women below the new middle class, chances for achieving the Steel-Engraving standard continued to be severely limited by knowledge, skill, and money, and also by physical infrastructure. As slums sprouted to house factory workers, city services were strained to the limit—and beyond. Refuse and human waste piled up in backyard privies, often running off into open trenches. One source of water might serve several city blocks. Lighting was insufficient inside and outside the homes. Rooms were damp, cramped, unpainted, and poorly ventilated. In such housing it was difficult, if not impossible, to produce the cleanliness, modesty, and muted demeanor among girls that the upper classes so valued. The resulting appearance was consistently taken to indicate corruption: "No one can walk down the length of Broadway without meeting some hideous troop of ragged girls, from twelve years old down, brutalized almost beyond redemption by premature vice, clad in the filthy refuse of the rag-picker's collections, obscene of speech, the stamp of childhood gone from their faces, hurrying along with harsh laughter and foulness on their lips, with thief written in their cunning eyes and whore on their depraved faces."[20]

Yet, in spite of all the obstacles before them, working girls were among the most visible consumers of the fashion economy. Young workers would come home and sew late into the night, many becoming quite skilled and most showing remarkable resourcefulness in creating good effect from little means. Groups of girls jointly purchased the fashion magazines, sharing them and then doing their best to reproduce the content. Because the ruling moralists worked from the presumption that chastity and fashionable dress were incompatible among lower-class females, however, the dress habits of young working girls caused more hand-wringing than those of any other group. (Note that immorality was inferred whether the girls' appearance was ragged and shabby or fine and finished. This paradox is a signal that class tension, rather than dress behavior, is the real problem.)

As time passed, the factories (and slums) were filled with wave after wave of immigrants. Although the attraction of democracy was certainly important, immigrants also came specifically to better themselves in the booming modern economy. As with the "native" commonfolk, these attractions were intertwined: The goal was a better life, which meant not only more money, but the freedom to spend it without the class strictures common elsewhere in the world.[21]

Some immigrants were skilled, but most arrived without much material wealth. Nearly all settled first in the urban slums and were considered little more than animals by the "native" community. Each time a new immigrant group came in, cities once again seemed likely to explode with the burden of providing housing, employment, and services. The additional people in areas already overcrowded and underserved bred still more disease and filth. In a perverse sort of reasoning, many Americans blamed the crime and dirt of the slums on the "inrush of degraded foreigners."

The fashion industry figured prominently in female immigrants' economic prospects, and its products were central to their aspirations. Those who could not get positions that required English (i.e., domestic service) or some other job that required literacy, refined manners, and a good appearance (i.e., sales work) usually went to the textile factories. Those arriving with marketable skills usually were trained in clothing production, such as sewing machine operation or dress cutting. Each new set of arrivals, therefore, took its place behind machines that produced fashion for America: after native-born girls, Irish, then eastern Europeans, and finally young Italian women.

Whole immigrant families worked in their homes, so that entire city neighborhoods in the cities were dominated by production of garments, hats, shoes, or notions. The tight relationship between the economy of immigrants and the fashion industry was quite visible to "native" observers. For instance, near the end of the nineteenth century, the Lower East Side of New York, where the ready-made garment industry and the Jewish community were concentrated, was like an enormous human beehive. The Second Avenue elevated train rode through half a mile of the garment district, allowing commuters to peer through window after window at garment workers stooped over their tasks.

Jews in particular benefited from the fashion industry, probably because so many had worked in clothing production in their home countries. Many young females had experience with sewing machines; many men were tailors. Jewish entrepreneurs formed networks to recruit skilled workers from among newer arrivals. Recruiters themselves often became manufacturers because only a small investment—about $50—was required for start-up. In 1885, of the 241 garment factories in New York, Jews owned 234. By 1895, 50 percent of the Jews in America worked in the garment business.[22]

A remarkable number of Jewish immigrants rose to fame and wealth by building tiny peddling businesses into department stores or mail order companies. Although many of these stores were absorbed by a larger chain long ago, a fair number of the immigrant names are still recognizable today: B. Altman, Gimbel's, Bloomingdale's, Bergdorf-Goodman, Saks Fifth Avenue, Neiman-Marcus, Filene's, Joske's, F. & R. Lazarus, Abraham & Straus, Rich's, Lord & Taylor, Henri Bendel, I. Magnin, Joseph Magnin, the Hecht Company, Sanger-Harris. Still other Jewish immigrants came to own and control companies named for others, such as Julius Rosenwald of Sears & Roebuck, and Lazarus, Isidor, and Nathan Straus of Macy's.[23]

Some of these success stories involved women. For instance, Mary Ann Magnin opened a small workshop for lingerie, bridal gowns, and baby clothes because she wanted to keep her husband out of the dangerous jobs that were open to him. Within a few years the business was so successful that she opened a downtown store. Mary Ann named it "I. Magnin" after her beloved husband, Isaac. She was the first woman to open a major American department store. Another retailing tycoon, Lena Himmelstein, immigrated from Lithuania at sixteen. She went to work in a sweatshop making lingerie. She then married a jeweler named David Bryant, who died after their first child was born. Lena pawned a wedding gift and bought a sewing machine. She set up shop making bridal wear and lingerie, but her business really began to grow when she diversified into maternity clothes. Lena opened a store and called it "Lane Bryant" ("Lena" became "Lane" through an error on a bank deposit slip).[24] Another American fashion institution was born.

The desire to gain upward mobility, typical especially of young immigrants, made personal appearance a priority. Frequently, buying a change of clothing was one of their first acts upon arrival to this country. Sophie Abrams told the story of her initiation into American dress habits: "I was such a greenhorn, you wouldn't believe. My first day in America I went with my aunt to buy some American clothes. She bought me a shirtwaist . . . a blue print with red buttons and a hat, such a hat I had never seen. I took my old brown dress and shawl and threw them away! . . . When I looked in the mirror, I couldn't get over it. I said, boy, Sophie, look at you now. Just like an American." Men did the same kind of thing, abandoning traditional caps and cutting their hair in favor of a clean shave, a stiff collar, and a necktie. But among all nationalities, young single women were most likely to show their assimilation through clothing. More traditional immigrants looked down on their behavior, but the girls continued. This persistent practice and the disapproval it engendered produced a gap between young and old, but also between the home culture and the new.[25]

"Real" Americans were shocked by the seeming profligacy of the new arrivals and insulted by their awkward attempts at imitation. This, coupled with anxiety over the success immigrants were having in the new industry, must have made the fashion revolution seem all the more ominous to conservative viewers. But without religion, law, and the rights of caste to force their "inferiors" to dress more demurely, the Yankee Protestant ruling class was forced to think of new strategies. What they came up with was "reform."

## THE RESPONSE

By the time of the incident at the 1852 Women's Convention, the two competing philosophies emerging from the post-Revolutionary struggle had produced a clear political split, with party alliances on each side.[26] Protestants, British descendants, and former gentry had coalesced as the "respectable" vote, represented by the Whigs. The Democrats purported to represent the "popular" vote, which included urbanites, non-British immigrants, workers, and Catholics. Whigs cast themselves as the party dedicated to moral progress, while the Democrats were more inclined toward social freedom.

Within the Whig party were pockets of extremists, including a group known as the ultraists, or ultras, whose influence was concentrated in the isolated Puritan enclaves of northwestern New York. Throughout the seventeenth and eighteenth centuries, New England Puritans had been aggressively expansionist, brazenly moving settlers to the Dutch communities of New York and then sabotaging their governments. After the Revolution, the Continental Congress settled disputes over this territory in a decision that ultimately resulted in an enormous migration of New Englanders into the area. In the rural regions near Seneca Falls, Syracuse, and Rochester, intense local conflicts over cultural issues echoed centuries of Puritan demand for cultural hegemony in the former Dutch settlements.[27] This background may account for the New York Puritans' higher level of social insecurity.

What distinguished the ultras from other Whigs was their comparatively greater willingness to use government powers to impose moral righteousness. Historian Lee Benson suggests their position can be summed up in the query of one minister: "For why should a good man stop who knows certainly that he is right exactly, and that all men are wrong in proportion as they differ from him?" In lieu of legislation, however, ultras were perfectly willing to try influence by other means. So, from this group emerged a cluster of social reform movements, all aimed at controlling the behavior of outsiders: temperance, dress reform, a broadly defined movement called "social purity," and a variety of Nativist groups, including the infamous Know-Nothings.[28]

The early feminists were personally, demographically, and ideologically aligned with the ultras—in fact, they used that term to describe themselves.[29] Susan B. Anthony, Elizabeth Cady Stanton, and their friends lived in the central ultraist communities and were active in the whole cluster of reform movements forming under that banner. Feminism was not the common thread holding these social initiatives together. The real agenda was sectarian: These movements originated in the Puritan community, expressed Anglo-Protestant interests, and were led by their clergy.

Anything associated with the new immigrant or modern communities—whatever marked them, sustained them, gave them pleasure or power—carried the stigma of the out group in the eyes of the in group. Even those initiatives that seem to us clearly aimed at a serious social problem had an underlying agenda of domination. Take, for instance, the temperance movement. The effort to curtail the consumption of alcohol was focused on working-class men, especially Irish and Germans. Irishmen did drink a good bit. But their pubs were also the centers of their political activity. Since Irish "machines" were in control of the politics of every major northeastern city within twenty-five years of the first immigration wave of the 1840s, closing the pubs through which the Irish organized promised unambiguous political benefits for the Anglos. Germans also loved beer. They started breweries to supply themselves with plenty of it; many became prosperous as a result. Just as the Irish derived political power from their pubs, the Germans accumulated the power of wealth in "Budweiser" and "Schlitz."[30] Thus, the temperance movement would "take out" the two largest immigrant groups of the period. It was not a coincidence.

The goals of social purity activists were wide-ranging: to eradicate prostitution, to give Puritans the power of public censorship, to provide alternatives to "vicious commercial recreations," and to teach "moral hygiene."[31] All these efforts drew from both the Puritan and genteel traditions. For instance, in addition to seeing moral depravity in fashionable dress, the Puritans had disapproved of most occasions for which one might "dress up." The early Puritan communities outlawed all sorts of entertainments. The Puritan clergy deemed plays sinful because they were fictional, produced to amuse, and allowed an occasion for pleasant socializing. Beginning in the early 1700s, theatrical plays were actually against the law in Connecticut, Massachusetts, Rhode Island, and New Hampshire. Similarly, circuses, menageries, and other forms of entertainment were unwelcome in the Puritan communities. Dancing, music, games, and other playful activities were also forbidden. One pastor even canceled the midweek church service because the congregation was enjoying the gathering too much.[32]

As in the pre-Revolutionary era, elites condemned the entertainments of the industrial working class on the basis of their commercial settings. "Respectable" women who regularly attended balls with great anticipation were horrified that working-class women liked to go to dance halls that charged a fee. Furthermore, many of the early immigrants had recreational activities that the Puritan community deemed sinful. Germans, for instance, were enthusiastic about picnics, dances, cards, and bowling. They organized all sorts of choirs, teams, and bands. They put on plays and parades. As harmless as these activities sound now, they were viewed negatively by American Protestants, particularly when practiced, as they often were, on Sundays. "Blue laws," restrictions on the activities allowed on Sundays, were often aimed at the recreations of immigrant communities.

The social purity reformers set themselves up as a moral Geiger counter, judging each play, exhibit, or dance. The leader was a man, Anthony Comstock; however, the ranks were filled with women. This group, the New York Society for the Supression of Vice, lobbied against art exhibits and shut down ballets in order to purge America of immorality. They allowed no distinction between a pornographic photograph being passed around a saloon and a nude in an art museum. They arrested art students as well as prostitutes, dancers as well as abortionists. Pictures in the popular press were seen as a major moral threat. Frank Leslie and other publishers had found enormous success producing cheap newspapers that were relatively easy to read and contained pictures to help the illiterate and non-English speaking comprehend the news. With its typical iconophobia—and an obvious interest in curtailing the dissemination of political information among the lower strata—the Anglo-Protestant ruling class decried the images of the industrial press. The most far-reaching success of this group was the enactment of the Comstock Laws, which governed "obscenity" and ultimately were used as often against feminists as against anyone else.

Among the social purity initiatives, "moral hygiene" was the agenda that involved regulating the grooming, dress, manners, and child-rearing practices of "less intelligent" women. The concept of "moral hygiene" reconciled the Puritan mistrust of personal grooming with the genteel aesthetic. Social purists not only believed that an acceptable appearance was an outward sign of inward grace, but also the reverse: An acceptable outward appearance could cure moral deficiencies. Thus, uppity common folk and "degraded foreigners" were to be morally uplifted by regular baths and demure manners. At the same time, however, social purists explicitly linked fashionable dress to moral decline. In one official document for child-rearing advice, for instance, "love of dress" and "extravagance of dress" are listed right along with "self-abuse" and "impure books" as primary causes of moral failure in children. Puritans traditionally had identified fashionable dress with religious heresy; the effort to control the appearance of immigrant women followed as logically from the desire for "social purity" as did efforts to control any other behaviors in which Catholics or Jews were engaged.[33] I doubt the negative impact dress reform would have on the immigrants' economy was lost on the Puritans, either.

The early feminists rebelled against some aspects of the Steel-Engraving Lady aesthetic, but they did not reject those expectations outright. They agitated for a Puritan version of simple clothing through the dress reform movement, but they used the moral hygiene platform of the social purity movement to enforce genteel ideas about personal cleanliness on the population at large. Thus, while some of their efforts involved trying to get women to pay less attention to their appearance in terms of clothing, they were, at the same time, insisting that women pay more attention to their grooming in terms of bathing and cleaning their teeth.

The reform movement took on a range of problems and adopted an array of forms and tools. Lectures and essays were a prominent means of disseminating the views of the disgruntled elite, but there were more active avenues as well. Demonstrations, some of them destructive, were not uncommon. Organizations were formed, societies founded, money raised, and buildings built. Several of the most powerful organizations involved were women's groups, such as the Women's Christian Temperance Union. To persuade through publishing and lectures only required a few productive rhetoricians; to be effective through demonstrations and organizations required large numbers of people willing to volunteer their time and resources. What gave the reform movements their ideological power was the Puritan ethos and the ruling class mystique. What gave them numbers, however, was the idle time of middle-class women.

Because gentlewomen still held that one could not work and be a lady, the new middle class had adopted the idea that a wife at home was a point of achievement in the struggle for material and social success. Many women of the middle class found their lives of domestic bliss unsatisfying, however. So to put their time to more productive use, they began working as reformers. Ironically, middle-class ambition ultimately gave political impact to the old elite's reform initiative.

## THE EFFECT

The reform movement had failures and successes. Usually feminist historians blame the failures on a mysterious but vaguely male group, such as "the liquor interests." In many cases, though, it seems quite clear that reforms failed because *those to be reformed did not wish to cooperate.* I invite readers to consider what was like to be on the receiving end of all this high-handed interference. Let's examine three groups that would have felt the brunt of the early feminists' efforts: female domestic servants, women employed by fashion, and women in the arts.

### WOMEN IN DOMESTIC SERVICE

Before the textile mills opened in 1814, most working women were servants. "Domestic service" continued to be the largest category of female employment for the rest of the nineteenth century; however, a strong preference for factory employment among working women caused a shortage of servants and a constant turnover in home service. Social workers and journalists investigating the issue reported that the preference for factory work stemmed from several working conditions typical of domestic employment. These conditions, taken together, apparently outweighed the fact that domestic service paid substantially better than factory labor. Although mill girls had long, grueling workdays, their hours were regular, allowing them to have time that was sure to be their own. Servants were expected to be "on tap" at all times, even when their regular duties were finished. Mill girls had active social lives and often lived with other young women. Employers of domestics, however, reserved the right to control who and how many servants entertained in the kitchen or their rooms. Servants often were lonely and had to endure indignities within the employer's household. Although they were called by their own first names, they had to address even the employer's children with deference. They might be referred to as "one of the family," but usually were required to eat at a separate table. Their looks, character, and manners were intently scrutinized because a servant's appearance reflected upon her employer's social standing.[34]

Wearing uniforms was one of the most frequently mentioned complaints about domestic service. "Livery" announced the servant's social inferiority just as a prisoner's uniform announces incarceration. The suit of clothing was usually selected and purchased by the "lady" of the house. One young woman reported an early experience with service, in which the mistress asked her to wear "the nurse's cap and apron" while caring for the children: "She was real good and kind; but when I said, 'Would you like your sister, Miss Louise, to put on cap and apron when she goes out with them?' she got very red, and straightened up. 'It's a very different matter,' she said; 'you must not forget that in accepting a servant's place you accept a servant's limitations.' That finished me. I loved the children, but I said, 'If you have no other thought of what I am to the children than that, I had better go.'"[35]

The same simple, uniform dress that signified superior spirituality when worn by Quakers expressed low caste when worn by a servant. The freedom to wear clothes of one's own choosing expressed individual dignity. Dress reform's aim of getting working women—most of whom were still servants—to adopt plain dress merely extended the control of the mistress to the infrequent leisure hours servants were allowed. It also denied them one of their few opportunities for expressing creativity and individuality. Such a political effort by wealthy women also must have seemed like an obvious attempt to turn back the clock on class relations.

When the dress reform movement began, the majority of domestic servants were Irish—indeed 80 percent of the maids in New York were from Ireland. After the famine in Ireland in the 1840s, economic opportunities for young women were quite bleak, much more so than for men. Thus, the Irish immigration was distinctively young and female. Those who crossed to America came expecting upward mobility; they were determined to better their circumstances regardless of what obstacles they might encounter. Unlike her upper-class American counterpart who viewed commerce as sinful, the Irish woman was entrepreneurial, attempting economic gain whenever she could. Irish women, in contrast to women of other groups, were willing to work as servants because domestic service was better paid than any other form of employment open to women except teaching. Prosperous Americans were so desperate for household help that Irish women could rely on steady employment, even when swings in the economy put everyone else out of work. The stable demand also allowed the Irish more leverage to negotiate pay and working conditions. When they didn't like the situation and could not persuade the mistress to do better, they simply packed up and walked out. Another job was always easy to find.

The record of the time is, therefore, littered with references to conflicts between Irish servants and their "mistresses" over money, manners, and housekeeping. Elizabeth Cady Stanton's papers refer to Irish servants with contempt, even including threats to "break the pate of some Hibernian" for housekeeping errors. The leading suffrage paper, the *Woman's Journal,* claimed that "the ignorant, foreign help occupying the field are a positive element of demoralization and barbarism in the household." Mary

Livermore, the *Journal*'s editor, echoed the rest of the group, saying that immigrant servants were "ignorant, thriftless, wasteful, insubordinate, unteachable."[36] The tension between "ladies" and their Irish servants was also the basis for many cartoons and stories aimed at the prosperous classes. "Bridget," the stereotypical Irish maid, is always fat, usually middle aged, and has an apelike look to her upper lip. Bridget dresses "excessively" and flirts shamelessly. Although a ridiculous figure, she can intimidate her employer and is always out to take advantage. Like Aunt Jemima, however, the figure of Bridget masks another reality.

The Irish girls who served in American households were younger and more attractive than the Bridget stereotype suggests. Lois Banner writes, "Young Irish women, according to a number of observers, seemed to be dressed in fashionable clothes as soon as they stepped off the boats at Castle Garden." Young Irishwomen became famous for their stubborn stylishness. One gentleman observed: "I have been amused, on a Sunday morning, to see two Irish girls walking out of my basement door dressed in rich moire antique, with everything to correspond, from elegant bonnets and parasols to gloves and gaiter-boots—an outfit that would not disgrace the neatest carriage in Hyde Park. These girls had been brought up in the floorless mud cabins covered with thatch, and gone to mass without shoes or stockings very likely, and now enjoy all the more their unaccustomed luxuries." But how do we square such focus on fashion with the economic astuteness that was also said to be typical of Irish women?[37]

The Irish servant girl's strategy was to live by the room and board the employer provided, but use the cash she was paid to send back to Ireland or to give to the church. Between 1848 and 1865 Irish immigrants, primarily women, sent $65 million back to Ireland. At the same time, they donated substantial sums to the fledgling American Catholic church. Their duty done, a number of them amassed a good personal savings and managed their money shrewdly, but once obligations to family and church were fulfilled, they also spent money on little luxuries, especially clothing, hats, and cosmetics. They were criticized for these spending habits, even by their own community.

By forcing plain dress on servants, the feminists' dress reform movement would have promised Irish women still further humiliation at the hands of well-to-do Yankee Protestant women. In this light, the aggressively fashionable dress of Irish women takes on a distinctly political cast—and it doesn't seem particularly puzzling that they continued to dress well despite the substantial criticism they endured for it.

The Irish girl's focus on genteel life, furthermore, had a long term payoff. Irish maids used what they learned about how the gentry lived to win social mobility for the first generation of American-born Irish. Mothers considered it their role to advance the status of their families, and they actively prepared daughters to continue the effort. The first generation of Irish laywomen and nuns built an impressive women's network through which widows could be helped, orphans fed, workers trained, and young girls educated. Indeed, the single-mindedness of this group in educating the community's daughters eventually produced a lopsided parochial school system that disadvantaged boys. (By the 1870s, the Catholics in America were running 87 schools for boys and 209 for girls.) The first American-born generation of Irish girls came to dominate schoolteaching and nursing as their mothers had dominated service. The economic and social progress of Irish women outdistanced any other group of immigrant females.

Irish women, fiercely loyal to their families, their community, and their church, were offended by the nativist rhetoric of the early feminists and opposed to their unorthodox views on marriage and divorce. These women weren't ignorant of the controversy over women's rights, but they were forced to choose between feminism and the dignity of their own community. The Yankee feminists, however, simply assumed that the lack of support for their ideas was due to the Irish women's "slavish" adherence to both the Catholic church and the desires of their "brutish" husbands. Yet with their economic autonomy, their strong ties to other females, and the activist network they built with Catholic nuns, Irish women were, in fact, closer to achieving the social structure imagined by feminists than were leaders of the woman movement themselves. When Irish women failed to join the ranks of the movement, their absence voiced ethnic, religious, and class conflict—both public and personal—that subsumed issues of gender.

## Women in the Fashion Industry

Much of the dress reform effort was funneled through the supervised homes and clubs that well-intentioned Anglo-Protestant ladies ran for the factory workers. Through institutions such as the Young Women's Christian Association (YWCA), "reform women" tried to protect the working girl, particularly her virginity, and to provide her with morally acceptable recreation and spiritual uplift. "Working girls' clubs" often emphasized activities directed toward encouraging sexual abstinence, including frequent morality talks and lectures on "modest" grooming, dress, and manners. The age difference between the reformers and the average workers shored up the "ladies'" maternal attitude toward their charges. The girls themselves, however, often chafed under such "protection," resented the intrusion, and worked toward renting homes with others like themselves instead.

Whether they lived at the Y, with relatives, or with their peers, working girls tried to wear fashionable clothing. The wealthy women who wanted to "reform" them usually chalked this behavior up to the inherent foolishness and misdirected vanity of the urban masses, but other suspicions were also aroused. The swelling numbers of stylishly dressed working women in the Boston community, for example, caused so much concern in the early 1880s that a large-scale social study—one of the first ever done in America—was undertaken to determine the moral status of this increasingly visible group. The reasoning was that since young working women could not possibly afford the clothes they were wearing on their meager wages, there must be a huge prostitution racket going on. The study was to uncover this unsavory activity, for which the only evidence in hand was the dressing habits of working women.

After interviews were conducted among over a thousand working girls as well as their parents, friends, neighborhood police, and employers, it was determined that there was no such connection between the stylish dress and the morals of the young women. Not only was no prostitution discovered, the researchers commented that the clothing was usually made at home after work, by the girl herself, and showed remarkable creativity and an astute use of means. Their analysis of the spending patterns of the young women showed that, at $67.75 a year, clothing was the second largest expenditure these girls made—food and lodging being the first—but the third largest expense, which followed closely behind at $67.33, was the support of others, usually relatives. The average annual savings was larger than either of these categories, at $72.15. The young women were fully exonerated. Despite this kind of evidence, the display of attractive dress among working women continued to be attributed to immorality.[38]

The fashion industry employed large numbers of women outside of the factories. In department stores, for instance, the department heads, stylists, promotion managers, buyers, and salespeople were nearly all women. Ambitious seamstresses became designers, opening small shops and showrooms of their own. Millinery also provided opportunities for skilled workers or proprietors. So, too, with jewelry design. A substantial number of women became "penny capitalists," often basing their businesses on a fashion innovation, a talent for design, or a new cosmetic preparation.[39]

The fashion press, even in its infancy, was written, edited, illustrated, and produced primarily by women. In addition to publishing instructions for acquiring the appearance of gentility, these writers played an important role in changing the genteel aesthetic to accommodate work without the loss of respectability. As the writers of fashion magazines were themselves working women, it was clearly in their best interest to propagate such a view.

Whether they were dress designers, shop girls, factory workers, or magazine editors, women who worked had to confront the attitude that attributed immorality to anyone who was not a lady of leisure, especially when she dressed well. Yet all the avenues that offered advancement required good English, genteel grooming, pleasant manners, and fashionable dress. And, in all these areas of opportunity, knowledge of fashion, an eye for color and style, an ability to present goods in an attractive way, and skill at persuading customers were the tools of the trade. Mastery of these elements won the cooperation and respect of coworkers and the promise of rising status.

The feminists' insistence on the immorality of fashion was unlikely to be persuasive to a woman trying to make a living in one of its many walks. From the beginning, women workers of all ethnicities felt that the movement had nothing to offer them. In fact, the early movement was insensitive to issues surrounding most work. It should be obvious at this point that it is not true, as is often claimed, that women of the day were excluded from the labor force. Common women—that is, *most* women—were not barred from employment at all, but worked hard on farms and in factories, as seamstresses and servants. However, for the early feminists, taking one of those jobs would have meant a loss of caste. The occupations that the founding feminists demanded be opened to them were those once defined as "leisure"—law, medicine, ministry—and so were appropriate for gentry. Most of these required university training.

Even before winning access to the universities, the early feminists were substantially better educated than most other women. Unfortunately, they exploited this advantage when they advocated an educational qualification for female suffrage—as a conscious attempt at excluding the working women they viewed as inferior.[40]

## Women in the Arts

The founding feminists challenged traditional standards of decency by giving speeches and publishing essays. By appearing in public, they opened themselves to being called "public women," a catch-all term referring not only to prostitutes but to any woman who displayed herself in public, who worked in public, or even who allowed her writing to be displayed through publication.

It's hard to imagine a situation in which a journalist or a poet would be essentially the same as a prostitute.[41] Think for a moment, though, about the practice of keeping "respectable" women wrapped in heavy robes or hidden behind walls in some parts of the world today. For those women, going out in public without heavy wraps is enough to impugn their reputation forever and can result in their being expelled from their own families, or even killed. To go out with one's face uncovered and speak to a crowd would be an unthinkable offense. Those systems of oppression through seclusion are historically related to the concept of the "public woman" in America. "Respectable" women were to be kept "under wraps," as it were, and any venture out into public life—whether it was literally putting oneself on display or merely putting one's thoughts on display—was an invitation to disrepute.

On this basis, feminist historians emphasize the risks involved in the public activities undertaken by the founding feminists—and rightly so. However, the same writers often belittle the public activities of women in other venues, such as actresses and dancers. Such selective judgment is consistent with the reform tradition. Through the social purity movement, the early feminists' energies were focused on measures designed to censure or stop the activities of other women in the public realm; feminists argued that *those* women were disreputable. The negative attitude that more recent feminist theorists have had toward women in the arts, particularly models and actresses, appears to be a vestige of this hostility between the Puritan feminists and women who offended the social purity movement by dancing, acting, writing, posing for pictures, or otherwise becoming public women.

These "Jezebels," as social purists called them, commonly painted their faces, which were splashed across the pages of popular newspapers, magazines, and posters, giving disreputable women unprecedented public exposure.[42] When today's feminists tell you that only "disreputable women" painted in the nineteenth century, they are including some women in that category who would be acclaimed, powerful, and respected today. Several famous journalists of the nineteenth-century were beautiful, flamboyant, strong, and always dressed to the nines, but to the social purity reformers they were just another group of Jezebels. Elizabeth Cochrane, Winifred Black, and Leonel Campbell O'Bryan wouldn't have been invited to a Yankee Protestant suffrage meeting on a cold day in hell.[43]

Far and away the most noticed group—by both audiences and reformers—was actresses. Because of their association with the "corruption" of the theater, actresses were definitely not considered reputable women. However, acting was highly lucrative and offered independence even to women. Therefore, American girls have been running away to join the theater for a long time. And, while the upper classes and diehard Protestants looked down on it, other, less self-righteous groups enjoyed the theater and admired the people who were in it. Theatrical fame could even overcome ethnic prejudice, as the popularity of Irish actresses during this period demonstrates. Even so, actresses could not be included in "polite" social gatherings until the 1910s and did not begin to have the kind of cultural currency they have now until the 1920s.

The nineteenth-century Jezebels were just as instrumental in pushing the boundaries of appropriate gender behavior as were the early feminists, contributing to the emancipation of women in both social life and economic activity. By their example, women in the arts challenged the notion that a well-dressed woman must be a weak-willed whore—a notion that feminists then and now have taken all too seriously.

Ironically, the most famous feminist of the early 1800s was widely considered a "public woman" in the worst sense. Frances Wright, a Scottish immigrant, was one of this country's first speakers and writers on the rights of women. Wright favored interracial breeding as the antidote to racial problems, talk that shocked "real Americans" who, like the founding feminists, thought purity of the Anglo-Saxon "race" should be preserved. She invited further censure by speaking to crowds that included immigrants, blacks, and "those of the meaner sort." She also advocated sexual freedom for women, known then as free love. The term "Fanny Wrightist," in fact, was a nineteenth-century pejorative for a feminist, particularly one with thoughts of sexual freedom. The Puritan feminists steered clear of this brave, articulate woman because they did not want their movement besmirched by association with her.[44]

## CONCLUSION

Let's return at last to our opening scene, in which Susan B. Anthony has just stopped Paulina Wright Davis and Elizabeth Oakes Smith dead in their tracks by accusing them of being too fashionably dressed. Now that we have drawn in the larger social context, a few additional details will help us to produce a more informed explanation for this event.

Most of the early feminists experienced the modern economy as a loss in stature compared to their parents rather than a gain. Paulina Wright Davis, however, had had a run of luck. Although born to a "good" Massachusetts family, she was orphaned early and sent to relatives on the frontier. After returning, she married one of the newly wealthy textile manufacturers, but he died before they had children, leaving Paulina independently wealthy. She remarried, this time to a jewelry manufacturer who was also loaded. When, at this very meeting, it was decided the group should publish the first feminist newspaper, Paulina Wright Davis promptly funded the *Una* out of her own pocket. Davis was already known as "a Fanny Wright woman," having scandalized New England when, in her zeal to improve the health education of young women, she had gone to female seminaries, teaching anatomy using a model of a naked woman.

Elizabeth Oakes Smith was a public woman because she was a paid journalist, a paid lecturer, and a paid literary figure. In the 1850s she was, quite literally, famous. To add further to her shame, she was the sole support of her husband and their four children. Smith was an unapologetic admirer of Fanny Wright. In fact, one of the only records we have of Wright's later lectures is the description written by Smith. Smith lectured for seven years on women's rights, speeches attended by the likes of Henry Clay, Bronson Alcott, and Henry David Thoreau as well as by immigrant laborers. She shared the platform with Ralph Waldo Emerson, Horace Greeley, and Henry Ward Beecher. In spite of the fact that Smith's speeches were well regarded and her essays circulated widely, her work is never included in the feminist anthologies today. And in histories of the feminist movement, Elizabeth Oakes Smith is mentioned only as the woman Susan Anthony felled from the platform because of her dress, if she is mentioned at all.[45]

Both Davis and Smith had opinions and allegiances with which the feminists were unsympathetic. Both were more cosmopolitan, more inclusive, and more open-minded than the other members of the convention. These two had already come to the realization that the movement needed to reach as many as possible, which meant building bridges to the poor and foreign women their contemporaries held in contempt. Although Davis and Smith both came from unimpeachable New England ancestry, neither accepted the tenets of its culture. Davis rejected the church early in her career and was already making "bold and direct" statements about marriage reform. She was also an outspoken advocate of "spiritualism," a powerfully popular alternative to the mainstream Christian faiths of the nineteenth century. Smith was volubly contemptuous of Quaker asceticism, and by the early 1850s she was flirting with joining the Catholic church, having been profoundly influenced by Bishop O'Reilly of New York. In 1851 Smith had lectured against dress reform in a talk called "Dress, Its Social and Aesthetic Relations," which was based on a pamphlet she had published earlier.

To the audience at the 1852 convention, Smith and Davis must have seemed the personification of all that threatened Yankee Protestant hegemony. The presence of several Puritan clergy in the crowd that day probably made the early feminists particularly sensitive to Smith's and Wright's associations. It is unlikely they would have wanted these men to see them vote for such unsavory characters as leaders. Perhaps they were relieved when an unknown Quaker provided them with an excuse to elect someone else.

The incident between Anthony and Smith was thus far more complex than the one-righteous-feminist-confronting-a-worldly-imposter story it appears to be at first. What occurred was a confrontation between worldviews: ultra and modern, religious and secular, ascetic and cosmopolite, intolerant and tolerant. My aim in situating the early feminists in their historical context is to raise readers' doubts about whether it is appropriate to adopt their philosophy of dress uncritically. The early feminists did not and could not speak for all women. Their view was no more privileged in its "correctness" than that of the ultras with whom they were associated. Their "reform" ideas about dress were conveniently appropriate for shoring up their preeminence as Anglos, Protestants, Whig sympathizers, Nativists, and gentry. If the dress reform movement was not the articulation of a universal premise but the rhetoric of a group reasserting its challenged social status, we need to rethink our acceptance of its principles in feminist politics today.

## CHAPTER 3

# MAKING THE MYTH

OPPONENTS OF THE WOMAN MOVEMENT ACCUSED ITS ADHERENTS OF BEING UNFEMININE. The founding feminists defended themselves in speeches and essays, quickly developing a strategy that would become a stock tactic in feminist rhetoric: discrediting femininity by ridiculing it. The feminists used their fledgling press to "revile and repudiate" more traditional women through exaggerated images of "frivolous, simpering gossips who were both physically and mentally weak." In acid tones, they recast the Steel-Engraving Lady's quiet manner as passivity; her desire to make others comfortable became hypocrisy. Her character, once thought the height of civilized achievement, became "viney, and twiney, and whiney." The great lady's famous judgments of taste were transformed into a slavish adherence to "fashion."[1]

The nineteenth century feminists were also aware that simply to condemn the Steel-Engraving Lady was insufficient. An alternative character had to be produced to exemplify their principles, illustrate their vision of the future of women, and win converts. Therefore, the core group of organizers began very early to discuss what the ideal of their new movement should be like, how she should dress and talk. Through their speeches and published works, as well as through the example of their own personal dress, this group tried to define a new "True Woman" for the society. Their readers, their audiences, their allies, and their adversaries took up the question as well. In the ensuing debate, the new character was named the "New Woman." Thus began the continuing controversy over what a good feminist should look like.

In the process of inventing the New Woman, Puritan feminists employed methods identical to those of the new fashion media, and they experienced some surprising success. Much of what happened, however, has since been retold so selectively that these uncomfortable facts have dropped from view. A great deal of mythologizing has gone on—some of it by the founding feminists themselves and the rest by those who followed.

## THE BLOOMER STORY

The dress question was brought into focus for feminism by the introduction of the bloomer in 1851. In feminist mythology, the bloomer story goes something like this. A small group of feminists adopted loose, gathered trousers as a challenge to the tyranny of fashion, whose long, heavy skirts oppressed women by fettering their freedom of movement and making them sex objects. The bloomers were offensive to the public because they looked like men's trousers and because they were such an affront to the elaborate tastes of the period. The bloomers also were not sexy, as the corseted looks of fashion were. This small group of feminists bravely wore the new costume despite unfriendly audiences and street crowds wherever they went. There were many frightening incidents, including one in which two feminists were threatened by a crowd of hoodlums in New York City. Eventually the public reaction became overwhelming, and the group abandoned the bloomers. The power of the fashion industry had simply been too much for them. The meaning of the event can be (and usually is) summarized in Stanton's words: "Yet such is the tyranny of custom, that to escape constant observation, criticism, ridicule, persecution, mobs, one after another gladly went back to the old slavery and sacrificed freedom to repose. I have never wondered since that the Chinese women allow their daughters' feet to be encased in iron shoes, nor that the Hindoo widows walk calmly to the funeral pyre."[2]

A closer look at the sequence of events reveals contradictions in the accepted mythology, however. In the early winter of 1851, Elizabeth Cady Stanton's favorite cousin came back from Europe dressed in an outfit she had seen on actress Fanny Kemble, an ankle-length dress with what were then called "Turkish trousers" underneath. Rich, eccentric Libby Smith Miller's costume was as luxurious as it was unorthodox. The dress itself was made of plain, high-quality black broadcloth, but Miller had accessorized it with a Spanish cloak, dark furs, and a beaver hat with feathers. Stanton quickly saw the practical advantages. The two cousins made up a new suit, and Stanton was thrilled with the freedom it gave her.

Days later Stanton and Miller went into Seneca Falls to show their radical new rags to the deputy postmaster, one Amelia Bloomer, who decided to try the outfit herself. Over the next few months Stanton and Bloomer persuaded others in their community to adopt the style. Then, in April 1851, Bloomer endorsed the costume in her women's temperance paper, *The Lily,* followed soon by sketches of herself and Stanton in their new clothes. Letters poured into the editorial office asking for a pattern. The editor obliged and from then on the costume, which had previously been known as Turkish dress or Oriental dress, was called Bloomers.

Through *The Lily,* Bloomer and Stanton offered suggestions for materials and accessories for women wanting to make the new dress. These bloomers were not an ascetic uniform, as the official story suggests, but were created in a variety of fabrics and colors and were accessorized with an eye to style. According to Stanton's biographer: "By adopting the bloomer style and advertising its convenience, Stanton hoped to set an example that would be widely copied. She urged that the outfit be made of 'the richest materials, not gaudy, but . . . tasteful.'" *The Lily* even published "fashion plates" of the costume. Both Bloomer and Stanton appeared in a daguerreotype in September 1851. In short, *The Lily* was operating in a manner similar to the fashion press, promoting a particular look and presenting its staff as arbiters of taste.[3]

The bloomer costume became quite the rage. Bloomers appeared in fashion magazines and ads and were favorably reviewed by *Harper's Monthly.* Bloomer balls were thrown in cities throughout the country, where dances called the "Bloomer polka" and the "Bloomer quadrille" were performed. Popular plays about "Bloomer girls" were written and staged.

These events turned Amelia Bloomer into a celebrity. During the first year of the bloomer, the circulation of *The Lily* grew from five hundred to four thousand and went from a monthly to a twice-monthly schedule, a phenomenon most attribute to women's interest in the new dress. Suddenly the postmaster from rural New York was on the national lecture circuit, drawing huge, admiring crowds wherever she went. The *New York Journal* wrote: "If ever a lady waked up one morning and found herself famous, that woman was Mrs. Bloomer; she has immortalized her name, and the Bloomer Costume will become as celebrated as Mary Queen of Scots' Cap, the Elizabeth Ruff, or the Pompadour Robe."[4]

By the 1851 Fourth of July celebrations, women all over the nation were wearing bloomers. At the Antislavery Festival that year ten women appeared in bloomers, all of them in bright colors with white trousers that Stanton reported "pleased me very much." Although the bloomer costume was very popular in New York and New England where the Yankee Protestant feminists were, it was even more popular on the frontier and in the West—and gained acceptance even in parts of the South. More than sixty women attended a ball in Akron, Ohio, in bloomer dress. The local newspaper reported that "long dresses hitherto hid from view all the graceful movements of the lady dancers; but here all was visible which related to the 'poetry of motion.'" Nearly every woman who attended an elegant ball in nearby Toledo wore bloomers, and it was said that at least two hundred were wearing them in Cleveland. The *Dubuque Tribune* reported that the new dress was spreading "like prairie fire" there. Thirty-one young women in Battle Creek, Michigan's Fourth of July parade wore bloomers. The *New York Tribune* reported that a dressmaker in California had put a fashion doll in her window and began wearing bloomers while in her store: "Men and women all over the city talked of nothing else. The general impression is decidedly favourable, and I should not be surprised to see it generally adopted." In September the costume spread to Florida, when "three of Alabama's fairest daughters magnificently dressed in the Bloomer Costume" arrived and "produced quite a sensation."[5]

The publicity initially generated by the bloomer fad put women's rights in a favorable light. It is important to stipulate, however, that there were other associations attached to the bloomers besides women's rights. Although the "Bloomer" name was affixed to the costume, it had been worn by actresses first—and continued to be associated with these popular heroines even as the Puritan feminists adopted it. Bloomer trousers also looked very much like pantalets peeping out below the skirt. Pantaloons, although new in America, had long been common in France. In fact, the associations with France had given pantaloons erotic content—so they had been worn mostly by prostitutes before their widespread acceptance among "respectable" women during the 1850s. Furthermore, the bloomer costume had been worn in Robert Owen's New Harmony commune during the 1820s and so was very much associated with free love and "Fanny Wright women." Therefore, to the contemporary observer, the costume was not just a masculine outfit, but also had "improper" associations with France, prostitutes, unmarried sex, and actresses—not to mention that the wearer simply looked like her underwear was showing.

Once the bloomer fad caught on, Stanton's brother-in-law, Daniel Eaton, invited Elizabeth and Cousin Libby to New York for a visit: "You and Mrs. Miller can keep each other in countenance, whenever you wish to promenade Broadway in 'shorts.' The novelty of seeing a Bloomer in New York is so effectually worn off that I hear of no more insults or annoyance being offered to such as choose to wear the costume. So please pack up your coats and trousers and come along." Excited about their trip to the city, the two made new bloomers from the best fabric and trimmed them with lace. They toured New York dressed this way and experienced no difficulties whatsoever. Stanton wrote to Mrs. Bloomer: "The talk about it being dangerous to walk the streets in the new costume, all humbug!" Stanton enjoyed the trip so much that, upon her return, she had a bloomer evening gown made in white satin and wore it to a ball. She danced until the wee hours and everyone said she looked wonderful.[6]

Bloomers, like hula hoops, were a short-lived fad, however. By autumn 1851 the outfit was waning in popularity and beginning to attract more ridicule than admiration. Some leading feminists, most notably Anthony, were quite late in adopting it. So some taunts that those women endured may have been the result of being seen in clothing that was already out of style.

During 1852 bloomers also took on a new political dimension. In January Susan Anthony had a bitter confrontation with the New York temperance clergy over including women in their meetings. Anthony formed the Women's State Temperance Society for the explicit purpose of challenging the clergy. She made plans to hold a convention that very spring. Anthony invited her new friend, Elizabeth Cady Stanton, to speak because she knew that Stanton would incite the group with her radical ideas.

Stanton took the stage in a black satin dress with trousers of the same material and black "congress" gaiters showing from underneath. Her sleeves were trimmed with white linen cuffs and at her neck she wore a white linen collar fastened with a gold pin. This outfit was not only more aggressively masculine than her other bloomer costumes, it also seems aimed to mimic clerical dress. By presenting herself in this way, Stanton implicitly challenged the male leaders of this movement, a challenge she made explicit in her talk. Stanton roused the women present to take control of their own funds, to deny their male members a vote, and to put together a group of traveling female lecturers. Stanton was voted president of the society, and Susan Anthony was made the general agent in charge of their new field effort. In the next issue of *The Lily,* Amelia Bloomer reported Stanton's address, including a detailed description of what she was wearing. Thus, the new political twist on the costume was quickly communicated to many of its adherents.

In the autumn of 1852, the men's temperance group met again. Bloomer and Anthony appeared, both wearing black bloomers. The exchange that ensued was heated, and the meeting degenerated into chaos. Again, the event was described in detail by Amelia Bloomer for *The Lily.* During the next six months, the bloomer issue was debated in the Yankee religious press. Throughout the winter, Bloomer reported later, the strongest objections came from the Puritan ministry. The debate was fought almost entirely on religious terms, with each side quoting Bible verses and claiming points of early Hebrew and Christian dress.

Bloomers also appeared in the antislavery arena during this time. Lucy Stone, already a famous abolitionist orator, was introduced to Stanton and Anthony in Seneca Falls in the spring of 1852. Impressed with their attire, Stone made herself a pair of black bloomers, which she wore to the annual New York antislavery meeting. She caused a stir but was allowed to speak as usual. For the next year Stone wore bloomers at speaking engagements throughout the Northeast, some of which drew crowds of two and three thousand people.

During 1852, therefore, the bloomer became the mark of a "radical cadre" rather than merely an amusing alternative fashion. It was then seen as "a political statement of the 'ultras,' . . . the most advanced, radical, and controversial of the woman's rights advocates." Remember, though, that becoming the "ultra uniform" meant more than just an association with women's rights; the ultras coalesced around abolition, temperance, and feminism, but also social purity, censorship, and Nativism. Solidly identified with Yankee Protestant elitism, ultras were consistently characterized as pompous and judgmental. Whether the feminists were offensive to the public or not, the ultras certainly were. In fact, the feminist movement had been criticized for its association with the "excesses" of ultraism from the beginning.[7]

The ultraist clergy retaliated against the new women's challenge by packing the females' temperance meeting of 1853 with conservative women. Stanton was voted out as president. Furious, she vowed to turn the movement into a forum for women's rights. It was at this point that the "woman movement" really began to have an impetus of its own; however, it was also at this point that Elizabeth Cady Stanton stopped wearing bloomers and began to discourage her colleagues from wearing them. So, although Stanton later blamed the demise of the bloomer on other women's sensitivity to disapproval, in truth all the other feminist leaders and many of their followers wore the bloomers far longer than she did.

Amelia Bloomer, for instance, continued to wear her bloomers for eight years, apparently without mishap. Bloomer, however, had continued to design her outfits in appealing, even stylish, ways. For instance, in June 1853 she appeared before a sellout crowd at Metropolitan Hall in New York wearing a dark brown tunic and bloomers trimmed with rows of black velvet topped by a red and black hat. The dress "had a large, open corsage, with belt and a diamond stud pin." There were three thousand in the respectful crowd that night, and many others were turned away for lack of seats. Bloomer toured Connecticut and was met by scores of bloomer-clad women of all ages. She was even invited to give the Fourth of July speech in Hartford, Connecticut that year, for which she wore bloomers. When she stopped in her hometown, former neighbors and relatives—many wearing bloomers—were so proud of her they begged her to speak at the church that night. So many people showed up that the church couldn't hold them all, so Bloomer stayed for a second night. This is not the way people treat a pariah.

Lucy Stone also continued lecturing in bloomers that year. Despite her fears that crowds would be unfriendly, she found that the bloomers were expected and so did not inspire as much controversy as she anticipated. Stone spent most of 1853 traveling to New England, Ohio, Michigan, Illinois, and Canada, wearing bloomers and breaking audience records the whole way. That year she drew the biggest crowds ever assembled in St. Louis and Toronto. Her rise to fame was so spectacular that reform leader Thomas Wentworth Higginson announced "Lucy is Queen of us all!" Stone was even invited to speak to the Massachusetts legislature in 1853, which she did in her bloomers. It was at that address that Lucy Stone's future husband, Henry Blackwell, saw her for the first time. Although he was not fond of the bloomers, they didn't stop him from chasing after Lucy trying to convince her to marry him.[8]

The actual harassment of Stone and Anthony by "hoodlums" takes on an expanded meaning in context. The incident apparently occurred when the two came to New York in September 1853.[9] The purpose of their trip was to attend the highly publicized meetings of the Anti-Slavery Society, the Whole World's Temperance Convention, and the Women's Rights Convention, which were all to take place within a week of each other. Legions of ultras went to town for this event. The convention, filled to "standing-room only," was covered by every representative of the press and produced a tidy sum in ticket sales.

The meetings held that week focused public attention on issues that were about to tear the country apart. The newspapers were predicting trouble. The event drew unruly crowds, including working class and Irish who were notably unreceptive to the ministrations of the Anglo-Protestant gentry. When Stone and Anthony ventured into the street that week, dressed in the black bloomers that had become the ultra uniform, they were surrounded by a group of "hoodlums" (read: working-class males, probably Irish), who teased them and wouldn't let them go. A friend who happened by called the police and they were rescued. According to Stone, the teasing, however uncomfortable it made the women feel, was good-natured. Given the riots that accompanied such confrontations in those days, the situation could have been worse.

Bloomers had a variety of effects on observers, depending on the occasion and the manner in which they were worn. It appears that bloomers began as a fashion fad and initially had meanings and proponents other than those they came to have in their second year. Far from being sexually neutral, bloomers clearly had an erotic appeal to some men. Like many departures from conventional fashion, bloomers were seen as silly or shocking and were worn mostly by the young. And, like other fashion innovations, the public eye appears to have become accustomed to them fairly quickly.

When linked to the ultras, bloomers usually were produced in an all-black, austere style, which clearly distinguished the uniform from its earlier, lighthearted form. Any serious controversy seems to have occurred within the old Puritan community, where the bloomer was presented as a challenge to the clergy and was debated on moral and religious terms, rather than on issues of comfort or practicality. So, generalizing the reaction of the Puritan clergy to the society at large, as is usually done, is probably not warranted.

It does not appear that the costume was ever a threat to the fashion industry. If anything, the early feminists seem to have enjoyed their moment as fashion arbiters and took advantage of the celebrity the costume brought them. Although some negative reaction to the costume among political "outsiders" seems to have developed by 1853, it is impossible to isolate feminism from the other social issues represented by the ultras and therefore unreasonable to attribute the reaction exclusively to gender politics.

The meaning of the bloomer costume differed even in the minds of the core group of feminists, however. Susan Anthony adopted it with a fervor that neither Bloomer nor Stanton nor Miller brought to the costume, and she discarded it only with tears and a great sense of failure. Afterward, Anthony wore only loosely cut black dresses in public. She loved colored clothes, but gave them up because she believed subjugation of self entailed wearing bleak clothing and that it was only through self-denial that the cause could be won. We can understand this thinking by learning something about Anthony's past. Doing so is particularly important since, as the century wore on, the New Woman was increasingly identified with the image of Susan B. Anthony.

## THE ANTHONY NEW WOMAN

Anthony grew up in a Quaker household where no toys, no music, no pictures, and no colored clothing were allowed. Although her mother occasionally dressed the children in plaids or stripes, she otherwise conformed rigidly to the norms of the Friends. Susan was educated in a female seminary that focused on beating self-esteem out of its students. This approach to child rearing, part of the Puritan tradition, was used with both sexes and has been described as resulting in "morbid self-abasement in the midst of morbid self-concern."[10]

Anthony first left home in 1846 to go to Canajoharie, New York, to teach school because her family was having temporary financial problems. When she arrived at this lovely village, she had only Quaker gray dresses in her trunk. Anthony was shy, young, and unsure of herself, even in the classroom. At the end of her first term, she was required to give a public examination of her students. She was scared to death. One of her non-Quaker relatives who lived in Canojaharie persuaded her to buy a blue and purple plaid dress with matching shoes for the occasion. A cousin braided Susan's hair in a more elaborate style than she usually wore it. The townsfolk were impressed with her appearance and said so. The examination also was quite successful. The impact of this event on Anthony was remarkable. She relaxed her teaching style, which had been rigid and authoritarian. She began to show a sense of humor. She wrote and produced a play. Her students, who had respected her, came to love her. She began going to parties and on buggy rides with men. She even tried to dance.

Susan's self-confidence, which had been pitifully stunted, grew. She described the change as a "greater flow of spirits." When her family's finances stabilized, she began to create a wardrobe for herself: a "gypsy hat," a fox muff, a plum-colored dress, and flowers to trim her bonnets. But she also stopped going home for visits. Her biographer suggests that she had become "independent, emotionally as well as economically." Then, as suddenly as she had adopted them, Susan rejected the clothes, the parties, the young men, and all that went with them. She claimed she had abandoned her new, happy lifestyle after seeing young men drinking at a party. She declared little Canajoharie "a hot bed of vice and drunkenness." She put away the pretty clothes and went back to her old, severe hairstyle. She became a temperance activist.[11]

During this same period Susan began obsessing about her mother's sad life. The deep depressions she had had as a child returned. In her dreams, Susan's mother was dying because her daughter had not come home. She began writing long letters to her mother. Finally she quit work and moved back to her family. Susan and her mother renewed their relationship. Biographer Kathleen Barry argues that this bonding with her mother was Anthony's feminist awakening. Certainly it was when the Susan Anthony the world would know—ascetic, humorless, and judgmental, as well as brave, persevering, and idealistic—came to the fore. But it was also a period in which Anthony experienced severe psychic distress and in which she sacrificed her financial and emotional independence, apparently out of guilt.

It is ironic that Anthony's conversion would be seen as an act of sympathy with her mother, since her return to ascetic behavior mimics the actual source of her mother's suffering. Lucy Read Anthony had renounced pretty clothes, music, and other innocent pleasures as the price of marrying the man she loved. Yet Daniel Anthony's church refused to accept his marriage to a Baptist. Susan Anthony's mother spent the rest of her life trying to outdo the Quakers' austerity. The once-vivacious young woman turned inward and became distant; she always had a sad look about her and a defeated tone of voice. She stopped singing, never even indulging in a lullaby to her babies. The only times that she exhibited any remaining ability to reach outside was when she dressed her children in plaids and stripes. Yet she never became a Quaker herself, contending that she was not good enough. This was precisely the kind of quiet hell the Puritan-Quaker community excelled in producing for women. I see no reason to heroize Susan Anthony for giving in to it.

Anthony's conversion was the first of the now-standard feminist renunciation of pretty clothes as the public proclamation of rebirth. More than a century later, in her book *Femininity and Domination,* Sandra Bartky supported the continued insistence that feminists should express their new politics by changing their clothes, their friends, their recreations: "To be a feminist, one has first to become one. For many feminists, this involves the experience of a profound personal transformation, an experience which goes far beyond that sphere of human activity we regard ordinarily as 'political.' This transforming experience, which cuts across the ideological divisions within the women's movement, is complex and multifaceted. In the course of undergoing the transformation to which I refer, the feminist changes *her behavior:* she makes new friends; she responds differently to people and events; her habits of consumption change; sometimes she alters her living arrangements or, more dramatically, her whole style of life."[12] This oft-represented epiphany usually evokes a profound sense of anomie and expresses itself in an aggressively austere outward appearance. Anthony's own transformation seems solidly situated in her own religious attitudes and cultural upbringing. The initial connection to overbearing Puritan-Quaker self-righteousness has now been forgotten. Nevertheless, the event has been reenacted by thousands of feminists like a sacrament of unknown origin.

Anthony's conversion, Stanton's address to the Women's State Temperance Society, Anthony's public condemnation of Elizabeth Oakes Smith, and Anthony's own adoption of the bloomer occurred, in that order, within a six-month period in 1852. We can see, therefore, that Anthony, like her arch enemies the Puritan clergy, leapt easily from her own austere choice to trying to police others into doing the same. When today's campus feminist groups pressure lipstick-wearing women to change their style or leave the group, they are repeating an old and long established phenomenon of feminist society.

Unlike her friend Susan, Elizabeth Cady Stanton preferred a mode of dress she deemed "sensible," which meant comfortable and practical, but also occasionally self-indulgent, and she was disinclined to sacrifice small pleasures for big principles. Until Cousin Libby showed up in Turkish trousers, both Stanton and Bloomer had been against any change in clothing that would resemble men's. Only a few months before Stanton published an article that said, "As to their costume, the gents need have no fear of our imitating them, for we think it is in violation of every principle of duty, taste, and dignity; and, notwithstanding the contempt and abuse cast upon our loose garments, we still admire their easy graceful folds." The sudden adoption, as well as the equally rapid abandonment, of the bloomer costume was typical of Stanton's attitude toward dress and, to some degree, her behavior in politics. She changed her mind whenever it suited her purposes, and she seldom saw the inconsistencies between her own behavior and her criticism of others. She regularly assumed any woman dressed in style was a weak-willed idiot, yet she herself unapologetically indulged her taste for pretty clothes and fine point lace. In 1869 Stanton wrote that "the true idea of fashion is for the sexes to dress as nearly alike as possible." But in 1873 Dr. Mary Walker, who attended feminist conventions in a black tux and top hat, outraged Stanton: "I endured untold crucifixion at Washington. I suppose as I sat there I looked patient and submissive, but I would have boxed that Mary Walker with a vengeance." By the late 1870s Mary Walker was barred from feminist conventions, but by then Stanton was again calling for androgynous dress.[13]

As we saw in chapter 2, there were women within the feminists' inner circle who were less threatened by fashion than was Susan Anthony. Some of these leaders wanted to present a New Woman image that could act as a counterargument to claims that woman movement members were unfeminine. Paulina Wright Davis, for instance, feared that the appearance and manners of her colleagues would alienate audiences unnecessarily. She wanted to present a dignified, "ladylike" image that would work against the emergent popular perception that feminists were bearded old women given to smoking and cursing.

As the century progressed, however, Susan Anthony emerged as the living incarnation of the New Woman, and both her asceticism and her attitude of moral superiority came to be identified with the new prototype. Furthermore, although most of the early feminists were married, Anthony pushed the coming era as an "epoch of single women." Anthony herself was single, and she often felt betrayed when a friend married. Much of her negative view of married women appears related to her belief that the sex act was an act of dominance that reduced the woman to an object fit only to service her husband's basest needs.

Anthony used ideas gleaned from contemporary fiction to develop her own self-concept as well as her articulation of the new ideal. She was particularly fond of the new women's novels then coming out of England, such as those by the Brontë sisters. Rachel Brownstein, in her 1989 book *Becoming a Heroine,* argued that the heroines of these British novels represent the development of a feminist persona that was still the basis of self-creation for intellectual feminists. As Brownstein points out (approvingly), the new heroine was pointedly plain and usually an outcast. Her strengths were her noble spirit and her great intellect. This heroine, according to Brownstein, became a feminist talisman because she is "a heroine of the mind" instead of "a heroine of the body." These two categories are presented as being mutually exclusive. You cannot be pretty and also be "a heroine of the mind." And you must be an intellectual ("a heroine of the mind") to be a feminist. In Brownstein's book, therefore, we see contemporary evidence of that process begun by Susan Anthony: defining "the good feminist" as plain, asexual, intellectual, ascetic, and antisocial.[14]

To take on the attributes increasingly associated with this New Woman meant becoming chronically alienated from the society and, essentially, living alone or with feminist friends, but never with a family. It also meant grooming to be plain and denying yourself sensual experience of almost any kind. Needless to say, it took a special kind of woman to find this ideal appealing. Had it not been for an alternative concept of the New Woman developed by Lucy Stone, the fledgling movement might have died for lack of new recruits.

## THE STEEL-ENGRAVING FEMINIST

At the time Lucy Stone moved into the Stanton circle, she was already a nationally known orator. She had been the first American woman to receive a college degree in rhetoric. Just like Ralph Waldo Emerson, Henry David Thoreau, Wendell Phillips, and William Lloyd Garrison, Lucy Stone could stir the passions of an audience, make them laugh, and move them to tears. Any well-trained orator knows that the tools of rhetoric include not just words but voice inflection, gestures, facial expression, dress, hairstyle, and the overall character communicated to the audience. It is axiomatic in rhetoric that all of these tools are to be employed as effectively as possible. Stone altered her accent and her vocabulary slightly to suit each audience, fitting her persona to frontier farmers or northeastern transcendentalists, as the occasion required. She was so good at this that she could stand up in front of an audience in the most extreme bloomer get-up possible and use her voice, words, and face to communicate the most ladylike of characters. She could appear before an unfriendly crowd and have them nodding agreement while remarking that she looked like a woman with a home, a baby, and a husband—even when she had none of these things.

In her youth, Stone never had sympathy with women who decorated themselves in even a minimal way. She herself dressed in plain calicoes and "Quaker bonnets." She also had a strong aversion to the idea of marriage and to sex in particular. Stone was, therefore, as natural an exemplar as Anthony of the "single blessedness" that was the ideal of the movement in the 1840s and 1850s.

Lucy was lonely, however, and the ardent Henry Blackwell was determined to convince her to marry him. Henry made promises and concessions to her fear of being entrapped in matrimony, and he honored them. Lucy Stone was the first American woman to keep her own name after marriage. The couple's marriage vows included a protest renouncing the rights of husbands over their wives' person, earnings, property, and children. They were reprinted in papers around the country.

Anthony, Stanton, and Stone had a falling out in the aftermath of the Civil War. A rift occurred in the suffrage movement and two separate groups were formed, the "radical" one led by Stanton and Anthony (the National Women's Suffrage Association, or NWSA) and the "conservative" one led by Lucy Stone (the American Women's Suffrage Association, or AWSA). As leader of the conservative organization, Stone allied herself with members of Boston's reform community, a dignified, elite group. Men were included and the women dressed, acted, and wrote "like ladies." Just as she changed her manner to appeal to people in farming communities across the country during her younger years, she tailored her appearance to her new constituency. She began wearing a lace cap and collar and imitating the tenor and views of a gracious lady. Lucy Stone became the role model for thousands of prosperous women reformers.

Stone's editorial strategy in her periodical, the *Woman's Journal,* paralleled her sartorial tactic. The voice of the *Journal* was consistently dignified, while Anthony's and Stanton's *Revolution* was scrappy, sarcastic, and sometimes mean-spirited. Both journals addressed issues of dress from time to time, but the *Journal* was more traditionally feminine in its outlook. The persona of the New Woman, as developed by the *Journal,* seemed reasonable, as compared to the more radical image put forward by the *Revolution.* The *Journal* was able to attract advertisers and, eventually, to reduce its price enough to gain a large base of subscribers. The *Revolution* was seen as so inflamed, opportunistic, and hypocritical that even the reform community would not support it. After eighteen months, the *Revolution* folded and left Susan Anthony saddled with a $10,000 debt. The *Journal* lasted long enough to become the main suffrage paper of the twentieth century and eventually the official publication of the League of Women Voters.[15]

So the feminist movement came to have at least two competing ideals: the New Woman as exemplified by the ascetic, unorthodox Susan Anthony and an image we might call the Steel-Engraving Feminist as exemplified by Lucy Stone. The New Women commanded more attention from the press, but it was the Steel-Engraving Feminists who eventually supplied the suffrage movement with the numbers to stage marches, push petitions, and influence legislators. Well dressed, well placed, and polite as a group, they were comparatively more difficult to ridicule than the New Women and damned harder to ignore.

It's not surprising, perhaps, that today's feminists like to honor the New Women, but criticize or patronize the Steel-Engraving Feminists. Yet many American women joined the suffrage effort in spite of, not because of, the image of the New Woman as she was first developed by Susan Anthony. Were it not for the insight of Lucy Stone, the persona of the good feminist might never have been made accessible to the mainstream of American women.

## COMMERCE AND THE NEW WOMAN

Today's feminist critique often criticizes those in business who adopt feminist messages or styles. Consistently, ad campaigns, beauty editors, or fashion designers who try to respond to feminist imperatives are charged with "co-opting feminism for commercial purposes." Yet even early on, the dress reform and feminist movement provided financial rewards that the leaders accepted happily.

Amelia Bloomer certainly found dress reform to be a financial windfall. Not only was she invited to give speeches in prestigious places and lucrative venues, Bloomer also benefited substantially from the increase in the number of subscriptions to *The Lily* that the bloomer introduction brought. The incremental revenue from 5,500 more subscribers over the three-year period would have been $2,800, at a time when working women were lucky to earn $1 a week. By 1853 Bloomer could command fees for her speeches that were equal to those of the most popular and respected male lecturers of the day—and she insisted on getting them. When she sold *The Lily* in 1856, it had a national circulation of 6,000, which would have brought a very comfortable income of $6,000 a year. As an asset producing a $6,000 annuity, *The Lily* probably went for a substantial price.

Just before Henry Blackwell met Lucy Stone, he told his sisters that he wanted to marry money. Blackwell, who had lost all his inheritance on ill-advised investments but retained a singular penchant for material luxury, announced: "I see but one way to get into a position to do something—and that is to find some intelligent, go-ahead lady with a fortune to back her go-aheadativeness." Lucy Stone fit that description perfectly. She had begun public speaking in 1848, the first of the Puritan feminists to lecture. Her initial appearance got great reviews, so her second appearance drew a large crowd. Over the first three years of her career as a speaker, Stone managed to save $7,000—a huge sum at that time. The conservative press used her financial success as a point of criticism during the World Slavery Convention of 1853: She was accused of taking money from rural innocents who didn't know any better and was even charged with selling discounted "season tickets." By the time of her southern tour in 1854, Stone was netting between $500 and $1,000 a week.[16]

Stone retired from lecturing when she gave birth, but was forced back by Blackwell's poor money management. She quickly recovered that money and then some, outdrawing even the most publicized event of her time, singer Jenny Lind's tour promoted by P. T. Barnum. Stone was wealthy when she died, leaving enough to support Henry in leisure for the rest of his life, yet the women's movement had been her only work.

Lecturing on tour was a recognized get-rich-quick activity in the nineteenth century, but Elizabeth Cady Stanton did not take advantage of the money-earning opportunities offered by the movement until after her children were through their infancy. She was engaged by the New York Lyceum Bureau in 1869 and she earned $2,000 in the first seven months. She continued to lecture for eight months out of every year, for twelve years, earning $3,000 to $4,000 per annum. In the crucial convention year of 1871, Stanton did not want to forgo income by interrupting her lecture tour, so she sent a $100 donation instead.

Near the end of her life, Stanton appeared in a national advertising campaign for Fairy Soap (see figure 3.1). Feminist historian Mary Ryan writes: "The commonsense advertisements of the Fair [*sic*] Soap Company even resorted to feminism, picturing Elizabeth Cady Stanton extolling the virtue of their pure, simple cleansing product, unadulterated by perfume."[17] But appealing to feminist sentiments was not a desperate measure. Fairy Soap was a leading brand, and the campaign seems to have been a straightforward celebrity appeal. Stanton was only one among the marketable figures who were signed to hype the soap.

By the turn of the twentieth century, the New Woman, in fact, had a definite commercial appeal. Her upper-class status, university education, and "progressive" ideas made her quite chic. The New Woman was identifiable in Gilded Age imagery by her bloomers, her bicycle, and, quite often, her smoking (see figure 3.2). Undoubtedly feminists today would charge the fin de siècle fashion industry with co-opting feminism for profit, but we need to bear in mind the humbling information that feminism's founders were doing the same thing.

Figure 3.1. Elizabeth Cady Stanton endorses Fairy Soap. *Ladies Home Journal,* September 1899.

Figure 3.2. The fashionable New Woman appears in advertisements. *Ladies Home Journal,* April 1896.

The feminist press, further, had its own fashion commentary and its own style tips. By advocating their style of dress, feminists promoted more than natural comfort or physical hygiene, but a whole range of political, moral, religious, and financial interests. Thus, it seems that there is no essential difference between the dress reform activities of the early feminists and any other fashion enterprise. Instead of allowing this discourse to proceed as one between "fashion" and "antifashion," we should alter our concepts to recognize that we are really observing the competition between one form of fashion and another.

## MODERN WOMEN

Beyond the circle of the Puritan enthusiasts, but within their same world, were other women who challenged existing gender norms and invented new images of womanhood in the process. These women were known to the founding feminists—indeed, in some cases they were friends—but did not belong to the temperance/social purity crowd. As a result, the routes they took to greater freedom are less well documented.

The "Modern Woman" of the nineteenth century was a person looking to make a name for herself, to acquire wealth or fame. A woman of this type pursued money or professional advancement in a way that the Victorians considered unsuitable. Today's feminists find the Modern Woman an equally unappealing exemplar because of her complicity with commercial culture and her presumed insensitivity to social issues. These Modern Women, however, are the forerunners of today's working professionals. Modern Women were often their families' breadwinners, so they had to juggle work and home life in the same stressful way that working mothers do today. Maintaining a good appearance—fashionable clothing, well-groomed hair, clean skin, good grammar, genteel posture, and so on—was central to the Modern Woman's ethos; a successful working life demanded it. Modern Women, therefore, were sometimes characterized as both excessively ambitious and overly fashionable.[18]

Here I introduce four women who aptly exemplify the Modern Woman ethos as it was expressed from within the emerging fashion industry: Sarah Josepha Hale, Ellen Curtis Demorest, Jane Cunningham Croly, and Harriet Hubbard Ayer. Each of these women was the undisputed authority in her respective field. Each also represents the first in a long line of strong female editors, designers, writers, and manufacturers, respectively. All of them were social activists, even though they all worked full time and raised families, and all should be better represented in feminist history than they are.

## The Editor

Sarah Josepha Hale was the first publicly known, independently successful woman of the press. She was also among the first to fight for women's property rights, winning the battle in Massachusetts in 1835, nearly fifteen years before the Seneca Falls Convention. Hale founded the first organization dedicated to higher pay and better working conditions for women. She started the first day nursery for working mothers. She was the first to argue publicly that women should be teachers, doctors, and nurses. Hale was a prominent leader in the fight for women's educational rights. Yet Sarah Hale is virtually unrecognized as an early feminist. In fact, she is regularly castigated for being an *antifeminist.* The reason is that, in addition to her contributions to women's rights, Hale was the editor of the first major fashion magazine in America, *Godey's Lady's Book.*[19]

One of the most famous essays to criticize Mrs. Hale, written by Gloria Steinem for *Ms.* magazine in 1990, lists her specific crimes: "Hale went on to become the editor of *Godey's Lady's Book,* a magazine featuring 'fashion plates': engravings of dresses for readers to take to their seamstresses or copy themselves. Hale added 'how to' articles, which set the tone for women's service magazines for years to come: how to write politely, avoid sunburn, and—in no fewer than twelve hundred words—how to maintain a goose quill pen. She advocated education for women but avoided controversy. Just as most women's magazines now avoid politics, poll their readers on issues like abortion but rarely take a stand, and praise socially approved life-styles, Hale saw to it that *Godey's* avoided the hot topics of its day: slavery, abolition, and women's suffrage." After Hale set the tone and advertisers became interested in her readers as consumers, Steinem argues, the women's magazines were able to attract male editors and so these periodicals (each now "one giant ad") came under the control of men, where they have remained ever since.[20]

Academic feminists charge that Hale used *Godey's* to invent and diffuse the cult of True Womanhood, thus burdening her with responsibility for hindering the spread of feminism with that system of beliefs. Sarah Hale is therefore regularly condemned as working against the liberation of women, particularly against their employment. It's an ironic charge: Not only was Sarah Hale far more active on behalf of working women than any of the founding feminists, she was herself a single working mother who challenged convention by her own life choices.

Sarah Hale was widowed suddenly in 1822, when she was thirty-four. Her young husband left behind five children and no money. She decided to try to write for a living, a daring step because at the time women writers were still seen as "immodest." In early industrial New England, widows were the only women given the leeway to earn a living without being condemned as disreputable. Perhaps it was for that reason that, after her husband's demise, Sarah Hale wore black every day for the rest of her life—some fifty-seven years. Her black silk dress announced her status as a widow to everyone with whom she dealt as an author, editor, social reformer, or businesswoman, thus reminding the community of her right to self-support, and protecting her from slander.

Sarah Hale was nevertheless beautiful, elegantly groomed, and gracious. She also wore crinolines, corsets, pantalets, and side curls. Her appearance and her occupation therefore fit the Yankee Protestant feminists' stereotype of the fashionable feminine woman. However, it would be unfair and inaccurate to describe Hale also as "viney, and twiney, and whiney." The historical record is clear: Although she appeared as if she fit the feminine ideal of the True Woman, Sarah Hale dedicated her life to making radical political changes in the world around her. Further, Hale's biographers insist that, by being less outwardly abrasive than the founding feminists, she actually was able to accomplish far more.

Hale began her career by publishing poems and stories. Encouraged by her success, friends offered to finance her start in a magazine. Hale's vision for the *Ladies' Magazine* was to be a venue for high-quality American fiction, particularly that written by women. There were biographical essays, critical reviews, and considerable coverage of social causes, including elevating the status of women. The magazine carried no fashion plates and no advertising. Steinem claims that Hale began a long tradition of women's magazines with "editorial copy directed to women . . . informed by something other than its readers' wishes." The truth is that Hale maintained a detailed and personal correspondence with her readers (as did many editors who followed). Readers of the *Ladies' Magazine* repeatedly asked that fashion plates be added. In this case, Hale bowed to their wishes, although it went against her own judgment. Her compliance, though, came with an attitude. She began by publishing the most ridiculous plate she could find and wrote a critical commentary to appear beside it. From then on, she included criticism of fashion, right alongside the popular plates.

Eventually, the *Ladies' Magazine* ran out of money. By that time, however, Hale and her magazine had come to the attention of publisher Louis Godey, who invited her to work on a magazine with him. Thus was born *Godey's Lady's Book.* Hale and Godey worked as equals in this enterprise. They had at least one major disagreement that we know about, however, and it was over whether to include fashion plates. Hale was still strongly against the pictures; Godey insisted on including them because they were very popular. We can speculate that Hale's arguments against the pictures—all the puritanistic, anti-Catholic, Francophobic fears we have heard already—may not have seemed very persuasive to Godey, who himself was the son of poor French immigrants. Godey won this argument, a decision for which he and Hale have been condemned for 150 years now, even though she consistently used the editorial section of *Godey's* to criticize women's adherence to fashion and Godey did not interfere.

As editor of *Godey's,* Hale often expressed daring opinions in support of women's rights to education, property, and professional careers as well as other issues. One media historian remarks, "Not a month passed during her entire half-century of editorship but that Sarah Hale proclaimed the gospel of equal education, equal economic rights, equal recognition under the law, and equal professional opportunity for women." Eleanor Flexner noted Hale's contribution in her landmark history of feminism, *Century of Struggle:* "Writing always with the greatest circumspection, Mrs. Hale waged a number of tenacious and uncompromising campaigns—for the higher education of women, for their admission to such professions as medicine and nursing, together with adequate training in the same, on the merits of physical education for women, the menace of corsets, and many more."[21]

Critics determined to discredit the popular press, however, have played fast and loose with their assertions about her politics. Keith Melder, for example, asserts: "Hale's influence, although conservative, was widespread because of her position as a popular writer and editor. The popular literature written during the 1840s for a female audience had little to say directly concerning the debate over woman's rights. Implicitly, however, in its overriding concern with domesticity, it reinforced conservative views." Like many early feminists, Hale tried to use the idea that women occupied a morally superior "sphere" from that of men as the basis for an assault on the social and economic limitations of that sphere. But we cannot fairly argue that she had "little to say" about women's rights: She worked actively and consciously against the system that oppressed women. Furthermore, from the perspective of national cultural politics, she was much less conservative than the Stanton, Stone, and Anthony clan. In contrast to the Whiggish sympathies of these founding feminists, Hale was an ardent supporter of the northern Democrats and was actively involved in campaigns for rent control and other issues, showing a more sophisticated consciousness about the means of oppression than was in evidence among those feminist history insists were so "radical."[22]

The criteria being used to judge the life of Sarah Hale have been unevenly applied. A comparison will help punctuate the point. Elizabeth Blackwell, who became the nation's first female doctor in 1849, now occupies a sacred place in feminist history. In her own time, however, Blackwell was one of feminism's most prominent foes. Believing that her medical practice suffered because of "the strong prejudice against me on the part of women, which is heightened by the vulgarity of the radical movement," Blackwell consistently denounced the efforts of activists to organize for women. Yet, as feminist historian Blanche Hersh comments: "In spite of this reluctance (and this is one of the ironies of the women's movement), Elizabeth Blackwell became a feminist heroine, an example of what women could become."[23]

Feminism turns a blind eye to the aggressively antifeminist politics of Elizabeth Blackwell, yet slanders Sarah Hale for minor deviations from a clearly feminist course. Where does this bias come from? I think it comes down to politics at its most mindless. Blackwell is lionized because she was a doctor. Hale is condemned because she was the editor of a fashion magazine. The long-standing animosity between feminism and the fashion press begins here: not with high moral distinction, but with selective pettiness.

Gloria Steinem, like other feminists writing on this issue, asserts that women's magazine editors since Sarah Hale have been men. Hale, however, was only the first in a long line of powerful women to edit major women's magazines. She was followed, in the nineteenth century alone, by Miriam Leslie at *Leslie's Popular Monthly* and Ellen Demorest at *Madame Demorest's Mirror of Fashion,* as well as by Louisa Knapp Curtis (the *Ladies' Home Journal*), Ellen Butterick (the *Delineator*), Mrs. George Bladworth (*McCall's*), Mrs. Josephine Redding (*Vogue*), and Mary L. Booth (*Harper's Bazaar*). From 1900 onward the list continues, interrupted only by a brief interlude in the 1950s. *In its entire hundred-year history,* Vogue *magazine, arguably the queen of them all, has* never *had a male editor.* At the time of this writing, *all* of the major fashion magazines in America are edited by women. Although most of these women support feminism in print, they are still repudiated simply because, as one feminist admitted, they are, after all, editors of fashion magazines.[24]

## The Designer

Ellen Curtis Demorest was the Donna Karan of the nineteenth century. Her products extended from formal dresses to children's clothing, from lingerie to gloves. Not only a talented designer, she was also a brilliant mass marketer. She revolutionized the distribution of fashion and invented a number of technologies by which clothing was made or worn. As one of the earliest participants in the women's club movement and the first fashion editor to actively support suffrage, Demorest was also a feminist activist. She practiced what she believed in her business by hiring women at every level, including women of color, and insisting that all work, eat, and socialize as equals.[25]

As a young woman, Ellen opened a small millinery shop in her hometown of Sarasota Springs. Within just a few years she moved to New York City, arriving in the metropolis about the same time as the Seneca Falls Convention. One day in the early 1850s, while watching another woman cut out a dress from a crude brown paper pattern, Ellen had an inspiration: to mass-produce patterns for a variety of sizes on thin paper that could be used to duplicate a particular dress design accurately every time. Within twenty years, the U.S. paper pattern industry had become international in scope and Demorest was the undisputed leader. Demorest sold her patterns through the mail and department stores, but also through a magazine, *Madame Demorest's Mirror of Fashion.* Other pattern makers did the same: the Harper Brothers founded *Harper's Bazaar* in 1867, Ellen and Ebenezer Butterick started the *Delineator* in 1872, James McCall started *McCall's* in 1873, and William Anhelt began *Pictorial Review* in 1899.

Today these magazines provide important records of what clothing was really like, since they include detailed suggestions for making each item, accompanied by pictures and recommendations for fabric and trim. These magazines also give us an idea about how the clothes were supposed to fit, since they were keyed to actual patterns used to produce the clothes. The smallest waist size was 20 inches around—a long way from the 11-inch waists we're told were "dictated" by fashion in those days—and the largest waist size was a rather generous 38 inches. Fashion historian Valerie Steele reports that the measurements of existing corsets made between 1856 and 1910, in the collections of costume museums, average about 21 to 22 inches. The smallest she found was 18 inches when laced completely closed (women usually left the corsets open a few inches in the back).[26] This information suggests that the tight-lacing phenomenon was not as widespread as dress reform rhetoric implies it was.

Before the paper dress pattern, acquiring a dress in the latest style was a complex and secretive process between a wealthy woman and her seamstress with "sources" in Europe. The coming of paper patterns and the pattern magazines was a key factor in eroding the class distinctions expressed through dress. From the beginning, Ellen Demorest saw her mission as producing fashionable clothing that ordinary women could wear in their daily lives. Keep in mind, though, that the mode of this period still took its cues from leisure-class women—a group that announced its aristocratic status by wearing clothes that effectively immobilized them. Demorest's approach was to adapt the clothing of the leisure class to a more active and democratic lifestyle by simplifying the clothes and making adjustments in cut, line, and fabric. She came to be seen as the leading figure in the emergence of a new, distinctively "American" style. This aesthetic valued comfort and practicality, was focused on clothes for everyday life rather than for special occasions, and was aimed at a large audience rather than being exclusively focused on the aristocracy. Demorest was followed by a veritable legion of female American designers: Claire McCardell, Miss E. M. A. Steinmetz, Lilly Dache, Hattie Carnegie, Sophie Gimbel, Mollie Parnis, Adele Simpson, Pauline Trigere, Betsey Johnson, Norma Kamali, Mary McFadden, Gloria Vanderbilt, Liz Claiborne, Adrienne Vittadini, Donna Karan, and Anne Klein are only a few.

Ellen Demorest became active in the women's movement while raising four children and running a worldwide business. One platform she used to advance women's rights was her pattern magazine, *Madame Demorest's Mirror of Fashions.* Take, for example, the frontispiece of the November 1885 *Demorest's* (see figure 3.3). "The Nineteenth Century Woman" shows traditional roles of home life on one side and business roles on the other. The accompanying essay explains that the first plate illustrates an older age, "the domestic age," which was "the age when man was willing to be leaned upon, and woman was willing to lean." "Then came the revolution," the essay announces. The second plate illustrates the post-Revolutionary age, in which woman follows the path of work to independence and happiness. The rest of this issue includes travel articles, reports on current events, stories, poems, and literary criticism, as well as fashion plates, household tips, and embroidery instructions. A column called "What Women are Doing" announces degrees won at the Sorbonne and papers presented at the Social Science Association, but doesn't mention a single wedding, debut, or birth.[27]

The *Mirror*'s 1860 circulation was reported to be 60,000 a month, growing to 100,000 within five years, when it was distributed by 1,500 agencies in the United States. The popularity of *Demorest's* raises an interesting question. Feminist histories argue that the "popular press" was antifeminist and limit their discussions of the feminist press to the *Una, The Lily,* the *Women's Journal,* and the *Revolution.* Yet the content of the *Mirror* suggests that exceptions are in order.

Figure 3.3. Frontispiece from *Mme. Demorest's Mirror of Fashion.* Demorest's Monthly Magazine, November 1885.

*Demorest's* had a much larger circulation than any of the feminist papers, and it was published longer than any save the *Woman's Journal.* With a substantially lower price and a secular (not sectarian) orientation, *Demorest's* probably reached a more diverse audience too. (For perspective, the annual subscription price of the suffrage journals was twice what an Irish servant made in a week.[28]) If the *Mirror of Fashion* persuaded a larger, broader audience of women to adopt the feminist perspective, its impact on the movement may have been greater than the others.

I can anticipate the objections. Since *Demorest's* was a fashion magazine, it cannot also be a feminist paper. Yet the feminist papers carried fashion too, advocating certain styles and promoting certain looks, just like any other fashion vehicle. *The Lily* provided "fashion plates" of bloomers and gave suggestions for making and accessorizing them. The *Una* covered fashion and did not support dress reform. The advice on dress and manners given in the *Woman's Journal* was as "ladylike" as that of *Godey's Lady's Book.*

Perhaps it is the attitude toward fashion that is different. A fashion magazine promotes fashion, while a feminist paper criticizes it. Yet the editorial content of *Demorest's,* just like *Godey's Lady's Book,* was consistently critical of women who followed fashion too closely or spent too much money on clothes or dressed in an overly fashionable way. *Demorest's* regularly ran articles in favor of simpler dress, including a campaign for a standard evening gown. Furthermore, although *Demorest's* helped women dress like ladies, it certainly did not encourage them to act like parasites. The consistent ideology of *Demorest's* was that women should be productive members of society rather than mere ornaments. Its favorite prototype was not the belle of high society nor the True Woman, but the working professional.

Perhaps it is the source of support to which we object. *Demorest's,* we assume, differed from the other journals because it was an advertising vehicle—which, to feminists writing today, makes it a mouthpiece of the patriarchy. Subscriber-supported papers are more "pure" because they are less commercial. The only suffrage paper that survived more than a few years was the *Woman's Journal,* which continued largely because it attracted enough advertising to reduce its price and, therefore, create a sustainable readership. The *Revolution* sought advertising support, but couldn't solicit enough to survive. Ironically, one of this ill-fated periodical's most faithful advertisers was Ellen Demorest.

## The Fashion Writer

The men of the New York Press Club anticipated, no doubt, that it would be a historic event when Charles Dickens came to speak to them during his American tour of 1868. They could not have anticipated, however, that the farthest-reaching impact of this engagement would begin when Jane Cunningham Croly was refused a ticket.[29]

Jane Croly was then the most famous newspaper woman in America. She had emigrated from England to America as a teenager and, after educating herself at home, went to work as a reporter. After marrying Irishman David Croly, a radical journalist, she had five children, one of whom was the famed progressive Herbert Croly, founder and first editor of *The New Republic.* Early in their marriage, her husband took ill and could not work, so Jane became the family's primary breadwinner. With her children, her work, and her household responsibilities, Croly had the kind of busy life that is well known to working mothers now. As a biographer commented: "She managed a busy home on New York's West 14th Street off Washington Square, entertaining such diverse personalities as Louisa May Alcott and Oscar Wilde. Her Sunday evening receptions were described as the nearest thing to the Parisian salon that America had to offer. She followed a hectic, but strict schedule. Every morning she spent three hours at home supervising household duties, and by noon she would be in her office working frequently until 2 AM."[30]

Jane Croly's journalistic career is legendary in media history. She was the first woman to work daily for a newspaper, and she was the first to teach journalism at the college level. Although she wrote mostly on fashion, Croly also covered news, reviewed books, penned editorials, and wrote social commentary. She usually wrote for several magazines and newspaper organizations at once, which magnified her impact on the culture of industrializing America. Croly's column was the first to be syndicated across the nation, under the pen name Jennie June, thus becoming the first of many women columnists who have written about women's interests and issues: Ellen Goodman, Dorothy Dix, Abigail Van Buren, Ann Landers, and others. She published several books on topics of interest to women, particularly working women. Jane Croly was the editorial voice behind *Mme. Demorest's Mirror of Fashion.* It was Jane Croly who took over *Godey's Lady's Book* when Sarah Hale retired. And it was Jane Croly who started the biggest organizational movement by women in American history.

The men of the New York Press Club really should have seen it coming. Smarting from the slight of being denied a ticket, Jane Croly enlisted influential women to form their own club, an unheard-of act at the time. After much deliberation, the club was named Sorosis, a Greek word referring to the growth of many things.

When the New York Press Club members heard the news, they were amused and unnerved but intrigued. They invited Sorosis members to breakfast as a peacemaking gesture. When the women arrived, they were treated to a lovely meal at which the men spoke to them and sang to them, but expected the women to remain quietly and decorously in their seats. This did not go over as well as the men may have hoped. Instead of stalking out in indignation, however, the members of Sorosis responded in kind. They invited the New York Press Club to tea. At the meal, the women spoke to the men, sang to the men, and even recited poetry to the men, but the men were told to remain quietly and decorously in their seats. The women paid the bill. The point was made. At last, the New York Press Club and Sorosis held a joint event, in which both men and women participated and where everyone paid their own way. A newspaper commented: "We believe we violate no secret when we say that the gentlemen were most agreeably surprised to find their rival club composed of charming women, representing the best aristocracy of the metropolis—the aristocracy of sterling good sense, earnest thought, aspiration, and progressive intellect, with no perceptible taint of the traditional strong-mindedness."[31]

The women who founded Sorosis were, in fact, of a very different stripe from the "strong-minded" Yankee feminists. Sorosis was cosmopolitan rather than provincial. Its members were not uniformly Anglo-Saxon, Protestant, or born in America. Most worked for pay and most were successful. This was a sophisticated group, in terms of dress, travel, and consumption. They were more pragmatic than ideological in orientation, and they had learned through experience to negotiate for their objectives without unduly straining the limits of convention. Consistent with this strategy, these women were demanding on issues such as equal professional recognition, but dressed and behaved "like ladies."

Within one year of its founding, Sorosis had grown to 83 members, almost entirely professionals. Soon, however, the membership expanded to include middle class women who wanted to invest their energies outside the home. Similar women's clubs were founded in other towns. In 1880 Jane Croly took the first step toward forming the General Federation of Women's Clubs by calling a national conference. The GFWC started with 52 member organizations. Within a dozen years the federation had 180 clubs and 20,000 members. By the turn of the century it had 150,000 members. There were 1 million women in the GFWC by 1910 and 2 million by 1915.

The clubs that composed the GFWC varied in purpose, size, and composition. They divided their efforts into specific social interests, such as promoting the arts, or eradicating child labor, or improving municipal services or conserving natural resources. The non-partisan and nondenominational GFWC held its members to no specific theory or creed. Ultimately, the GFWC provided money, workers, publicity, and influence for the suffrage movement. However, it's important to understand that the club movement did not rely on suffrage workers; the suffrage movement relied on the clubs. The sheer size and scope of the federation made the suffrage organizations look like small, narrowly defined projects.

The founding of Sorosis, therefore, marked several firsts. Sorosis was the first organization dedicated specifically to furthering the shared interests of women as a class. Sorosis, as it turned out, ultimately spawned the GFWC, the largest single association of women in American history, which would become the organizational machinery of the suffrage movement. In a very concrete sense, then, the feminist organizations of today, such as the National Organization for Women, are descendants of Sorosis. The founding of Sorosis was also the first challenge to the exclusivity of men's professional clubs, which was to become an enormously important feminist issue a hundred years later. Finally, Sorosis was the first organization with a feminist consciousness centered on the interests of educated women who worked for pay. The strength and concerns of the Second Wave of feminists would come from growth in the number of educated working women. So perhaps we should have studied the history of Sorosis with the same respect and intensity with which we have pored over the early abolitionist and temperance groups. But, of course, we have not.

The founders of Sorosis are little known to American history scholars; they make no appearance at all in the historical education of most Americans. Why not? One reason is that the lives of these women do not fit the ideology of feminism as it has developed. These women were not Puritans. They were attractive and dressed fashionably. They were indignant, but they were not unpleasant. They were bright and beautiful, but they were not arrogant. If American women knew more about early feminists such as the group that established Sorosis, it would be hard to maintain the blind acceptance of the rule that says good feminists cannot be feminine or fashionable.

## Cosmetics Manufacturer

Harriet Hubbard Ayer grew up in Chicago, where she was a member of the elite of new wealth. When she and her husband divorced in 1883, however, Harriet was left to support her two children. She moved to New York, where she went to work as an interior decorator. Ayer had been known as one of the great beauties of high society, so New York socialites made the trip down to the shop where Ayer worked just to get a look at her embarrassing position. Ayer had a distinctly modern attitude toward the aristocracy's condescension: she didn't care why they came as long as they bought something. This outlook led her to establish what was then a shocking line of business.[32]

On a trip to Europe scouting for furniture, Ayer returned to the chemist who had supplied her with cosmetics during her heyday as a society beauty. He sold her the recipe for a face cream that had been used by Madame Recamier, the French courtesan of the Empire period who had been renowned for her young, white skin until well into her old age. Upon returning to the United States, Ayer researched the production and packaging of the cream until she could produce it at an affordable price. She borrowed $50,000 from a client, Jim Seymour, and began her business, placing ads for Recamier Cream in fashion magazines. In what would have seemed like the first step toward the whorehouse, Harriet Hubbard Ayer put her own name on the jar and in the ads.

Recamier Cream was a tremendous success, becoming one of the first nationally branded beauty creams in America. Ayer repaid Jim Seymour, more familiarly known as P'izen Jim, almost immediately, but he wanted Ayer's business for himself. He had Ayer kidnapped and put in an insane asylum. It took eighteen months for Ayer to get out: the ensuing lawsuit was long, ugly, and public. During the suit, the still-beautiful former socialite went on the road to speak out against the conditions of asylums and for the rights of the mentally ill. Ayer gave the proceeds to mental health organizations formed in response to her appeals. She amazed her audiences by first appearing on the podium dressed in the clothes she had been forced to wear during her incarceration. The fact that Ayer had not been allowed to change clothing or footwear for this entire period apparently impressed audiences more than any other aspect of her talk. Then she would retire for the intermission and return to the stage dressed as Harriet Hubbard Ayer, the famous socialite and cosmetics magnate. The contrast left her audiences breathless.

Although she won the lawsuit, Ayer could no longer afford to run her company. She sold the business to other people, who ran it under the name "Harriet Hubbard Ayer" until the 1950s. Then the former socialite and entrepreneur walked into Joseph Pulitzer's *New York World* and asked for a job as a reporter. The editor, Arthur Brisbane, challenged her to write a column on the spot. She stood at the window (the men in the city room would not offer her a seat) and wrote a beauty column. Brisbane hired her.

Rather than addressing debutantes and demure middle-class daughters, Ayer wrote her column to working girls. In this, the first nationally syndicated beauty column, Ayer advised that health was more important to beauty than anything else. She concocted home remedies for a variety of uses, which she printed or sent by mail to readers. She denounced the corset and advocated tailored dress for work.

The mail poured in. Many of the letters were pleas for help in areas other than personal grooming: women contemplating suicide, women being brutalized by their husbands, women in prison, women with addictions. Ayer became deeply involved in efforts to help these women, joined a small feminist group made up of working women, and became what we would today recognize as a feminist activist. In the meantime, her popularity and her responsibilities at the *World* grew. She became the editor of the woman's page. She did exposés of tenement conditions, interviewed murderers, and published books. Eventually her operation at the *World* was so huge it had to be moved to separate quarters.

When Harriett Hubbard Ayer died in 1903, the *World* flew its flag at half-staff (never done for a woman before) and published these remarks: "The achievements of her lifetime constituted a history of courage that misfortune, no matter how severe or frequent, could never affect. It is seldom that one woman has so thoroughly commanded the respect and admiration of the reading public, as well as the love and friendship of all who came within the wide range of her personal influence. For her to hear of a case of need was to relieve it. It mattered not whether its object were a friend or a total stranger. She often said that her religion in life might be summed up in two words—'lift up.'"[33]

## JEZEBELS

If, in nineteenth-century terms, a woman was seen as "disreputable," she is unlikely to show up in feminist history books. You have to look hard in most feminist histories for the acknowledgment that Fanny Kemble originated the bloomers. Lola Montez and Lillian Russell, both popular "Jezebels" of the age, lectured for women's rights, but you would never know it from the histories of feminism. Russell, herself the daughter of a "strong-minded" feminist, was as committed as any suffragist. She lived to walk with 50,000 other women in the 1914 suffrage march in New York, making perhaps the most marked impression on audiences of the time—but she is *never* mentioned in the historical accounts.[34]

Another "floozy" who contributed to the movement was Miriam Leslie. In 1865 this former dancer from New Orleans became editor of a magazine in Frank Leslie's enormous publishing empire. When Leslie divorced his wife to marry Miriam, their affair became a national scandal. The new Mrs. Leslie was one of those fashionable nouveau riche women who dressed extravagantly in gowns and jewels. Frank Leslie eventually ran into financial difficulties—some said his new wife spent all his money—and died in bankruptcy. Before his death, Frank told his spouse to "Go to my office, sit in my place, and do my work until my debts are paid." So, when he died, Miriam took over the business by legally changing her name to "Frank Leslie" and assuming all debts. Under her direction, the publishing company was brought back to profitability. "Frank Leslie" was once again a wealthy woman. When she died, Mrs. Leslie left her entire estate to the women's suffrage movement and named its leader, Carrie Chapman Catt, as trustee. This money was a major factor in putting the suffrage movement "over the top," by paying for educational and promotional materials in support of suffrage and by allowing the movement to buy back the *Woman's Journal,* which had been sold. Yet most histories of suffrage never mention Mrs. Leslie or her generous gift.[35]

Possibly the most telling omission, however, is Victoria Woodhull. A great beauty, a free lover, a radical politician, a self-made millionaire, a professional clairvoyant, Woodhull was the foremost feminist in the minds of the public in the last thirty years of the nineteenth century. Sadly, her name is now unfamiliar to most Americans, although she held a number of important "firsts":

- the first woman to address the U.S. Congress on suffrage, or any other issue
- the first woman broker on Wall Street
- the first female candidate for U.S. president
- the first publisher of the *Communist Manifesto* in America
- leader of the first American chapter of International Workers of the World (IWW)
- the first person arrested under the Comstock Laws.[36]

Despite these distinctions, Woodhull has been relegated to a relatively obscure place in feminist history for reasons that are not terribly complex: Woodhull's life story was a Whig-Republican's nightmare.

Victoria Claflin was born to a poor family in rural Ohio, one of seven children. Her mother was an illiterate German servant and her father was a one-eyed con artist. Victoria and her younger sister, Tennessee, claimed to be clairvoyants and healers from an early age. For much of Victoria's childhood, the family had a traveling medicine show, in which Victoria and Tennessee told fortunes, healed the sick, and sold magical potions. They were constantly on the move, always trying to stay one step ahead of the tar-and-feather party.

Before she was sixteen, Victoria married a young doctor from a "good family" in Rochester, New York, but the doctor turned out to be a philanderer and an alcoholic. He could not practice medicine because of his drinking, so Woodhull supported him and their two children as a cigar girl, a seamstress, and an actress before returning to her most lucrative option, fortune-telling. The young couple thus continued to roam with Victoria's family, living in their catch-as-catch-can manner. Woodhull's first husband continued to live with her even after she married her second husband, Captain James Blood, who introduced her to radical politics.

Like every capable witch, Victoria Woodhull had a powerful personal presence. She was well dressed, very beautiful, quite articulate, and had a look in her eye that sometimes made people fall in love with her and other times gave them the creeps. Her personality "compelled," and she could speak to an audience "like a prophetess aflame with a message."[37] Her talents served her well in the political world.

In 1868 Victoria and Tennessee went to New York where they became spiritual advisers to Commodore Cornelius Vanderbilt. Vanderbilt set the two sisters up as brokers on Wall Street. They became national celebrities, called "the Bewitching Brokers" by the popular press. They were not shunned but admired; they attracted many customers and became millionaires.

The sisters' success caused many Americans to compare them to the Yankee aristocrats working for women's rights. Although Victoria told the press she was doing more for women's rights by carrying on a daily business than the founding feminists were with papers and speeches, she soon stepped into the ring of feminist politics.

On April 2, 1870, a long letter from Victoria C. Woodhull headed "First Pronunciamento" appeared in the *New York Herald.* Referring to herself as "the most prominent representative of the only unrepresented class in the Republic," she announced her candidacy for president. She described her qualifications as follows: "While others argued the equality of women with men, I proved it by successfully engaging in business; while others sought to show that there was no valid reason why women should be treated, socially and politically, as being inferior to men, I boldly entered the arena." Many found the idea preposterous, but her announcement was greeted positively by the press. The *New York Herald* responded: "Mrs. Woodhull, the lady broker of Broad Street, independent of all suffrage tea parties and Grundy associations, proclaims herself as a candidate. . . . Now there can certainly be no objection to such a competition as this; it possesses the merits of novelty, enterprise, courage and determination. . . . Now for Victory for Victoria in 1872!"[38]

Next, Woodhull followed a tradition already established by the suffrage journals and began publishing her own newspaper. *Woodhull and Claflin's Weekly* was distributed nationally and, due to the sisters' fame, was never as obscure as other reform newspapers had been and, due to their money, looked more permanent and authoritative. Fifty thousand copies of the first issue were sold—a very large number for the time. The new weekly was favorably reviewed by journalists, and it soon overshadowed other women's rights papers.

Through her broadening circle of radical acquaintances, Woodhull became friendly with a Civil War hero, General Benjamin Bradley, who had become congressman for Massachusetts. Bradley and Woodhull formulated an argument that women already had the right to vote under the Fourteenth and Fifteenth amendments. Woodhull was invited to present the case to Congress on January 11, 1871. Coincidentally, the National Women's Suffrage Association was holding a convention in Washington on the same day. Learning about the speech from the local newspaper, the suffragists were disappointed, then outraged. They refused to go hear such a disreputable woman, regardless of the validity of her argument or the importance of the audience. Finally, a friendly senator counseled them: "This is not politics. Men could never work in a political party if they stopped to investigate each member's antecedents and associates. If you are going into a fight, you must accept every help that offers." The women begrudgingly decided to go.[39]

Even in the antechamber of the hearing room, though, the suffragists were planning to snub Woodhull. One man who overheard them said, "It would ill become these women, and especially a Beecher, to talk of antecedents or to cast any smirch on Mrs. Woodhull, for I am reliably assured that Henry Ward Beecher preaches to at least twenty of his mistresses every Sunday."[40] At the time, both suffrage organizations had titular male leaders: AWSA was led by Henry Ward Beecher, the well-known minister of a fashionable church, and the NWSA was led by his protégée and best friend, Theodore Tilton. Beecher, a major figure in the Yankee reform community, was sleeping with Tilton's wife. Several suffragists, including Stanton and Anthony, knew of the Beecher-Tilton affair, but they were helping to keep the scandal quiet. So, when the congressman in the antechamber confronted them, the whole group fell silent.

When Woodhull entered, the suffragists were taken aback by her appearance: "They had expected to find a bold, aggressive woman decked out in bright colors and furbelows. Instead they saw a beautiful young woman, plainly and tastefully dressed, with every appearance of refinement." Woodhull's speech was well argued and elegant, but passionate. She made a terrific impression on the congressmen and on the feminist delegation. Susan Anthony insisted Woodhull return to the NWSA convention and repeat her address. The hall buzzed with gossip as Woodhull mounted the platform, but when she spoke, hearts were won. She explained her idea about voting under the Fourteenth and Fifteenth amendments, and the convention adopted it as the central premise of a fresh strategy they called the "new departure." Under the new departure, women would go to the polls, register, and vote—and then would probably be hauled to jail. But the new departure gave a needed boost to the spirit of the movement, and Woodhull developed a following among the ranks.

Woodhull differed from the founding feminists on many other issues, however. She supported the Catholic church at a time when anti-Catholic sentiment was running very high. She favored regulation of prostitution when most in the movement were devoting much time and energy to criminalizing it. She was a proponent of free love while movement rhetoric was infused with ravings against "animal instincts" ("Votes for women; chastity for men!" was the rallying cry). Woodhull's past also evoked charges that the woman movement was leading America into a moral decline. The NWSA began losing substantial numbers to their rival, as Lucy Stone called suffragists to "purify" the movement by excluding those of dubious reputation or beliefs.

On November 20, 1871, Victoria Woodhull admitted in a public appearance that she was in favor of free love: "Yes! I am a free lover! I have an inalienable, constitutional, and natural right to love whom I may, to love as long or as short a period as I can, to change that love every day if I please!" At the next convention, Susan Anthony tried to bar Woodhull from the dais. Woodhull nevertheless swept up the platform, catching the audience with her power of oratory. While Anthony pounded her gavel, Woodhull continued speaking. Anthony peevishly shut off the lights in the hall. Everyone stumbled out in the dark. The next morning, however, six hundred people appeared at Woodhull's meeting in another hall, while a small, tense group attended the NWSA.[41]

While the moralists were distancing themselves from Woodhull, the Beecher-Tilton liaison began to create conflict. Finally, too tempted to resist exposing the hypocrisy of the reform group any longer, Woodhull told the story to an assembly of spiritualists in Boston. But the next morning, not a single Boston newspaper nor any major paper reported the story. So, she published a special issue of *Woodhull & Claflin's Weekly,* exposing one of the biggest scandals of the time. The price readers paid for this one issue went from fifty cents to five dollars, then ten, twenty, and finally forty dollars. Some people even rented the paper from others.

Woodhull and her sister were promptly arrested for sending obscene materials through the mail. They were kept in jail for nearly a month, and all proceedings were held out of public view. Although the two were officially charged with violation of the Comstock Laws, it was clear to many that Victoria and Tennessee really were being held for hurting Henry Ward Beecher's reputation. Woodhull reassured reporters repeatedly that she was waiting for "powerful friends" who would come and save them. She apparently believed that whatever differences there had been, the leaders of the New York suffrage movement would show their solidarity by coming to the sisters' aid. But none came forward, although several, including Stanton and Anthony, had direct knowledge that the charges against Beecher were true. Eventually the court found the sisters not guilty, but they still were shunned by the suffragists, who never invited Woodhull to another women's rights convention.

Stanton, Anthony, and others in the movement thought of this incident as a narrow escape from infamy. Suffragists in New York and Boston became more obsessed with appearing "pure," with tragic long-term consequences for the movement. After the turn of the twentieth century, the movement's antisexual orientation would keep it from developing livable approaches to issues that the next generation considered crucial, thus costing it the respect of the "New Feminists" of the Jazz Age.

## BLUESTOCKING RHETORIC, BLUESTOCKING HISTORY

In the earliest days of the bloomer craze, Amelia Bloomer wrote disapprovingly: "There is a class of men who seem to think it their especial business to supervise the wardrobes of both men and women, and if any dare to depart from their ideas of propriety, they criticize."[42] Though Stanton, Bloomer, and Anthony felt that the men of their community had no right to proclaim what was proper in their own manner of dress, none of them hesitated to declare the dress of other women improper or to "dictate fashion" when they had the opportunity.

Certainly the community at large recognized that this group was trying police other people's dress and habits. We can tell this by two terms frequently used to describe them, "Mrs. Grundy" (or "Grundyism") and "bluestocking." Feminists today usually write off both of these terms as derisive names for strong or educated women. Such translations do not accommodate the true meanings, however. "Bluestocking," popularly translated by feminists today as "a male term for an educated woman," in fact refers specifically to a female pedant, an intellectually pretentious person. This term did not refer to all educated women any more than the term "holy roller" now refers to all people who go to church. In nineteenth-century American usage, the term further connoted rigid adherence to a creed and loyalty to New England. (The name "Blue Stocking" was rejected by Jane Croly's first group, specifically because Sorosis members wanted to be "hospitable to women of different minds, creeds, and habits of work and thought.") "Mrs. Grundy" refers specifically to a fictional character in Tom Morton's play *Speed the Plough,* who was the self-appointed arbiter of both taste and morals in her community. The play was first produced in 1798, but by the mid-1800s, "Grundy" was a commonplace shorthand for the way censorship is enacted in everyday life through people with rigidly conventional views. A poem published in the 1890s describes Mrs. Grundy:

> She also is convinced that man is very, very bad,
> And that most women go about far too sparsely clad;
> She holds "the times are out of joint," but deems it "cruel spite"
> That she's been born (or thinks she has) to quickly set them right;
> And to the Decalogue, which now we say at church on Sunday,
> Would add this new Commandment—"Serve no God but Mrs. Grundy!"

For all the earnestness of the founding feminists, therefore, their model could be easily pulled into unflattering shapes. That doesn't mean there wasn't some *semblance of truth* to the parodies. The feminists and their ultra compatriots *were* quite judgmental and *did* go around telling other people what to do. Furthermore, they *did* use their better education as a blunt instrument against others, and they *did* believe in the general superiority of the New England Protestants.[43]

Today, feminist writers angrily dismiss such "ugly feminist" images as a fabrication of the patriarchy. This position, however, is not honest. For better or worse, the leaders of the women's movement have often been plain and prudish. Many were active in initiatives designed to control the behavior of others. Failing to acknowledge these facts only makes feminism look defensive, insensitive, and hypocritical. Furthermore, the early feminists themselves often unfairly distorted the ideals of others. Stanton's inclination to trash more traditional women as "viney, and twiney, and whiney" probably cost the movement sympathy on many occasions. Indeed, when trying to reconstruct the past from feminist writings, we must remember that the feminists themselves were engaged in rhetoric—and thus the images they created of the rest of the culture were often distorted for a purpose rather than being objectively true.

We must be particularly cautious of rhetorical effects since works written by this small group have become the core source for the history of the movement. A substantial portion of the material we have documenting the early woman movement was written by either Elizabeth Cady Stanton or Susan Anthony. Their prejudices and jealousies are easily observable in what they have omitted from the story. For example, their *History of Woman Suffrage* originally covered the period between the Civil War and the 1880s without a single line about Lucy Stone or the AWSA. In this same history, Victoria Woodhull and Jane Croly have a couple of throw-away sentences and footnotes. The movement's history was thus construed to support a particular group of women, their morals, their religion, their class loyalties, and their mode of dress.

Identification of feminism with this one narrowly defined group continued through the twentieth century. This is true even though we now also know that women in the West, on the prairies of Kansas, and in the elite enclaves of the South, worked for freedom with as much intensity and intelligence as the Yankee Protestants did. Professional women, thinking through the burgeoning feminist consciousness of the early Industrial Age, shared neither the dress attitudes nor the moral precepts of the New England group, but in histories they are overshadowed by the dominance of the Yankee Protestant ruling class feminists. And the "disreputable" women of the nineteenth century simply disappear, regardless of how differently today's culture may view their "public woman" activities. As a consequence, the story of feminism has been developed as a mythic basis to support a grim, pleasure-free, Puritanistic worldview. It didn't have to be this way. It still doesn't.

# CHAPTER 4

# READING THE POPULAR IMAGE

CHARLOTTE PERKINS GILMAN THOUGHT THE GIBSON GIRL PERSONIFIED THE NEW Woman of the twentieth century. In *Women and Economics,* first published in 1898, Gilman argued that the Gibson Girl not only looked differently, but behaved differently from the heroines of fiction and theater who had characterized the century then drawing to a close. The fabulous popularity of the beautiful young women Charles Dana Gibson drew signaled, in Gilman's mind, the demise of "the false sentimentality, the false delicacy, the false modesty, the utter falseness of elaborate compliment and servile gallantry which went with the other falsehoods." Yet when we look at the Gibson Girl today, she hardly seems as noble, strong, honest, brave, healthy, able, and skillful as Gilman claimed she was. In fact, she seems the quintessence of traditional femininity, with her "wasp waist," her upswept hair, her too-pretty face, and her ladylike air. From the twenty-first-century perspective, the cartoon in figure 4.1 seems to be yet another threadbare reference to the wiles of the feminine woman—"dangerous" only to her unsuspecting male prey and her female competitors.[1]

Is it possible that Charlotte Perkins Gilman, one of the most brilliant and unorthodox minds feminism has ever produced, was simply so enthralled by the power of this mass image that she couldn't see what it was really doing? Such a suggestion seems to me overly insulting to Gilman, as well as an unwarranted self-congratulation. But if, as feminist criticism consistently suggests, figures operate on us through universal symbols and unconscious means, and if natural womanliness is timeless and unambiguous, then the Gibson Girl should not look radically free of artifice to Charlotte Perkins Gilman and still seem the epitome of scheming femininity to us.

At the turn of the twentieth century, furthermore, there were many contradictory opinions of the Gibson Girl.[2] Some agreed that she was free of artifice, but others claimed she was merely crude and clumsy. Some said she was lavishly feminine; others cried that she was offensively "mannish." Some said she had an appealing manner,

Figure 4.1. A Gibson Girl cartoon

while others dismissed her as having no manners at all. The Gibson Girl was smarter, livelier, and more athletic than the Steel-Engraving Lady, and she was prettier, funnier, and less prudish than the Anthony New Woman. If, however, you were a fan of the Steel-Engraving Lady—which many turn-of-the-century viewers still were—the Gibson Girl appeared to have no manners, no grace, no accomplishments, indeed no redeeming characteristics of any kind. Gibson's heroine stomped around in stout shoes, stood with arms akimbo, and crossed her legs when she sat. She was not in awe of the men around her. If they did not show her the deference due a lady, she did not seem to care. She could be impertinent to the point of insult. She was maddeningly smug about her educational accomplishments, and she selfishly planned a career with no thought of home or children. From the viewpoint of True Women, the Gibson Girl was the herald of civilization's end. She was clearly dangerous.

But if you were a dyed-in-the-wool Puritan—which many turn-of-the-twentieth-century viewers still were—the Gibson Girl was too secular, too frivolous, and too flirtatious. She loved novels and parties as well as sports—and seemed to have no religious sensibilities whatsoever. Worst, she was uncowed in the presence of her elders. If this girl had the vote, she probably couldn't be counted on to continue the tradition of reform. She was dangerous, very dangerous indeed.

Despite the reservations of conservatives, the Gibson Girl had strong appeal across a widely divergent group of viewers. And because Gibson drew young women in many circumstances and walks of life, his sketches provided a basis for several different groups to identify with his heroine. The Gibson Girl appeared as a single girl, a bride, a married woman, and a widow. She was sometimes in her teens, usually about twenty, but occasionally appears to be thirtyish. The Gibson Girl appeared as a maid, a nun, an actress, a judge, a soldier, and even a priest. Although her hair was nearly always dark, the facial features of Gibson's girl varied quite a bit. Her fans among the elite were quite sure she was pure Anglo, but others argued that she was of mixed parentage.

A brisk debate flourished about who the "real" Gibson Girl was—was she upper class or working class, Anglo-Saxon or "of foreign stock," was she Gibson's sister, or the reigning socialite, or an up-and-coming Irish actress? The "reigning beauties" of New York asked to pose for Gibson; he respectfully allowed these princesses to come to his studio, but he found that they were not particularly good models. So the young women who "sat" for Gibson regularly were working girls. Several were Irish. When Gibson married southern belle Irene Langhorn, he drew many pictures using her as a model. In the unceasing speculation about the "true" identity of the Gibson Girl, these examples could be brought forward as "evidence" for the superior claim of the elite, the working class, the Irish, and the South to "ownership" of this heroine. Each group saw, with their own eyes, something of themselves in this charming young woman.

It would be difficult to choose any one turn-of-the-century viewer as having understood the "true meaning" of the Gibson Girl when we know there was so much disagreement. How could we presume, from the distance of one hundred years, to be able to divine her true meaning ourselves? Yet several feminist critics, including Lois Banner, Patricia Marks, and Martha Patterson, have purported to do just that.[3] Feminist writing on the Gibson Girl is typical of the approach to image evaluation taken by most feminists. In this literature, pictures usually are treated as having powers that work on us in ways that we can't see ourselves. This body of work makes little, if any, effort to situate a particular picture in the surrounding discourse, to document what was intended by its makers, or to demonstrate any actual impact on real females viewing it. In the end, the feminist literature treats images as if they were magical mysteries and claims knowledge about their dangers that is unavailable to the everyday viewer. The resultant aura of iconophobia is worthy of its Calvinist heritage.

## THE IDEAL AND THE REAL

Even turn of the century viewers understood that the Gibson Girl was an idea about womanhood in picture form and not an accurate reflection of the real world. Yet today's feminists remark that the Gibson Girl was too idealized to be real, as if this were an insight. Indeed, the most frequent feminist complaint about any female image, particularly in advertising or the fashion press, is that the woman shown is "unrealistic." Such critics treat the idealized picture as a deception, dishonest to whatever degree it diverges from recording the real, and further insist that ideal images force women to try to be what is impossible to achieve.

Yet in our own culture, as in most other cultures around the world, many pictures go beyond mere reflection to make complex statements. Indeed, many are purposely fictional, even fantastic. Such images cannot accommodate demands that all pictures be "the accurate representation of things and events as they occur in real life." This aesthetic equates "fantasy" and "falsehood," and suggests that the realm of the imagination should be forbidden territory. Very little art could survive such a guideline.

The philistinism implicit in this standard is worrisome enough, but the way feminist critics use the term "realistic" varies so much it would be difficult even to establish what the standard is.

When a woman in a picture is beautiful, the demand that the picture should be more "realistic" usually means the woman pictured should be less attractive. The critic insists that "real women" are ordinary-looking, which in turn implies that either no real women are beautiful or that all beautiful women are fakes. Thus, "realistic" comes to mean "not beautiful."

"Realistic" is also used to mean "representative," in the sense of "providing fair representation for everyone." A picture can also be said to be "unrealistic" on the basis that it does not show the "whole woman." The "whole woman" can refer literally to including the entire body within the frame of the page, or it can refer more metaphorically to all the roles a woman plays. In this aesthetic, therefore, every picture of any woman must be equally representative of all women in all moments of their lives in order to be acceptable to feminism, a demand that is, among other things, pictorially impossible.

"Natural" is another synonym for "realistic," particularly when applied to pictures of women. As we have already established, "natural" here doesn't mean unwashed or uncombed or uncivilized, but refers to a woman without makeup, with a conventionally simple hairstyle and conventionally modest clothing. Such a look doesn't challenge the standards of acceptability, as is often claimed by feminists, but in fact perpetuates them by asserting their "naturalness."

"Real" can also mean "authentic" in the orthodox Marxist sense. The preferred picture would be an accurate reflection of nature unsullied by the distortions of the social, specifically the marks of patriarchal oppression. It could not be a picture that "sexualized" women or showed them engaged in traditionally female tasks (i.e., mopping a floor) or in an attitude of deference (i.e., serving a man some coffee). The "authentic" picture, therefore, would be an instance of what is also called "positive imagery." Positive images would show women in prestigious occupations or engaging in nontraditional activities or in which men were mopping floors and serving coffee. That is to say, "authentic" or "positive" images are those that conform to a feminist world view and so are not really ideology-free at all.

All these notions of realism are often applied in the same essay, without definition or distinction, causing a tone of militant confusion, like a machine gun going off on its own. There are several reasons for this conceptual chaos. One is the biased treatment of the real and the ideal. When we want a positive image of women, we are asking for the representation of our own ideals. When we then complain that other people's idealized images are not "realistic," we are being inconsistent. What we really are asking for is not realism, but that our own ideals be represented to the exclusion of the ideals of others: pictures of happy pilots but not happy housewives; pictures of strong women but not pretty ones. Whether such a political objective is appropriate is a matter for further discussion, but we should at least be cognizant that what we are using as a standard is not reality, but a *feminist* ideal.

The more fundamental cause for confusion, however, is the narrow conception of images that the demand for realism serves. By insisting on realism as the first and last principle of picturing, we ignore the range of purposes for which images are employed as well as the broad spectrum of forms that picturing takes. Images then are robbed of their expressive qualities, and the skills required for reading them are reduced to mere object recognition.

## THE GIBSON ETHOS

Whenever a picture is created, the setting, the angle, and all other visual elements must be chosen. As a result of each selection, all other potential choices are rejected. So, all pictures necessarily exclude some alternative view. If someone photographs a woman's face, they must exclude the back of her head. If they draw her walking in sunlight, they haven't shown how she looks lounging in the moonlight. If they choose to show her smiling, then we won't see her crying. The same would be true of any picture of any person or object. No one picture can *ever* be said to offer a complete or unbiased view of *anything.*

Just as the choice of words, tone of voice, facial expression, and gestures impinge on the meaning of a spoken statement, the selection of pictorial elements impinges on the meaning of an image. Sometimes the maker chooses to reverse, magnify, abstract, or stylize in order to make a complex statement that goes beyond pointing to an object. Interpreting the image, therefore, depends on the viewer's ability to correctly "read" the message, using *all* the pictorial cues given, not merely recognizing the object pictured.

In the case of a line drawing like the Gibson Girl, the peculiar quality of the artist's "hand" is one of the pictorial clues that readers use to help them interpret the meaning of the image. Having recognized a particular drawing style, we may also situate the character in the context of a pictorial "world" we have learned through past experience—through, for instance, reading a comic strip regularly. We distinguish women drawn by artists whose style we have learned to recognize: Women from *Doonesbury* and little girls from *Peanuts* are distinctive enough that, even if we do not know the cartoonists' names, we can recognize a woman drawn by Garry Trudeau or a little girl drawn by Charles Schulz. Merely by recognizing the artist's hand at work, we invoke a certain worldview—a *Doonesbury* strip has a fundamentally different voice from a *Peanuts* cartoon. We also learn to recognize specific personalities within that picture world: Consider the number of women "characters" in American culture who exist as nothing more than line drawings: Betty Boop, Betty and Veronica, Tank Girl, and others. But, as easy as it is for us to do this, someone very far away (say, a hundred years into the future) would be hard pressed to infer the difference in character between Marge Simpson and Wilma Flintstone communicated by the manner of drawing. Similarly, the girls drawn a hundred years ago by Charles Dana Gibson were as clearly associated with a certain authorial character, or ethos, as these characters are in our own time. Therefore, to comment intelligently on the "meaning" of the Gibson Girl, it is essential to re-create that context.[4]

"Gibson Girl" did not refer to a specific character, such as Wonder Woman or Jessica Rabbit, but would be more accurately translated as "a girl drawn by Gibson." When the public first saw Charles Gibson's drawings, he was illustrating fiction in popular magazines and books. Therefore, the heroines Gibson depicted initially were not of his own creation, but their characters must have become entwined with the drawings, as is the nature of illustration. Although these characters ranged from brides to bicyclists, they did have some characteristics in common.[5]

The fictional heroine Gibson illustrated was usually unimpressed by money or status. She was friendly and rather impulsive. She spoke her mind, sometimes without thinking. She foolishly rushed into places and situations where she didn't "belong." In spite of her lapses in judgment, she was loved by everyone, especially the young men of her acquaintance. This heroine had a face "full of a fine intelligence and humor" and "something of a challenge in her smile." She often wore tailored clothing, sometimes including a "high mannish collar," a man's hat and coat, and even a tie. Men in the stories were drawn to her because she was active, "jolly," and "clever," rather than passive and retiring. Often these stories assert a distinctively modern view of courtship and marriage, where the relationship between man and woman is "companionable" rather than formal.

Eventually, Gibson became most widely known for his own satirical cartoons and his protagonist was a girl who, by incorporating many of these traits, spoofed traditional America. Gibson drew for *Life,* a sophisticated New York humor magazine that included parodies of politics and social life, stories of "modern" situations, reviews of New York stage plays, and many smart little cartoons. Founded by four college men, *Life* was somewhere between the *New Yorker* and the *Harvard Lampoon* in spirit. The political attitudes of the *Life* editors came through its pages loud and clear: They were contemptuous of Puritan reformers, supportive of education for women, dismayed by Comstock's crusades.

Many incarnations of the New Woman, as the character of the feminist was by then familiarly known, appeared in these pages. The political stance of the editors was essential context for reading them. For example, figure 4.2 appears to be a spoof of the Susan Anthony New Woman, an antifeminist cartoon that intends to undermine the movement by stereotyping feminists as unattractive. Figure 4.3 is more ambiguous. Is this artist trying to belittle the "shackles" of womanhood by referring to them as "bracelets"? Or is he ridiculing the way antifeminists refused to see their own unfairness, covering up for unpleasant realities through elaborately sentimental metaphors? The turn-of-the-century reader had to decide by inferring intention from the context provided by the magazine itself. As it happens, both of these cartoons appeared in a special edition of *Life* (October 9, 1913) devoted to supporting women's suffrage. So, the viewer presented with the "shackles" cartoon would have been unlikely to interpret

Figure 4.2. *Life* cartoon spoofing the Susan Anthony New Woman. October 9, 1913.

it as an attack, but instead would have understood it to be ridiculing feminism's foes. And what of the jab at the Susan Anthony type? Again, the vehicle acts as frame. Opposite the masthead, fifty pages before the cartoon of the Anthony-style spinster chained to her policeman, is a drawing of the great suffragist herself, this time heroized in the Mount Rushmore fashion. Underneath, a few passionate paragraphs writ-

"TAKE OFF YOUR SHACKLES?
WHY, MY DEAR, THEY ARE
BRACELETS AND MOST BECOMING."

Figure 4.3. Profeminist cartoon in *Life.* October 9, 1913.

ten by the artist, Arthur Young, conclude: "The spirit of revolt as shown in the action of this splendid woman is abroad in the land. A new generation of women is imbued with Susan B. Anthony's purpose to vote for the right as they see it, and help make the laws that rule the lives of their children."[6] The reader of this issue of *Life,* therefore, would have had little doubt as to the supportive sentiments that its editors had toward women's rights in general and Susan B. Anthony in particular. And yet more than one cartoon makes fun of the dried-up-spinster-as-feminist stereotype. How can we explain this? It seems to me fairly simple. For most people, it is possible to be in support of a cause and still laugh at the excesses of some of its more zealous proponents. Amusement does not necessarily indicate antipathy.

Unfortunately, feminist criticism often mistakes humor for condemnation. For example, Patricia Marks reluctantly praises *Life* for its contribution to a positive mythology for feminism, but when its cartoons poke fun at changing gender roles, she consistently reads the humor as contempt or alarm. Marks makes such judgments repeatedly despite ample instances in which *Life* also makes fun of traditional women (not to mention traditional men), reformers of all sorts, ministers, lawyers, doctors, politicians, old people, young people, and even prosperous college men like themselves. Are we to conclude that *Life*'s editors harbored deep fears about every group in American society including their own?

The need to account for editorial context is further illustrated by Marks's reading of bicycling images. The adoption of the bicycle is considered an important event in the history of feminism because the invention gave women mobility and because cycling required changes in clothing that dress reform had been unable to bring about. Bicycling was a huge fad between 1888 and 1898. *Life* often spoofed women riding bicycles, which Marks takes as fear of the New Woman. However, if we look at *all* cartoons in *Life* during the bicycle craze, we find everybody who took to wheels ridiculed, from immigrants to socialites. *Life* seems intent on poking fun at the fad itself: A cartoon about a woman cyclist seems no more a criticism of feminism than one about cycling clergy would be a rage against the church. Further, the bike-riding New Woman was romanticized as often as she was lampooned, as in the Gibson drawing in figure 4.4.

Gibson drew cartoons for *Life* for four years before the "Gibson Girls" began to appear. Like his compatriots at the magazine, Gibson had little regard for Puritan moralists. He took on a variety of social and political issues as they appealed to his sense of the outrageous, unfair, or absurd. In one particularly memorable cartoon, he spoofed the social purity crowd by showing them driving carriages drawn by modestly dressed horses. Below the image ran the legend: "A Scene in the Moral Future: When the suggestive reformer shall have 'purified' America and *Life* alone refuses to be Comstockianized." Gibson led the standard against the trustees of the Metropolitan Museum of Art, who refused to open the museum on evenings or Sundays so that working people could attend. He attacked the Episcopal Church's attitude toward divorce. The early Gibson political cartoons, therefore, suggest an author who is irreverent, egalitarian, enthusiastic, idealistic, and contemptuous of prudery and social climbing.

Once the Gibson Girl was invented, she appeared nearly every month and eventually was so popular that a double-page cartoon appeared in the center of each magazine as a regular feature. The cartoons remained satirical in nature; in fact, they are so often ironic that familiarity with the ethos of the artist is essential to understanding them. In the picture world of Dana Gibson, the young American woman made her way through a country full of silly socialites, stuffy old women, ridiculous fops, pathetic European aristocrats, self-righteous conservatives, and a garden variety of snobs. The Gibson Girl was smart and independent as well as pretty. She pushed the limits of conventional behavior with a determined charm. Although she was dogged by suitors who were smitten silly, the Gibson Girl was not dainty or blonde or given to flattery. Instead, she was dark, regal in bearing, quite tall, and had a casual air toward men. She had a variety of outfits, but she was generally associated with the new "mannish" look, which included a dark skirt, a white blouse, and a tie.

Figure 4.4. Gibson romanticizes the New Woman

The Gibson Girl had a counterpart, the Gibson Man. Like the Gibson Girl, he was very tall and very handsome. In the new etiquette of the times, the two made their own appointments and went without chaperones. The lovers held hands at tables and stared, absorbed, into each others' eyes. They also fought and pouted, stamping their feet and turning their backs on each other. Theirs was a very modern relationship, one that differed profoundly from courtships of the past. But unlike other characterizations of the man who escorted the New Woman, there was nothing weak about the Gibson Man. He was the sort of "man's man" that you could imagine on African safari alongside Teddy Roosevelt. He was not, however, authoritarian, cool, or abusive. He was sophisticated enough for the cafés of Paris, but he was too decent, too democratic, too "American," to be a snob, an intellectual, or a bully. Gibson thus created an imaginary man who was not merely *tolerant* of the independent woman but who was *worthy* of her.

As his cartoons' popularity increased, so did Gibson's personal fame. By 1895 *Life* claimed that Gibson's name had become a household word. His signature implied a particular authorial personality that readers carried from one cartoon to another. An example of the mistakes that can result when the viewer is unfamiliar with the Gibson ethos is supplied by Martha Patterson, a critic who attacks the Gibson cartoons about people who marry for money. Such folly was indeed one of Gibson's favorite targets. Patterson, however, claims: "Viewing subjects could never be assured of gaining their love objects since both the Gibson Girl and Gibson Man may marry for money rather than love." Readers of his time, familiar with Gibson's well-known views on the subject, would not have inferred that Gibson condoned people marrying for money just because he drew them. Such a suggestion is comparable to saying that just because Garry Trudeau often drew cartoons about Ronald Reagan, he must have been a Republican.

## AMERICAN GIRL

Feminists writing about the Gibson Girl assert that she was "the dominant image of women" at the turn of the century and thus women were "forced" to try to be like her. The reader isn't given any sense whatsoever of what "dominant" means in this context. Is it based on popularity? On frequency of appearance? On public reception? The reader is usually left to infer—erroneously—that the Gibson Girl had few, if any, competitors in the pictorial discourse about women at the time. Without alternatives, it seems obvious that women were "forced" to be Gibson Girls. In truth, however, there were many images of pretty women in the popular magazines, books, and posters when the Gibson Girl appeared. Several famous illustrators, such as Harrison Fisher, Maxfield Parrish, James Montgomery Flagg, and Coles Phillips, were well known for their pictures of pretty girls.

The Gibson Girl herself was recognized by viewers as belonging to a specific subgenre of pretty girls, known as the American Girl. Other artists of the day, such as Howard Chandler Christy, were also known for images of the American Girl type. The American Girl also appeared in fiction, drama, and essays. In fact, the American Girl as a cultural character predates the Gibson Girl by about three decades and has had a great deal of staying power since. Originally she was called "the Girl of the Period," a term first used by Eliza Lynn Linton in 1868. Linton, a first-class stick-in-the-mud, wrote a series of articles complaining about the looks and manners of the girls of her time. The term passed into the vernacular. Just like "hippies," "beatniks," and other neologisms, "the Girl of the Period" referred to a social phenomenon that many Americans could observe going on all around them: girls of the West who put on pants and learned to shoot, young immigrants who wore American clothes and used slang, working girls who sneaked out to the dance halls, farm girls who ran away to join the circus, debutantes who eloped with unsuitable matches.[7]

The adventurous nature and straightforward attitude associated with the Girl of the Period appealed to some as exemplary of the American spirit. So by 1900 this impudent charmer was popularly known as the American Girl—and many of her attributes are clearly feminist. Writing in 1894, a contemporary observer commented: "American girls have shown they . . . are fast developing a bright, clear, intelligent, self-reliant, courageous, and refreshing variety of the human race. . . . in a country like America, where social classes are not permanent or rigidly defined, the daughter as well as the son of the house contemplates the possibility of self-support, and the harem view of the sphere and occupation of women, however modified, wholly disappears. From the marriage service the word 'obey' gradually vanishes or is smoothed away by interpretation, and the ideal of woman changes and improves. These social conditions foster self-respect and self-reliance."[8]

The American Girl was also the very embodiment of the popular "melting pot" concept, having "successfully appropriated to herself the best qualities from all the different races to which she owes her origin." Indeed, illustrations of "American Girl" behavior can be found in many ethnic contexts. An Irish father in a popular Chicago humor column had a Gibsonesque daughter named Molly Donahue who tried to convert her mother to New Womanhood and unexpectedly took up cycling: "No wan knowed she had th' bicycle, because she wint out afther dark an' practised on it down be th' dump. But las' Friday evnin', lo an' behold, whin th' r-road was crowded with people fr'm th' brick-yards an' th' gas-house an th' mills, who shud come ridin' along be th' thracks, bumpin' an' holdin' on, but Molly Donahue? An' dhressed! How d'ye suppose she was dhressed? In pa-ants, Jawn avick. In pa-ants. Oh, th' shame iv it!"[9]

Although the American Girl was a character well liked by many, public commentary was still full of remarks about the impertinence, sloppiness, bad manners, and outrageous behavior of young females: "The egotism of the girl is colossal, and in its train it brings selfish disregard of others' rights, ingratitude and rudeness. The mother she so unmercifully bullies is to be pitied, but any others who submit to her exactions are not in the least deserving of sympathy." The Gibson Girl, as one of the American Girl species, evoked this kind of reaction too. One commentator wrote of the Gibson Girl: "She exhibits the audacity of the unlicked schoolboy"—and called for her parents to give her a thrashing. Despite the fact that feminist historians consistently portray the enculturation of young girls as stultifyingly restrictive and fully focused on producing passivity, the number of complaints in the historical record about the intransigence of girls is striking. The patriarchy was undoubtedly *trying* to keep these young ladies under control, but it appears that their actual success was limited.[10]

In the decades since, the American Girl has appeared in many incarnations. She is Holly Golightly, Scarlett O'Hara, and Nancy Drew; we find her in the TV series *That Girl* and *Clueless.* She is Patty Duke's American twin. She is Cyndi Lauper singing "Girls Just Wanna Have Fun." From these characters, even though they differ, we can draw a broad outline of the American Girl prototype.

The American Girl is energetic and sociable. In fact, she talks too much. The American Girl is a flirt. She likes to dress up and go to parties, but she would rather be staked to an anthill than go to Sunday school. She is neither stuffy nor self-righteous. Like Huck Finn or Tom Sawyer, the American Girl is disobedient. Indeed, she *likes* to raise eyebrows. Her favorite target is her own mother. The American Girl leaves home: She goes to college, she joins a road show, she tours Europe. The American Girl is smart but not intellectual; she is compassionate but not a reformer. She intends to get ahead. She may seem, at once, outrageously materialistic and truly heroic, like Scarlett O'Hara driving a mill wagon while pregnant. Whether she seems hopelessly without guile, like Daisy Miller, or full of frank theatricality, like Holly Golightly, she has a puzzling sort of innocence. We find ourselves, in spite of our "better judgment," liking her immensely.

The American Girl always dresses in a way that is both the height of fashion and the edge of fashion. Her look, shocking in its own time, becomes the cliché of an era. At the turn of the twentieth century, she dressed in tailored clothes. In the 1920s, she wore lipstick and rolled her stockings. In the 1960s, she wore jeans and pierced her ears. Today her nose may be pierced too. The American Girl has been both trashed and adored in every generation (see figure 4.5). At each step along the way, older observers have pined for the American Girl of their own generation (who suddenly seems tame) and have announced the end of girlhood as we know it. She survives every time (see figure 4.6).

Historically, the American Girl, in pictures, on stage, in film, on television, or in real life, has been particularly offensive to older-generation feminists. In their judgment, the American Girl is *never* suitably political, *never* appreciative enough of the trials they have endured for her sake, and *always* too secular for their tastes. But although the American Girl may not have been a social activist, she nevertheless acted to change the world, and the status of women in it, by her own challenges to convention.

The American Girl is a generational emblem, the expression of an emergent cohort. She always walks within a discourse of other ideals that compete for attention and ascendancy. At no point in Gilded Age culture was the Gibson Girl the only image available for women to model; indeed, if that were so, we would not see so much discussion about the value of her influence. So, sketching in some of that pictorial discourse will not only help to illuminate the meaning of the Gibson Girl, it will help us to understand how the images of the day formed a set of symbols for their viewers.

## FIN DE SIÈCLE PICTURE WOMEN

The technology of image production that revolutionized the press of the 1890s created new possibilities of thought and signification through pictures. With the emergence of halftone printing and color lithography, both photographs and illustrations could be

Two Extremes

"I don't know whether to go and see a show that glorifies the American girl or a play that drags her through the dirt."

Figure 4.5. Two views of the American Girl coexisted

reproduced with an exactness that was previously impossible. Many of these new forms of picturing included pathbreaking ways of representing and "reading" women.

The Art Nouveau movement, for instance, was born about the same time as the Gibson Girl and became popular with comparable speed. This movement was first known as the Decadence because of the luxuriant, self-indulgent, and aggressively erotic attitudes of the artists and writers who formed its original incarnation in Europe, especially in England. Today art historians recognize Aubrey Beardsley, a British illustrator, as most representative of the Victorian Decadence and the first to influence American Art Nouveau. Beardsley's drawings often showed subjects that Victorians found shocking ("perversion, eroticism, corruption, and depravity"), generating controversy on both sides of the Atlantic. His women were so distinctive that the phrase "Beardsley Woman" entered the vernacular, along with "Gibson Girl." The Beardsley Woman was usually rather sinister in looks—and was openly sexual. Feminist critics today, in fact, argue that Beardsley's oeuvre aided the advancement of the New Woman through the liberation of her sexuality.[11]

Although the sexuality of the Beardsley Woman is taken as a positive sign for feminism, Martha Patterson writes that the "unbounded sexuality" of the Gibson Girl's heroic body indicated that she was intended to produce children instead of political

Figure 4.6. The American Girl of an older generation seems tame when the new one appears.

change. Yet pictures of the Gibson Girl as a mother are quite rare. In a discourse where ridiculously romanticized images of motherhood were everywhere to be found, in fact, the Gibson Girl was notably childless. Although her full figure may suggest fecundity to us now, other signs in the Gibson Girl's manners, dress, and recreations made it clear to readers at the time that this character was not a fertility symbol. Quite the opposite:

Her implicit challenge to the family was one of the most controversial things about her. Beardsley's women, in contrast, removed as they were from depictions of everyday life, offered little on the politics of kinship or motherhood. The Gibson Girl, like the Beardsley woman, was less sentimental than other popular images. The Gibson Girl, however, was *far* more concretely associated with feminist attitudes in her own time than the drawings of Beardsley.[12]

William H. Bradley became known as The American Beardsley, although his pictures were not openly erotic. Instead, his images were drawn in the aesthetic spirit that came to characterize Art Nouveau: a reorientation toward the pictorial plane, in which the purposes of representation were subordinated to the objectives of design. For example, Bradley's bicycle poster in figure 4.7 pictures the women and the bicycles in a pattern that is more akin to fabric design than to traditionally realistic painting. But feminist historian Ellen Gruber Garvey criticizes the use of Art Nouveau in bicycle posters, particularly the one shown here by Bradley, on the basis that the "feminine" lines of the style made bicycles more socially acceptable for women to ride. In Garvey's estimation, "feminizing" bicycle riding took the subversive bite out of the activity.[13] Yet Art Nouveau was seen in its time as a break from traditional artistic practice *and* as a manifestation of the most modern social trends. It was condemned with as much Puritanistic disgust as traditionalists used to decry the bicycle, just as one might expect for a manner of drawing known then as the Decadent style. To have associated bicycles with Art Nouveau would have made a logical connection with progressive ideas in the minds of Gilded Age viewers, but would hardly have made cycling more palatable in conservative eyes. If Garvey had investigated the use of Art Nouveau to promote bicycling by men, she would have found many posters, including several by Bradley. Does that mean that bike riding by men was feminine too? As is so often the case, this critic has read the images without due attention to the circumstances of use.

Another poster artist, Maxfield Parrish, was as famous for pictures of young women as Gibson. Parrish painted in an otherworldly style and he often illustrated fairy tales and other flights of fancy. Although the Parrish girls were seldom modestly dressed, Parrish's works were considered appropriate to hang in "respectable" homes and given as gifts even to young girls. The moral status of Parrish's work is important because of the controversy over nudity in pictures that came to a head at this time. Anthony Comstock and his social purity activists had taken to ransacking the studios of any publisher, artist, or photographer who produced pictures of the human body in a state of undress. One of these was a rather innocent painting called "September Morn," which had been quite well received by critics in France and was reproduced by *Vogue* in the United States. Comstock's vandalizing of the gallery where "September Morn" was displayed came to epitomize the conflict between reformers and the

Figure 4.7. Will H. Bradley designed art nouveau bicycle posters for men and women. Back cover, *Life*. January 16, 1896.

culture at large over the question of pictorial nudity. Comstock, as always, held that all nudes were pornographic. But amid the increasingly sophisticated pictorial discourse, Comstock was beginning to look ridiculous. Covers of leading magazines (*Scribner's, Century,* and even the *Ladies' Home Journal*) sometimes featured nudes, as did children's books, such as *Poems of Childhood* illustrated by Maxfield Parrish. In the proliferation of pictures brought by the new mass press, the American public had learned to make distinctions among nudes, deeming some erotic and some innocent and some even appropriate for children.[14] This is a skill some feminists today would do well to cultivate.

Among those pictures Comstock found obscene were those of female athletes because the clothing they wore was revealing by the standards of those times. Even in the context of "suggestive" pictures of athletes, however, there is evidence of the contemporary viewer's ability to "see critically." For example, "Lavare Charmion, the Perfect Athletic Girl" was a celebrity who toured the country showing off her athleticism, as well as her body, to enthusiastic audiences. When she arrived in Denver in 1904, the *Post* published a large full-length picture of her in tights, along with two photos of her "pumping iron." The headline reads: "Ladies, How Does Your Figure Correspond with the Measurements of Charmion?" To the side of her image, in prominent type, appears a complete list of her measurements, including her ankles, her wrists, and even her shoe size. The paper claims that her bust is 36 inches, her waist is 20 inches, and her hips are 36 inches. Since she is only 5' 1" and weighs 125 pounds, it seems improbable that she would have such a tiny waist. (The photograph does look touched up in that area.) Rather than compliment Charmion's figure, however, the author of the accompanying story, Florence Heath, sets right out to debunk the measurements: "Observing this small person at close range, one is apt to conclude either that the eye deceives or figures lie. For Charmion's form, generally symmetrical, seems not to tally with the measurements, which could hardly be called correctly proportioned." This critical article suggests that viewers were not incapable of discerning implausible differences between representation and reality in contexts where such judgments were necessary and appropriate.[15]

Mass reproduction of images also brought rumblings of modernism to the American viewer. Because this new movement broke radically with representational techniques of the past, viewing these works was a skill that had to be learned, even by sophisticated viewers. The first Cubist painting, "Les Demoiselles d'Avignon," produced by Pablo Picasso in 1908, required that the viewer assemble a plane of fragmented images to "see" five women on the canvas. Modern works were reproduced in the popular press, teaching new ways of "reading" pictures to a broad audience. Therefore, the prevailing techniques of representation were at a pivotal point in the early 1900s and so, necessarily, were the community's skills of pictorial perception.

Graphic artists responded with creative techniques of their own, and these, too, required an active, informed viewer. One of the most popular was invented by Coles Phillips in 1908, the "Fadeaway Girl" (see figure 4.8). Omitting the demarcation between the woman's dress and a background of the same color was a novel idea, rather like reversing the technique of silhouette, that appealed very much to Gilded Age readers. As art historian Ernst Gombrich and others have shown, viewers put together the suggestive lines and shapes on the flat plane of a picture in such a way as to actively construct the image in their own minds. Not only will viewers "make and match" a picture based on minimal visual information, but the more effort required, the more they enjoy the image. To produce such an effect, the artist's technique must hover at the viewer's horizon of expectation: It must challenge viewers, but not confuse them. This suggests that popularity of the Fadeaway Girl was a function of the effort it took to visually create the dress in the absence of a clear demarcation.[16]

Without knowledge about the emerging graphics environment, the feminist interpreter might be tempted to develop a critique asserting the Fadeaway Girl's erotic subtext. We could say, for example, that the visual ambiguity allows the viewer to "undress" the figure and thus "sexualizes" her. However, what was fun about the Fadeaway Girl was the perceptual effort required to "see" her dress rather than the titillation of seeing her "undressed." It would also be quite au courant nowadays to critique the Fadeaway Girl on the grounds that she is "fragmented" or "symbolically dismembered," but this criticism would miss the whole point of such graphic innovations. The picture is designed to play with the boundaries between figure and ground in just such a way as to encourage the viewer to put the picture *together.*

Assessing the impact of an image on any viewer would substantially depend on our understanding of the mental processes of pictorial perception and our awareness of the viewing strategies available at a particular moment in time. Unfortunately, feminist criticism of images neither recognizes the complexity of visual perception nor acknowledges the cultural and historical conditions on which the perceptual act depends.

## LEARNING TO SEE

Much of the feminist critique of pictures relies on the assertion that pictures operate on our unconscious, that we are influenced by this "irrational" form in ways that do not occur with written text. This critique glosses over the complexity of pictorial perception and the learned skills that are required for even "ordinary" women to read pictures. Implicit is the assumption that because we are born seeing, interpreting pictures is an activity based in biology and thus unmediated by culture or judgment. Yet a new-

Figure 4.8. Coles Phillips' "Fadeaway Girl," *Life,* 1908.

born lives in a world of sensory nonsense, learning to see a variety of familiar objects only over time. The truth is that seeing is a skill that, while it is learned early in life, is acquired only with some effort, guidance, and concentration.[17]

Ambient vision and pictorial perception, although closely intertwined, are different. Looking around ourselves in the environment involves constant and purposeful movement of the eyes. Not only do we move our heads and our bodies, thus changing the position of our eyes; we look at the environment by constantly moving our focus in a kind of visual sweeping. Having learned to use binocular vision to discern depth and distance, we employ early childhood lessons about the visual properties of motion, height, shape, and size as we make our way through space. Viewing pictures, in contrast, requires negating or counterbalancing the very visual strategies we depend on in ambient seeing. The traditional western system for translating three-dimensional space onto a two-dimensional plane assumes the scene is viewed from a single, stationary point. Because humans are binocular animals who see only through movement, we must always adjust our ambient mode of vision to recognize flat, static pictorial shapes as familiar objects.

The ability to interpret pictures thus develops alongside the acquisition of ambient vision, but it is a learned skill, with requirements that diverge dramatically from the ability to see the environment. In our own culture, an adult will hold the child and point to simple pictures of objects, usually in a book made for this purpose, saying the word for the object and repeating it many times. Often children are shown a variety of picture books in various places. They learn to recognize apples, bears, and cats in many different patterns of lines, colors, and shapes. The three pictures of ducks in figure 4.9, for instance, represent a sample of the current fare available for the eight-month-old reader. A child of this age may have seen pictures of ducks already—on sheets or pajamas or wallpaper—and may even have a rubber duck. Each is likely to be different from all of the others, and many of them will bear only a vague resemblance to any actual duck. When we tell this child that each of these disparate shapes is a duck, we are essentially asking her to create a huge regression of images under an abstract cognitive category "duck." This process necessarily requires the use of memory, abstract thinking, and mental spatial manipulation. When the child does finally see the real bird and is told that this, too, is a duck, she probably treats it as one more instance of the general genre of "duck," rather than realizing right away that all previous viewings were merely paraducks and this, at last, is the real thing. Therefore, the learning of a category of pictures called "duck," has occurred independently of actual contact with web-footed birds. The same is true for "elephant," "pig," "tiger," and other cognitive categories created using picture books, but often not preceded by experience. In our theories, however, we often assume, without giving it much thought, that people know a picture of a duck refers to a duck simply because it looks like one.

Figure 4.9. Pictures of ducks from current baby books

Reading pictures often requires viewers to move into a figurative interpretation when the picture doesn't seem to fit with the observed world. For instance, to "read" the bloomerized duck in figure 4.10 required that readers, knowing that ducks are not often fashionably dressed, recognize the picture as a metaphor, fantasy, or a joke. Without the ability to shift into metaphorical thinking, viewers would be forced into absurdly literal translations. Children learn how to make such shifts early in childhood—preschoolers can recognize Daffy and Donald, but they don't usually expect real ducks to spit when they talk.

The act of looking at a picture, therefore, requires a complex battery of skills and knowledge: the ability to override the "natural" mode of ambient perception, familiarity with various formulas for representing objects, and a mental catalog of cognitive abstractions like "duck." Because there are so many possible formulas, categories, methods, viewpoints, and purposes for representing any one object or concept—and because our pictorial language is constantly changing—we must bring learning and judgment to bear on *each and every picture we see.*

Yet feminist critics stubbornly insist on readings that fail to accommodate such tacit knowledge. Lay readers can easily get the impression that feminists are crude and dogmatic because they so often ignore an intention that seems obvious or fail to employ visual conventions most of us invoke as a matter of course. The resistance to applying these normative visual strategies to pictorial artifacts casts doubt, in my mind, on the effects that some critics claim images have. If the proposed impact requires reading the picture in a way that we can presume few, if any, of its viewers actually would have done, how can we believe that the argued effect took place?

Feminist critics often justify their readings by saying that their theory does not require establishing intent to be valid, or that they are reading deep structures that lie beneath surface manifestations such as style, or that they are interpreting symbols so universal that no other information is required. As we have seen, both the inferred intentionality and the style of a picture profoundly affect its meaning. Pictures, further, are so culturally and historically specific that the usefulness of "universal readings" is very limited. A far sounder practice, in my opinion, would be to flesh out our interpretations of images with information about the makers and to balance that with evidence of the actual response. So far, I have tried to do the first by providing information about the making of the Gibson Girl and the discourse in which she appeared. Now I want to address the second issue by looking at evidence about the actual response from viewers.

## THE GIBSON GIRL AS EQUIPMENT FOR LIVING[18]

Clippings of the Gibson Girl appeared in backstage dressing rooms, mountain cabins, boarding schools, freight trains, and college dormitories. Women who admired her wore tailored clothes, swept their hair into casual knots, and walked in long strides. But male admirers were as likely to signal their own identification with Gibson's work as the women were: "Gibson also created a type of man the square-shoulder, firm-jawed, clean-shaven, well-groomed, wholesome youth . . . and the American young man, less self-consciously than the American girl, set himself to imitate the type. It was Gibson's pen which sent mustaches out of fashion and made the tailors pad the shoulders of well cut coats." Other images had their own associated ways and looks. DuMaurier's Trilby, who was nearly as popular as the Gibson Girl but much more bohemian, inspired Trilby shoes and coats. So women who adopted the Gibson Girl chose her as a model from among other possibilities. Others chose different models and, therefore, a different manner of displaying themselves. Furthermore, a woman

Figure 4.10. A Gilded Age joke using a fantasy duck. *Life.* November 19, 1896.

might combine a Gibson Girl hairdo with another character's skirt. Instead of being blindly imitative, that sort of emulative behavior was highly creative.[19]

Other ways of emulating the Gibson Girl were visible in behavior. A "companionable" way of conducting a courtship or a manner of posture, for example, could evoke the Gibson ethos. Furthermore, the attitudes that underpinned such behavior were also a form of (and basis for) identification: Support for women's athletics or education would both have been consistent with the Gibson Girl ethos, as would disdain for those who married for money. Nevertheless, as we have seen, many in America at the turn of the twentieth century disapproved of women's athletics, thought posture was important, and maintained a traditional practice of matrimony. As we know some people *rejected* the Gibson Girl, we cannot argue that anyone was *forced* to be like the Gibson Girl or that she operated on the human consciousness by flying under the radar of rationality.

The response to the Gibson Girl, for our purposes here, may be further broken down into two types: the response of a group (an act of social identification), and the response of a person (an individual adaptation for a singular set of circumstances). I address the first by looking at the three groups most clearly identified with the Gibson Girl at the turn of the century—college girls, athletes, and office workers. Then I look at two fairly unlikely candidates for individual adaptation, a poor black girl and a rural runaway.

## Group Identifications

*College Girls.* When Inez Haynes Irwin, one of the radicals among feminists at the turn of the century, wrote *Angels and Amazons: A Hundred Years of American Women,* she called the chapter on her own generation "Gibson Girls." The Gibson Girl, as the heroine of reading material aimed at the college-educated, was a natural for these young women to emulate. The new college woman, far from being a marginal character, was highly glamorized by the popular press, particularly if she went to one of the prestigious schools from which many feminist leaders graduated. Attention focused on the elite "Seven Sisters" colleges; a mystique developed around these "young girl graduates" that was based in no small part on their own exclusivity. William O'Neill noted in *The Woman Movement* that these turn of the century feminists, as graduates of the eastern women's colleges, "regarded themselves, quite rightly, as an elite with special privileges and responsibilities."[20]

The self-consciously elite status of the college girl sometimes led the Gibson Girl's critics to feel she was a little too pleased with herself. A contemporary satire by Caroline Ticknor, "The Steel-Engraving Lady and the Gibson Girl," skewers the Gibson Girl for her self-importance. This particular Gibson Girl boasts: "You see,

I've had a liberal education. I can do everything my brothers do; and do it rather better, I fancy. I am an athlete and a college graduate, with a wide universal outlook. My point of view is free from narrow influences, and quite outside of the home boundaries." The young woman then turns toward the Steel-Engraving Lady. "But tell me," the Gibson Girl said condescendingly, "what did your so-called education consist of?" After the Lady's exit, the Gibson Girl exclaims to herself, "She surely is an extinct type! I realize now what higher education has done toward freeing woman from chains of prejudice." Thus, college girls were easily observed emulators of the Gibson Girl, but some contemporary Americans did not approve. The behavior was taking place among educated women who were consistently identified with feminism and this very identification is part of what made the Gibson Girl threatening to more conservative parties. A similar dispute occurred among another of the Girl's fan groups, the athletes.[21]

*Athletes.* Because Gibson often pictured her biking, golfing, and swimming, the Girl was a model for women athletes. Like her real-life comrades-in-arms, she drew fire from conservative quarters. Our heroine's large size and easy movement, her physical training and athletic activity, were said to result in an "atrophy" of "girlish modesty and decent reserve." This "hoyden" (or "tomboy") used too much slang, and her manners were shockingly casual. As one observer sneered at the Gibson Girl type: "She will enter a hotel dining room with her sleeves rolled up above her elbows, and her hands in the pockets of her short skirt, treading on the big heels of her clumping boots as solidly as any grenadier. Her usual form of salutation to her friends, young men or women, indifferently, is 'Hallo!' in a tone that is like a slap on the shoulder. On a golf course recently a player waiting for a very pretty and well-dressed girl to play out of his way was entertained by her comment on her stroke, after she had made it: 'Holy smoke! what a bum swat!'"[22]

Fashion magazines jumped on the sports bandwagon, nevertheless. As early as 1890, the *Delineator* recommended bloomers enthusiastically in its update on spring fashions, praising the garment's practical qualities, especially its appropriateness for cycling, and offered a pattern to readers. *Demorest's* also endorsed the bloomers. *Vogue,* the arbiter of taste for high society in the 1890s, endorsed cycling in 1894, published a special issue about the bicycle in 1895, offered bloomer patterns, and ran numerous commentaries on how to dress for cycling. The *Ladies' Home Journal* editor remarked approvingly in 1895 that bicycle makers had accomplished more for dress reform in two years than reformers had since clothes had come into use.[23]

*Office Workers.* Beginning in the late 1880s, after the invention of the typewriter, a new class of white-collar women workers arose. It grew at such a pace that, as a percentage of total working women, it outdistanced domestic service and factory work by 1915. In 1900, working women had to choose between humiliating, grueling, often dangerous, low-paying jobs such as factory work or domestic labor, and the relatively greater respect, job security, safety, and pay that came with an office job. Many women studied and worked very hard to get such work.

The stigma that always had been attached to working women was carried over to office work, however. From the earliest days of office work, feminists were writing in rather nasty tones about office clerks' excessive dress and heavy face paint. Often they attributed greater industry and morality to plain women in the office: "It is the same bureau, where you find the assortment described, and that is most of them, there is perhaps a minority of female clerks with whose dullness and demeanor it would be difficult to find fault—women working like horses, scarcely taking time for lunch, making books of records second to none, and copies of important papers with wonderful rapidity and correctness."[24] By the turn of the twentieth century, such judgments about the dress of office workers had resulted in the development of a specific set of appearance requirements.

Advice columns instructed clerks to dress very plainly and to be scrupulously clean. The ideal was a "trim and spotless shirtwaist," a dark skirt, and a tie, accessorized with heavy gloves, a plain hat, and low-heeled shoes. All this "so might the woman who worked for a living remain something of a lady nevertheless." Inez Haynes Irwin believed that "business women" should avoid jewelry, high-heeled shoes, ruffles, or any other feminine touches "like the pestilence." "Nevertheless," she wrote later with an air of resignation, "the business women clung to such coquettish touches as watches affixed to golden bowknots or fleurs-de-lis at the bosoms of those aforesaid shirtwaists—watches facing straight forward, so that all the world except the wearer could see the time. And they did their best to look like the lovely, candid-eyed, goddess-featured models of Charles Dana Gibson." Apparently, office workers were trying to soften and individualize the effect of an aggressively asexual and undifferentiated manner of dress. The Gibson Girl's example may have provided the model for remaining feminine, attractive, and individual in spite of the self-conscious unobtrusiveness of one's uniform.[25]

As a clerical worker advanced into higher-level secretarial jobs and then into supervisory roles, the need for bland clothes and good grooming became even more important. Helen Rosen, the daughter of Russian Jewish immigrants, had an excellent preparation for Vassar, but both her financial situation and her ethnicity precluded following that option. Her education left her ill-equipped for any job, so Helen spent her first year out of high school struggling to find employment in the new office bureaucracies. She studied shorthand and attended evening classes, finally breaking into office work by learning to use the newly introduced Dictaphone. Once inside, her education, level-headedness, and appreciation for a challenge served her well, and she quickly moved up. After being promoted to a position managing other stenographers, she became keenly aware of the importance of appearance to career advancement. She remembered a difficult case:

> I had another secretary, a bright Irish girl who had been studying shorthand at night. She was able and alert, but came from a rough neighborhood and was one of the few girls I have ever seen in any office who was not clean. Her waists—all girls then wore white shirtwaists to work—were frequently wet through with perspiration. Her hair was untidy and unwashed. It was impossible to have her about, in spite of her good work. One of the more important executives in another department needed a new secretary and I thought she could earn more money there, but the promotion seemed hopeless because of her personal habits. So one day I said to her:
>
> "Miss Mahoney, there's a better job for you in this place. You will get four dollars a week more at once. I wonder if you'd be willing to change—er—er—to do some things differently—in order to get it. I don't like to say what I'm going to say to you, but I feel it must be said.
>
> "You really are a mighty bright girl. You're a good stenographer and you will make a lot of money before you get through. But men are peculiar. They—they like a girl always to have a nice fresh shirtwaist. You'd think they wouldn't notice about hair—but your hair is very strong and healthy and probably needs washing at least once a week—."
>
> She thanked me, adopted all the suggestions, was promoted, was thereafter always trim and neat. She never forgave me.

By cultivating the look and manners of genteel women, office workers were able to carve out a peculiar class position of their own, one somewhere between the college-educated suffragist and the factory laborer:

> The girls in offices did not consider themselves working-women; they "went to business." And they neither wanted to be condescended to by "society" women taking up suffrage, nor did they want for a moment to be classed with the members of labor unions. They had the white-collar feeling completely, and they thought themselves independent and ladies. . . . They live by the standards of the whole western world, which looks down on them because they work for a living. If they were women of education working for a living, this condescension would be less. If they were women of wealth working for fun, it would not exist at all. So naturally they pretend to both education and wealth.

Just as the social stratifications between working women and leisured women were articulated through dress and grooming, so were the class levels among working women: "I would walk into the dressing room in my unbecoming black skirt and white shirtwaist, wash my hands, throw on my hat. The rest of them were putting on rouge and powder before the mirror. Not to use make-up was an unpardonable affectation of superiority in their minds. I considered it a real sign of superiority." The white shirt and black skirt of the Gibson Girl signified "office worker" in the dress language of the day, but status within the work world was signified by other elements, such as the use of rouge. These quotations suggest a relatively complex system of social marking, not a blanket drive to emulate a single ideal.[26]

## Individual Adaptations

Women who were far removed from the relatively privileged atmosphere of colleges and offices also could use the example of the Gibson Girl.

*The Entrepreneur.* Sarah Breedlove, for instance, was the first member of her family to be born free. As a child of the aftermath of slavery, Breedlove struggled to establish herself at the most basic levels of economic life. She went to work as a laundress, a brutally difficult job, requiring heavy lifting as well as constant contact with hot water, harsh soap, and high-handed mistresses. The pay was minimal and uncertain. Early on, Breedlove decided that escape from domestic labor in another woman's home was the only way to real independence. The question was how to get out. It took her twenty years.[27]

Breedlove admired the long, upswept hair of the Gibson Girl and wanted to come up with a way to enable black women to have that look. After experimenting with homemade hair preparations, the treatment she developed consisted of several chemical and mechanical steps that seemed to result in hair that grew longer but also looked straighter. About 1900, Breedlove began selling the treatment in her own neighborhood. Later she traveled by train, selling door to door. She was briefly married to a newspaper man named C. J. Walker, who helped her to write and place advertising in local papers. She took his name for her business, and, within two years, it had grown from $10 to $1,000 a day.

The former laundress and daughter of slaves became America's first black millionaire. "Madame C. J. Walker" designed a system of distribution that would help others escape from servitude in the white woman's home. "Walker Agents," who wore black skirts and white shirts in the manner of the Gibson Girl, became familiar sights in African American communities around the nation. The first agents trained others and soon a network of delivery spread over the country like a fine web.

Madame Walker wanted to be sure that her good fortune was reinvested in the black community. She shared her profits liberally with her employees—a number of them became wealthy. She established "Walker Clubs" in every community where a Walker Agent worked to channel funds to needy families, deserving students, and others whom a little could money help. She put students through college, worked tirelessly in the antilynching movement, and built parks and playgrounds. Walker forced organizations of black men to deal with her on the grounds that she was more economically successful than any of them. In her will, Madame Walker left two-thirds of her estate to African American organizations working to help black people achieve equality. Educator and activist Mary McLeod Bethune eulogized her: "Madame Walker was the clearest example I know of what the Negro woman can do. She has gone, but her work still lives. She will be an inspiration to the world."[28]

The benefits of Madame Walker's treatments to black people as a race, however, were mixed. From the beginning, Walker was criticized for selling products that made black people "look white." Walker was adamant that she was trying to help black women grow long, healthy hair, not encouraging them to look like whites. She argued, as did many other black leaders of her time, that pride in race should involve pride in appearance. Walker also contended that black women needed to be encouraged to go into business for themselves if they were ever going to achieve economic independence. "I have left the washtub for a better job," she said. "The girls and women of our race must not be afraid of business." Her advertisements emphasized both points: the economic independence that could be had by selling the products and the social benefits and personal pride that could be had by using them.[29]

This particular grooming controversy illustrates again the limits of the feminist critique. Sexual allure was not the issue here. Both men and women used Walker's products until the 1960s. Straight, shiny hair became the standard for "good hair" for both sexes and was an aesthetic that was seen by all to be rooted in racial prejudice. When black women began wearing their hair "natural" in the 1960s, their men were doing the same. In both cases, the "Afro" hairdo was a political statement about race, not gender. Late in the twentieth century, young black girls who wanted straight hair had to struggle with their mothers, whose concern was not over communicating sexuality but with the way straight hair signaled a backward movement in race relations.[30]

*The Showgirl.* Although white women in rural areas had limited access to fashion, they often followed the careers of actresses with jealous fascination. Thus, a classic American Girl story is one where a young girl goes to the city to become a star of the stage. A young Kansas girl, Belle Livingstone, fantasized about her future: "I could neither sing nor dance, nor was I a beauty. Yet with the soaring self-confidence of seventeen I knew no qualms. Give me a part, give me a costume and I had not the slightest doubt that I could hold an audience in the hollow of my hand." Although her family was poor, Belle's mother was determined that Belle would marry and be a respectable woman. But, like so many American Girls, Belle had no desire to live out her mother's scenario. In 1892 she ran away to join the chorus of a road show. Among the chorus girls, she got a new education: "The chorus, I found, was divided into two classes, the wise virgins and the foolish ones. . . . To my surprise, it was the foolish virgins who taught me the most. My mother would have told me that the wise ones would fare best in the end—that those sterling souls who always had a clean handkerchief would attract the greatest admiration and the most flattering offers of marriage. But as I learned life, it was the foolish ones—who may have neglected to wash their necks or mend their stockings—who married the rich men." The "foolish virgins" worked hard for their performances and made a sufficient living but used the rich men who attended shows to get luxuries.[31]

Soon Belle aspired to join in the glamorous world of foolish virgins, rich men, and glittering nightlife. Once in New York City, she landed a part in popular musical. Although she did not have a pretty face, Belle was tall and had long "poetic" legs, which her costume showed to advantage. She felt confident in her new role, but was still anxious about her "Junoesque" looks and her lack of fashion skill. One day, as she was standing in the lobby of the theater, she saw a man admiring her picture. He walked over to the ticket window and asked for a front-row ticket. The ticket seller struck up a conversation.

> "Say, you must like this show. How many times have I sold you a ticket?"
>
> "Fifteen, mister. I go just to see that showgirl—" nodding in the direction of the poster. "Boy is she a stepper!"
>
> The ticket seller dropped his head and began to whisper. I knew he was telling the man that the original of the picture was standing in the lobby. The man turned, gave me one look, and his countenance altered so dramatically that I didn't know whether to laugh or to cry.
>
> "My God!" was all he could say, as he grabbed back his five-dollar bill and fled.

This "yelp of disappointment" persuaded Belle that she would have to change her off-stage style: "Here was a man spending his money just to look at me across the footlights. Think what he might have spent for nourishing steaks and chops if only I had lived up to his expectations in real life." Belle was tired of other girls "padding over shaggy rugs in softly lighted restaurants, getting a run for their teeth on terrapin to the strains of 'Tales from the Vienna Woods' while I was boiling a cup of tea on a gas plate." She made a resolution that would change her life: "At that moment I had never had a cocktail or a regret. I decided to try both."[32]

Belle took her next paycheck to one of New York's top fashion designers. She told him: "I know I'll never be beautiful—look at this pug nose and red hair! But I want dash, splash, flash. I want to look like Paris. Can you make me over completely? Do whatever you like—I won't even look in the mirror." The couturier dressed her in a manner that took advantage of her Amazonian figure and topped off each outfit with a provocative hat.[33]

In her new couturier look, Belle became part of the nightly go-round of dinners and parties that had become a kind of alter-institution for elite men as well as a social stage from which actresses promoted themselves. One observer recounted: "The famous beauties, whose pictures were in the lobbies and whose names were in the feature stories, knew just the right moment for their entrance into the crowded restaurants. The wise orchestra leader knew his cue and, as a headliner appeared at the door with her escort, he gave the signal to his men and the strains of her song hit greeted her. She was always just so surprised; fluttered nervously with the great bouquets of violets or orchids which her well-repaid admirer carried for her and finally, with every eye upon her, walked slowly to their reserved table." Groups of revelers would enjoy the evening together, often going from place to place until dawn. Belle recalled: "On those rollicking nights of the Nineties the idea of fun was not to go out on a twosome. Showgirls like to see and be seen by as many as possible, and parties rolled up like snowballs." The next day, however, it was as if the men and women had never met: "In those days, New York showgirls were given a big rush from midnight to dawn in Sherry's but overlooked next afternoon in Central Park."[34]

Needless to say, the women in the parlors of the elite did not approve of their men going out with actresses, nor of the restaurants, champagne, and wee-hour revelry. From their point of view, the men were using their money to buy sex and indulge in dissipated behavior. The actresses were allowing themselves to be bought for the pleasure of the men—or were luring the men into the webs of their own sinfulness. Belle described it like this: "Everybody loved it, except the prunes-and-prisms ladies who preferred to remain away. Certainly the men flocked there. I am a man's woman. I don't know why men like me, unless it is because I am tolerant of their peccadilloes, but they have always sought out my company, a fact that in itself is enough to get me hanged, drawn, and quartered by the sewing circle."[35]

Now Belle was happy. Then an odd event propelled her to stardom:

> One morning I awoke in the brass bed to find myself famous. The artist Charles Dana Gibson, whose Gibson Girls were the pin-up models of the Nineties, had been for some time popularizing the full-bosomed type of feminine beauty. The Gibson Girl rage may or may not have been responsible for what had happened, but one day the *New York World* published a full-page picture devoted to the measurements of the ideal feminine figure. Hoyt's enterprising publicity agent immediately phoned the *World* that my own measurements corresponded to a T to their specifications. As a result every Sunday

> newspaper carried stories and pictures of the "ideal woman"—me. The form I had thought a liability because of its goddess-like proportions was now the envy of all my showgirl friends.

The publicity agent continued to ply the press with Belle's Gibsonesque measurements and she became a national celebrity. "Immediately things happened. Even Hollywood could not have asked for more. I began to get top billing, and the show played every night to SRO [standing room only] . . . I knew well enough I was no beauty, but I had learned how to make the most of my buxom figure. It began to dawn on me that I could go further and faster on proportions, personality, and publicity than on a picture face."[36]

Belle Livingstone was famous in the theater and popular in the nightlife, and she made a good salary for herself. Oddly, although she had never been very interested in matrimony, she began to think about marriage. Friends who had gone to Europe looking for husbands among the wealthy and titled were writing to her of their successes. Belle decided to try her luck, again becoming part of a distinctive Gilded Age phenomenon: "This was the day of the great invasion of England by America, not by shock troops but by shocking little troupers—hordes of showgirls, each one intent on making a wealthy and, if possible also, titled marriage."[37]

Society "belles" were also looking for titled marriages in Europe during this time, as documented often in the satires of Dana Gibson. Society women claimed the advantage in their "breeding" and "refinement," which were still defined largely by British aristocratic standards. But in England, the women of the American stage became popular among the aristocracy and were treated with as much respect by day as they were by night. If they chose to marry, they had as much access to the titles of Europe as did their social superiors back home. The would-be nobility of America were beaten at their own game.

In the face of competition, the elite moved toward a "refined" dress, which emphasized lines and subtlety over the more obvious grandeur of the past. The women of the stage, however, dressed in a publicity-seeking way with huge hats, elaborate gowns, feather boas, lots of beads and spangles—"dash, splash, and flash." These costumes bespoke more than just "educated" versus "uneducated" tastes, and more than simple sexual availability. The difference between muted colors and flashing rhinestones expressed a huge philosophical chasm. On one side was the exaltation of the mind, the fear of the body, the drive to reform the world to one's own specifications, and the ascetism that paves the way to everlasting life. On the other stood the appreciation of worldly luxury, the willingness to risk mistakes, the toleration of opportunism, the desire to see the world in all its variety, and the determination to live life to the fullest.

Belle Livingstone married four times, including a millionaire and a count. She acquired and lost fortunes with the abandon most of us save for umbrellas. Her salons in Paris and London were filled with people from the arts, both famous and infamous, for which one journalist called her "the Most Dangerous Woman in Europe." The former showgirl ran a military hospital, a soup kitchen, and a prototype of the U.S.O. out of her huge home in Paris during World War I. This escapee from the midwestern prairie knew Diamond Jim Brady, Isadora Duncan, and Lily Langtry. Once she went around the world on five pounds sterling just to win a bet. In short, she lived a life of daring and romance the likes of which most people experience only in fiction. She finished her autobiography just before her death in 1957. In it, she asked that her gravestone be engraved: "This is the only stone I have left unturned."[38]

The life that Belle Livingstone created for herself made use of the Gibson Girl by turning her large proportions into a public relations asset. But the Gibson Girl was only one very small piece of this magnetic and unconventional persona. As her autobiography shows, Belle took a great deal from the model provided by nineteenth-century actresses and courtesans as well as from entrepreneurial modern women and rollicking Western girls. In choosing the materials from which to create her own persona, Belle also set herself up *in opposition to* the Steel-Engraving Lady ("the prunes-and-prisms ladies," "the sewing circle"), as well as the temperance women, and the long-suffering pioneer women. So, by taking bits and pieces from models she admired (or was stuck with anyway) and by refusing to display the signs of those she did not wish to be, Belle Livingstone created a strategy for living life and a unique self to live it. It is in this way that, for all of us, images become equipment for living.

## CONCLUSION

If we are sincerely interested in determining the social effects of pictures, it is essential to engage in a study of the ways in which pictures are produced, visual strategies invoked, and images incorporated into daily life. We have seen that the viewer of popular pictures, even in the early days of photoengraving technology, had to confront and make sense of an enormous range of factors that affected the meaning of each image. We have observed the extraordinary difference that the vehicle, the medium, the technique, the historical period, and contemporary social standards can make, even among pictures of the same subject, a beautiful young woman. Before critics can legitimately comment on the impact of a particular image on the culture, therefore, they must carefully reconstruct the visual context in which the viewers read that image. In all the analysis of popular feminine images I have read within the feminist corpus, I have yet to see anyone try to accomplish this.

Feminist criticism of images instead is full of incompetent readings masquerading as privileged insights. What allows this kind of thing to be passed off as knowledge is the assumption that images communicate to us in ways unavailable to ordinary consciousness. This belief is central to the theories feminists have used most often to interpret pictures: Freudianism, structuralism, and Marxism. These same interpretive theories also provide the basis for ignoring the actual circumstances under which pictures are produced and read.

In Freudian interpretation, pictures are approached as if they were dreams, in which the illogic of the unconscious is expressed in distorted images so that the ego will be unaware of desires that threaten it. The forces at work are presumed to be independent of history or class or contingencies. The activities of conscious, cognitive processes are not considered, nor are the public, historical forces that shape pictorial statements. Consequently, the model of the mind implied by such interpretations is devoid of judgment, unable to make selections, and oblivious to fine distinctions. No wonder women are easily manipulated in this model; who wouldn't be?

In structuralism, the "true meaning" of any statement lies in its "deep structure," an abstract grammar that axiomatically ignores the intention, style, situation, and reception of the actual message. The interpreter's work is to "brush away" surface elements of the message—such as the manner in which it is rendered—to get at the deeper, presumably truer structure. Once the picture is dispensed with in this summary way, the interpreter goes on to attribute all sorts of unseen meanings to the "structure" beneath it—without considering whether there is any likelihood that such messages were actually exchanged between maker and viewer.

In Marxism, every artifact in capitalist culture distorts reality in a way that is invisible to the uninitiated. The only good picture is the one that copies the world as it really is—or, rather, the world as it appears to those who don't suffer from "false consciousness." Because of its initial reliance on resemblance, a Marxist approach to images is always doomed to confusion. Because the approach presumes only Marxists see the world as it really is, you can't argue with it. You may as well try to convince a member of the religious right that there are other authorities besides the Bible.

All three of these theories depend on a sensitized oracle to pull away the surface illusions of a message and reveal the "true" meaning underneath. None requires any empirical validity, historical corroboration, or even reasonable probability. None addresses the complex processes through which pictures are read. Yet all purport to explain the "effects" of images on a culture.

Having the kind of training that feminist critics have—in Marxist cultural theory, semiotics, and Freudian interpretation—cannot and will not substitute for the everyday training that real viewers use to interpret pictures. In this very important way, the data entry clerk reading a fashion magazine on her way to work is as qualified in the interpretation of pictures as the self-proclaimed feminist expert. The knowledge necessary to "decode" popular pictures does not depend on special terminology or obscure grammars, but is most clearly available in the daily lives of the people who view them.

CHAPTER FIVE

# THE POWER OF FASHION

A BEAUTIFUL DEBUTANTE CARRYING AN AMERICAN FLAG LED THOUSANDS OF WOMEN, all dressed in white, down the empty canyon of Fifth Avenue. Crowds cheered as the suffragists marched through the bright autumn day to 42nd Street. As the pretty leader's standard pitched and flapped in the wind, a New York city policeman rushed over to help adjust her pole. At 31st and Fifth, the men from the Knickerbocker Club leaned from the windows to wave at their lovely friend. The dark-haired beauty led her sisters another ten blocks, then she stopped to salute the president, who stood in the grandstand, smiling. In response to her salute, he lifted his top hat and waved it in the air. The watchers and marchers thrilled to the experience, glad in the knowledge they all shared: The moment for women's suffrage had come.[1]

In a sense, the Fifth Avenue suffrage march of 1917 was the culmination of sixty years of feminist effort. Yet there was no denying that recent years had brought something new to the movement: feminism had become fashionable. The daughters and granddaughters of the nineteenth-century nouveau riche, now entrenched in their social position, had conferred on suffrage the same prestige they bestowed on the dress designers, beauty salons, and hairdressers they patronized. To the new "mass" magazines for women, they leaked the details of their newest clothes, described their beauty routines, and promoted women's causes with savvy enthusiasm.

We're not used to thinking of feminism as something actively promoted like face cream or toilet water. For years now feminist critics have railed against the methods of marketing as if promotion and persuasion were totally alien to them. This chapter aims to demonstrate that feminism and fashion are both part of the commerce of women's culture and thus are difficult to clearly separate. And because the fashion world is marked with the same hierarchical patterns and barriers of exclusion that characterize women as a social group, the ability to control what is fashionable is a form of power women wield over each other. By leveraging these social differences against the influence of the women's magazines, the socialites of the 1910s made feminism fashionable, a strategy that built coalitions among women of all classes.

With the force of this huge movement behind it, suffrage for women was finally achieved.

## IN *VOGUE*

Having made room for the Vanderbilts, the Astors, the Goulds, and the Rockefellers, the first families of America still were continually assaulted by new elites in publishing, finance, and the arts. They decided to mark their turf by publishing a magazine; they called it *Vogue.*

An explicit effort to "maintain the standards of morality and taste" being challenged by new elites, *Vogue* was intended to stipulate who and what was "fashionable" in the exclusionary sense that the term was still used. The editors and writers, socialites themselves, accomplished this feat by reporting on certain parties but not others, drawing some party dresses while ignoring the rest, and itemizing the politics, table manners, skirt lengths, religious preferences, and home decor that marked those who were included. The entire magazine was designed to announce that, in the words of a regular columnist: "We rule with a golden rod and our social word is law."[2]

*Vogue*'s first editor, Mrs. Josephine Redding, was a woman whose own social position was unassailable. Perhaps that was why she felt no discomfort in using the magazine's editorial page as a feminist forum. It seems strange, I know, to think of feminism being advocated in such a vehicle, but Redding expressed her attitudes so frequently and consistently that there can be no doubt of her intentions. For example, in a barbed attack on the misguided opinions of "no less dignified a medium than the *Atlantic Monthly,*" she wrote: "When man consents to acknowledge that he is simply a male variety of human being, no whit superior to the female type, except to 'brute force,' the woman critic will cease from troubling him. So long, however, as he continues to give himself his old-time airs of superiority, he may expect to be made to undergo the process known as being taken down. The New Woman can be trusted to give him his deserts in this particular." When a bishop spoke against the New Woman in a commencement address to female graduates, Redding could hardly be restrained. "If the conservatives would only bring themselves to investigate the facts of to-day, and not keep their faces turned so persistently toward conditions that the world has outgrown, they would be able to realize that the girl of this age confronts problems that did not enter into the life of her ancestor," she wrote with acid condescension. Mrs. Redding offers instead that, "progressive people consider it only just to women to train the whole sex, without any reference to the 'sphere' idea, and to encourage all girls to be self-reliant, setting before them the incentives to work and to achieve that have inspired men to 'arrive' in art, science, commerce and industry." Week after week, the foolishness of conservative men was exposed with the withering sarcasm only a Leader of Society could bring to the task. Feminism, it is clear, was the required view of the refined few.[3]

When loyalties of gender came into conflict with values of class, however, there was no question to which direction *Vogue* was inclined. In spite of Redding's support of vocational training for women and her periodic pleas on behalf of working girls, *Vogue*'s message comes through distinctly that all people who work were unambiguously "common." As a writer explained: "I have always divided people into two classes, equals and inferiors, and with this classification I admit no shading nor do I recognize a half-way house. I am always civil to tradespeople, to persons who wait on me in shops, in the same manner as I am to my valet or to any unfortunate individual who has to hire out his personal services . . . but I have never expected that they would for a moment imagine that I would place them upon the same social level as myself." Socialites who were forced by economic misfortune to go to work in order to live immediately became "common" and were then ruthlessly excluded: "I think that as soon as one becomes crippled in one's finances it is much better to face the world bravely, take up the burden on one's shoulders, and do anything rather than be humiliated by being an object of charity to others. Then, although it is hard, and it may seem cruel, one should draw the curtain at that moment. Society has no place for poverty, however honorable." Participating in "trade" was unthinkable. Even at *Vogue*'s office, the high-born "preferred not to sully their hands with the commercial elements of their slim journal," so little attention was paid to advertising, circulation figures, and other "such vulgar matters." As a result, between 1900 and 1909, a time when the total revenue of American publications was growing at 50 percent a year, *Vogue*'s circulation dwindled to 14,000 and its advertising to $100,000.[4]

Condé Nast acquired *Vogue* in 1909. Although he built his business on the tastes of the elite and was married to a "well-born" woman, Nast's own forebears could not have withstood the critical eye of his audience. He came from a poor midwestern family, a second-generation German immigrant on his father's side, the descendant of a French St. Louis fur trader on his mother's. He was a Roman Catholic. Through the generosity of an aunt who had married well, he attended George Washington University. From there he became a successful advertising executive, having built his friend Frank Collier's magazine into a giant through ingenious promotion.[5]

Nast acquired *Vogue* as an attempt to build a business for himself, according to a clearly conceived philosophy of publishing that seems obvious to us now but was a radical idea in those days when the *Ladies' Home Journal* and the *Saturday Evening Post* threw shadows across the rest of American publishing. Nast believed that a magazine offering a select audience, perfectly suited to the needs of a particular group of advertisers, could make more money than one with an undefined audience that included "waste" readership. Nast's avowed intention toward *Vogue* was to turn it into just such a vehicle by putting the providers of luxury goods in touch with *only* those who had the money to buy. Under Nast's management, the advertising rate for *Vogue* was increased to $10 per thousand readers, as compared to $2–$3 per thousand for the national women's service magazines, which also covered grooming and dress. In spite of its smaller circulation and higher rates, however, *Vogue* soon carried 44 percent more advertising than the *Ladies' Home Journal,* 78 percent more than the *Delineator,* and 292 percent more than its nearest competitor, another society book called *Harper's Bazaar.* Advertisers in *Vogue* paid a substantial premium for the quality of the audience—and did so eagerly.

This is the point in the story where we have learned to expect the ugly faces of top-hatted capitalists to become visible behind the fashion machinery. In this case, though, the situation is not quite so clear. Most *Vogue* advertisements in the 1910s were placed by small businesspersons, mostly women trying to make money off the tastes of their wealthy sisters by selling cosmetics, exercise programs, and salon services. In one issue, *Vogue* reported recent success stories among their advertisers: four shopping commissioners, four dressmakers, two children's tailors, one lace manufacturer, one selling agent, one specialty shop, one hairdresser, one milliner, one tea room owner, and one counselor.[6] So, although the ostensible readers of *Vogue* were an aggressively homogeneous group of wealthy families, the advertisers were a heterogeneous assemblage of working people, many of whom were women. The really big capitalists were the ones reading *Vogue,* not the ones publishing it or advertising in it.

*Vogue* became increasingly attractive to advertisers as the magazine developed its role as "arbiter of taste" for the elite social set in New York and then for the smaller but equally jealous elites in towns around the country. The person most responsible for the rising authority of *Vogue* was the first editor of Nast's own choosing, Edna Woolman Chase. Chase, "a woman as remote from Society, in the class sense, as an Eskimo," had grown up in a modest Quaker home. She had joined the magazine at eighteen, glad for employment addressing envelopes. Chase was obsessed by her work, even when young, and referred to nonworking women as "civilians." Although she was a warm, unpretentious person in private, on the job she was tough, unflinching in her criticism, and unwavering in her judgment. She ran the *Vogue* office as if it were the mutant child of a military school. Chase required employees to wear black silk stockings, white gloves, and hats at all times. She expected all clothing to be of high quality and to show good taste. She strongly disapproved of women who dressed in an overly feminine or sexual way in the office, but she equally disliked women who came to work dressed like men. She and Nast were close friends as well as colleagues, and appear to have held each other in equal esteem, much like Sarah Hale and Louis Godey.[7]

Both Nast and Chase were enthusiastic supporters of the trend for women to work. For their editorial staff, they hired women almost exclusively. There were the "Society girls," fresh from college, who spent their days pretending to work. These young women made it very clear to their employers that *Vogue* was just a stopping-off place for them and they did not expect to give or get very much. The Society girls irritated Chase, but because they provided important ongoing "connections" to her readership, she put up with them. With another class of worker, however, it was a different story. Women of ambition were given real assignments, were carefully taught the business, were expected to work hard, were held to high standards of performance, and generally were nurtured as professionals. Many fashion editors of the twentieth century first learned their craft from Edna Woolman Chase and Condé Nast.

Just like their advertisers, therefore, the publisher, editor, and staff of *Vogue* were a mixed bag. The frictions and interdependencies of class must have been felt all the more acutely because of the day-to-day contact. Those who were at *Vogue* to make a career had to flatter and indulge those who were not, since the more privileged women were a crucial conduit to the audience, as well as the content, of the magazine. Yet the high-handed manner with which the Society girls must have treated the career girls can be easily imagined from the class attitudes expressed in the magazine. As editors trained at *Vogue* moved out into the growing world of women's magazines, the sense of social stratification probably followed, even where the socialites did not.

In its earliest days, *Vogue* discussed dress designs, but the attention was focused on the clothing of the Leaders of Society, regardless of where the clothes came from. By the 1910s, however, the editorial features of *Vogue* increasingly glorified Parisian designers. The very word "Paris" became a magical instrument capable of turning a dress into a totem and was invoked to glorify everything from the cut of a skirt to the feathers on a hat. Nevertheless, it is difficult to pinpoint the concrete impact of the French designers on actual clothing worn in America. The French designers had very little distribution in the United States. Ads by Paris designers are very rare. As a practical matter, to buy a real French designer dress, a woman either had to go to Paris or have a dress brought to her from there. Either way, both money and "connections" were necessary to accomplish the purchase, connections that were difficult to acquire and cultivate.[8]

Women who had neither the social standing nor the wealth to buy directly from the couturiers could buy one of very few originals brought to the United States by the department stores. Showings of Paris originals were used to lure consumers into the stores, where women were more likely to buy one of the copies offered at a lower price. *Vogue* also published highly detailed drawings of dresses seen at the Paris salons for the express purpose of allowing American dressmakers to copy them. (The actual reach of the Paris couturiers was so limited that they made no attempt to curtail copying until after World War I.)

For a few women, then, buying a dress from Paris was a possibility. For the majority, however, the race was to get *information* about what was new in Paris—and therefore likely to be "fashionable" among the Leaders of Society. *Vogue,* as well as local stores and dressmakers with "sources" in Paris, provided this valuable social data. A credible claim to Paris connections, therefore, was a powerful market advantage, which suggests that the desirability of French design was due to its *inaccessibility* rather than its ubiquity. Among the many advertised claims of the department stores, smaller retailers, and local dressmakers, however, it is impossible to tell who, if anyone, actually had information about French fashion and who was merely using "Paris" as promotional puffery.

Even for the rich, the Paris gown was a special item. Most other clothing was made by local dressmakers or purchased ready-made from local retailers. By 1910 some American dressmakers had enough success to open boutiques or showrooms where wealthy women would come by appointment to view locally designed clothes modeled by pretty working girls. American designs were not as prestigious as were copies of the latest Paris originals, however, so ads for American dressmakers alluded to their "Society" client list instead. A reputation as one of the preferred dressmakers, therefore, was also a valuable economic asset, one that could help make up for a lack of connections in France.

When World War I cut off America's information about French fashion, *Vogue* was left with a lot of blank pages to fill. Edna Woolman Chase had the idea of holding a charity fashion show featuring New York designers—sponsored by leading Society women to give the clothing the necessary prestige. However, such a project would require that leisure class women cooperate with the economic interests of local dressmakers. Nast told Chase right off that her readers wouldn't do something having such close connections to trade—not to mention the fact that they were unlikely to appear in public in the company of their dressmakers. The injection of "charity" into the exchange helped the matter somewhat, but the prospect of Society participation still seemed unlikely—unless some social benefit to the "women of refinement" could be cooked up.

Chase's solution was to use the hierarchy among the fashionable to facilitate her project. Members of Society preferred to follow one or two women who, by claims of superior "breeding," set the rules for the rest. The continued approval of one of these leaders was treated as a constant gift that must be continually reciprocated; a person who lost favor with one of these leaders for any reason could be excluded from the social circle. Given this power structure, the endorsement of a top member of Society could recruit the cooperation, even if begrudging, of the rest of the sheep.

At the time, one of the key leaders was the formidable Mrs. Stuyvesant Fish. Chase knew that with Mrs. Fish's blessing, the rest of Society would stampede to the show.

When Chase arrived at the Fish residence, however, the Leader of Society refused to see her. In a rather brazen swap, Chase promised to consider publishing illustrations by the son of Mrs. Fish's personal assistant in return for intercession with the recalcitrant dowager. At the assistant's urging, therefore, Chase was given an audience with Fish. During the meeting, Chase was able to convince her to support the charity show herself and to recruit others to do the same. As the magazine editor left, Mrs. Fish was already phoning Mrs. Astor, telling Chase, "She will certainly be a patroness, and so will the others. Can't afford not to."[9]

In this transaction, we can see again a phenomenon already observed in preindustrial America—one that is, in fact, typical of all economic systems. The "commercial" transaction eventually takes place because of a series of other personal transactions, only some of which include money. Some trades are devised on the spot, such as Chase's deal with the personal assistant. Others involve the calling in of favors or *obligations to reciprocate* for past transactions as yet uncompensated.

The fashion show was a huge success, even though the fact of socializing with dressmakers and models made the "refined women" uneasy. That same year Chase's own dressmaker, Anna White, experienced that prejudice firsthand. White had come to the United States from Dublin after her husband's death. She built a dressmaking salon into a lucrative business, becoming successful enough to live in an elegant apartment and send her daughters to a posh girls' school. White was patronized by elite women and had an interesting social circle that included many leading artists and writers of the day. But when Anna White's eldest daughter, Carmel, became engaged to Arthur Fitzpatrick in 1914, his high-society mother insisted on calling off the engagement when she found out the bride's mother was "in trade."[10]

Heartbroken, young Carmel went off to France to work for the American Red Cross. After the war, she went back to work in her mother's dress shop, once again to watch and listen to the great ladies pluming themselves for grand occasions. Then Carmel was offered a job as an assistant fashion editor at *Vogue.* Although she found the ladylike atmosphere at *Vogue* "la-di-da to a fare-thee-well," Carmel became one of the magazine's best people. Eventually she married a man named Palen Snow, with whom she had three children. However, she never quit working. She stayed at *Vogue* until 1934 and then was hired away to be editor of *Harper's Bazaar,* where she remained until her death in 1961.

Under Carmel Snow's direction, *Bazaar* became a serious competitor for *Vogue.* Although Carmel herself was a conservative dresser, she had a widely admired ability to identify new fashion trends. The fashion establishment in Paris treated Mrs. Snow like royalty. The shows would not start until she arrived, because the couture houses believed she was powerful enough to make or break a dress designer. Indeed, Paris gave both Snow and Edna Woolman Chase more deference than it did to New York

Society women. In a world where information about Paris design had such social value, those with consistent and unimpeachable access to it automatically assumed power over other women. The American press described both women in overblown terms, such as "the High Priestess of Fashion," "the idol of the American fashion world," "the final authority in all matters of fashion." It can't have pleased the elite to be so publicly under the influence of a poor Quaker and an Irish dressmaker's daughter. Nor can the irony have been lost on Chase and Snow.

Power over the fashionable world was also used to forward the cause of suffrage, causing the fledgling movement to become as au courant as Parisian gowns among the readers of *Vogue.* The leading dowager in the feminist movement was Mrs. O. H. P. Belmont. Formerly Alva Vanderbilt, the daughter of a wealthy southern family, she had caused the social scandal of the day by divorcing William Vanderbilt for adultery. She had also scored the social coup of the day by marrying her daughter, Consuelo, to the Duke of Marlborough. In her suffrage days, she was rich beyond belief, having won a huge settlement from Vanderbilt and, by 1910, become the widow of multimillionaire Oliver Belmont. This very powerful, very wealthy woman was focused almost obsessively on issues of women's rights. She was attached to the most militant ranks of the suffrage movement, which she supported with money, introductions to Society women, and the publicity value of her name or presence.

Belmont was an intimidating woman, known among the social elite as the Bengal Tiger. She held meetings in the homes of supplicant socialites to recruit for suffrage. Members of Society felt obliged to attend whether they were suffrage enthusiasts or not. At the meetings, Belmont's radical friends gave speeches. The audience was expected to volunteer time, money, signatures, influence, and whatever else they could offer to the suffrage cause in exchange for the continued approval of the Bengal Tiger. At one of these meetings, the beautiful debutante who led the Fifth Avenue march was recruited:

> . . . on a close afternoon the following summer, [the housel was packed with society dames, fresh from their lunches of eight courses, who controlled their skepticism about suffrage, and the speaker Miss Alice Paul, since the young woman was sponsored by Mrs. O. H. P. Belmont. . . .
>
> However, after examining the issue steadily for a few moments at the instance [*sic*] of Mrs. Belmont, I seemed of a sudden magically aware that suffrage was necessary, inevitable, without a true argument to be made against it, except by frumps, fools and knaves. So, throwing my hat into the ring, I was at once joyfully accepted, and exploited.[11]

This young woman awoke the next morning to find her name and photograph in the papers as a new convert to suffrage. Despite her genuine commitment to the cause, she soon realized that her social position and beauty were being used to lure new recruits.

Alice Paul, who was the leader of the suffrage militants as well as Belmont's protégée, had worked with the radical British suffragist Christabel Pankhurst in England. Feminist history emphasizes that, up to that time, the British suffrage movement was quite a bit more militant than the American movement particularly because it had already utilized dramatic strategies such as hunger strikes and pickets. What is *not* noted is that the ranks of the British movement were filled with aristocrats. Because the American social elite continued to emulate the British ruling class, nothing could speak so well for suffrage as the commitment of that sacrosanct group. In its September 1, 1910 issue, *Vogue* reported that the British suffragists "are leaders in the social world, the petted daughters and wives of the rich, who have had since babyhood hosts of servants at their beck. Yet now, for the good of the 'Cause,' they are spending bodily strength, sacrificing reserve, in chalking pavements!" Accompanying this article is a portrait of New York Society beauty Inez Millholland, a Vassar graduate who had once led a suffrage parade down Fifth Avenue herself and who had since gone abroad to participate in this *très chic* movement.[12]

Backed by Mrs. Belmont's money and considerable social influence—and blessed by the halo of the British aristocracy—Alice Paul's group, the Congressional Union, soon rivaled the NAWSA (the combined organizations founded by Anthony, Stanton, and Stone) in its ability to get attention, if not in actual numbers. The "women of fashion" who supported this final push to suffrage, however, were hardly marginal or disempowered. If they were "forced" to conform to "fashion"—as they used the term—it was only to maintain their position of privilege. This social position, however, did endow them with a peculiar power to "force" less privileged women to follow them all the way to the ballot—in the name of "fashion."

## GETTING THE TREATMENT

One glorious spring day in 1912, Florence Graham did something she had never done. Instead of working through lunch, she "removed her white coat, discreetly dusted her nose with some face powder, slipped into the jacket of a smart walking suit, put on a smashing Gladys Ogilvie original replete with pink ostrich feathers, and announced that she would be out to lunch." As her staff watched, dumbfounded, from the window, Graham walked up the street to where a crowd was gathering. "In a voice that resembled nothing so much as a sergeant major's, a portly matron was shouting orders at the almost 15,000 women queuing in the middle of the avenue. Florence joined the marchers with pride. She was now a 'suffragette.'"[13]

Until that moment, Graham had held only contempt for the suffragists who marched in the streets past her business. She felt that those who thought the vote would liberate them were ridiculous—in her mind, the only way to freedom was through acquiring wealth. Earning her own wealth was to buy Florence something besides freedom: social status. For these two goals, she worked tirelessly. The daughter of a Welsh farmer who had immigrated to Canada, Graham had been sensitive to the indignities of her poverty since childhood. Suffering under the patronizing gazes of the aristocrats who employed her father, she vowed not to remain poor herself. When she came of age, Florence went to America to find her fortune.

On arriving in New York in 1908, Graham found a job as a cashier in what was then a new kind of beauty establishment. Owned by an Irishwoman named Eleanor Adair, this salon was dedicated to caring for the complexions of elite women. Adair had opened successful salons in Europe before coming to New York to introduce her facial method, the Ganesh muscle strapping treatment. After strapping the client's head in a leather muzzle, Adair and her "treatment girls" tapped and patted facial skin with skin tonics, muscle oils, and creams.

By setting high prices and cultivating an elite clientele, Adair had created a novel phenomenon, the high-society beauty salon. Scores of imitators had followed, each announcing her services in the advertising pages of *Vogue.* A number used the reputations of prestigious clients as leverage on which to do business. Indeed, the "treatment-plus-socialites" formula became so common that bankers would finance start-ups with only the right client names as capital. The scheme was so simple that treatment girls often left their employers after learning the skills, only to reemerge as competitors, opening a shop on a shoestring and growing on a combination of assumed prestige and promotion. Established proprietors could only splutter impotently at the usurpers, again through ads in *Vogue.*[14]

When Florence begged Adair to allow her to be a treatment girl, her employer reluctantly agreed. Sure enough, a year later Graham went into partnership with another treatment girl, Elizabeth Hubbard, to open a new salon. These two new partners named their preparations and technique the "Grecian" treatment because they didn't like the guttural sound of "Ganesh." They opened a salon on prestigious Fifth Avenue and offered their service at a slightly lower price than Adair's. Although they had few customers, they advertised themselves as a salon serving socially prominent women. The new salon did not last, however, because Graham and Hubbard did not get along. Within a year they parted, and Hubbard moved to new premises a few doors away. Graham was on her own. Since she could no longer use "Grecian," she called her products "Venetian," again, because she liked the sound. She borrowed money to decorate in a "Venetian" style and improved on her products by scenting them with perfume, giving them a delicate tint, and packaging them in pretty jars with pink ribbons about the neck. The proud proprietor painted the salon door bright red and mounted a brass plate with the name "Elizabeth Arden" on it.

"Elizabeth Arden" was just a name Graham made up. She liked the sound of it and the way it looked in script. At first the new salon owner called herself "Florence Graham" and pretended that "Elizabeth Arden" was a real person who simply traveled a lot. She even ran ads announcing that Arden had gone to Paris to observe new techniques to bring home to her clientele. Around 1914 Graham started using the name "Elizabeth Arden" for herself, but she never legally changed her name. Throughout her life, she maintained the odd habit of referring to this absentee owner as if she were someone else. As late as 1956 a journalist remarked: "Miss Arden has put Elizabeth Arden on a pedestal. She invented her and she actually works for her as though she were a real person." When faced with a difficult decision, the cosmetics tycoon would stare into the air and ask aloud, "What would Elizabeth Arden do in a situation like this?"[15]

While selling her services to the rich, Florence Graham became a different person in many ways besides her name. She joined charities for the explicit purpose of rubbing elbows with the upper echelons of society. She became an ardent Anglophile. "To be Catholic or Jewish isn't chic," she would declare. "Chic is Episcopalian." Her biographers argue that the only reason Arden joined the suffrage movement was to make society contacts: "In the brief two years since 1910, suffrage had become fashionable. . . . It was not so much the cause that Elizabeth admired as those who espoused it. Such a prestigious social aegis could only lend distinction to anybody who walked in its shadow. Elizabeth might have looked like a reformer, but she was actually only making another grab at the hem of the hobbled skirt of fashion." Elizabeth Arden thus presents an interesting twist on the feminist critical formula. Instead of customers creating themselves according to the perceived demands of the cosmetics dealer, we have the cosmetics dealer re-creating herself in the image demanded by her customers. As *Fortune* magazine commented decades later: "She has been at it so long that she, least of all, could qualify as a witness on whether or not some of her qualities are real or faked. It no longer matters." A reporter for the *Post* interviewing her in 1957, however, observed that her face had a "vague, fixed look" and that "the over-all picture she presents is peculiarly fascinating in an unreal sort of way." It was a phenomenon as pointless as it was pitiful. As a woman who made her living by rendering personal services, Elizabeth Arden was doomed to occupy the lowest social position in the commercial strata already disdained by those whose respect she craved. They would never have accepted her as an equal, no matter how elegant and wealthy she became.[16]

Although she was not the first to open a salon, Elizabeth Arden became known to fashion history as "the mother of the treatment business." Arden's first salon was a huge success. By 1912 she had begun taking mail orders for her products, which she also advertised in *Vogue.* Soon the Arden preparations were being sold by a select group of stores around the country: I. Magnin on the West Coast, Marshall Field in Chicago,

Neiman-Marcus in Dallas. Because her products were premium-priced, Arden could make a profit even on a small sales volume. The wholesale business quickly became the most lucrative part of her operation. The salons' select addresses demanded high rents and the level of service made labor costs astronomical, but their exclusive clientele reinforced the Arden mystique, so Graham continued to operate her salons long after they had become unprofitable. Because of the national distribution that manufacturers like Arden eventually gained, however, the treatment houses of the 1910s are considered the forerunners of the major cosmetics corporations. Therefore, Arden is also usually named as "the founder of the American cosmetics industry."

All but one of Arden's early competitors fell in her wake. Helena Rubinstein opened her first U.S. salon in 1916, having already established salons in Paris and London. Both Rubinstein and Arden were immigrants, and both were poor as children. Beyond that, however, they had little in common. Whereas Arden affected the speech, tastes, and views of the Anglican elite, Helena Rubinstein was a Polish Jew with eclectic tastes in clothing, furnishings, and art. Arden was small, blonde, and feminine; Rubinstein had an exotic face, which she emphasized by wearing her black hair pulled back into a knot. Where Arden was dignified in gowns by Worth, Rubinstein loved the sensuousness of Poiret and the humor of Schiaparelli. Arden's jewelry was discreet and tasteful. Rubinstein owned an enormous jewelry collection that she kept in a huge tangle under her bed. She piled on multiple necklaces and rings every morning, mixing costly stones with the cheapest costume jewelry. Arden was obsessed with having the right clothes, the correct manners, and the proper surroundings. Rubinstein drank alcohol, belched out loud, ate huge amounts, and wiped her mouth with the back of her hand.[17]

The difference in personal style between these two women was reflected in their salons, their products, their clients, and their advertising. Arden's salons were pink, with "bon-bonesque" treatment rooms. Rubinstein salons were dramatic, colorful, decorated with modern art and furniture. Arden spent lavishly, particularly on her business, and never wanted to know the impact of her ways on the bottom line. Rubinstein, it was said, reacted to every proposal with the words "too much." Elizabeth Arden's customers were well-bred socialites, but Helena Rubinstein's clientele tended in the direction of the theater. Arden's employees were hired to seem as waspish as her customers; Rubinstein always hired foreigners for their exotic appeal. Arden avoided the mention of money in her salons and trained her employees not to offend by calling attention to the commercial nature of the encounter. Rubinstein, however, told her employees: "You have got to look right down into their pocketbooks and *get that last nickel.*"[18]

Each made all the decisions about her business, mixing her own creams, signing her own packages, and naming her own colors and treatments. Rubinstein used the same high-quality ingredients that Arden did and charged the same high prices. Both wrote their own ads. But while Arden's graphic "look" was old-fashioned and conventionally

178 LADIES' HOME JOURNAL October, 1929

# ELIZABETH ARDEN IS REAL!

*And her preparations are personally planned for you*

THE name of Elizabeth Arden is a symbol of loveliness to more than ten million women. But Elizabeth Arden is so much more than a name. She is a real woman, an exciting personality, whose enthusiasm for Beauty has placed the priceless gift of charm within reach of every woman.

Miss Arden understands the exquisite care of the skin, and knows that faces do not just stay in shape, but must be held in shape by good strong muscles and firm healthy tissues. This means regular care and exercise—to strengthen the muscles and quicken the circulation so that the blood comes dancing to the cheeks to invigorate the tissues and clear the skin.

Elizabeth Arden's Treatments and Preparations keep muscles vigorous, tissues toned up, and your skin smooth and tight so that your face simply does not get a chance to droop. Ask for Elizabeth Arden's book, "THE QUEST OF THE BEAUTIFUL," which will tell you how to follow her scientific method in the care of your skin at home.

*Elizabeth Arden's Venetian Toilet Preparations are on sale at smart shops all over the world.*

VENETIAN CLEANSING CREAM

Melts into the pores, rids them of dust and impurities, leaves skin soft and receptive. $1, $2, $3, $6

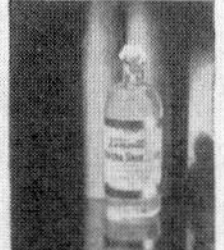

VENETIAN ARDENA SKIN TONIC

Tones, firms, and whitens the skin. Use with and after Cleansing Cream. 85c, $2, $3.75, $9

POUDRE D'ILLUSION

A pure, vaguely scented powder made for those who demand the extreme of quality. In eight lovely shades. $3

VENETIAN SPECIAL ASTRINGENT

For flaccid cheeks and neck. Lifts and strengthens the tissues, tightens the skin. $2.25, $4

VENETIAN ANTI-WRINKLE CREAM

Fills out fine lines and wrinkles, leaves the skin smooth and firm. Excellent for an afternoon treatment at home. $2, $3.50

## ELIZABETH ARDEN

NEW YORK: 673 FIFTH AVENUE

PARIS: 2 rue de la Paix LONDON: 25 Old Bond Street BERLIN W: Lennéstr. 5

CHICAGO: 70 East Walton Place PHILADELPHIA: 133 South 18th Street WASHINGTON: 1147 Connecticut Avenue DETROIT: Book Building
BOSTON: 24 Newbury Street SAN FRANCISCO: 522 Powell Street LOS ANGELES: 600 West 7th Street ATLANTIC CITY: Ritz-Carlton Block
BIARRITZ: Arcades du Grand Hôtel, Place Clémenceau CANNES: 3 Galeries Fleuries MADRID: 71 Calle Alcalá ROME: Via Condotti 65



Figure 5.1. This fantasy figure may have been Elizabeth Arden's ideal self. *Ladies Home Journal,* October 1929.

feminine, Rubinstein's was modern and avant garde. In contrast to Graham's referrals to the elusive "Elizabeth Arden," Rubinstein's ads were written in the first person and usually included her own picture.

By the early 1920s, a new fantasy figure had become a distinctive mark of the Arden advertising (see figure 5.1). This strangely virginal image may have captured the self that Arden wanted to show to the world. The figure's head, neck, and shoulders are closely wrapped in white veiling, hiding the hair and framing the face in a way distinctly like a nun's habit. Initially the photographs were taken by society portraitist Baron DeMeyer. The image bore his signature style, already familiar to readers of *Vogue,* a glowing, soft-focus effect very popular among Society ladies. Often DeMeyer imposed a halo of light behind this figure's head. Oddly, this virginal vision is heavily made up, particularly around the eyes. The combination of headgear, photographic style, and makeup presents an eerie, almost supernatural person to the viewer. This oddly nunlike vision became the central image in virtually all of Arden's ads up until World War II.

Arden's own lack of sexual interest in men was legendary. She pointedly avoided courtship and marriage until she was well past thirty. The men she liked best were the ones who made a good appearance (well dressed, good dancer), but otherwise stayed out of her way. Although she was married twice, apparently she did not have a carnal relationship with either of her husbands. Before her first marriage in 1915, Arden made a regular practice of inviting one of the treatment girls to go home with her for dinner, where she would lose track of the time and insist that the girl stay the night. Arden and her guest would then give each other treatments and retire to the same bed. After the lights were out, Arden would ask, in a child's voice, that the girl hold her hand until she fell asleep. Even after she was married, Arden avoided traveling with her husband, preferring to take her current favorite among the treatment girls. She booked adjoining hotel rooms and left the door between them ajar. Arden took her traveling companion to the theater and to elegant dinners. Then they would retire to the hotel to give each other treatments, put up their hair, and go to sleep. Even though most of these relationships were ephemeral, several women who worked for Arden stayed for decades. She promised them she would take care of them forever, and she kept her promises. Even after her death, her estate supported them for the rest of their lives.

The most important relationship in Arden's life, however, was with Elisabeth Marbury, one of a group of blue-blooded lesbians prominently involved in the arts and in leftist politics, including the feminist movement. Marbury's set, known in New York society as an Amazon enclave, was reputed to have "Sapphic orgies" at the Sutton Place home of Anne Morgan (J. Pierpont Morgan's daughter and president of the American Women's Association). Although this group, which included Marbury's longtime lover, Elsie De Wolfe, were definitely understood to be lesbians, they were considered quite chic.[19]

At the time she became friends with Elizabeth Arden, Marbury had a huge home in Maine. Arden bought the estate next door, at Marbury's suggestion, and the two spent weekends there together, although Arden was married. When Marbury died suddenly, Arden bought the first house and, combining the two estates, opened her now world-famous spa, Maine Chance. The idea was to create a monument to Marbury by celebrating the beauty of women. No men were allowed. The women spent the day dancing, exercising, and having treatments. In the evening, however, they dressed up and floated about the spa displaying their beauty for their own collective pleasure.

There is not enough evidence to say conclusively that Arden was a lesbian, but she exhibited many behaviors that point in that direction. We can at least say that Arden's view of the world was singularly woman-centered. Her notion of beauty was spiritual and Sapphic, but with a social cachet. The desire to please the male gaze does not seem to have figured prominently in her mind. If the cosmetics industry is built on male demands for sexual allure, as feminists claim, then Elizabeth Arden seems an unlikely character to have been its founder.

## WOMEN'S SERVICE

The prestige skin treatments, the pages of *Vogue,* and the status of those who consumed both represent the top level of female commerce and social stratification during the 1910s. Although certainly wealthy and influential, this group alone cannot account for the enormous success of the women's movement at this time. For the full explanation, we must look at the next level, where middle-class women formed a political coalition powerful because of its size, its commitment, and its mainstream respectability. These activists were known as clubwomen because they worked through the same nineteenth-century women's clubs of which Sorosis was the original. In fact, the overarching umbrella for all the women's causes of the 1910s—which included not only suffrage, but labor reform, consumer advocacy, and other charges—was the very group founded by Jane Croly, the General Federation of Women's Clubs (GFWC).

The middle-class activists (often referred to in history as the "social feminists") looked to leaders who were quite different from the suffragists in terms of style, strategy, and substance. Several leaders of the suffrage movement at this time, such as Alice Paul, Anna Howard Shaw, and M. Carey Thomas, fit the angry, ugly, man-hating feminist stereotype like a glove. They lived alone or with other women. They dressed in plain, pointedly unflattering style. Most of them were associated in some formal way with the all-female Ivy League colleges that held so much prestige among both feminists and the Leaders of Society. The social feminist leadership, however, often "challenged the feminist stereotype on every count." Feminist historian William O'Neill writes: "Lillian Wald, Florence Kelley, Jane Addams, and Margaret Dreier Robins, to name but a few, gave women a well-deserved reputation for intelligent generosity and high accomplishment." These women were known for their diplomacy, their grace, and their desire for the greater good. O'Neill continues: "However, most of these great women, although suffragists, spent their energies on the struggle for social justice. Woman suffrage, while desirable, was not to them of overriding importance." The middle-class women who peopled the ranks of social feminism, although generally prosuffrage, were unimpressed with the "scholastic suffragists," who showed little interest in practical initiatives and whose ties to prestigious universities were foregrounded, from the clubwoman's point of view, rather too much.[20]

The suffrage leader who did win the respect of the social feminists was Carrie Chapman Catt. Catt was one of Susan Anthony's protégées, but she was not as extreme in looks, lifestyle, or tactics as the scholastics. Like most clubwomen, Catt was feminine, dignified, and married. She had a broad social conscience and was an astute political strategist. Alice Paul's militant suffragists were often the center of attention in the press, but Catt's much larger NAWSA learned to stage some pretty successful photo opportunities of its own. There were marches and candlelight vigils, for which dress and color schemes were carefully planned—the suffrage dress was usually white, with banners and other accents in purple and gold. Her picket lines had themes: One day the pickets would be debutantes, the next teachers, and so on.[21]

The clubwomen thus followed the lead of Society to a degree in their politics, as well as in dress and manners, but they infused each with an ethic of their own. The magazines they read, such as *Good Housekeeping* and the *Ladies' Home Journal,* were ideologically distinct from *Vogue* and *Bazaar.* Even though they featured articles on dress for the whole family, the "women's service magazines," as they are even now known, were also much concerned with the women's issues of the day, which included a broader reform agenda than suffrage alone. Thus, the name "women's service" describes not only the services that the magazines purported to offer their readers in the form of fashion and homemaking advice, but also refers to the ongoing passion of their many readers—the service women were then offering to their communities through the clubs.

Far from representing a ghetto in the world of the press, the women's service magazines of the 1910s were among the largest and most lucrative periodicals. Three of them—the *Ladies' Home Journal,* the *Woman's Home Companion,* and the *Pictorial Review*—grew during the decade to circulations in excess of 2 million readers with ad revenue of about $7 million each. At the same time, the combined circulations of three other women's magazines, *McCall's, Good Housekeeping,* and the *Delineator,* went from 750,000 to 3.3 million. Thus, the gross circulation of the top six women's service magazines at the end of the decade was about 10 million readers, representing 30 percent of the total adult female population. These magazines exerted a significant influence by reaching nearly a third of the adult female population, but it is important to keep in mind that the women's service magazines did *not* reach fully 70 percent of that population. The demographic profile also shows the class status of the reader base: Up through the 1930s, the leading women's service books were read by about 50 percent of the top two income groups but by fewer than 5 percent of the lower two tiers.[22] Because of their limited and homogeneous audiences, the term "mass magazines," although often used, really does not properly apply to these publications.

In their critique of the women's magazines, feminists focus exclusively on the *Ladies' Home Journal* and its editor during the suffrage years, Edward Bok. Bok, it is said, despised women, feared feminism, and used his magazine to contribute to the oppression of his readers, at the same time catering shamelessly to the desires of his advertisers. Feminists then transfer by assertion this model of magazine management to all women's magazines throughout the twentieth century. The women's magazines have become a linchpin in feminist ideology, as they are said to be both the conduit for antifeminist sentiment and the concrete manifestation of the "necessary" connection between capitalism and the oppression of women. Yet a closer look at the *Journal* can cast doubt on this theory. The fortunes of its competitors during this key period in both feminist and publishing history tends to undercut the argument altogether.

Bok was editor of the *Ladies' Home Journal* from 1889 to 1919. He did not invent the *Journal,* but took it over as an established enterprise from its founder, Louisa Knapp Curtis. Curtis can be said to be at least proto-feminist and definitely antifashion. Bok continued her attitude toward fashion by being a vociferous advocate of dress reform. Several of the other stands he took on "women's issues" were seen as "Progressive." Bok was an outspoken temperance advocate, a position that endeared him to the Women's Christian Temperance Union, the largest single women's organization in the country at this time (and one solidly identified with feminism). Importantly, Bok was also a leading muckraker in the patent medicine controversy and an activist in the campaign for the Pure Food and Drug Act—a legislative issue of substantial concern to many women's organizations. Under Bok's tenure, such progressive luminaries as Jane Addams published columns on social issues. And Bok himself could be quite radical, using the ultra-respectable *Journal* as a forum to support sex education and to fight venereal disease: For example, Edward Bok was the first person to use the word "syphilis" in an American popular magazine. Although Bok did not think women should work outside the home, but he was very much in favor of equal pay for equal work when they did—a position that won him support among the labor reformers, also a core feminist group. The single issue that has brought Bok so much ire from later feminists was suffrage. And, frankly, it made some of his contemporary readers furious too. When Bok announced that he was against suffrage because, after careful research, he had determined (in his infinite wisdom) that it was not in the best interest of his readership to vote, angry women wrote him hate mail by the truckloads. Entire women's clubs threatened to boycott the *Journal* (an act he prevented by threatening to sue the clubs under the Sherman Act).[23]

Even though Bok's opinions about women's issues were sometimes conservative, he did not espouse them merely to please advertisers. In fact, a key aspect of Bok's politics was that he did not allow advertising interests to influence his stands. Further, he often punished industries of which he did not approve by refusing to run their ads in the *Journal.* In addition to banning patent medicine advertising from the *Journal* as part of his campaign against what was then the largest group of advertisers in America, he excluded ads for makeup, tobacco, and liquor. All these were expensive decisions. Bok was also an activist in the campaign to outlaw outdoor advertising, something that did not endear him to commerce. In spite of his independent attitude toward advertisers, the *Journal's* annual advertising revenue exceeded $11 million under his editorship and circulation climbed from 440,000 to 2 million, making it the largest circulation magazine in the world. But this was a period in which American magazines were on a steep upward trend, and, to some degree, a rising tide will raise all ships. Thus, the growth figures of the *Ladies' Home Journal,* while impressive, disguise the magazine's gradual loss of standing among the other women's periodicals; its share of total readers declined by half, from 41 percent to 21 percent between 1910 and 1920.

Growth in circulation went instead to the *Pictorial Review,* the *Woman's Home Companion, Good Housekeeping,* and *McCall's.* Looking at the editorial strategies of those four magazines yields surprising insight into the relationship between the women's press and the women's rights movement. *Pictorial Review* was established by a pattern maker in 1899 and had a circulation of 200,000 in its first year. By 1910 circulation had grown to 1.5 million, placing *Pictorial Review* second only to the *Journal* among the women's magazines and third in the nation. However, the advertising revenue of the *Pictorial Review* lagged behind, in seventh place. The magazine's management approached the J. Walter Thompson advertising agency to study the problem and recommend a way to bring advertising sales more in line with the circulation figures. The agency found that *Pictorial Review* did not have the prestige that other women's magazines did and "decided to place the *Pictorial Review* in the public mind as the most *progressive* of women's magazines—to gain recognition of a genuine leadership it had in recording the development of women's activities" (emphasis in original). Publicizing the magazine's outspoken emphasis on progressive politics took *Pictorial Review* to a circulation of 2 million in one year and increased advertising by nearly 70 percent. At the end of the decade, the "new" *Pictorial Review* was even with its two major competitors in circulation and was second (to the *Ladies' Home Journal*) in advertising revenue at about $7 million.[24]

Gertrude Battles Lane became editor of the *Woman's Home Companion* in 1912, when the magazine had a circulation of 737,000 and advertising revenue of about $1 million. Throughout the teens and early 1920s, Lane published articles on women's issues, often written by suffragists including Shaw, Catt, and Thomas. By 1919 the *Woman's Home Companion* had a circulation of 2 million and about $7 million in advertising sales.

*Good Housekeeping* was created in 1885 as "A Family Journal Conducted in the Interest of the Higher Life of the Household." By the 1910s, however, its approach to housekeeping would be best described as a consumer information service. The magazine taught nutrition, discussed pricing, and published articles on the effects of national and global economic policies on the availability and cost of consumer goods. It published critical analyses of the effects of profit taking on both prices and wages, and also printed floor plans and discussed developments in architecture, showing a particular interest in the safety of public buildings. It printed features about fashion only occasionally, even though it offered a line of dress patterns. In spite of its overtly genteel attitude, *Good Housekeeping* could be quite radical: The Russian women's Battalion of Death was featured in a highly complimentary article complete with photographs of the officers posing in uniform, caps removed, and shaved heads on display. *Good Housekeeping* maintained ties with the women's clubs and published serious articles about their activities. It was solidly prosuffrage, and, although its mission was definitely family-oriented, *Good Housekeeping* strongly supported advanced education and expanded social roles for women. In short, there was nothing about the old *Good Housekeeping* that could be said to insult the intelligence and plenty that contributed a genuine service to women and to the public. Under this editorial policy, the circulation grew from 55,000 in 1900 to about 1 million in 1919.

*McCall's* during the 1910s can be distinguished on several levels. First, its price was only five cents, compared to fifteen cents for the *Ladies' Home Journal,* the *Delineator, Good Housekeeping, Pictorial Review,* and *Woman's Home Companion* and twenty-five cents for *Vogue* and *Harper's Bazaar.* That price put *McCall's* within reach of more women, which probably accounted for a good bit of its increase in circulation from 200,000 to over 1 million between 1900 and 1920. Unlike the other women's magazines, the editorial staff of *McCall's* is not listed by name on the masthead; however, the leadership was definitely female, as were the editors of all the "departments." The dialogue between *McCall's* writers and readers has a very pleasant woman-to-woman quality about it. One reason for this was probably the structured interaction between the editorial staff and its readership. Each major women's magazine received enormous numbers of letters from readers, and, to their credit, all endeavored to answer them. *McCall's,* however, actively sought readers' advice on magazine content and layout. Apparently, the results of McCall's reader surveys showed that romantic fiction was preferred because editorials refer frequently to efforts to get more of it. All the women's service magazines published fiction, but none went for "love stories" with the unabashed ardor of *McCall's.* Condé Nast firmly refused to publish fiction at all because he feared it would draw a lower-status clientele than he was selling to advertisers. Interestingly, two radical feminists of the time, Inez Haynes Irwin and Mary Heaton Vorse, were regular contributors to *McCall's.* Both wrote stories with the traditional plots and players, but with a clear and intentional feminist message. Thus, while *McCall's* may appear on the surface to be catering to traditional romantic interests, those who trouble to read the stories today may be surprised by the subtext. Another notable difference between *McCall's* and the other women's magazines is the implicit assumption, evident throughout every issue and nearly every feature, that the readers are interested in making and saving money. This presumption appears in advice to young girls, in plans for working girls' weddings, in ideas for selling the fancywork featured in its columns, and in the advertisements. Ads appear that are clearly aimed either at saving money on household needs, especially clothes, or at giving readers access to jobs. There are employment ads for sales agents for a variety of products, including corsets, bicycles, and women's magazines. Many home work jobs are offered, such as weaving rugs. There are also advertisements for nursing schools, dressmaking and tailoring schools, millinery training, commercial art instruction, and other vocational education institutions. Unlike *Vogue,* there are few dressmaker's ads, but many trade items for dressmakers are advertised, particularly style catalogs, and quite a few instructional courses and books. *McCall's* even had a regular column addressed to selling goods made in the home. One column tells the story of a woman who earned money by making box lunches every morning and then selling them to passengers at the train station. The very idea would have made *Vogue*'s readers apoplectic.[25]

The only major women's service magazine to lose share of readership besides the *Ladies' Home Journal* was the *Delineator.* During the first decade of the century, the *Delineator* had built its circulation to 1 million. Given the atmosphere of the times, some of this growth probably was due to public concerns brought to the magazine by its editor, author and social critic Theodore Dreiser. After Dreiser returned to writing novels in 1910, however, the *Delineator* took a more conventional approach. From then until 1920, circulation rose slowly, but like the *Journal,* it did not keep pace with the growth of the overall market. Consequently, its share of women's magazine circulation dropped to 12 percent.

The big winners in this important growth period for women's magazines were those that took the most progressive attitude toward women's rights and a proactive role in social reform: *Good Housekeeping,* the *Woman's Home Companion, Pictorial Review,* and, although it used a more personal and practical orientation, *McCall's.* There is certainly no evidence to suggest that siding with progressive reform in general or with suffrage in particular was punished by a withdrawal of advertising support. In fact, the record suggests the contrary. The women's service magazines of the 1910s were attuned to the middle-class level of the American feminist movement. Their emphasis on reforms such as consumer protection, labor laws, nutrition, and public health accurately reflects the scope of social feminism. By addressing these issues in a serious, consistent way, the leading women's service magazines attracted large, prosperous readerships and the generous advertising placements that come with such audiences.

Advertisers at this level were quite different from those in *Vogue,* however. The bread and butter of the women's service magazines in the 1910s came from national toiletry companies, such as Pond's Creams, Andrew Jergens, and Colgate-Palmolive. The makers used these vehicles to market midpriced beauty aids that were sold in drugstores and some department stores around the nation. In this decade toilet goods advertising shifted from small, black-and-white entries to full-page, four-color splashes. In fact, in the years between 1910 and 1920, the most visible change observable in these magazines is the growing advertising presence of such brands, because of the employment of color and space.

Probably because of the visibility of these ads, today's feminists often carelessly attribute to the women's magazines a willingness to acquiesce to advertisers' desires at the expense of readers' interests. To suggest that magazines were not influenced by advertisers would be foolhardy, but to say that they were completely controlled by them is an exaggeration. By 1910 all of the major women's magazines had instituted quality control systems to keep deceptive advertising or poor products out of their pages. *The Delineator,* the *Ladies' Home Journal,* and *Modern Priscilla* (another major magazine at the time) had guaranteed products advertised since the 1890s, promising to reimburse readers for any loss incurred from buying a product cited in their magazine. Under Condé Nast, even *Vogue* guaranteed its advertising. *Good Housekeeping* was the first to promote testing of products in its own laboratory, but the other magazines all had to do the same, if not with the same rigor, to honor their guarantees. The *Journal* adopted strict codes for censoring advertisements, as did the *Delineator* and others. Early twentieth-century magazines were, in fact, willing to turn away advertisers rather than allow their readers to be deceived or harmed.

Although these magazines reviewed products and fashion items in columns, products names were not cited in the text. Instead, readers had to write in for the information, and staff members had to answer requests individually. It was policy everywhere not to review any product that did not meet the editorial staff's honest judgments of quality. The reason for this discrimination is clear—and was equally clear to the advertisers. If the reader couldn't have confidence in the magazine, circulation declined, and both publisher and advertiser lost. As the number of good magazines willing to make these judgments rose, any consumer who feared deceptive advertising in one could simply choose to read another.

The administration of these product reviews must have been quite burdensome. Not only were individual responses required to audiences that in some cases exceeded 1 million readers, but the magazines had to be responsible for a burgeoning variety of goods. It's not surprising, therefore, that as national brand names gained in strength and reputability, the accountability to the consumer shifted from publishing medium to manufacturer. Eventually the magazines stopped guaranteeing products and instead started publishing brand names in features and reviews. Thus, the product reviews that critics often read now as an unethical form of collusion between manufacturer and magazine actually evolved over time as a way of distributing product news, while making it clear that responsibility for each item rested with the maker, not the magazine. All these efforts to control the quality and claims of the products advertised were in perfect accord with the efforts of the women's clubs to put pressure on manufacturers to standardize quality, produce under sanitary conditions, and so on.

Each of the leading women's service magazines included fashion articles, and, because most of them started as pattern books, most offered patterns for sale. The relationship between these books and Paris design is considerably more tenuous than that of *Vogue,* however. The *Delineator* and *McCall's* often refer vaguely to "Paris" without naming the designers. Why would they promote French designs, after all, since both were in the business of selling patterns for their own designs? *McCall's* ran a fashion column that included remarks on fashion in Paris that season, but these descriptions are so vague, the tone so precious, and the details so sparse that the entire column seems a fiction. *Good Housekeeping* made no pretense of trying to cover Paris design at all. The *Ladies' Home Journal* was aggressively anti-Parisian in its approach to fashion; Edward Bok repeatedly ran columns and commissioned articles encouraging women to drop the French designers in favor of American style. The large department stores dominated the clothing ads in all these magazines. Thus, the influence of Paris on middle class women was filtered through the marketing sensitivities of the American department stores, garment manufacturers, and middle-class magazines, which inevitably affected the designs of the clothes themselves. The charge that American women slavishly followed the "dictates" of Paris—frequently made then as now—probably overstates the facts in actual practice.

Society women in New York were adamant that they set style in America, not Paris designers. Regardless of where the clothes were purchased, they argued, the only reason the styles were accepted in the United States was that they were endorsed by "women of fashion" (meaning themselves). There seems to be a great deal of truth to this claim, based on the tenuous connection to Paris fashion that the American middle-class press had. The pretension to Parisian connections that the magazines often made may reflect instead the way their readers looked to Society women as role models in several arenas, including politics.

## COMMERCIAL COUP

In the bright sunshine of Fifth Avenue, a group of office workers stood together. Some were secretaries and some were professional advertising copywriters. All of them worked for the largest advertising agency in America, J. Walter Thompson. An immaculately groomed woman who "looked like a Rosetti" circulated among them, handing each a purple, white, or green campaign hat. This thirty-year-old woman was the day's organizer, but she was also the supervisor of these women and, in a very real sense, of the men back at the office too. They all loved and admired her because she took a personal interest in them and because her brilliant, daring mind was a wonderful thing to watch. Excited, the adwomen waited until it was time to march, and then followed their confident leader who, in turn, fell in behind a beautiful, dark-haired debutante carrying a large American flag. After the glorious parade was over, the agency treated the marchers to a big dinner at the Savoy Hotel.[26]

Marching for suffrage was an action consistent with Helen Lansdowne's commitment to women's rights in everything she did. Her own mother had taught her the importance of being self-reliant. Helen grew up in a fatherless home. Her mother worked and raised nine children on her own. Helen remembered her mother's warnings, repeated throughout her childhood, that she should never get caught without a way to support herself. She took the lesson to heart. Upon graduation from high school, she got a job. As time would make clear, Helen Lansdowne was intelligent enough to have been successful in college, but that option was beyond the reach of a poor girl from Covington, Kentucky.

In 1907 she went to work auditing for Procter & Gamble in Cincinnati. She changed jobs twice, first writing ads at the newspaper, next for a streetcar company. Along the way, she met a Yale graduate named Stanley Resor, whose family had been prosperous but whose business had failed. Stanley and his brother opened a Cincinnati office for J. Walter Thompson (JWT) advertising agency in 1908 and they hired Helen Lansdowne to be their only copywriter. She proved her talent early and was promoted to the New York office in 1911, as was Stanley Resor.

Shortly after the suffrage march of 1917, Helen married Stanley. By then the two of them had acquired a controlling interest in the agency from its founder. Stanley was in charge of business and strategic decisions, while Helen was responsible for creative work. Under their guidance, JWT became the largest agency in America, a position it held for fifty years.

Helen Lansdowne Resor was an important influence on the development of advertising as a career for women. From the early years of the twentieth century, advertising was known as an industry where women were paid more and had better opportunities for advancement than most others. In the large national agencies, women were usually organized into "women's departments," in which a self-contained group handled the strategy, research, media, planning, art, and copy for products that were thought to need "a woman's touch" in their messages. Because women, even then, were the buyers for some of the most heavily advertised goods, the women's department handled accounts that were among the most profitable in any agency.

At JWT, the women's department had its own separate space and culture. Helen Lansdowne Resor insisted that the decor of the department be beautiful and conducive to inspiration. She paid her women well and encouraged them to buy nice clothes, furnish their own apartments, buy tickets to the theater, and the like. She appears to have been actively concerned with building the self-esteem of the women who worked for her.

The women's group was a cohesive unit, a world unto itself. When the Second Wave of feminism broke in the 1970s, the "girl group" was a major grievance among women in advertising. Although reforms did occur, vestiges of this practice were observable in some agencies even in the late 1980s. In its time, however, this organizational form provided a way for women to have influence and independence that was probably unparalleled elsewhere in the white-collar world. On some products, the women's group at JWT had nearly complete autonomy in the management of product design and marketing.

Helen herself hired the young women who joined this group, and her selection criteria were consistent. She wanted the college-educated woman who could "really dig out the causes of things, think for herself, enjoy thinking for herself." She also wanted budding feminists, women whose mothers had been "constructively minded, seeing a big future dawning for women over the horizon," and who had filled their daughters' minds "with the vision of a new day for women when they should stand squarely beside men on the platform of achievement."[27] The women who worked at JWT were, therefore, feminist in orientation, even though they wrote ads to sell cosmetics and toiletries. Obviously, however, their feminism was probably different from that of the socialite suffragists on questions of work, fashion, and commerce.

As head of the women's department of JWT in New York, Helen Lansdowne Resor had substantial control over the leading national accounts in soaps (Woodbury), creams (Pond's), and manicure products (Cutex). Since these products were rapidly becoming the lifeblood of the women's service magazines, Resor had considerable influence in the press world. Resor herself was publicity-shy; however, the campaigns she developed are some of the best known in advertising history.

The campaign for Pond's creams was one of the biggest coups of Helen's career. Pond's Extract, a patent medicine, had been a client of J. Walter Thompson since 1886. Two creams, Pond's Vanishing Cream and Pond's Cold Cream, were developed about 1907 to be distributed through drug and department stores. The first Pond's cream ads appeared in 1910; Helen Resor took over the account in 1912. The sales of both creams grew dramatically for several years and then, nearing the end of the decade, began to slow.[28]

The JWT women's group undertook an enormous research project to determine why the Pond's business had slowed. They conducted five hundred personal consumer interviews in Cincinnati, Hamilton, and Middletown, Ohio; Covington, Kentucky; and Topeka, Kansas. They gave blind product tests and canvassed a rural county in New York, and sent out nearly 2,000 questionnaires across the nation to a representative cross-section of ages and classes. The group also spent two weeks selling creams in Lord & Taylor's Fifth Avenue store, Bloomingdale's Third Avenue store, and Marshall Field's in Chicago.

The findings revealed that 86 percent of American women used face creams and that habitual use was well established even among the middle class. The four major midpriced creams—Pond's, Daggett & Ramsdell, Elcaya, and Ingram's—had 36 percent of the market, but were quickly losing ground to the status products being offered by the Arden and Rubinstein treatment houses. Pond's creams were seen as good and reliable, but not "up-to-date, smart, and prestigious." The JWT women concluded that the creams being sold by treatment houses were actually gaining market share because of their higher price, which consumers took as indicative of social standing: "It was apparent that Pond's Two Creams, leaders in their field, had begun to suffer from their very leadership. Reasonable in price, used by everyone, many women had begun to think that they could not be as good as creams that were more costly or that were imported. Their popularity had brought them loss of caste; they lacked exclusiveness, social prestige."[29]

JWT's advertising strategy was to lift Pond's creams out of the class of middle-level creams and to give them a prestige that would place them on a level in public esteem with the higher priced and imported products of the socialite's treatment salons. Resor's group decided to execute this strategy by getting testimonials from socialites and having them photographed by society portraitists. Yet how would such a campaign be executed when socialites were not supposed to meddle with commerce?

The first endorsement came from the Bengal Tiger herself. The headline was: "An Interview with Mrs. O. H. P. Belmont on the Care of the Skin." It opened with a signed statement from Alva Belmont: "A woman who neglects her personal appearance loses half her influence. The wise care of one's body constructs the frame encircling our mentality, the ability of which insures the success of one's life. I advise a daily use of

Pond's Two Creams." The endorsement emphasizes Mrs. Belmont's role in the women's movement. Italicized "callouts" say that she is president of the National Woman's Party and "known all over America for her active services in securing the suffrage for women." The endorsement also mentions her work in other women's reform activities. According to the Thompson archives, Mrs. Belmont was chosen as the first endorser because she was "a woman of great wealth and social position, who is equally noted as a leader of women throughout the country and for her wide interests in all women's causes and movements."[30]

As one could have predicted (and as JWT women's department no doubt expected), once Mrs. Belmont was in a full-page ad for Pond's running in magazines all over America, other ambitious socialites wanted to follow suit. There were Biddles and Vanderbilts and Roosevelts. Mrs. Condé Nast and Mrs. William Randolph Hearst posed for full-page ads. Dame Margot Asquith, no beauty but an innovator in personal appearance, actually wrote her own copy: " . . . we have all known women who have more than made up for their lack of features and general homeliness by the play of their expression, the grace of their carriage or the beauty of their complexion. I can only speak for myself. . . . I have used Pond's Creams for my skin more years than I can remember; and though I have never been beautiful and I am not young, I have not got a wrinkle in my forehead." Anne Morgan announced beneath her Baron DeMeyer portrait: "I should like to see the dressing-rooms of our new Club House of the American Woman's Association equipped with Pond's Two Creams."[31] The Queen of Rumania and the Duchess of Marlborough chimed in, along with princesses, ladies, and countesses.

In the truest tradition of the fashion press, each ad was designed to reflect the identity of the endorsers by describing their homes, their personality, their social activities. But the campaign also made use of a blatantly commercial practice, the coupon. Each coupon, redeemable for a sample of cream, contained a mailing code that keyed it to both the particular ad and the magazine in which it ran. In that way, Resor's colleagues knew whether suffragists "pulled better" in *Vogue* and princesses better in the *Delineator,* or whatever. The rule of aristocracy was harnessed for the purposes of commerce.

Elizabeth Arden was furious. Jealous of Helen Resor for having pulled the promotion off at all, Arden was particularly irritated because, as she claimed, the women in the ads were actually her customers. (Asquith, however, was a Rubinstein regular.) Arden herself had been too concerned with being accepted as a social equal to have asked Society leaders for help in a commercial matter. And, indeed, she was probably right to refrain from such a request, as it was bound to cause offense.

So why did Mrs. Belmont agree to endorse Pond's creams? That is the question I want to focus on, although I have no definitive answer. Alva Vanderbilt Belmont took a huge social risk when she agreed to do this, and, although she was certainly known as a risk taker, she was not a fool. She would have agreed to endorse this product only if an equally valuable favor was given in return, something she could not get another way. That rules out money.

The interview was conducted by one of Helen Resor's "girls," Peggy King, in Alva Belmont's home. King's notes suggest that Resor set up the Belmont interview for her. Now, Resor was an important woman, but she was not of the social class that would normally have given her access to Mrs. Belmont. The most likely way these two women could have met was through the women's movement. Somehow these women not only met, but a debt was incurred. In some way, the beginning of a connection of obligations was formed: the obligation to give, to receive, to reciprocate. Mrs. Belmont, I'm guessing, owed Helen Resor a big one. What was it?

What comes next is pure speculation on my part. Mrs. Belmont's passion was suffrage. Whatever was exchanged between these two was probably something that Resor could do for suffrage that was uniquely hers to do, just as Mrs. Belmont's endorsement was uniquely hers to give. It may have been something modest: Perhaps Helen Resor offered to develop a publicity campaign or write press releases or any number of things that J. Walter Thompson could have easily done "in house." Or—and in my mind this is more likely—it may have been that Helen Resor used her influence with the women's magazines to gain favorable treatment for suffrage. We know that Belmont and company were sensitive to (and sophisticated about) press treatment. And no one, male or female, in America at this time was in a better position to influence the women's magazines than Helen Resor. Not only did she manage the campaigns for the big advertisers in all of those magazines, she was also giving marketing advice first to *Pictorial Review* and, later, to the *Ladies' Home Journal.* It would have been a win-win situation for Resor to convince the *Pictorial Review* to cover women's suffrage to increase the magazine's prestige and then to provide an introduction to someone in Mrs. Belmont's entourage. In any case, I believe there was an exchange of favors, gifts of equal weight. Since all Resor had to give—and all she could have used in return—was some kind of marketing influence, I'd be willing to wager that the nature of the trade was a boost for feminism in return for a face cream endorsement. But of course there is no way of knowing that now.

## IN THE SHOPS

We have addressed two levels of the highly stratified society of women in the 1910s to determine their relationship to each other, as well as to women's issues, to fashion, to the market, and to the media. We have found a well-developed and clearly hierarchical system of protocol and exchange being used for a variety of purposes—and we have seen that each group had its own communications vehicles in the form of magazines directed to them.

Yet we still have not looked at the majority. Even in 1910, the largest group of women was not the middle class but the working class. It was not until the end of the decade that magazines, national advertisers, and cosmetics manufacturers would address this group directly. That does not mean, however, that the largest class of women was uninvolved in these areas. On the contrary its numbers and its labor underpinned the distribution of goods and magazines. Further, working class women, as the target for many reforms, continued to have a problematic relationship with their social "superiors." This relationship was made more complex by the roles working women took in the world of fashion.

A good case in point is the department store sales force. The manners and appearance of sales personnel were considered key to the genteel environment that could attract leisured women and prosperous housewives. Therefore, department stores were highly selective in hiring saleswomen and insisted on controlling their clothing and grooming. Standards were strict: It was not unusual for a woman who came to work in "unacceptable" attire to be sent home to change and her pay docked for the time. Sales personnel came from working-class backgrounds and had limited resources. As a result, some owned no clothing other than what they worked in. Store policies essentially forced the workers into feigning the appearance and manner of the higher classes. Saleswomen had to do this in a convincing way, all the while denying the reality that the saleswoman was employed in a service relationship to the customer—and therefore, by definition, was not of the class that her appearance indicated.[32]

Saleswomen were encouraged to develop advisory relationships with their clients, so sales could be made as part of an ongoing relationship rather than by chance. They began by keeping cards on each client, listing color preferences, sizes, and favorite styles. Then they would surprise customers by "remembering" these particulars on subsequent visits. Once a relationship was established, the salesperson might phone or write the customer when an item came in that was suited to her budget and tastes. Eventually, a saleswoman might insinuate herself so thoroughly into a customer's life that she could have unsolicited items delivered directly to the home and simply bill the customer's account.

Many customers, however, resented the impertinence of working girls who offered advice to "women of intelligence." Some shoppers, in this very class-conscious age, were abusive toward sales personnel, treating them in an imperious way and rebuking them if their manner was too "familiar." In response, store personnel developed coping strategies to "get back at" rude customers. These tactics ranged from sounding a special signal when a difficult customer entered the store to authorizing the delivery of clearly unwanted merchandise. In these ways, the sales counter could become a battlefield between a working woman and "a woman of refinement."

At the same time, one of the most successful social feminist groups focused on relieving the working conditions of retail salesworkers. The National Consumers League (NCL) was founded on the concept that the biggest political weapon prosperous women had was their spending power. The women in the NCL pressured stores to improve labor conditions by threatening to withhold their patronage. Their standards included weekly minimum paychecks, limits on hours, required breaks and days off, paid vacations, minimum ages for workers, and various amenities at work, such as lockers, lunchrooms, and seating behind counters. The league boycotted stores that did not meet these standards. Since the National Consumers League had affiliates in twenty states and went beyond boycotts to lobbying and legislation, a threat from this organization was taken quite seriously. Thus, it became the "militant and highly articulate conscience of the buying public."[33]

The efforts of organizations like the National Consumers' League were often successful in producing reforms, but sometimes they led to friction between reformers and workers. A bourgeois woman would come in to shop, but linger to ask blunt questions about a worker's pay or hours, as if she were a social policeman who could grill a worker with impunity. Many took offense at such violations of privacy. Tension between the "refined woman," who felt it was her right to ask about work conditions, and the saleswoman, who felt it was her job to advise on intimate matters of appearance, must have been exquisite.

A considerable number of well-to-do women were involved in labor reform, including, prominently, Mrs. O. H. P. Belmont. She and many others concentrated their support in the Women's Trade Union League. The membership of the WTUL was divided into two groups, the workers and their "allies." The "allies" were prosperous women who attended strikes with the workers, walking arm in arm with them during demonstrations. This gesture achieved several things. First, the police and the employers were more hesitant about instigating violence against the strikers if they were so closely attended by bourgeois women. Second, when violence did break out, which it often did, the allies were there to act as witnesses to the brutality, thus providing evidence to be used later in legal proceedings, press reports, and negotiations. Third, since the police were unlikely to arrest the allies (who could be easily identified by their dress and grooming), they could follow arrested strikers to ensure that civil rights were honored, as well as post bail. The allies also raised money and provided relief during long strikes in the form of food and heating. With the allies' role clearly defined in terms of support, therefore, the workers could take responsibility and leadership for the labor negotiations themselves.

The credit for the success of this system has been given to the gracious and beautiful Margaret Dreier Robbins, who, as president of the WTUL, was able to create a tolerant environment, smooth over the rough spots, and work effectively with both sides. One contemporary commentator remarked that Robbins was able to refrain from trying to enforce upon the working girls the "alien ideals and capacities of another class." In return, the workers respected and appreciated her efforts to help them. Thus, in the words of one historian: "Mrs. Robbins demonstrated that one could be both feminine and a feminist, that a great cause could be fought for without compromising the dignity and self-respect of those it was supposed to help, and that, terribly difficult though it was, lines of empathy could be thrown over the barrier of class."[34]

Florence Kelly, the leader of the NCL during this decade, was a Marxist. Although she retained her belief in the goals of socialism, she directed her activities toward putting an end to abuses and suffering as she found them. This activity draws criticism today. As a Marxist, the right thing for Kelly to have done was to withhold "bourgeois reformist efforts," so that "the Revolution" would be hastened: "Nonetheless, Mrs. Kelley's decision did her credit. It requires a certain hardness of character to put abstract propositions, like The Revolution, ahead of human wants, and to work for a distant event when present evils are so compelling."[35] Here we have another paradox produced by the Marxist loyalties of recent feminist writers. In spite of the long, admirable record of American social feminism in putting pressure on both business and government, today's radical feminists belittle "liberal" reform efforts as a matter of principle. In this way of thinking, virtually none of the major feminist initiatives—suffrage, the Equal Rights Amendment (ERA), the pro-choice movement, the antipornography movement, the push for equal education rights, the work toward divorce reform, the assertion of property rights—can be held to be anything but weak liberal backsliding.

The emphasis on social activism among the middle-class feminists and the narrow focus of the "scholastics" on suffrage produced a rift within the movement, even before the suffrage victory. Both sides anticipated a showdown in the aftermath. After the vote was won, the Woman's Party, represented by Alice Paul, immediately announced it would begin to pursue the Equal Rights Amendment. Many of the regulatory gains won by organizations such as the WTUL and the NCL hinged on the cultural assumption that women, as a class, needed additional protection under the law. The social feminists therefore saw the ERA as a direct threat to their fifty-year effort to achieve labor protection for women. The militant suffragists, for their part, were utterly unwilling to listen to concerns raised by the social feminists. Thus, a schism opened up between the social feminists—a broadly motivated, "ordinary," feminine, and dignified group of women who pursued social reform through specific action—and the former suffragists—a single-minded, elite, masculine, and angry group of women who pursued legalistic remedies for abstract reasons—that continued for many years. Because the history of the women's movement is today popularly understood as the history of suffrage, it shouldn't be surprising that the looks and style associated with the scholastic suffragists still signify ideological purity, while the gracious manners and sympathetic attitudes of the social feminists have become the signs of weak "liberal" sisters.

The reform efforts aimed at factory and retail labor offered little relief for the millions of women who engaged in various forms of informal wage earning and market transactions from their homes and farms. Yet here too we can see the effects of fashion and feminism, however distantly reflected. Individual field agents, virtually all women, sold the national magazines around the country. The agents' sales organizations were conceptualized and presented as "clubs" rather than as employment, even though the objective of making money was certainly not hidden. Thus, the magazines of the "clubwomen" had clubs of their own: clubs of commerce. Those who sold subscriptions were repaid in cash and gifts. Each club also provided a path of achievement. For instance, the *Woman's Home Companion* had an "Inner Circle" of their Pin Money Club. Once a woman sold twenty-five subscriptions, she was inducted into the Inner Circle and received a small Tiffany pin with a diamond chip and $15 in cash.

Those who administered the subscription clubs—also female—found that their organizations provided cash and a sense of achievement, but also the occasional luxury, the odd diversion, and a form of social exchange for women who were often bored and isolated as well as strapped for money. The field agents wrote frequent and personal letters to their "friends" at the magazines in New York. One administrator of several subscription clubs remarked on the level of intimacy that the field agents expected from her: "My purely commercial department brought letters asking for advice about intimate, sometimes tragic problems. Some of these women were desperate for someone to talk to. . . . To me at that time, it was new, and I was moved and astonished. The girls sent presents, too, and invitations to visit. . . . Every department of a woman's magazine gets such letters. This faith is less now [in the 1950s] than it used to be, but not much less."[36] Sarah Josepha Hale and Harriett Hubbard Ayer both received frequent and personal correspondence from readers in the early years of fashion magazines and beauty columns. Indeed, this kind of intimate correspondence is characteristic of the relationships that women's magazines *always* have had with their readers. It is remarkable that, at least up until about 1930, most of these magazines struggled to answer each and every letter personally. It is therefore inaccurate to say, as Gloria Steinem and other feminists have done repeatedly, that the women's magazines were not in touch with ordinary women—whether readers or field agents—and that they were oblivious to the interests and concerns of American females.

The first national magazine aimed at working-class women grew out of just such letters. Bernarr MacFadden, the publisher of a controversial fitness magazine, *Physical Culture,* also received a great deal of mail from his readers. So many letters came from young women writing about love affairs that his wife suggested a new magazine as a vehicle for their stories. Introduced in 1919, *True Story*'s cover announced: "Truth is Stranger than Fiction!" and "We Offer $1,000 for Your Life Romance!" With its unadulterated interest in relations between the sexes, to elite observers *True Story* epitomized the "degraded" level of popular culture, but local five-and-ten-cent stores couldn't keep it on the shelves. Even though *True Story,* at twenty cents an issue, was fairly expensive, it passed *Good Housekeeping* in circulation by 1924, reached a readership of 2 million by 1926, and pulled even with the two leading magazines, the *Ladies' Home Journal* and *McCall's,* in 1927.[37] Imitators of *True Story* followed, which created a new genre of magazine, the "romance" or "confessional" magazine.

*True Story* soon became the leading magazine among the lowest two tiers of income groups in the United States.[38] This group had less spending power on a per capita basis, but because it was much larger than those served by the fashion and women's service magazines, it was still a legitimate market segment for many advertisers. *True Story* can be said to represent the first truly mass magazine for women. Even though the circulations of the romance books approached those of the genteel women's magazines, however, the leading advertising agencies were initially hesitant to put "respectable" clients' ads in them. The early issues of *True Story,* therefore, are full of ads for get-rich-quick schemes, mechanic's and beautician's schools, muscle builders, self-improvement courses, and the like, rather than nationally distributed cosmetics or prestigious dressmakers.

A second type of magazine also found its way among working girls, although it caught on a little more slowly. Movie magazines started about eight years before the romance magazines, but they hit their stride of popularity at about the same time. *Photoplay,* the first and largest, struggled as a pamphlet for several years before being sold to different publishers in 1914. As the movies grew in popularity during the 1910s, particularly among single working girls, the readership of *Photoplay* grew as well. By 1920 the circulation of *Photoplay* was double the circulation of *Vogue;* within another decade, the nation's leading movie magazine had more than three times the circulation of the leading high-fashion magazine.

Neither of these magazines ever reported on Society events or Parisian fashions. When Society women appeared in the fiction of *True Story,* they were villains of false values to be overcome by the virtuous working-girl heroine. In *Photoplay,* Leaders of Society were relevant only as movie roles. At this level, in fact, the effective role models were neither middle class matrons nor socialites but actresses, particularly those who had risen from the ranks of the poor. Indeed, middle- and upper-class activists were involved in reform efforts that brought them into direct conflict with the readers of *True Story* and *Photoplay.* Continuing the practices of the nineteenth-century social purity movement, many reformers attacked the romantic stories in magazines and movies. Several of the women's organizations of the Progressive era—from around 1900 to 1920—with the support of the middle class women's magazines, especially the *Woman's Home Companion* and the *Ladies' Home Journal,* were intensely involved in these censorship campaigns.

Beauty products continued to be something that working-class women exchanged among themselves. Commercial enterprises that took advantage of this subcultural economy also were born. One of the most successful was the California Perfume Company, which, although it was established in 1886, didn't advertise until after World War II. David McConnell, the company's founder, recruited female factory workers as sales representatives. Using their neighborhood contacts, these representatives became an effective form of distribution that worked independently of the advertising and promotion other cosmetics companies relied on. By the century's turn, there were 6,000 representatives, who became known as Avon ladies only after the company changed its name in 1939. Throughout most of the twentieth century, in fact, cosmetics sold by Avon and Mary Kay have outdistanced the so-called national cosmetics houses such as Arden and Rubinstein in terms of total sales.

The readers of the fan magazines and confessional books, however, also proved to be a remarkably lucrative market for advertisers. As national companies began testing their way into campaigns in these vehicles, they found this group notably responsive, particularly to beauty products—and often in categories not acceptable in the higher-tier books, such as lipstick. There are several reasons for this. One, obviously, is the sheer difference in numbers; the market was simply bigger. Another difference is probably that the more limited access this group had to luxuries made them more sensitive to such appeals in the early years. The novelty of buying through an ad rather than a friend may have had an impact too. Finally, a different aesthetic often operated at this level. Working class women were not always happy simply to ape the practices of their "betters," whether the choice was cosmetics, reading materials, or political efforts. Thus, products pitched at this group often fared differently than they had with the other strata. The difference in aesthetic also implies an alternate set of models and another touchpoint of inspiration. In this case, the inspirations were screen actresses and Hollywood rather than socialites and Paris.

## THE ENDS OF OBLIGATION

If we step back and look at the system of exchanges suggested by the content of the magazines, we can imagine a network of obligations from coast to coast: obligations between seamstresses and patrons, designers and fashion editors, socialites and their followers, women's editors and freelance feminist writers, saleswomen and their customers, treatment girls and their employers, manufacturers and field agents, the Avon Lady and the local corset agent, Pin Money "girls" and their contacts in New York. Each obligation branches out in all directions: The treatment girl is obligated to her employer and to her customer, each of whom is, in turn, obligated to her and to each other. The nature of the obligation is not just a matter of cash accounts: the customer is obligated to the saleswoman who helps her keep up with the clothing needs of her family, and, in turn, the saleswoman is obligated to the customer who joins the National Consumers League to help her get better working conditions . . . and so on.

The edges of a social system can be marked where no exchanges exist. Marginalized groups often have restricted market access. For example, throughout the country at this point, but most famously in the South, blacks could sell or shop only among themselves. Much of the tension that caused lynching and Jim Crow legislation during this time was related to African American efforts to participate in the marketplace by selling to or buying from whites. The politics of fashion shows these rifts as clearly as do other commercial interactions.

There are no black models, products, services, features, or advertisers in the fashion or women's service magazines of the 1910s. Instead, the media in the early twentieth century—and well past its midpoint—was completely segregated. Not only was access to magazines a problem for black women, but access to the information in the fashionable retail environment was also denied because black women could not be served in stylish stores. Indeed, they were considered only for jobs that kept them at an acceptable distance from genteel customers.[39]

The limited buying capacity of the impoverished black community made it difficult to maintain a business base sufficient to support its own press. Nevertheless, between 1910 and 1919, several black magazines were started: the *Crusader,* the *Messenger,* the *Champion,* the *Half-Century.* Only one, the *Half-Century,* begun by Kathryn L. Williams in 1916, was what might be called a women's magazine. Williams tried to emulate the Curtis Publishing Company magazines, the *Saturday Evening Post* and the *Ladies' Home Journal.* She addressed social questions and community initiatives. The magazine carried fiction, but also current events and reports on club activities. There was a fashion page and a beauty column. The spirit of the magazine was definitely activist; Williams was involved in many black organizations, including the black women's suffrage movement. The *Half-Century* ran for seven years and had a circulation of 20,000 at its highest point (7,500 more than *Vogue* had when Condé Nast acquired it).

The advertisements all seem to come from black-owned companies. Nearly all are pushing bleaching creams, hair straighteners, hair pomades, hair switches, and the like.

Yet, although clearly the magazine would not be in business without such ads, the editorial content suggests that readers knew the contradiction between black pride and these businesses. For this and other reasons, the *Half-Century* emphasized repeatedly in features from editorials to club reports the need for black people to start and patronize their own businesses.

The beauty columns of the *Half-Century* were devoted to practices we would now consider "basic grooming": how to brush your teeth, shampoo your hair, clean your face, manicure your nails, how often to bathe, and so on. The fashion page presented photographs of attractive African American women wearing clothes made by black dressmakers, tailors, and milliners. Not only did the magazine print the names of the makers, but it offered to help any interested reader buy the featured products. Here the general desire to support black businesses seems to have overridden any impetus to keep commerce out of the fashion pages.

The small column that always appears under the fashion pictures is written by "Madam F. Madison" and titled "What They Are Wearing," a phrase that mimics the titles of similar columns in *Vogue,* such as "What She is Wearing, "What They are Reading," "As Seen By Him." The precious tone and content of this column seems equally out of place. One feature talks about upcoming activities at New York's exclusive Piping Rock club; another even refers to "our Puritan forefathers." At times the *Half-Century* fashion columnist says things that are so ridiculous you wonder if she is plagiarizing *Vogue:* "Buckskin will not be used very much this season for the very good reason that there is practically none to use, so slippers of white kid will be worn with the sports costume on the days when one is not wearing white kid." In other places, *Vogue* obviously is the source material, but it has been grossly misinterpreted: "And so we have searched up and down Fifth Avenue together—the street with the interesting little French shops which dictate the fashions of the world." There was no way the readers of the *Half-Century* were going to gain access to the Fifth Avenue shops, to couturiers, or to the Piping Rock club. How is it that the mandarin voice of *Vogue* echoes as far away as the *Half-Century*?[40]

The intention of *Vogue* was to set the standard by which others would live. The effectiveness of that strategy can be seen in the *Half-Century.* Among a group struggling to be accepted as full social and economic members of American society, there is this habit of copying the tone of the power elite no matter how irrelevant and inactionable the content may be. The *Half-Century* was mimicking *Vogue* because New York Society women were the dominant women in the culture. If those New York women had been wearing Thai clothes, then columns from Bangkok would have appeared in the *Half-Century* (and in *McCall's* as well). So, these odd little columns reflect the power of the New York socialites, not the Paris designers. By adopting the grooming practices, clothing, and etiquette of the elite, blacks were making a bid for power. This is *not* blind slavishness, but a clear-eyed assertion of intentions. Although the practice is imitative—in fact, especially *because* it is imitative—it announces "I am as good as you are."

The *Half-Century* offers a microcosm of the way racial prejudice and tension were expressed by beliefs about grooming standards and by access to dress. An incident in suffrage history illustrates the same phenomenon with a more poignant result. In 1917 militant suffragist Alice Paul and her followers began picketing the White House. The picketers were arrested several times. Small groups were incarcerated at various times in the Occoquan workhouse, which also held a number of black women prisoners. Upon their arrival at the workhouse, the suffragists were treated to an indignity that lingered long in their minds: They were forced to undress and shower in front of black women. After their showers, the suffragists were given clean clothes to put on. These clothes were also, in their view, a form of mistreatment, as they were heavy and crudely made. The workhouse clothes the suffragists found so offensive, however, had been taken from the black prisoners, laundered, and made available for the new arrivals. So, what the suffrage prisoners were insulted to wear were actually the prison's "good clothes," and the black prisoners had to wear less acceptable clothing so that the higher-class prisoners might have the best. The feminist prisoners were further shocked to find that they were expected to shower with "the colored women" and even share the same soap. Also horrifying was the demand that they sleep in the same room and eat at the same tables, but the forced nakedness, showering, and shared soap seems to have struck a chord that was unparalleled by any other incident.

Because suffragists were prominent women in Society and the professions, their ordeal was widely publicized. The government was forced to back down. One woman was pardoned by President Wilson himself after only three days in prison. When a few picketers went on a hunger strike in the workhouse, there were forced feedings and beatings. Nevertheless, the prisoners *were* released. Having observed the success of suffragist hunger strikes, the black women asked for help. A suffragist wrote:

> One of the heart-breaking handicaps of the swift, intensive warfare of the pickets was that, although they did much to ameliorate conditions for their fellow prisoners, they could not make them ideal. Piteous appeal after piteous appeal came to them from their "comrades in the Workhouse."
>
> "If we go on a hunger-strike, will they make things better for us?" the other prisoners asked again and again.
>
> "No," the Suffragists answered sadly. "You have no organization back of you."

This explanation doesn't fully account for the difference in treatment, of course, but the fact that suffragists said, "You have no organization back of you" is telling. Clearly, grand names for organizations representing "Women" really referred only to white women, since these poor black prisoners, in the suffragists' eyes, had no organization back of them.[41]

During the entire history of suffrage, black women were excluded. The women's clubs would not allow African Americans into their organizations because they believed black women were dirty and immoral. Therefore, the black community produced its own women's movement and clubs, made up of the children and grandchildren of slaves who had managed to achieve prosperity in the post–Civil War period. The women who belonged to these clubs were educated and made a point of looking genteel and acting refined. Teaching personal hygiene was consistently among their major concerns. From within their own community, they worked to provide education and healthy leisure pursuits, to stop lynching, to create jobs.[42]

When the National Woman's Party convened for the first time after suffrage, whether to include black women was a major issue. Alice Paul, its new president, refused to address black women's concerns, including their voter registration problems (a race issue, not a gender issue, according to Paul). Black women's organizations, therefore, continued to be separate from those of white women, just as were their shops, beauty parlors, fashion magazines, and advertisements. Thus, the feminist movement stopped at the same place that the market did; and beyond that there was no obligation.

## CHAPTER SIX

# SEX, SOAP, AND CINDERELLA

ONCE UPON A TIME, THERE WAS A YOUNG GIRL WHO, THROUGH NO FAULT OF HER OWN, was reduced to working as a maid in the home of three cruel women. Her employers not only required her to work to exhaustion, they degraded and humiliated her at every opportunity. They gave her rags to wear and did not allow her to wash herself or comb her hair. Then they laughed at her dirtiness and called her names. Having no place to go and no other skills, the young girl quietly tolerated their cruelty, did her best to please them, and dreamed of escape.

One night her dream came true. Through the forces of magic, the girl was groomed and dressed beautifully and carried in a coach to a royal ball. The prince was struck by her beauty and asked her to dance. He was so entranced that he kept her with him throughout the evening.

The next day, after the magic was over, the young girl was back in the home of the three cruel women. They treated her even more harshly because of the impertinence she had shown by appearing at the ball. When they heard the prince was looking for the young girl he had met, the three women tried to hide their servant's identity. But she made herself known to the prince and he asked her to marry him.

The three women were now ashamed of their previous treatment of the young girl. They feared and expected reprisals. The new princess, however, being as good as she was beautiful, forgave them. And they all lived happily ever after.

The story of Cinderella has been a favorite target of feminist criticism for many years.[1] The feminist reading casts the prince, rather than the three cruel women, as the enemy, and Cinderella as a weak-willed underachiever—a mere "heroine of the body." The self-interested maternalism and false sisterhood of the three women who hold Cinderella prisoner are completely ignored, as are the class implications of the narrative. Particularly unnoticed are the strategies for control adopted by the stepmother and her daughters: To keep Cinderella down, they keep her dirty, restrict her dress to rags, refuse her recreation, and, perhaps most important, erect as many barriers as they can think of between the kitchen maid and her prince.

In the 1920s a conflict arose between a whole generation of Cinderellas and the mothers of the suffrage movement. This era brought a wave of sensualism, in which legions of young women—particularly though not exclusively those of modest means—asserted themselves by their dress, their dancing, and their romances. The feminists of the previous generation, "Progressive" as they may have been in their own time, were still so rooted in the values of social purity that they quickly condemned the behavior of the new generation, even though much of it posed a challenge to gender roles. In their zeal to censure the new ways, the Old Feminists, as they were known in the 1920s, became allied with conservatives on a number of issues. Before the Roaring Twenties came to an end, the controversy had been carried from feminist essays to public debates and was reflected in the pages of popular magazines and even the advertisements. We can discern echoes of the resulting rift in feminist politics today, as a new generation questions the attitudes of older feminists toward dress and romance.

## DANCING IN GLASS SLIPPERS

The central figure in this whirlpool of sin was the "flapper," a term coined initially to describe young working-class women, but eventually expanded to include young women of all classes who challenged traditional norms in distinctive ways. The flapper drank, drove, smoked, and danced new "immoral" dances to a modern musical style called "jazz." She read banned books and went to the movies every week. She wore lipstick and bobbed her hair, and her clothes differed dramatically from those of the previous generation

Dress trends of the 1920s made the most noticeable break with past styles since the early 1800s. The signature elements are by now familiar: cloche hat, straight silhouette, bare arms, short skirt, and masses of jewelry including dangling earrings, long necklaces, and multiple bracelets. Although arms and chest had been exposed in the fashions of the Victorian period, legs had not been visible during any time in American history. The flash of foot that had appeared occasionally was concealed in boots or covered with thick, dark hose. Now the wonders of industry brought transparent, leg-shaped stockings to the market at affordable prices, and short skirts showed them off. Dresses were made in light, fluid fabrics and decorated in creative ways, with asymmetrical hems, elaborate patterns, spectacular trims. Voluptuous accessories, such as jeweled cigarette cases and enameled compacts, were the rage. For the young, the new look demanded only minimal underwear. Light girdles were made to hold stockings up, but the fad among flappers was to go without a girdle and just roll the stockings around the knee. So, the New Girls, as the flappers were also known, not only wore short skirts and had unrestricted waists, but were more bejeweled and befeathered than had previously been thought respectable.

The flapper's dress was particularly suited to her nightlife. Going without a corset left the girl free to move—and all the fringe, beads, and spangles shimmied with her. Just as has happened with every other musical sensation coming from the African American community in the twentieth century—ragtime, swing, rock, blues, rap—the conservatives charged that jazz would corrupt the morals of white youth. Calling attention to the "sensual stimulation of the abominable jazz orchestra with its voodoo-born minors and its direct appeal to the sensory centers," community leaders everywhere attempted to eradicate the jazz scourge. Most of the new dancing, however, went on in places unsupervised by middle class moral leaders: "It is the cheaper night clubs and dance halls which most endanger poorer, less beautiful and less intelligent girls. These scrubby places, which offer inexpensive dancing and amusement to tired workers, abound in the East Side of New York and, I suppose, the more congested sections of other cities. . . . Most young girls, I am convinced, go at first to these resorts with no intention of wrongdoing." But "wrongdoing"—that is, sexual expression by young working girls—seemed certain to come from the corrupt rhythms: "The road to hell is too often paved with jazz steps," declared the *Ladies' Home Journal* in 1921.[2]

The number of times that critics blamed the New Girl's clothes for her immoral behavior is almost humorous. A conservative judge wrote: "They read in the newspapers of gay places enjoyed by those in better circumstances, about beautiful clothes, and they devour the fashion pictures in the rotogravure prints. Exhausted after a day's drudgery, craving stimulation and amusement, what is to offer in a restricted, often unclean and unhappy home? And what often happens?" Anything might happen to such a girl, I guess, but it was said that most of them were driven into prostitution to feed their fashion cravings.[3]

Given the way elite Americans still viewed the practice of trade, the most unsettling thing about the flapper may have been her market orientation. Although conservatives of the 1920s and feminist historians of today disdain this period's "sexy saleslady," the young women who staffed department stores, wrote press releases, edited fashion magazines, and otherwise made their living in the booming market economy appear to have admired those of their sisters who showed a talent for commerce. In *Photoplay*, for instance, the flapper could read a popular, long-running serial entitled "Peggy Roche: Saleslady." "Here is the first of the Peggy Roche stories," announced the editors when the series began. "The adventures of an American girl in a new field of industrial endeavor. . . . Peggy is the intrepid, unique American business woman—plus." Peggy's stories were said to be full of "the romance of commerce."[4]

As much as they may have loved the "romance of commerce," however, the flappers were best known for romance of a different kind. The New Girl often was charged with reading too many romance magazines and watching too many movies about love, becoming the nemesis of reformers who, having just achieved Prohibition and having finally outlawed prostitution, now concentrated on the last plank of the social purity platform, censorship. Worse, these girls also seemed determined to exert their own "amatory license," as one observer of the times called it.[5] This heady combination of independence and sensuality drew young men to the new Cinderellas in droves, again rearranging the hierarchy of courtship, marriage, and, thus, kinship in America.

Jazz Age contemporaries used the term "New Woman" or "New Feminist" interchangeably with "New Girl" and "flapper." So, accurate or not, most people associated short skirts, frenetic dancing, shared flasks, and public necking with feminism. Can we, from the distance of seventy-five years, view such a Cinderella as a feminist role model? Not within the framework of behavior advocated first by the Puritan feminists, next by the suffragists, and now by the "New Victorians" of the millennium's turn. No, for this, we must look to a different tradition of feminism.

## SEX AFTER SUFFRAGE

As expected, the tenuous coalition of women's groups that characterized the suffrage movement fell apart after the vote was won in 1919. The new National Woman's Party redefined itself around the new single-issue battle, the Equal Rights Amendment. Alvah Belmont and others who had once championed worker's rights became alienated from the labor movement. In fact, during the 1920s, the National Woman's Party formally allied itself with the Republican party, the very guardian of capital. The new party's leadership tried to define the objects of feminism as those aspects of oppression unique to women, but not resulting from class or race prejudice. As a result, feminism once again became a movement dedicated to improving the lot of women whose class and ethnic backgrounds were unproblematic—Anglo upper and middle class. When sexual issues were pressed on the political front by either young women or poor women, the older feminists refused to recognize the importance of the questions, just as they refused to recognize the importance of labor and race issues.[6]

The birth control struggle illustrates the way class differences clouded the discourse on what we would see today as unambiguously women's issues. In the nineteenth century social purists had made distribution of contraceptive devices a crime. Nevertheless, middle-class women of the early twentieth century generally had access to birth control through their doctors. Estimates suggest that more than of 70 percent of married middle-class women used birth control by the 1920s, yet there was general ignorance of family planning among the working class. Many former suffragists felt that the lower classes should simply learn to control their lust better; others were inclined to support birth control among the poor just to reduce the numbers of ethnic minorities. The very idea that a poor woman had the right to enjoy sex without fear of unwanted pregnancy flew in the face of such prejudices. Many older feminists were personally uncomfortable with sex and preferred not to think about it, never mind talk about it. The idea that a single woman might want the freedom to engage in sex was simply beyond their ken. So the question of women's sexuality was once again deferred by the "mainstream" movement, left to be considered and defended by more controversial groups.[7]

The spokespersons for this new assertion of sexual freedom for women were the political granddaughters of Victoria Woodhull, not Susan B. Anthony. Like Woodhull, these newer thinkers were braver in their approach to life, more likely to take risks, less sheltered. They went out in the evenings without chaperones, lived alone in big cities, and crossed class and race boundaries in a way the old suffragists would not have done. Margaret Sanger, Emma Goldman, and Crystal Eastman belong in this group. These new leaders were not only more likely to be allied with socialism and "free love," as Woodhull was, but they were also more likely to come from modest circumstances and despised ethnic groups. Emma Goldman, for instance, was a Jewish immigrant whose first job in this country was as a cigar factory worker. Like many girls in the first generation of Irish born in America, Margaret Sanger was a nurse. Neither woman had the attitude toward pleasure that Anglo-Protestant Americans shared. The difference in antecedents between those who championed women's sensuality and those who preferred purity was once again an important backdrop.

Charlotte Perkins Gilman defined the poles of debate by naming the two factions the Human Feminist and the Female Feminist. The Human Feminist lived a life of the mind that made her indistinguishable from men. The Female Feminist expressed her essential femininity by her concern with the life of the body, including both sexuality and motherhood. Human Feminist ideology was designed to discredit those "heroines of the body" who demanded rights to sexual freedom and physical pleasure. Psychologist Ethel Puffer Howes responded, in a now-famous essay, naming the dangers inherent in this mind/body split: "Yet that disaster is what we are now inviting, not on principle, but through pure obstinate stupidity, in opening all doors to women, without providing for the woman's love life as the ordinary social setting does for man's. Various writers set up a straw-woman, the 'brain-woman.' . . . the present social framework does not allow the natural and necessary development of woman's affectional life, along with . . . exercise of her intellectual powers. The man demands of life that he have love, home, fatherhood and the special work which his particular brain combination fits. Shall the woman demand less?"[8]

Behind this philosophical difference were cultural origins and values that, in the xenophobic milieu of the 1920s, could be evoked in highly inflammatory ways. "Red Emma" Goldman, by far the most politically radical of this generation, championed sexual expression, freedom for the arts, the beauty of the body, and the importance of sensuality—"Moral Bolshevism," as one conservative judge put it. In public addresses, Goldman repeatedly emphasized the origins of public prudery: "The history of New

England, and especially of Massachusetts, is full of the horrors that have turned life into gloom, joy into despair, naturalness into disease, honesty and truth into hideous lies and hypocrisies. . . . Puritanism no longer employs the thumbscrew and lash; but it still has a most pernicious hold on the minds and feelings of the American people. . . ." Goldman did not spare the leading feminists: "The great movement of *true* emancipation has not met with a great race of women who could look liberty in the face. Their narrow, puritanical vision banished man, as a disturber and doubtful character, out of their emotional life." In unapologetic contrast to the so-called Human Feminists, Goldman refused to repudiate the notion that the love between a woman and a man, or between a woman and her child, was important.[9]

The fault line across the movement is illustrated by an issue of *Current History,* dated October 1927, devoted to discussion of that decade's New Woman. Essays by Carrie Chapman Catt and Charlotte Perkins Gilman both focus on legal and professional gains. The other writers all address the moral questions posed by the New Girls. Joseph Collins, a neurologist and supporter of feminism, suggests New Women saw themselves in a fundamentally different way: "In her discoveries of herself she has stumbled upon the fact that, far from being what man has always asserted she was, timid, prudish and monogamous, she is bold, immodest and polyandrous. She is making short business of adapting the existing code of morality to her new interpretation of it." Further, Collins wrote: "Man, be he pietist, puritan or pagan, must eventually realize that woman of the future is not going to sit back supinely and observe him suck life's honeycomb. She is going to have pleasures and pastimes equivalent to his. . . ." Martha Bensley Bruère, writing in the same issue, saw hope in the larger view of morality posed: "Formerly sin was to us a purely personal matter, usually a sex transgression, to be atoned for individually; whereas, the great community immoralities, public corruption, class oppression, ignorance and exploitation, concerned us very little. The new code now developing includes virtues and vices quite unconnected with monogamy."[10]

The morality of the New Girls was, therefore, a *different* morality rather than an absence of morality. According to some, the new outlook represented a more humane moral order, one in which all persons had the right to pleasure, love, and care—and in which compassion was valued over censure. But to more traditional (and powerful) Americans, including the Old Feminists, their own forebears' moral code was a universal standard. With characteristic self-righteousness, they worked to quash the "immorality" that now confronted them.

## SCULLERY MAID'S REVENGE

The postsuffrage Cinderella was out of the kitchen, and she wasn't going back. At least that was the conclusion reached by Ida Tarbell when she surveyed members of the

YWCA for the *Woman's Home Companion.* Young women gave the same reasons for shunning domestic service they had given for years: long hours, lack of respect, no social life. "It is described as a feeling that she is 'owned,' is 'everybody's servant,' is 'one who should not have any social standing,' 'one who ought not to have any pleasure,'" writes Tarbell. Genteel housewives and working girls had been struggling over dress, pleasure, and sexual relations a long time. But in the 1920s, more than ever, single working girls seemed determined to elude the best maternal wishes of "refined and educated women." And, more than ever, Cinderella seemed to understand that efforts to control her pleasures and her romances were, in fact, attempts to keep her down in the kitchen.[11]

The young single woman who could earn her own money didn't have to mind her superiors any more. She played wherever she wished. She could love whomever she could win. And she could dress however she liked. The working girl, rather than the moneyed housewife, was now seen as the fashion trend-setter: "The best dressed women in the United States, according to widely diversified and representative masculine testimony, are not the wives, who have to wheedle clothes money out of their husbands, or even the debutantes, who have to wheedle it out of their fathers, but the smart little working girls, who earn their own money and buy their own clothes."[12] The working girl's autonomy and her ability to keep up with the times threatened the hegemony of the socialite over fashion and the bourgeois matron over the marks of gentility. She became, for the first time, the one who was envied rather than pitied. That made the desire to control her all the more pressing.

Many commentators of the time thought the New Girl's romantic impulse stemmed from her ability to support herself. Because she could afford to marry for love, Cinderella seemed to have found a freedom that eluded others. Economic considerations were still primary in marital arrangements, even among the middle class, but the younger generation was rebelling against this idea. We can see early evidence in a *Good Housekeeping* survey conducted in 1910 among 500 middle-class bachelors around the country. They were asked how much money they needed to get married. The answers came as a backlash for romance—and a surprising vote of confidence for the working girl. A "Springfield man" wrote: "Romantic idealists do not attack the question of matrimony with a careful weighing of material evidences and a close system of reasoning, nor do we try to pare down original estimates like a contractor figuring on a construction job. Such mental processes in connection with the discussion of matrimony are as inconsistent as an attempt to reconcile our religious faith with a rational scheme of the universe." *Good Housekeeping* next asked these men whether they thought the girls "of their set" were well prepared for marriage. The answers were overwhelmingly negative, not because the girls weren't good cooks or laundresses, but because the girls were spoiled and too concerned with social life.[13]

In contrast, these same young men described a different ideal wife: "'Sporting spirit' is an unusual term to apply to a woman, but it describes that spirit of taking adversity with a smile and going ahead that I find in many women. Many a girl that is 'rightly brought up and trained' for matrimony in the eyes of the world lacks just that." Consistently, these young men preferred to have a "business girl" as a mate: "I believe the girl who would make the best wife is the one who has earned her living. She has a truer appreciation, not only of money but of everything in life." One bachelor expressed a belief that many seem to have held: "I do not think the simple fact that a girl works for her living makes her less likely to marry the man she wants to, although it may give her greater freedom to oppose the old maxim, 'Better married poorly than not married at all.'"[14]

Surprised by these responses, *Good Housekeeping* then invited young women to write. Their letters show that the girls, too, believed that love rather than financial arrangements should be prominent in the decision to marry. Their statements also suggest, however, that they believed "business girls" were in the best position to choose a mate and that, in any case, business girls lived better than married women because they had their own money to spend. Throughout the texts of both the men and the women appears the feeling that businesswomen marry for love because they don't have to marry for money.[15]

The very essence of the romance ethic was, as always, to destroy the economic basis for marriage, thus also threatening class barriers in kinship. In the 1920s romance was, in many ways, a threat to the institution of marriage itself, at least as traditionally conceived and practiced. For instance, although the relationships between wealthy men and working girls had been the subject of cartoon and conjecture for decades, only rarely did the privileged male leave his wife for his downscale lover. Yet in the 1920s, the relationships between prosperous men and working girls seemed to take that turn more often. In *Woman's Coming of Age,* Winifred Raushenbush wrote:

> The working woman, who lived alone, and kept her own hours, had learned that there were at least two possible routes to marriage, and that the second route, in which the first step is being a mistress, and the second is being a wife, was perhaps the more reliable. She had also discovered that married men were attractive lovers, and that, as discontented husbands, they were potentially marriageable. She therefore decided that the married woman had no rights to her man which other women were bound to respect. The ultimatum which the working woman served on the married woman during the middle years of the twenties did not appear on the front page of any newspapers. But it reached its destination; and war was declared.[16]

Competition between the woman "rightly brought up and trained for matrimony" and the pleasure-seeking working girl appears frequently in the fiction, plays, cartoons, and films of the decade. As with the Steel-Engraving Lady, the Anthony New Woman, and the American Girl, the character of the new challenger was represented in both positive and negative terms, depending on the viewpoint of the person making the representation. Thus, an unconventional young woman of lower-class status who has caught the attention of an elite man frequently appears, but a wide range of tones and narratives provides context. She is referred to by various labels—gold-digger, chorus girl, vamp, and flapper—sometimes applied with derision and sometimes with affection. In works read by elites, the girl's appeal is reduced to sex and artifice—she is either an empty-headed sex toy or a painted schemer. Such a characterization, obviously, was the most palatable way of explaining the phenomenon to the elite.

The increasing interest of younger men in female counterparts who could work, as well as play, in ways that weren't open to the traditional woman is also remarked upon repeatedly. This new couple becomes a common conceit in the popular culture of the 1920s, much as the Gibson Girl and her beau had a decade before.

In material aimed at the broadest audiences, the working girl is clearly the star. This can be seen not only in story lines for movies and magazines but in comic strips, beginning with *Polly and Her Pals* in 1912 and continuing through World War II with *Winnie Winkle the Breadwinner, Somebody's Stenog, Tillie the Toiler, Etta Kett, Ella Cinders, The Kid Sister, Dixie Dugan, Dolly and the Follies, Flapper Fanny,* and *Fritzi Ritz.*[17] Polly, Winnie, Tillie, Dixie, Fritzi, and their comrades are pretty, energetic, independent, and always stylishly dressed and groomed. These characters reflect the broader culture's admiration for the pretty, "plucky" working girl.

The most enduring of these characters, Betty Boop, came from the Fleischer Studios, one of the first film animation studios in the United States. The Fleischer brothers were sons of a poor Russian tailor and his very independent wife, who fled Austrian persecution of the Jews during the late 1890s. The Fleischers' father started a penny arcade in America, which introduced his boys to the entertainment culture that would make them famous. The two young men opened their own studio in 1921. They created cartoons for the audience they knew best, which meant that their work, in the eyes of elite critics, was characterized by raw peasant humor, bad drawing, poor timing, and simpleminded stories. The Fleischer cartoons, however, were very popular with mass audiences.[18]

Betty Boop made her first appearance in 1930, evolving from a popular vaudeville and film character, the "Oop-a-Doop" girl. From the beginning, Betty was too sexy for Puritan tastes, but she was immensely popular with everybody else. Betty Boop was quite independent and a working girl. She had a Brooklyn accent that would have embarrassed Clara Bow. The early cartoons were often accompanied by a jazz score, sometimes by famous bandleaders, such as Cab Calloway. Betty danced and sang, but mostly she worked in an amazing variety of jobs: short order cook, race car driver, judge, secretary, pilot, soldier, teacher, leader of a cult, singer, actress, patent medicine huckster, and presidential candidate. She also starred in an early feature cartoon as "Poor Cinderella."

In spite of her wide range of professional abilities, Betty was a sex object, even to the anthropomorphized dogs and rabbits who were her costars. Assorted animal friends kissed her, grabbed her, and just generally tried to ravish her whenever the occasion presented itself. Betty, however, was nobody's victim. If she was not in the mood, she simply grabbed the nearest frying pan and made "no" sound like "no." The most amazing thing about Betty Boop, however, is that sometimes she *was* in the mood. Not only does she sometimes "give in," she often makes the first move. In fact, Betty shows no hesitation in being just as pushy and grabby toward the objects of her own desire as the "men" of her acquaintance.

Needless to say, Betty Boop was not the favorite character of the heirs of the suffrage movement. Social purists had her banned in Philadelphia and, eventually, pressured the Fleischer brothers into making her more of a lady (well, at least giving her a longer skirt and a more modest neckline). Like many other fictional working girls, Betty Boop was an offense to the establishment, whose members felt that the pretty girl heroines, lower-class origins, revealing clothes, and sexy repartee that had come to characterize popular culture were a threat to the purity of the body politic.

## YOU OUGHTA BE IN PICTURES

Ground zero for conflict over the working girl's recreation, sexuality, and social aspirations was the movie house. Small storefronts called "nickelodeons" arose first in poor Jewish neighborhoods. They were very popular among the working class and immigrants for several years before they were even discovered by the middle class. Usually the theater owners were also immigrants, often Jews—which further stigmatized movies in the eyes of reformers. Films were seen to be advocating values that were too different from those of the middle-class Anglo Protestants, while at the same time they offered, as had the fashion industry, economic opportunities to other ethnic groups. Cinema historians acknowledge that the effort to censor early films was rooted in status insecurity, much as the temperance movement was: "As the Progressive movement began to take form early in the century, it drew much of its energy from the middle class's discovery that they had lost control over—and even knowledge of—the behavior and values of the lower orders; and the movies became prime targets of their efforts to reformulate and reassert their power."[19]

Clubwomen around the country enthusiastically pursued the "Better Movies" movement. Much of the discourse about this effort, therefore, took place in the women's service magazines. In particular, the *Woman's Home Companion* took the initiative in setting up a national network of upper- and middle-class activists who made it their business to attend local movies, pass judgment on the films, and then take steps either to reward the exhibitors for showing "clean movies" or to pressure them into allowing the groups to censor what they showed. On a national level, the *Woman's Home Companion* itself reviewed movies as they were released, passing judgment on their suitability.

The new romantic comedy was the movie genre most frequently attacked by the middle-class ladies' magazines. These films shared much with traditional romantic comedies in prose, poetry, and drama, including the ritual ending, usually a marriage. In at least one very important way, however, the early Hollywood romantic comedies are distinctive: The happy ending demands a cross-class marriage. The female is usually the working-class character, but there is also the "formulaic" story where the leading man is a poor but worthy suitor and the woman is an aristocrat also exists. In the storyline of the Hollywood comedies, the person of lesser status prevails by being of better character and truer intentions than his or her well-born competitor. The triumph of the working girl inevitably involves exposing the superior manners of the upper crust as a cover for false values. In both its class-crossing courtships and its stabs at genteel pretentiousness, therefore, the romantic comedy was offensive to the upper classes and those who emulated them.[20]

The "Better Movies" reviewers writing in the women's magazines suggest the attitudes that club ladies had toward such films. The *Woman's Home Companion,* for example, recommends a short list of movies in its December 1916 issue. About the film *Saving the Family Name,* the *Companion* declared: "A chorus girl's story from an entirely new angle features pretty Mary MacLaren as the girl forced by misunderstanding into an unwelcome notoriety." Also recommended is *The Social Secretary:* "A bright, breezy comedy drama handling the old story of the pretty stenographer's temptation in a new and wholly entertaining way. Norma Talmadge effects an amusing transition from beauty to homeliness." And finally, *The Revolt:* "The first shopgirl's story to be developed sincerely just as it might occur in any department store. There is a certain unpleasantness, but the moral tone is good." These reviews are clearly written against an already-established genre in which chorus girls, pretty stenographers, and shopgirls get to play Cinderella a little too often for the tastes of the stepsisters. A "fresh" treatment, therefore, becomes one where the chorus girl is humiliated or the shopgirl meets unpleasantness, and the test of "realism" is whether she is kept in her place.[21]

Today's feminist film critics have not been much kinder to the romantic comedies so loved by Jazz Age Cinderellas. Such critics identify as "conventional" (and therefore oppressive) any denouement where a happy marriage occurs between the leading lady and her man; they overlook the very unconventional aspect of the cross-class marriage.

Critics have shown no more respect for the viewers than for the films. Marjorie Rosen writes in *Popcorn Venus* that the first female movie audiences were "as impressionable and malleable" as children and, therefore, would "be susceptible to misinterpreting" images of "experiences far removed from their own." Historian Mary Ryan writes that "even the greenest immigrant girl could decipher the message on the silent screen" and then goes on to trash female movie fans, reducing Cinderella's behavior just as surely as the moralists of the 1920s had done: "These same women aped the hairstyles, apparel, and gestures of screen heroines. The silver screen demonstrated the new priority of twentieth-century women: attracting the male through sexual allure, and very few women could escape exposure to this message."[22]

The power of the silver screen and its heroines was evident to all, however. The film audience was huge: 35 million people went to the movies every week in the early 1920s, more than read the top ten national magazines. By mid-decade, the audience had more than doubled: 20,000 "picture theaters" all over America served a weekly audience of 90 million people.[23] Public willingness to follow screen stars on a variety of issues came as an unwelcome surprise to the reform-minded at a time when their own control over the masses was slipping away. Overnight, it seemed, screen actors had usurped cultural leadership. And nowhere was this more observable than in the admiration flappers had for the new film actresses.

## QUEENS OF COMMERCE

The movie actresses presented a powerful and very different role model. Unlike the socialite, the actress was fundamentally engaged in commerce and a "public woman" in a way that was very much admired. The actresses of the 1920s were the epitome of upward mobility—self-made women in every way. They were unabashedly sensual and unconventional. And not only were most of them of lower-class origins, many were immigrants.

The biographies of the first movie stars—Mary Pickford, Marguerite Clark, Lillian and Dorothy Gish, Mae Murray, Mae Marsh, Blanche Sweet, Clara Bow, Esther Ralston, Joan Crawford, Mary Astor, Fay Wray, Mary Brian, and others—are remarkable in the consistency of their narratives. Almost without exception, the first generation of stars came from painfully impoverished families. By far the majority were either orphans or were raised by single mothers. Nearly always, their motivation to get into the movies was to support a starving family that included one or more younger siblings. In some cases the young girl is pushed by an older person into pursuing a career on stage, in the movies, or in modeling, as a last-ditch effort to attain a decent income. In others, the girl seeks a screen career against the wishes of her parents, who persist in seeing acting as indistinguishable from prostitution. Clara Bow's mother (who was mentally ill) actually tried to kill her rather than allow her to become an actress. This woman's words, though they come from a dangerously sick source, typify the attitudes among some of the older generation: "'You ain't goin' inta pictures,' she ranted. 'You ain't gonna be no *hoor.*"[24]

Another notable characteristic of this group is their cultural diversity. Many were Jewish, as were Carmel Myers, Sue Carol, Theda Bara, and Sylvia Sidney. Some of them were eastern European immigrants, as was Pola Negri, while others were from western Europe: France (Jetta Goudal, Renee Adoree, Lily Damita), Germany (Marlene Dietrich), Russia (Olga Petrova, Alla Nazimova), Scandinavia (Greta Garbo, Greta Nissen, Anna Q. Nilsson). Tsuru Aoki was from Japan. There were Americans of Italian ancestry (Mabel Taliaferro), as well as Chinese (Anna Mae Wong), Irish (Mary Pickford, Peggy O'Neill, May McAvoy), German (Mary Astor, Eleanor Boardman), and various mixes, such as Latin and Celtic (Geraldine Farrar). Particularly once the industry moved to California, women of Hispanic origin emerged among the list of favored stars: Dolores del Rio, Lupe Velez, Marina Said, and Maria Montez. Poor women from the South, including Mae Murray, Corinne Griffith, Marguerite Clark, Joan Crawford, and Mary Brian, were often drawn to the movies. Most, however, came from the urban slums of New York, Detroit, and Chicago.

Because the early movies not only drew from the lowest levels of society but played to them as well, the ethnicity and humble beginnings of an actress were nothing to hide, but instead were the best sort of fuel for the emerging publicity machine. The fan magazines positively thrilled to the discovery stories of poor girls who became famous overnight, and they were delighted to reveal the Irish, Italian, Hungarian, or Polish antecedents of a popular screen star. Young working women from various ethnic groups could therefore feel an identification, even a kinship, with screen actresses that they could never have felt for Astors and Vanderbilts.

Inevitably, some fans were stage-struck. For most of them, dreams of fame on the silver screen were probably unrealistic. But the second generation of movie stars had themselves been among the first generation's audience: Mary Astor, Clara Bow, Esther Ralston, Fay Wray, Joan Crawford, and others sat in the darkened theaters of the late 1910s, most of them hungry, shoeless, or abused. Their rise to stardom fed the aspirations of still more poor girls. Feminists today would chastise the movie industry for having produced "false hopes" in the breasts of these youngsters. Much better, in their view, for these girls to become something *substantial,* to hope for something more *realistic,* such as being a doctor or a lawyer or a university professor. Yet the life stories of the early screen stars make it heartbreakingly clear that these women's hopes of becoming famous actresses, improbable as they were, were more likely than their chances of receiving a college education.

Although actresses had endorsed fashion and beauty products in advertising for many years, they had never before had the broad fashion leadership that came to the screen stars of the 1920s. Even the Sears catalog shows their influence, with "Clara Bow hats" and other items named for the stars. The personal magnetism of the screen stars gave them particular authority in matters of grooming, so, as fashion historian Stella Blum writes, "the female stars' most significant influence was on face and figure, coiffure, posture and grooming."[25] Several started their own businesses: Carmel Myers and Mary Pickford, for example, introduced cosmetics lines.

Screen stars also had an impact on the stages of undress that Americans found acceptable, thus boosting the fashionability of short, bare-shouldered dresses considerably. *Life* magazine complained about underdressed actresses in 1920s movies: "Dorothy Mackaill, Clara Bow, Olive Borden, Esther Ralston and Madge Bellamy are all talented young ladies, but I advise them to get a new act. I for one am sick to death of watching them undress." Nudity on screen became a specialty of some directors. Cecil B. DeMille, for example, was said to have invented the "bathroom scene," a frequent favorite in the early silents. In DeMille's *Male and Female,* Gloria Swanson "stepped in a sunken bath the size of a small swimming pool, revealing a momentary glimpse of her breasts." Luxurious bathrooms also became a DeMille signature: "The bath became a mystic shrine dedicated to Venus, or sometimes Apollo, and the art of bathing was shown as a lovely ceremony rather than a merely sanitary duty."[26]

The leading ladies of the new silver screen almost never lived conventional lives. Promiscuity and divorce among movie stars became stock for jokes. The studios may been hushed up their love lives as much as possible, but the multiple lovers of Clara Bow were hard to hide, as was the fact that John Gilbert moved from Letitia Joy, to Ina Claire, to Greta Garbo, to Dorothy Bush in a very short time. Although knowledge of such things may not have made it to the dining tables of the bourgeoisie, the lesbian community believed that both Greta Garbo and Marlene Dietrich were gay. Louise Brooks fed rumors that she was a lesbian, and she starred in a film, *Pandora's Box,* with lesbian scenes.

The roles played by the early screen actresses were not necessarily passive or sweet or retiring, even though feminist film criticism may lead you to believe otherwise. The "quintessential Mary Pickford role," for example, was an underclass urchin who would fight the rich bully, twist the prissy schoolmate's nose, or kill a fly with her bare hands for the sheer entertainment of it. The leading roles in the early movies were not all for fairy princesses, but for abused children, gum-chewing shopgirls, Russian peasants, country bumpkins, dissipated flappers, and all sorts of other strange and wonderful characters with a negligible connection to True Womanhood.

The movies thus represented an entirely new social order, one that arose suddenly from the ranks of the immigrant working class, had unparalleled power, was controlled by Jews, and made national heroines out of young women who were not "well bred," Protestant, Anglo, or even particularly concerned about being respectable in the eyes of those who were. Thus, the emergence of actresses as the heroines of America was one clear sign among many that a new order had once again conquered the old.

## SIBLING RIVALRIES

Two of the most famous ad campaigns of the twentieth century, for Woodbury Soap and Lux Toilet Soap, were involved in a head-to-head competition that occurred right in the thick of this power shift among women. The fortunes of these two products tell a clear story of this profound change in social stratification. Both soaps were in the hands of the J. Walter Thompson advertising agency during the 1920s—and both were managed by Helen Lansdowne Resor, the suffragist who persuaded Mrs. O. H. P. Belmont to hawk face cream.[27]

The Woodbury Soap campaign represented by figure 6.1 was outrageous from the time it first appeared in 1911. Hard-bitten advertising men doffed their hats in respect for the sheer brazen brilliance of it. Dozens of others rushed to imitate the new "sex appeal" in ads for powders, creams, and hair ointments. By the mid-1920s, such appeals were no longer new, and even Woodbury had moved on to something else, but "A Skin You Love to Touch" had won its place in history. Today this campaign is often named as the first to use sex to sell a commodity as well as the first to use women as sex objects. Therefore, Woodbury's campaign has a uniquely ignominious status within a genre widely charged with responsibility for the oppression of women.[28]

The Woodbury Soap campaign was not, in fact, the first advertising campaign to sell with sex. Nor was it the first to present women as sex objects. Trade cards in the nineteenth century pictured scantily clad or seductive-looking women. However, such cards were relatively rare because most consumer products even then were purchased by housewives, who were not thought likely to be swayed by sex appeal. This readership, concerned as they were with maintaining the appearance of mental chastity, would have been horrified by a reference to sex in an ad, no matter how indirect. Therefore, we can search the nineteenth-century women's magazines in vain for an ad using sex to sell. So, when Woodbury Soap hinted delicately at a woman's desire for physical affection, it *was* a first among advertisements running in the leading women's magazines; never before had the promise of sex been used to sell something *to women.* Sales of Woodbury Soap, sluggish since the 1890s, blew through the roof.[29]

The unprecedented impact of the Woodbury campaign foregrounded a reality with which America was still quite uncomfortable: that women, like men, were sexual beings. By playing upon her desire to be loved and touched, Woodbury speaks to the reader not as a sex object but as the *sexual subject.* The idea that a respectable woman would want to be touched by a man, even her own husband, was shocking to some in the early decades of the twentieth century. Historians today know that, despite the

Figure 6.1. This advertisement is typical of the early "sentimental" version of the Woodbury Soap campaign. *Ladies' Home Journal,* March 1915.

rhetoric, there actually did exist nice, educated, middle-class, married women who privately looked forward to sex with their husbands, even in the Victorian era.[30] So, the Woodbury Soap campaign touched on a desire that, although usually unacknowledged in public, was a powerful motivator for some readers of the "ladies'" press. The unique genius of the Woodbury campaign was the way it alluded to women's sexual desires without making the women look like whores. ("The Skin *He* Loves to Touch," for example, would have gone too far.)

The Woodbury campaign also debuted during a period when personal hygiene habits of Americans were under considerable pressure to change. Infrastructural limitations—such as the lack of plumbing and the price of soap—had kept most of America pretty dirty until 1900. In addition to the physical barriers to cleanliness, American attitudes toward bathing were still influenced by the peculiar heritage of the Puritans.[31]

Cultures throughout history have emphasized bathing, although their methods have varied greatly. In most cultures, washing is done in a highly ritualized manner, is considered as much a benefit to the spirit as to the body, and is highly social in purpose and often in practice. In early Christian times, both the Romans and the Hebrews valued bathing. Because the early Christians wished to distinguish themselves from both these groups, a tradition quickly developed against personal washing as an overly sensual act of self-indulgence. Except for a brief respite during the Crusades (when Muslim influences temporarily revived an interest in bathing), this attitude held through the Middle Ages in western Europe, policed rather strenuously by the Catholic church. In western Europe and Britain, a dirty body actually became a sign of piety.

In England, the Puritans eventually distinguished themselves from both Catholics and more liberal Protestants by their stand on bathing: from their point of view, it was flatly immoral. The Puritan immigrants to the New World, therefore, had perhaps the most negative attitude toward bathing in the history of humanity. Englishmen down the Atlantic seaboard drew from the same tradition, if with a lesser passion, and so they too had an aversion to bathing. Over the next two hundred years, Anglo-American attitudes changed little, and the lack of bathing technology provided no encouragement.

The American "cleanliness revolution," as it is sometimes called, was caused by concern over runaway disease in the cities that sprang up as a result of industrialization. However, the connection between personal cleanliness and the transmission of disease was not understood until 1900. The first city clean-up efforts focused mostly on garbage collection, installation of sewage systems, the removal of standing water, and the like. Once it was understood that dirty hands and faces were the friends of disease, reformers embarked on campaigns to encourage better washing habits, especially among children, immigrants, and the poor. These efforts involved an array of institutions, including government agencies, schools, churches, women's clubs, and magazines.

In 1900, substantial differences in the washing habits of Americans were discernable across subgroups. For instance, in 1890 the staff of *Vogue* felt it "absolutely necessary" for a human being "worthy of respect" to take at least two baths a day. In the same year Edward Bok devoted a *Ladies' Home Journal* editorial just to telling readers that respectable men should bathe at least once a day. But in small towns and rural areas, aggressive attempts were made to enforce compliance with much looser standards: Aurora, Illinois passed an ordinance requiring every resident to bathe at least once a week or be jailed. When Standard Manufacturing Company began promoting stationary bathtubs to the general public in 1890, their ads opened with the 36-point headline: "DO YOU BATHE?" As late as 1919, *McCall's* beauty columnist wrote:

> Whenever I think of bathing as a means to health or a means to beauty, I always remember a letter I had from a woman who was suffering from a body-skin affliction. I knew she subconsciously felt what her difficulty was, when she wrote:
>
> "Do not advise me to take a bath every day. I take a good, sensible one once a week." This statement worried me, because I felt there must be many such women going along on the assumption that one bath every week or so can take the place of the daily one. Too bad this young woman did not know that, in the future, there will be a great social gulf between those who bathe regularly and those who do not!

Any people whose skin was dark—Italian, eastern European, Hispanic, African American—were believed to be chronically dirty, regardless of their actual washing habits. Teaching personal hygiene therefore became an aggressive part of "Americanizing" newcomers. Immigrants understood quickly that cleanliness was required to win respect and "get ahead" in America. Because poor neighborhoods continued to be underserved in terms of water and plumbing, however, immigrants were often at a loss to act on the instructions given them by immigration authorities. Consequently, upward mobility among immigrant families was often manifest in their restless quest for better bathrooms.[32]

Facilities were limited at every level, however. At the turn of the twentieth century, only 25 percent of American homes had running water. Indeed, bathrooms did not become common in urban middle class homes until about 1920. Even then, bathtubs were available only in white, which fit nicely with the sanitation ideology that put them there and clearly communicated that the purpose was antiseptic, not sensual. But by the end of the decade, fully 30 percent of urban and 75 percent of rural American homes still did not have bathtubs.[33]

The cost and availability of soap was also a barrier. Therefore, the emergence of national marketers for inexpensive bar soap significantly changed the possibilities for cleanliness. In 1879 an unbranded soap made by Procter & Gamble was given a name, "Ivory," and a full-page advertising schedule in the leading monthly magazines was initiated. Sales quickly built to 30 million cakes a year. Over the next thirty years several soap manufacturers such as Resinol, Fairy Soap, Pearline, Sapolio, Packer's Tar, and Gold Dust, invested heavily in advertising. As sales and advertising increased, the quality of soap improved and its cost to consumers went down.[34]

Initially the new manufactured soaps were touted for household cleaning as well as personal use. Patent medicine men, however, offered soap for health needs, including facial afflictions. Dr. John Woodbury, a dermatologist, invented a line of ointments, soaps, and salves in the 1880s. The products were popular, but when suspicion of patent medicines began to hurt Woodbury's sales, he sold the rights to the Andrew Jergens Company. Jergens tried to rid Woodbury of its patent medicine image by launching a beauty campaign, but the effort failed to increase sales. The company turned over the Woodbury account to J. Walter Thompson's Cincinnati office in 1910, almost on a dare.[35]

JWT undertook an enormous research effort on soap, skin, and washing practices. It contacted a number of physicians and retained one of them as a consultant. Then the agency conducted a large door-to-door study among female consumers. A list was produced of the skin problems that most concerned women *and* could be positively affected by the use of the soap: excessive oiliness, sallowness, blackheads, blemishes (pimples), and conspicuous pores.

The agency found that face-washing practices still varied tremendously, so the campaign it developed was a series of small-size magazine ads that showed different skin problems and provided elaborate instructions for using the soap: using hot or cold water, steps of lathering, motions of application, and so on. This "treatment copy," as it was known within the agency, instructed a populace whose grooming practices were still being formed, by providing a set of ritual steps as characteristically accompanies bathing and washing. At the time the treatment houses in New York were just getting started, so the Woodbury strategy caught a new trend toward elaborate skin regimens. At twenty-five cents a bar, Woodbury was expensive compared to the mass-produced household soaps, but it was quite cheap compared to skin treatments offered by Arden and Rubinstein and similar in cost to traditional patent medicine soaps, such as Cuticura.

In May 1911 the "Skin You Love to Touch" campaign, which JWT called "the sentimental copy," appeared for the first time. Between 1911 and 1914 the sentimental copy went from fractional to full-page advertising, and the image began using the entire visual field. The amount of sentimental copy run by JWT increased, going from 30 percent to 60 percent of the ad schedule in three years. Between 1914, when the sentimental copy began to dominate the campaign, and 1921, Woodbury sales experienced a steep upward growth curve.

Woodbury Soap sales were down in 1922 for the first time in ten years. JWT quickly reemphasized the sentimental copy, but it seemed to have no impact. Promotions and "trade deals" were instituted, but nothing revived the brand. Sales continued to drop.

A number of changes had occurred in the marketing environment by this time. The discourse about sex had become more open, and the notion that women liked sex too was gaining more voice, even acceptance in some quarters. The flappers were pushing the culture's shock threshold with their own sexual aggressiveness, and the movies were taunting censors with nudity and kissing. Similar changes had occurred in the discourse of beauty advertising. By the early 1920s both *True Story* and *Photoplay* were booming. Agencies began to write ads especially for the audience of these magazines, adapting the provocative headlines and language of the romance confession. For a while advertisers produced separate ads for the middle-class magazines, but eventually many began using the "tabloid approach" for advertising across the board. Thus, "sex appeal" became more blatant, even in the dignified pages of the *Ladies' Home Journal.* The formerly shocking Woodbury campaign lost its edge of distinction and even came to look rather demure by comparison to surrounding material.[36]

Whether people believe that soap will help them attract romance or not, once all soaps make that promise, one soap cannot be selected over another on that basis. Consequently, people must make their decision based on other attributes, such as scent, color, wrapping, consistency, and price. In the case of Woodbury Soap, a consumer choosing on quality and price alone was likely to pick another brand. Household soaps had become cheaper and more plentiful. In the resulting competition, some manufacturers tried to differentiate their products for special uses and users by claiming complexion benefits. New toilet soaps such as Palmolive had also been introduced at prices similar to the household soaps. So Woodbury was now well above the going price for complexion soap. At the same time, inconsistent production had resulted in a number of consumer complaints about Woodbury Soap's quality. With poor quality control, an inflated price, and a romance campaign that was no longer distinctive, Woodbury seemed destined to spiral downward.

Jergens refused to consider cutting the price on Woodbury (or to see quality as serious problem). Unable to change the price, JWT decided to try increasing the soap's prestige. At this point, the Pond's Society endorsement campaigns had been in the field a year and the results were good. The agency could hardly borrow the Society testimonial idea wholesale from another client, however. So it came up with an idea built around a theme of prestigious institutions. Woodbury was said to be the preferred soap of the women who went to Vassar, summered at Newport, had their debuts in Philadelphia, stayed at the Ritz-Carlton, and the like. Nevertheless, sales continued their downward trend.

In 1923 Lever Brothers, another long-term JWT client, decided to introduce a cake form of Lux household soap flakes. Jergens graciously allowed JWT to run the marketing campaign for this beauty soap, even though it posed a direct competitive threat to Woodbury's.[37] The concept of "conflict of interest" had not yet developed in the advertising world, and both clients were convinced that having the same agency would actually protect their respective markets.

JWT's response to the problem of having competing soaps under its own roof was to try to target mutually exclusive audiences. By giving the two soaps different graphic looks, different messages, and different prices, the agency and their clients thought they could keep the products from competing with each other. The Lux toilet cake was introduced in 1925 for ten cents, with this advertising theme: "Here is a fine white soap made as the finest French Soaps, but costs you only 10 cents." There were no treatments, no cosmetics claims, and no references to romance. An Art Deco graphic look, still quite distinctive among advertisers in 1925, was used for both Lux Flakes and Lux Toilet Soap, while Woodbury was switched to drawings by John LaGatta, a popular artist of the decade whose style looked new, but not Deco.

For almost three years, Lux Toilet Soap was successfully sold as a ten-cent French-milled soap. However, Woodbury sales continued to drop. Jergens began to envy Lux's success. Agency and client still differed strongly on the causes for Woodbury's decline. Jergens felt that the advertising did not have enough focused, logical, product-based appeal and that the romance element should be reintroduced, only with a more obvious tone that the new "sophisticated" reader would respond to: "At the same time, of course, the atmosphere of refinement and good taste, which has always distinguished Woodbury advertising, must not be sacrificed in the process of giving it modernized expression."[38] By asking for a product-oriented, dignified, but provocative romance campaign, Jergens was essentially asking for the old campaign of the 1910s, but expecting it to have the same impact in 1929 that it had had in 1911. This was not going to happen. So JWT tried to move Jergens toward approaches that were working for other clients, such as Pond's. The "personality advertising" that JWT was doing on Pond's was not, in Jergens' opinion, an effective way to sell soap, however, and the soapmaker only became irritated by the agency's continued search to use a similar approach with Woodbury.

Once Jergens had rejected the "personality" approach for Woodbury, the agency felt free to use it on Lux. So, in 1928, a huge campaign for Lux appeared in newspapers from New York to Los Angles, announcing that nearly 100 percent of the Hollywood screen stars used Lux Soap. Each ad was crowded with pictures of actresses claiming to use Lux. Soon magazine ads appeared with testimonials by the stars as well as from a platoon of film directors, who claimed that only Lux could give a woman the kind of complexion that looked good in a close-up. The next year the campaign alluded to famous bath sequences by showing film actresses in sumptuous bathrooms.

Lux ads were not the first to use screen star testimonials, even in the cosmetic soap category. But the number of stars, the names of directors, the glamorous photographs, the fancy bathrooms, and the sheer impact of a huge media budget trumped every other actress endorsement campaign. By 1930 Lux was the largest-selling toilet soap in America, a position it maintained for three decades.

The Lux campaign broke with existing precepts about bathing as much as the 1911 Woodbury soap advertising had challenged ideas about women's sexuality. The actresses in the Lux ads included women known to be from a variety of ethnic backgrounds and to have a range of moral profiles—as opposed to previous actress advertising, which had tended to focus on more "respectable" actresses, such as Lillian Russell. The bathrooms point neither to ghetto hardship nor to the antiseptic ethic of the Anglo middle class. Instead, the dress, attitudes, and surroundings suggest the sensual and social antecedents of bathing in cultures with traditions markedly different from the Anglo-Protestant history of washing—and they evoke the luxurious bathroom scenes of the movies.

On November 5, 1929, Jergens put J. Walter Thompson on notice that failure to increase sales in 1930 would result in the agency being fired from Woodbury account. Sales did not increase in 1930. JWT lost the Woodbury Soap account after nineteen years of service and one of the most famous advertising campaigns in American history.

The stories of Woodbury and Lux pose a number of conundrums regarding feminism's attitude toward sex and sensuality, particularly in a commercial context. For instance, feminist criticism of advertising treats the implicit promise of romance as a manipulative strategy of unfailing power. But from this perspective, the change in the Woodbury campaign's effectiveness is inexplicable. If it worked once, an appeal to sensuality should have worked every time.

In contrast, according to conventional wisdom of the advertising business, novelty is the key to getting and keeping a consumer's attention. Using this rule of thumb, we would expect that, as Woodbury's distinctiveness disappeared, its power to persuade would have worn away. Furthermore, other ads that appeared, while they presented a notable new trend, would each have been less distinctive than Woodbury's had been in 1911 and, therefore, by definition less novel and interesting. After a while, sex appeal would likely lose its power precisely *because* of its increasingly commonplace appearance. Feminist theory notwithstanding, the efficacy of sex appeal would have had an inverse relationship to the number of ads that used it.

To fully understand why the Woodbury campaign lost its power, we have to look at such factors as price and product quality, as well as some that seem rather far afield, such as the historical moment in bathing. To interpret and evaluate a single ad correctly, we must place it into a particular discourse of ads at a specific point in time. The norm in feminist criticism, in contrast, is to take one or two isolated, unrelated ads and build an entire theory around an interpretation of the selected texts alone. These interpretations consistently imply a theory of "how ads work" that relies on sexual imagery or subliminal manipulation, but never on an understanding of the practical and discursive influences that actually form any one of these texts. Such theories further imply that consumer response is automatic and certain, but in fact the Woodbury case demonstrates the reality that advertising, like any other form of rhetoric, is limited in its ability to motivate behavior.

Critics also argue that advertising enforces the dominant class standard of beauty, behavior, and morality. Yet J. Walter Thompson's attempt to differentiate between Lux and Woodbury led the agency to make use of the ongoing social competition between clearly identifiable subgroups of women, one dominant and the other emergent. JWT's hope of success depended up the audience being able and willing to comprehend *competing* standards of beauty. Therefore, it was in the interest of the advertisers in this case, as in many others to come, to create and support more than one ideal. The Woodbury/Lux case illustrates that the advertising industry actually depends, to a large degree, upon cultural heterogeneity as the basis for differentiating otherwise homogeneous products.

When it comes to the advertising of consumer goods, the feminist consensus also insists that products are inappropriately imbued with "social values," causing us to consume them for "irrational" reasons, such as the desire for affection or status. So as long as we consume soap and toothpaste to keep free of germs and cavities, it seems, we are "rational" consumers, buying and using things for the "right" reasons. But the right reasons are no less socially defined and politically motivated than the wrong ones. As we have seen, the "basic" grooming practices we take for granted are recently introduced, reflections of the grooming aesthetic of the former aristocracy, and the result of concerted political effort to achieve compliance. Even the assumption that it is OK to bathe for sanitary reasons, but not sensual or social ones, is an artifact of our ascetic Christian heritage and a recent past filled with plagues.

## THE POLITICS OF PURITY

Feminist criticism today consistently interprets an ad (or a film or a fashion) until it can be shown to be a temptation aimed at the male gaze—and then the critics stops. The implication is that if a dress, a picture, or a hairstyle is sexy, it is ipso facto oppressive. Underpinning this kind of writing is the assumption that "respectable women" do not have legitimate sexual desires of their own—that sex is something done *to* them. Here we see the lingering influence of the social purity activists, just as surely as we can see it in the failure of the Old Feminists to engage with the birth control issue. Indeed, Ellen DuBois and Linda Gordon, writing against the grain of late-twentieth-century feminism, observed: "Today, there seems to be a revival of social purity politics within feminism, and it is concern about this tendency to focus almost exclusively on sex as the primary area of women's exploitation, and to attribute women's sexual victimization to some violent essence labeled 'male sexuality' is even more conservative today because our situation as women has changed so radically."[38]

The mistrust of material pleasure and the denigration of popular art forms, too, are evident as vestiges of Anglo-Protestant ideology in today's feminist critique of consumer culture—just as they are easily seen in the moralists' reaction to the sensuality of the Jazz Age. Like other ascetic movements in history, the Anglo-Puritan wing of American feminism has forbidden a variety of worldly pleasures, including theater, amusement parks, dancing, and popular songs, as well as fashion and liquor, lumping them all into a category of "immorality." Their judgments, however, are nearly always applied selectively, showing a persistent prejudice that condemns the preferences of the masses in favor of the cultural materials associated with educated elites.

The class prejudices that infused asceticism with urgency and vigor in the 1920s are equally present in the discourse today, though we may deny it. Furthermore, the continuing habit of valuing the professions and achievements that require access to advanced education (those vocations in which a woman works with her mind) over those based on other, less status-dependent gifts (those careers built on the abilities of the body) is also profoundly grounded in centuries of class discrimination. The unthinking privileging of the "heroine of the mind" over the "heroine of the body" so typical of today's feminist discourse is just another manifestation of the insidious cultural categories that separate humans based on the advantages of birth.

Ironically, most feminists writing in the past thirty years would assert an allegiance to Marxism as evidence of their concern with class inequities. Yet they persist in rewriting history and formulating theory in a way that shores up long-standing aristocratic imperatives. Rather than rethink the Victorians' assumptions, some seem determined to rehabilitate the censorious activities of the Old Feminists and their forebears, while also ignoring their relationship to capital. Their antipathy toward romance is remarkable in its blindness to the class implications of this ethic for kinship. Views characteristic of Emma Goldman, Margaret Sanger, Crystal Eastman, Ethel Puffer Howes, and their colleagues on sex, family, beauty, and art are dismissed as "conservative," thus robbing the movement of a far more legitimately "radical" tradition and a much more genuinely class-sensitive outlook.

The strain to give credit to an outmoded view of sex and pleasure also costs us the legacy of the New Girls of the Roaring Twenties. Although feminist historians often argue that freedom of dress and freedom from the double standard were important goals for the women's movement, the flappers' considerable accomplishments in these areas are dismissed as "illusory" or worse.[40]

Today's "New Girls"—Rene Denfeld, Katie Roiphe, and even Naomi Wolf, among others—contest the morality of their generation's "Old Feminists" by emphasizing their own sexuality. The Old Feminists of the postmodern era rail against these New Girls, charging "antifeminism"—or dismiss the challengers' ideas as the naïve illusions of a new generation of Cinderellas. The echo from down the decades is deafening.

Through these arguments, made in many venues, a continuing maternalism gives "women of education and refinement" license to tell "the less intelligent girls" how they can dress, what they can read, what they can see, and how they should behave to avoid a fate worse than death: becoming sexually involved with a man (e.g., a sex object). So, although the majority of young working girls made it out of the kitchen long ago, they still must endure a lot of self-interested mothering and jealous sisterhood from those who pretend to be their superiors.

## CHAPTER 7

# RETHINKING NECESSITIES

CHARLES REVSON STARTED HIS BUSINESS IN THE WORST YEAR OF THE GREAT DEPRESSION, 1931. He and his brother, sons of immigrant Russian Jews, had only $300 in capital and a few square feet in a cousin's lamp factory in which to work. Their single product, a brightly colored opaque fingernail polish, was a novelty compared to the slightly tinted polishes then on the market. The Revsons had no money for advertising, and their only means of distribution was to persuade local manicurists to use the new polish on their customers. Charles himself peddled the product from one beauty parlor to another, while his brother filled bottles and applied labels by hand.

Nail polish had no utility, strictly speaking, and the Revson brothers had no access to modern marketing methods that "manipulate" women into buying things they don't need by "dictating" to them how they should look. The Depression put severe limits on disposable income at all class levels. By conventional reckoning, therefore, their product should have been a flop. Instead, Revson's nail polish was an immediate success. The new company, called Revlon, had $11,246 in sales the first year and $68,000 in sales the second year. At the end of the decade, sales were $1 million. By the time Charles Revson died in 1975, Revlon annual sales were $606 million and the company, which *Forbes* called "the General Motors of cosmetics," had become the largest U.S. over-the-counter cosmetics manufacturer.[1]

The 1930s were, in fact, an important period of growth in the history of the American cosmetics industry. After a brief but precipitous decline in the first years of the Depression, cosmetics sales held firm and then regained enough growth to support several entrants—Dorothy Gray, Germaine Monteil, Revlon, Charles of the Ritz, and Almay—and to expand existing corporations—Elizabeth Arden, Helena Rubinstein, Max Factor, and Maybelline. The growth in cosmetics was fueled by the remarkably rapid diffusion of full-blown face painting—not only reddened lips and cheeks, but elaborately colored eyes as an accepted practice among diverse groups of women. Other fashions that seemed to flaunt frivolity in the face of economic crisis appeared with puzzling frequency; fake jewelry with huge stones and gilt settings was wildly popular and a fad for collecting tiny charms in a multitude of shapes swept the country.[2]

Given the economic values most of us have been taught, we can only look for the dysfunctions that caused such unreasonable consumer behavior in a time of great material scarcity. Because our notions of rational economic activity would have predicted a decline in purchasing unnecessary goods such as hand lotion and manicure sets, never mind frivolous charm bracelets and colored nail polish, we must explain the fads of the Depression era by some widespread moral failure, or an unwelcome intervention, or a patriarchal conspiracy. When we advance such sinister explanations, however, we treat constant patterns in human behavior as aberrations and cast aspersion on time-tested survival strategies.

People need novelty, pleasure, and play to stay healthy and sane. When their survival is threatened, humans must maintain social conventions and expressions that shore up their dignity, or else fall into despair. In a time of widespread hardship, we should be heartened, not dismayed, to see evidence that playful, pleasurable, imaginative impulses are being expressed in modest ways—such as brightly colored fingernails—and that basic social standards—such as keeping a neat appearance—are being maintained. Indeed, the absence of play and the abandonment of social grooming standards among any subgroup should be cause for concern.

Disapproval of such "irrational" economic behavior further presupposes a consensus on what are considered to be necessary—and therefore "rational"—acts of consumption. As we have seen, American ideas about grooming and dress were forged amid the conflict of specific subcultural beliefs, a fluid social order, and major changes in technology. Some of the practices we now take to be natural, such as the daily bath, actually are recent innovations that appeared and spread in the context of democratization, industrialization, urbanization, and even plague. In the Depression, therefore, a nation with newly adopted "necessities" was suddenly confronted with the need to trim consumption down to the bare bones. Instead of condemning their purchase choices, we might instead consider their decisions as instructive examples from which we can learn what people really do need.

## THE TYRANNY OF NECESSITY

The impact of the Depression was quick and visible. The government shifted into a public relief mode that was unparalleled in American history. Social worker Louise Armstrong, for instance, was hired to administer the Emergency Relief program in a northern Michigan county. Her instructions were unequivocal: She must first gain the trust of the people to be helped and, from there: "No suffering must occur in this county which we could possibly prevent. No tragedies must happen which we could possibly forestall."[3]

Winning the trust of the poor turned out to be less difficult than gaining the confidence of those who still had jobs or investments. As long as the national effort lasted, citizens who had escaped the impoverishment that befell their neighbors charged that "chiselers" were "living in sinful luxury" on relief. Program managers were pressured to maintain records proving that the people they helped were truly in need, were not spending their grants on luxuries, and were generally deserving of help. Before granting aid, therefore, caseworkers visited applicants' homes, painstakingly cataloging their worldly goods, listing their unfilled needs, and assessing their prospects. Some case workers resented the position social selfishness put them in, but others took their "police work" quite seriously and treated their cases like criminals. In this way, the government, despite good intentions, often became a tyrant in the lives of the poor as well as a source of aid.

Although strict guidelines were drawn up for each relief unit, in many ambiguous situations relief workers struggled with the power of small particulars to bring big benefits to the despairing people under their care. A New York social worker recalled a family where the father was ill, the daughter was mentally handicapped, and the son's biggest source of pride was that he owned a toothbrush. The mother, wrote the manager, was the real relief worker because of her purposeful, though often "frivolous," use of aid to shore up the dignity of her fragile family: "Her mother confessed to me that she used some of the food budget to get this little girl a permanent. She was scared to death I was gonna scold her. But that was one of the things that helped this girl out of her condition. She found a job."[4]

Not only were Depression caseworkers reluctant to approve "luxury" expenditures, they also were concerned to assist only those who were not "chiselers." So they frequently "sized up" applicants by their appearance. As one labor organizer warned: "Try to get into the Y.W. without any money or looking down at the heel. Charities take care of very few and only those that are called 'deserving.' The lone girl is under suspicion by the virgin women who dispense charity." Anyone requesting aid had to strike a balance between appearing to *need* help and looking creditable enough to *deserve* it. One caseworker recalled: "In many cases, we tried to pick the nicer of the deprived and avoid the less-nice. We had absolutely no insight.'" A certain level of grooming was required for a person to be "deserving," including regular baths, clean teeth, trimmed hair, and manicured nails. Without these, a female was unlikely to get help, because her unkempt appearance was read as a warning sign that she might be a prostitute.[5]

As Scarlett O'Hara learned when she appealed to Rhett Butler for help in *Gone With the Wind,* the best-selling novel of the 1930s, the illusion of respectability must be consistent right down to the fingertips. Manicuring, however, was a new habit to most Americans in 1930. At the opening of the 1920s, only 25 percent of American women did anything to take care of their nails. By the time the Depression struck, however, the proportion had been reversed: 75 percent of American women manicured their nails and only 25 percent did not.[6]

The manicure preparation market was completely dominated by Northam Warren and his line of products called Cutex. The advertising was handled by Helen Resor's team at J. Walter Thompson, who began by researching the current habits of American consumers. Working-class and farm women, they concluded, were not an appropriate audience: "The market to be obtained for Cutex was limited to people above a certain standard of living, under which people simply could not take care of their nails." Instead, they decided to appeal to middle-class women who were already concerned with grooming as a requirement of respectablity.

The 1917 ad campaign sold the Cutex system of products by explaining hand hygiene in detail. Northam Warren himself orchestrated a huge program among health education classes in schools across the country, bringing the "necessity" for keeping nails clean and trimmed into public consciousness. By 1925 nearly everyone—male and female—was expected to be manicured. The regular manicure, like the daily bath, had become one of the minimal requirements for a socially acceptable appearance. Even the dispossessed were to avoid unclean nails if they wanted to appear "deserving."

Not only might a poor personal appearance jeopardize one's chances of receiving government aid, it could scare away the assistance of average citizens. Ophelia Tatham, eleven years old when her family drove to California looking for work in 1934, vividly remembered worrying, when their Chevy broke down, that passersby, thinking they weren't "decent people," would not stop to help: "She felt ashamed. . . . They'd always had furniture and clean clothes. Her mother had sent them to school dressed beautifully. . . . Sitting on the highway, now, Ophelia wondered how people would know that."[7]

Self-presentation also affected employability. Women without jobs shared clothes and grooming resources in order to help each other maintain the appearance required to get work. When these arrangements fell through, homeless women tried to be prepared to present a respectable appearance. Female hobos packed skirts and stockings in their bindles while wearing men's clothing to travel. The bindles kept "good clothes" protected for interviews or visits home. With so much riding on personal appearance, the first relief or employment check a person received often went to grooming and dress.[8]

Maintaining grooming practices was thus central to survival. Consider the American Woman's Association study of the Depression experiences of 180 professional women. Their primary finding was that sociability was the determining factor in the strategies of those who found new employment versus those who were pulled under. By staying "in circulation," survivors not only kept up their spirits, they heard jobs discussed, made important contacts, got the right introductions—thus gaining through sociability renewed economic viability. Staying socially active necessarily meant continuing to dress and groom rather than succumbing to despair and losing concern with one's appearance.[9]

Failure to show concern for grooming is one of the telltale signs of true despair. At that point, reasoning ability also fails, disorganization takes over, lethargy sets in, and sociability disappears into a desire to withdraw—all making the hopeless person less capable of saving herself. Once she succumbs to hopelessness, others are less likely to offer aid because paupers appear to be "beyond help." Maintaining one's own appearance expresses the will to survive and, at the same time, raises the chances of survival.[10]

The imperative to maintain grooming even under the worst circumstances is testimony to the principle outlined by Adam Smith that the most basic needs are not "biological" but involve those goods, *whatever they may be,* that allow a person to be seen as "creditable" in the eyes of the community. As sociologist Michael Schudson points out: "Human needs are for inclusion as well as for survival, for meaning as well as for existence. For purposes of social analysis, the notion that there are basic biological needs that can be separated from artificial and created social needs does not make good sense. All needs are socially constructed in all human societies. What people require are the elements to live a social life, the elements to be a person."[11]

## ECONOMICS AND THE SOCIAL FABRIC

Mapping the pattern of exchanges to identify social relationships has been standard practice in anthropology since Marcel Mauss analyzed the economy of the Trobriand Islands in *The Gift.* These islanders, who made their living by trade, exchanged sacred pieces of jewelry, which functioned both as ritual adjuncts and as a proto-currency, in geographic circles. Necklaces went to neighbors to the west, bracelets, to the opposite direction. Secular goods followed the sacred exchanges, creating a predictable series of trading circles east to west and west to east: "these precious things and objects for use, these types of food and festivals, these services rendered of all kinds, ritual and sexual, these men and women, were caught up in a circle, following around this circle a regular movement in time and space." Transactions were conducted on credit (a promise in the context of trade), and so related exchanges were separated in time. The first anthropologist to study the Trobriand islanders believed that the goods exchanged were gifts, but Mauss demonstrated that all the transactions were part of a system of exchange in which every party was obligated to others for past and future trades, but in which self-interest was a key factor. Therefore, no exchange was really a "free gift." Nevertheless, this network of extended transactions, typical of nonmonetized societies, is still conventionally known as a gift system.[12]

Similar trading systems had occurred in preindustrial America. Farmers in Kentucky traded agricultural and homemade goods for manufactures imported from Baltimore by local dry goods merchants. Sellers usually were paid once or twice a year, usually in some form of produce. Merchants would ship the produce downriver to New Orleans, where it would be traded again, this time for sugar, cotton, or indigo. Merchants would ship these items around Florida to the Atlantic seaboard, then trade them for manufactured wares, imported and domestic. The manufactures would move overland to frontier dry goods sellers, who would trade them for the produce of local farmers—and the whole circle would begin again. Potential profit existed at each point of trade. Because specie was scarce, exchanges were repaid, after a delay, in kind. Within each local economy, thousands of smaller transactions were conducted on a similar basis: one item exchanged for another, then used to repay an obligation from the past. All transactions were thus interwoven with promises, favors, affections, and the mediation of relationships.[13]

Because our exchanges today are usually accomplished through a medium (money), the social relationships among buyers, sellers, and distributors are more obscure than they would otherwise be. Cosmetics seem to appear in stores as if by magic. Yet modern market distribution is also put together, point by point, as an elaborate web of mutual obligation and self-interest. The two distribution systems that were initially devised by Charles Revson and his competitor, Northam Warren, are good illustrations. Although these two systems ran in a parallel fashion, they are both marked by the centrality of interpersonal indebtedness.

Warren himself initially sold manicure products person-to-person. Between 1913, when he invented Cutex Cuticle Remover, and the mid-1920s, when manicuring had become a "necessity" and Cutex dominated the market, Warren expanded his personal selling system into a national distribution network. This was accomplished through a system of "gift" exchanges, one going in the direction of consumers and the other going toward distribution middlemen, known as jobbers. Consumer advertising offered a sample set for a token price of three cents. These offers proved extremely popular: One ad in the *Ladies' Home Journal* brought over 8,000 requests. After using up the sample set, 80 percent of coupon respondents purchased the regular set. So, a substantial number of consumers subsequently went to stores looking for Cutex.

In response to consumer requests, local tradesmen contacted Northam Warren to buy stock. The order slip they filled out read: "Please send me *through my jobber* the following items" (italics mine). The wording of the slip thus automatically created an exchange relationship between the retailer and the regional jobber. Because jobbers were provided the regular sets at a 15 percent discount, they accrued a profit on any filled order. This policy built the distributors' business as quickly as Cutex grew, spreading the wealth Warren created throughout the system, resulting in considerable loyalty to that line of products. The combination of "gifts" to consumers, "gifts" to retailers, and enforced trading obligations put Cutex in drug, discount, and department stores across the United States by 1920.

The Northam Warren brand was so dominant that retailers often kept competitive manicure preparations out of sight, so customers looking for another brand often had to ask for it. In department stores, Cutex actually employed the sales clerks for manicure products. Indeed, the leading manufacturers of all types of cosmetics commonly employed clerks at the point of purchase. Sometimes the clerks were paid directly and in full by the manufacturer; other times a combination of gifts, rebates, and discounts was added to their regular salary. In all cases, something was paid for selling the preferred brand but not for selling competitors' products. This arrangement cut department store labor costs, which in turn increased the stores' loyalty to the leading manufacturer in each category. Furthermore, clerks paid by manufacturers often cooperated informally with each other; for example, the saleswoman for Pond's would sell Cutex when manicure products were requested, and the Cutex saleswoman would reciprocate by selling Pond's to face cream customers. At the retail level, therefore, a complex interlocking system of payments, gifts, shared obligations, informal cooperation, and understood reciprocity made the distribution system for Cutex practically impenetrable.

This system was maintained by visitors from both Northam Warren and J. Walter Thompson. The staff at JWT toured the country regularly, talking to druggists and department store managers, interviewing sales clerks, and just generally keeping themselves informed about the market at the local level while making the people in the distribution chain feel integral to the operation. Direct contact with the public taught the agency how customers felt about the products, what the complaints were, and whether there were any competitors to be watched.

Revlon first achieved distribution through the one area of the cosmetics business in which Cutex was weak: the beauty salons. Warren had not attempted to cultivate beauty shops and, perhaps as a result, manicurists were prejudiced against Cutex. By playing directly and exclusively to this market, Charles Revson took advantage of Warren's oversight. Revson regularly visited each of his contacts in salons, talking with them about their tools and their customers' tastes. Revson was so zealous that he himself wore nail polish, a different shade on each nail, so that he could show his customers the colors. Until Revson came along, a manicurist bought supplies at retail just like any other consumer. With Revlon, however, both shop and manicurist got their cut, just as distributors of Cutex shared profit with Northam Warren. Manicurists benefited when they sold customers the polish, so it was in their interest to sell Revlon, just as it was in the department store clerk's interest to sell Cutex.

By distributing his products through beauty salons, Revson tapped into one of the few areas of the economy that was healthy and growing throughout the Depression.

Hair care had grown to be an important beauty service right alongside skin care: in fact, Elizabeth Arden shared her first commercial space with two sisters, Clara and Jessica Ogilvie, whose names also became household words in American culture. Between 1920 and 1930, the number of beauty salons had grown exponentially, employing thousands of women and making some rich.[14]

Salon growth during the 1930s overshadowed even those gains. The Depression-era surge in business is largely attributable to the introduction of products, including Revson's, that were made available only in salons. For instance, Gerald Gidwitz and Louis Stein simplified the permanent wave process with their "machineless" waving pads, increasing the popularity of these treatments significantly, but they made it available only to hairdressers. In 1937 their company, Helene Curtis, introduced Suave Hairdressing, which salon customers liked so well that the company allowed shops to sell small bottles at retail (with a margin, of course). Also during the 1930s, Lawrence Gelb introduced Clairol hair coloring products, which made hair coloring much safer, cheaper, and more predictable. The Clairol products surpassed the flat, painted look of previous hair dyes and offered a wider range of colors—but they were sold only to salon owners.

The woman who became Revson's archcompetitor, Estée Lauder, also started selling through salons during the Depression: "With each sale, I'd give the ladies a tiny sample of something they hadn't tried, to take home—maybe I'd shave off the tip of a lipstick, put a few teaspoonfuls of powder in an envelope. It was my secret weapon. Once I could get them to try something, they'd be back next week to buy it." The Lauder "gift with purchase" became one of the cosmetics industry's most common selling tools. To this day, the Estée Lauder gift promotions are big retail events.

Like Revson, Lauder, Gelb, Gidwitz, and Stein all were poor Jews who had immigrated themselves or were the children of immigrants—thus none of them, even the males, can be said to have been part of the existing power structure. All established their foothold in the beauty business through the salons, and all of them emphasized personal contact in their selling and training.[15]

An equally important factor was the beauty salon's evolving role in community life. By 1930 the local beauty parlor had become the women's equivalent of the men's club: the place women went to be with each other. Beauty shops appeared at every level: small towns, big cities; black neighborhoods, white neighborhoods; rich areas, poor areas. Local women opened beauty salons as a way of making money from their own cosmetic skills. In most cases, beauty salon customers were drawn by word of mouth (just as they are today), and so the clientele was likely to be local in orientation and already affiliated with each other as neighbors, friends, relatives, and coworkers. Most services had to be repeated regularly, so the same group of women would show up at the same time on the same day, week after week. Shirley Abbott recalls the beauty salon in the hometown of her youth: "The neighborhood beauty shop is one of the foundations of society in small Southern towns. You go there to get your hair 'fixed,' but that isn't the real reason, any more than men congregate at the county courthouse to transact legal business. . . . It was an all-female society—no man would dare enter the place—and here, if nowhere else, women said what they thought about men. And what they thought was often fairly murderous. . . . They would gossip, of course. Every teen-age romance or impending marriage, separation, illness, operation, or death got its going-over."[16] Participating in the social occasion of going to the beauty parlor, therefore, was as important a reason for going as getting your nails done or your hair set.

A manicure provided another important mode of social contact: touch. Getting a manicure is one of those acceptable ways of being touched by someone who is not necessarily an intimate. Primates of all sorts will sit for long periods of time grooming each other, apparently enjoying both the company and the contact. People in preindustrial societies do the same kind of thing. Even in the dirty history of premodern Europe, people who never considered taking a bath would sit for hours having the lice picked off them while at the same time picking vermin off others. In such instances grooming is a concrete collective experience, one that would be impossible to divorce from the social realm.[17]

So, if forced to give up the salon for "necessities," these ladies would have lost a lot more than colored fingernails. They would have been robbed of a central meeting place, a grooming ritual, a social occasion, a tap into the community network, a time for touching, and lots of small physical pleasures. They would not have given it up easily. Even when money was scarce, the weekly trip to the salon may have been the last "luxury" to go.

The actual delivery of a Revlon manicure was an economic interaction between two women that was meaningfully grounded in community life. The economics of the salon was, in turn, dependent on a regression of social experiences, such as local gossip and visits from national sales reps. In each gesture of exchange, from filling the bottle at the factory to painting a finger, relationships and obligations were forged and reinforced. Thus, in many ways, the lacquered fingernail represented an opportunity for inclusion. In the end, the beauty parlor as a cultural institution cannot be distinguished as *either* social *or* economic, but is irreducibly *both.*

Economic subsystems such those that distributed Revlon and Cutex can be imagined as a system of circles like those of the Trobriand Islands, in which women exchanged products—nail polish—and services—manicures. In the process of ordinary exchange, an enormous variety of human needs were met: Jobs were created and salaries paid, while satisfying the group's hunger for beauty, desire to be touched, requirements for dignity, and so on. If we think of the American economy as a composite of many circles of exchange—of food, of medical services, of natural resources—we can view the Depression as a time when several of those circular systems failed, slowed, or stopped. One circle that kept going distributed cosmetics among women. That particular subsystem kept women employed—so that women, as a group of *workers,* benefited from the way women, as a group of *consumers,* spent money.

Over the course of the decade, women actually improved their job status, a substantial percentage moving from domestic service and factory work to proprietorships, management jobs, white-collar work, and service employment. Some scholars believe that women survived better because many of these positions were stereotypical jobs—such as cosmetic services—that men didn't want and wouldn't do. Within the protection of the beauty economy, women as a class were better able to get through the Depression.[18]

## MARKS FOR WOMEN

The beauty parlor's rituals and objects merged with other practices that signified inclusion in the circles of womanhood. Just as rites of initiation in other cultures often are made visible by a change in appearance—wearing a veil, shaving the head, tattooing the face—a tube of lipstick or a vial of nail polish given to a young girl became a signal that her coming adulthood was recognized. Moments of inclusion occurred gradually, across many small rituals rather than in one initiation ceremony, so subtle variations in age were readable: A teenager might have a permanent, for example, but was unlikely to have dyed hair or wear dark lipstick because her mother (and the "mothers" of the community) would not allow it.

From the salons of Fifth Avenue to the back-porch parlors of the deep South, grooming rituals figured prominently in mother-daughter relationships. Shirley Abbott's memories reveal the contradictory impact of the mother's association with grooming: "She was an excellent mother. Oh, how tired I got sometimes of her excellence, the cleanliness, the godliness, the puffed sleeves, the hundred strokes of the brush on my hair."[19] Grooming and dress often are practices where mother and daughter are joined, but a persistent conflict attends the daughter's need to differentiate herself. This tension nearly always involves a presentation of sexuality that diverges substantially from the asexual appearance the mother prefers for her child. Such ambivalence is evident, I believe, in the responses of many women to feminist directives about dress. Some don't want to be cheated out of their birthright to the beauty parlor (and all its secret pleasures). Others don't want to be told how they must dress (chastely) and wear their hair (simply) by a bunch of women who are not their mothers (but who seem to think they are).

Differences in ethnic, geographic, and economic subgroups also were expressed in these rites. Feminist and African American scholar bell hook's memory of the hair treatments of her girlhood echoes practices that have taken place in black women's kitchens since the time of Madame Walker: "For each of us, getting our hair pressed is an important ritual. It is not a sign of our longing to be white. It is not a sign of our quest to be beautiful. We are girls. It is a sign of our desire to be women."[20]

Grooming was a sign of membership, but it also could be used to express rejection of the home community and affiliation with outsiders. For instance, Shirley Abbott's mother, having been raised on a farm in Arkansas under conditions that were both poor and primitive, rebelled against her rural origins. Farm women in Velma Abbott's time had drastically different grooming practices from their sisters in the cities and a dismissive attitude toward the new ways. Questions about Cutex in rural areas "brought forth sardonic laughs; the women in these districts were even a little bitter at the idea that anyone should think a farmer's wife could take care of her hands, or that there was any use in trying to." But Velma, though she was a no-nonsense, hard-working woman, did adopt cosmetics: "Her generation was the first in the farming South to look toward town, to break the terrible old rule of utter self-sufficiency, to dare to cross the bridge into civilization. She and her sister were the first of their line to buy ready-made dresses or hear a radio or have electric lights or drive an automobile." Velma's use of makeup, therefore, was a purposeful step *outside* the line that defined conventional behavior for her own subgroup.[21]

As women like Velma Abbott adopted cosmetics, the practice of face painting, along with the use of colored nail polish and related products, spread quickly, reaching a substantial portion of the population within about five years (1930 to 1935). As adoption diffused through the population, the vividness and variation of color also steadily increased. The cosmetics industry grew largely because of the sudden spurt of sales in lipstick, rouge, eye shadow, mascara, eyebrow pencil, nail polish, and hair dye, all of which seem to have been part of a trend toward an intensely color-oriented aesthetic.

The rapid diffusion of full-face painting contrasts sharply with the acceptance of powder and rouge, which had been much more gradual, probably due to their "immoral" connotations. Few "respectable women" used any form of makeup in 1850; however, ads for facial powder were common even in the most conservative ladies' magazines by 1890. Ads for skin care products began to allude obliquely (in the fine print) to the availability of rouge during the 1910s. Some companies such as Rigaud, also offered lip "pomades" between 1910 and 1920, but it is difficult to tell how much color they had, if any. Lipstick advertising became prominent only in the late 1920s. By the mid-1930s, however, rouge and lipstick no longer had any connotation of immorality. In fact, it was considered "indiscreet" *not* to use powder.[22]

The high-fashion magazines and the working-girl magazines both tracked noticeably ahead of the women's service magazines on the makeup trend. For example, *Vogue* conceded as early as 1912 that "a little discreet paint would enhance a lady's appearance." The occasional ad for "lash growers"—which one suspects to be mascara—began to appear in *Vogue* in 1910. The first mascara marketed for everyday use, Maybelline, was invented in 1915. T. L. Williams created it after watching his sister, Maybell, apply Vaseline to her lashes to emphasize them. He began selling the mascara by mail in 1917; soon after his ads began to appear in *True Story* and *Photoplay.* At that time, mascara ads could not run in the *Ladies' Home Journal;* under the editorship of Edward Bok, it did not accept advertising for such "immoral" products. Mascara use really took off in late 1932, when Maybelline achieved distribution in the five-and-ten cent stores patronized by working girls. Soon eye shadow came into general use, as did eyebrow pencil. By mid-decade, eyes were as important to face-painting as lips and cheeks. Even Yardley, the most status-conscious and Anglophilic of cosmetic advertisers, was offering lipstick, cream rouge, and eye shadow by 1938.[23]

The last time makeup had been in style in the United States was just before the American Revolution, when painting the face white and coloring the lips red was the right of aristocrats of both sexes. The use of makeup receded among the American aristocracy in the early 1800s, but makeup usage did not cease completely. Instead, in the breakdown of the sumptuary customs, the usage pattern flipflopped, face painting now finding acceptance among the lowest classes. Thus, those who continued to use makeup were "disreputable"—common folk. The shifting of a self-adornment practice from the upper class to the lower classes, accompanied by the rapid abandonment of the same practice by the upper class, is a common human pattern, regardless of the particular habit in question. As lower classes pick up a fashion from the upper classes, the stratification markers must be revised quickly, in order to maintain the distinctions.

Why, after over a hundred years of dormancy, would face painting reemerge and spread in such a short period of time? And why these particular products and colors, applied in this particular way? Speculation about the "meaning" of lipstick and other colored cosmetics appears frequently in the feminist and popular press today. Most turn to a sexual explanation. Some say that emphasizing lips and cheeks with red paint creates a visual analog to the vagina and so mirrors the ape behavior of "presenting" the reproductive organs. However, if the use of red pigment were based in social biology, we would expect this practice of reddening the lips from all human females. But body and face painting, although quite prevalent among humans, takes a variety of forms, colors, and patterns.[24]

Some claim that reddening the lips and cheeks derives from the Egyptians, who used rouge to imitate the natural flushing of cheeks and lips at times of sexual arousal. However, the Egyptians, although they did redden their cheeks and lips, focused their attention on the eyes, painting them green, black, and gold. It is rare for human eyelids to turn gilded green under conditions of sexual arousal—or under any other circumstances, for that matter.

Furthermore, between ourselves and ancient Egypt lie long periods in which no reddening was done, in which people used no makeup at all, and in which the aesthetic focus of the face was elsewhere—the shaved eyebrows of the Renaissance, for example. Between ourselves and the Egyptians also come the blue-painted Picts, who are closer to many Americans in ethnicity as well as in time and space. The peoples who were native to North America nearly all painted themselves, but none reddened their cheeks and lips as Europeans did. In the colonial period, the taste for red lips and cheeks came and went, as did fashions for mouches and wigs. Twentieth-century lipstick use came into fashion after more than a hundred years of being quite unacceptable, so the example of the Egyptians explains nothing about its sudden reemergence. Neither the social biology nor the Egyptian explanation can tell us why twentieth-century women would suddenly begin to paint their *entire faces.*

Actresses continued to wear rouge and lipstick throughout the 1800s, both on and off stage. They also, as a matter of professional practice, darkened their lashes and brows, shaded their eyelids, and changed the color of their complexions with theatrical makeup. Therefore, the basic techniques used by actresses on the stage were the same as those that diffused through the rest of the population during the Depression, a similarity that is of striking consequence. There is no particular reason why the makeup of the western stage should have come to look the way it did—Kabuki actors, for example, followed an entirely different system, and the Greeks wore masks. Yet there is also no particular reason why the face painting of the average American woman should have taken the form it did—as noted, face painting occurs many places, but its exact form is quite variable. The connection here between professional use and its popular adoption is distinctive and, therefore, probably meaningful.

Before the entry of Maybelline and similar companies, mascara, pancake makeup, and other color greasepaints were available only as stage makeup. And, although there were recipes for lipsticks and rouges in the beauty books of the nineteenth century, none could be purchased already prepared except from theatrical supply sources. These theatrical supplies continued to be used in the early silent pictures. However, the lip colors were unsatisfactory because they photographed black. A Russian immigrant named Max Factor solved this problem, by developing red lipsticks that looked softer on film. Factor applied the lipstick to many film stars, developing a signature application that involved putting two "thumbprints" on the top lip and one on the bottom, leaving the edges of both lips "white." This method created the "beestung" look that became the characteristic fashion of the 1920s, after Max Factor's products were made available to the public. Clara Bow drew her upper lip somewhat differently, inventing the often-imitated "cupid's bow." Joan Crawford, shifting from her 1920s flapper persona to the "strong woman" persona for which she became famous in the 1930s, drew the color out to the corners of her lips, a technique that many soon followed.[25]

As we have already seen, the trend toward emulating actresses was a powerful force in forming the grooming habits of young American women in the early days of the silver screen. The demographic group that read fan magazines was the first to adopt lipstick, mascara, eye shadow, pencil, pancake, and rouge. As makeup use diffused into the rest of the female population, magazines for different groups all characterized makeup as a way to create a mood or character—a theatrical rather than a baldly biosexual intention. I think it's fair to infer that the turn to makeup was originally related to the emulation of actresses.

The popular notion today among both feminists and journalists is that makeup use came directly up from prostitutes. As the status of prostitutes never rose, however, there is no reason why other women would suddenly decide to imitate them. Some feminist historians assert that only prostitutes wore rouge before 1920, when wealthy socialites allegedly brought the practice into "respectability." This theory does not fit the data available. As we saw in chapter 5, clerical workers wore rouge in the mid-1800s. Although they dressed more conservatively by 1900, entry-level clericals continued to use makeup, producing a mark of stratification even within the workplace. Furthermore, by 1900, the Sears catalog included rouge and powder. The very appearance of these products in a national, grass-roots vehicle such as the Sears catalog suggests a broad-based, national demand for both items. It's certainly reasonable to infer that prostitutes were not the primary consumers of rouge, either in fact or in public perception, if Sears was selling it. Nor was it the province of the very wealthy, if it could be offered in a mass vehicle at mass prices.

Wearing lipstick had also been one of the signs of the New Girls of the 1920s. Although makeup was initially considered to be immoral when worn by these women, the practice soon took on the connotation of sophisticated rebelliousness that, while very threatening to the more conventional, was not necessarily unflattering. For example, Carmel Snow, who became editor of *Bazaar* in 1934, recalled that her first copywriter at *Vogue,* Lois Long, was also the first woman she knew who bobbed her hair and wore lipstick. Long, a "typical flapper" and a brilliant writer, moved back and forth between *Vogue* and *Vanity Fair* for several years before taking a job as a regular columnist for *The New Yorker.* Her pseudonym at the new job: "Lipstick."[26]

According to statistics collected by J. Walter Thompson, as late as 1927, the use of both lipstick and rouge was still concentrated among women under twenty-five and strongly skewed toward metropolitan areas. At subsequent age breaks, usage declined regularly; virtually no older women wore makeup. This pattern suggests recent adoption, since the products had not had time to filter into other age groups, as we know they ultimately did. Of particular interest, however, is that usage was also strongly skewed by education and employment: College girls and "businesswomen" used rouge and lipstick, but housewives generally did not. The pattern of diffusion, therefore, appears to have originated with actresses, moved next to young working women in factories and offices, eventually included college women and high-status businesswomen, and finally gained acceptance among middle-class housewives. Thus, makeup was used first by the most independent women in the culture, *not* the most dependent ones, and reached the bourgeois housewife *last.* Use of soap and manicuring products moved from the "respectable" circles outward to the larger circle of the "common" community; the use of makeup, hair dye, and colored nail polish can all be documented as having moved to the middle ground from what had once been the margins.

This pattern of adoption of lipstick and rouge is symptomatic of changes in the composition of fashion leadership, first of actresses and then of working women, particularly those in business and with college educations. By 1930 college graduates in business were a particularly glamorous group, especially if they were employed, as many were, in some aspect of fashion design or promotion. Several new publications aimed specifically at working women were introduced during the 1930s, and two, *Mademoiselle* and *Glamour,* were among the few magazines begun during that decade that survived to the present day. Their editorial content, tone, and style stressed career over marriage, education over looks. These magazines published information on new beauty products, services, and styles as well as on job opportunities and economic trends, all of which would have been important to the "subeconomy" of women.

The successful businesswoman came to epitomize "glamour," the new social grail of the era. A 1935 *Mademoiselle* cover feature questioned males around New York on who and what was glamorous. The respondents overwhelmingly named businesswomen: "the varying qualities of intelligence, astuteness, chic, sociability and compelling attractiveness that are the warrant for a woman's commercial or professional career are, at the same time, the attributes which serve to make her glamorous to many men." Among her many attractions, the businesswoman was as *capable* of femininity as the housewife or ingenue but was not as restricted by it.[27]

The women who wrote advertising copy at J. Walter Thompson certainly considered themselves glamorous. Employed in well-paying, high-status jobs, most were college-educated, many coming from prestigious schools. They were part of a fashion elite, but they weren't as up-to-date on what was "hot" as they would have liked to think. Furthermore, their own sense of status often caused them to resist fashion innovations from lower strata of women. This is what caused the JWT women to make a serious strategic error in their management of the Cutex account.

In 1924 market research indicated that a new demand was growing for tinted liquid nail polish. However, the JWT women dismissed the trend as coming from "younger girls, and on the whole a cheaper trade." Mature middle-class women—the bulk of the Cutex consumer franchise—thought the very term "nail polish" was "a dirty word." On that basis, a copywriter rejected the early signs: "There is a certain small class of women—mostly of the 'flashy' type—who do use it and who will create a small steady demand. . . . I should think that extensive and aggressive advertising of the Cutex Liquid Polish might turn out not only a loss, but a boomerang." So, in 1925, the Cutex team was caught lacking when liquid polishes offered by small competitors were suddenly selling like hotcakes—even at high prices.[28]

Northam Warren quickly scrambled to formulate a tinted liquid polish, but the technical challenge kept them from the market for another three years. The JWT women aimed the initial introduction toward "a younger and less conservative type of woman—a type far readier than any other to accept new departures in the field of personal adornment." They pursued the remaining market cautiously, using a kind of "rollout" plan whereby sales were first made to "flappers" who read *Vogue* and *Photoplay,* then gingerly extended to the ladies' press. By 1930, JWT was running a series of ads in which identifiable subgroups of women were asked whether it was acceptable to wear colored polish: Career women, banker's wives, athletes, debutantes, and socialites are featured. The campaign gives us a feeling for the range of types who were admired in the 1930s and should give us pause in thinking that any single "ideal," such as Jean Harlow, had an exclusive hold over American women.[29]

If we had been present as ethnographers to analyze the display of lipstick (or nail polish or rouge) in the American culture of the early 1930s, we would have noted that these possessions appeared only among a few clearly delineated social groups and that they were considered immoral by other, equally identifiable groups. If we had stayed long enough in the field, however, we would have observed these items consumed by an ever-widening circle of women until adult members of nearly all female groups wore some kind of makeup or nail color. Eventually, the use of lipstick or nail polish would have constituted a mark of gender (and adulthood), but would no longer, by itself, have additional distinguishing value. Importantly, however, as the color trend proliferated, new distinctions developed about the color worn, the method of application, the coordination of the rest of the facial colors, and the selection of occasion, which created fresh ability to articulate categories of women.

In preindustrial cultures where body painting is the norm, the practices also vary according to gender, age, and other roles. In some societies rules for painting are codified, but in others the paint is governed by a more general aesthetic that allows creativity to individuals. Some cultures are concerned more with the painted patterns than the body beneath and aim for symmetry, color, and even abstraction. In others, the goal is to enhance the body itself, through shading or highlighting. Rather than being a symptom of insecurity or a strictly sexual sign, body and face painting creates, overlays, and reinforces patterns of categorization and gives play to the whole range of distinctions that human imagination can produce.[30]

## PLAYING WITH MAKEUP

American men complained loudly about makeup (as they have done with every other significant change in women's fashion in a century). Women ignored male objections (as they had also done for a hundred years), becoming increasingly brash in their use of facial color. With the men complaining about the new trend in makeup, it was inevitable that *some* ads would seek to differentiate themselves by promising a more "natural" effect. For instance, lipsticks were offered that weren't supposed to rub off, that stained the lips rather than "coating them with sticky paste," or that magically turned the lips the "right" color without looking artificial. Most of these ads used shame appeals, stating that men disliked the overly artificial look and invoking lower-class antecedents of lipstick. These ads seem to have had little effect on the trend, however. Over the course of the 1930s, women applied more lipstick, bought more dramatic shades, and extended the application of lipstick to the corners of the mouth, to create what was called a "slash" or "gash" of color on the face. Concurrently, shades of eye shadow went to a range from subtle to garish. Disguising flaws or creating a deceptively "natural beauty" does not seem to have been a primary motivation. The watchwords were not "natural" or "undetectable," but "dashing," "gay," and "bright."

The cosmetics houses were by no means unified in their approach to makeup. So, for instance, Elizabeth Arden and others charged that makeup was being used to conceal flaws. Arden's headlines of the late 1920s are aggressively antimakeup: "Cosmetics Can Neither Cure Nor Conceal your Skin Blemishes"; "Makeup is a Cheap Makeshift"; and my own favorite, "A Painted Face is Disgusting." The Arden ads have the tone of whistling in the dark, since their declarations were clearly out of step with what was actually happening. Arden probably felt that the trend to color threatened her skin care business. Arden's rival, Helena Rubinstein, on the other hand, went into colored makeup early. Both women regarded Charles Revson as the incarnation of the devil, not because of his use of color but because of the shrewd competitor he became.[31]

American women of the 1930s seem to have been drawn to the bright colors and outright artifice of makeup. Beauty columnists began devoting considerable space to telling their readers how to choose and use colored makeups. A notion of color harmony and appropriateness, as well as specific message content, emerged. Certain colors were said to "go together." Other colors were said to be "alluring," "fresh," "smart," "dashing," "debonair," or "refined." There were nightclub makeups as well as vacation makeups. Columns declared what looked well on whom: "Pale women, older women, thin women and sick-looking women should avoid bright red or orangey rouges and lipsticks. . . . Bright red is for the moderately young and for medium complexions. . . . Swarthy women should use the darker reds. Women with clear olive skins who use no rouge can wear a very vivid lipstick." Varying application and color according to occasion or the specific message to be communicated was also stressed. One columnist offered this: "Q. What should determine choice of make-up? A. Suitability and becomingness. You must consider type, age and individual coloring, as well as occasion, frock, hat, lighting, time of day or year, perhaps even the mood of the moment."[32]

Advertisers suggested a variety of color-coordination schemes. Max Factor's "Color Harmony" makeup was very popular (the fact that he was "makeup man to the stars" didn't hurt). Richard Hudnut's cosmetics house suggested making up to match your eyes. Cutex, Coty, and Rubinstein offered lipsticks and rouges to match. Several advertisers suggested color-coordinating with clothing (a tactic that incidentally sold more makeup by requiring different schemes for different outfits).

Women reading all this advice were being asked to bring a good deal of thought and creativity to their makeup application. And, although feminists may be right that some women were intimidated by the task, many women—just like their sisters in other body-painting cultures—were delighted to give the new practices a try. Shirley Abbott's mother, down in the hills of Arkansas, became quite adept: "My mother thought that make up was one of the fine arts. She had an enormous dressing table, a yellow satin-veneer piece with a kneehole and a mirrored top, and a vast standing mirror that reflected the whole bedroom. There was a little low-backed bench and four drawers; in them she kept all her wonderful implements of beauty. Not every day, but once a week, or any time she was going out shopping, she would bathe, put on her stockings and a lacy slip and high-heeled shoes, and sit down to paint. I would abandon dog, swing, book, or any other pursuit in order to watch her." Standing beside her mother, Shirley observed the heady pleasures of the newest rituals of womanhood: "The open drawers gave off the most ravishing smells. Down in their depths sat little white jars with pink lids, black cylinders trimmed in silver, pink glass things with tiny roses on top, high-domed boxes with face powder inside (if you opened these on your own, they'd blow dust all over the table top), fresh powder puffs, miniature caskets with trick openings, compacts with pearl lids that shut with a glamorous click." Shirley would watch her mother "make up," while taking the tops off all the lipsticks and unscrewing lids off jars, hoping "to have a say-so in what she applied next." Velma Abbott, sitting at her yellow dressing table in the rural South, even developed a "day face" for shopping and a "night face" for the movies.[33]

## RITUAL, ART, AND PLAY IN MATERIAL CULTURE

Makeup now was more than imitation of actresses: It had become a mode of self-expression, an avenue for play, and a system for marking the differences among women. It is clear, however, a major stimulus was the sheer desire for novelty—a frequent but usually unrecognized motivator for economic behavior.[34]

A sewing project initiated by Louise Armstrong among her relief cases in Michigan provides another good illustration of the need for novelty and variation. Armstrong offered the poor women in her community an opportunity to work for aid by joining a sewing circle. The relief agency provided materials and the women produced blankets, baby clothes, and other garments needed by local households. Even those who did not have to work for their aid joined the group just for the pleasure of being with other women. The work was monotonous, however, so the group soon began to tire of the products they were making. Concerns were raised that the sameness of the children's garments suggested orphanage or prison uniforms—sure to cause stigma in the playground. "We also felt it worth while to bring into those bleak, dreary homes whatever we could that was attractive and in good taste, whether it was clothing or household necessities." One of Armstrong's assistants, a Mrs. O'Donnell, began to suggest tiny details that could differentiate the garments from one another: "A plain white outing flannel baby dress, hem-stitched in pink or blue, could be quite attractive, and little muslin collars with colored stitching added greatly to a child's percale dress. The fact that many of the things we gave our cases were not only useful and adequate, but pretty, brought many a pleased smile to dull and anxious and careworn faces."[35] None of these garments was warmer or sturdier or better fitting because of having a bit of lace applied. Still, a blanket with a little decorative stitching justifies itself in a small but necessary way.

The very concept of "novelty" implies a continuing search, since each new thing discovered eventually becomes known. Psychologists and anthropologists, however, have explained that there is a limit to how much sameness the mind can endure, but there is also a limit on how much differentiation a human can tolerate. When each sight, sound, or object is unique and unpredictable—as in the perceptions of a newborn—a condition of total heterogeneity is reached that is ultimately as disconcerting as total homogeneity. The essential task of culture, therefore, is to provide ordered ways of stabilizing experience, thus achieving a balance between too much differentiation and too little. By naming, ranking, narrativizing, and creating relationships among objects—things that "go together" or "look good" together—we organize the novel into a cognitive structure we can use.

For any product that depends on novelty appeal, keeping a sense of "newness" is very important, but so is maintaining a practicable order. By 1937 Revlon already offered twenty-one different shades, all some variation of red. Thus, as the colors proliferated, the choices might have become too many for consumers to recognize and remember. Novelty would have become a negative experience; pleasant stimulation would have devolved into chaos. A predictably human way of dealing with the need to recognize single shades from among an array that varied within a limited range would be to give a different name to each. And that's just what Charles Revson did, in the process creating another legend in marketing history. While his competitors were still offering shades with flatly descriptive but not distinctive names, such as Deep Red or Light Pink, Revson gave a memorable name to each new shade—Suez, Nassau, Tartar—providing order within continuing novelty by doing so. Names not only helped users situate each new shade in an existing framework, it helped them to return to shades they liked and wanted to use again.

Revson's problem of providing classification systems for mass-produced products is, in fact, endemic to modern consumer culture. "From a cultural perspective," writes anthropologist Igor Kopytoff, "the production of commodities is also a cultural and cognitive process: commodities must be not only produced materially as things, but also culturally marked as being a certain kind of thing." In other realms of social life, humans announce the names and categories of culture through rituals. Because our own society treats economics as an abstraction, however, we don't tend to think of commercial exchange as a ritual occasion like a baptism or a bar mitzvah. Yet trade in preindustrial cultures frequently involves liturgical requirements, such as special dress and responsive speech, and is usually attended by ritual songs, chants, or stories that imbue the objects to be traded with names, powers, affinities, inclinations, and even genealogies. These rituals not only regulate the flow of trade, they also mark goods for further use in the communication of cultural categories.[36]

We ourselves accomplish economic transactions through forms of ritual that, although they occur on a vastly larger scale, are essentially the same. Because all the potential parties to a postindustrial trade cannot be present at once, the ritual has been transferred to the virtual "space" of magazines or the actual space where people listen to the radio or watch television. All those "present" by virtue of being readers or listeners learn the names and qualities being used to mark goods. Using ads, manufacturers name products ("brand" them) and give them a personality (an "image"), just as traders do in preindustrial societies. We also use chants (slogans), songs (jingles), and stories (TV commercials).

The Revson brothers weren't able to afford advertising until 1935, when they began to run simple, small black-and-white ads telling readers about new colors. Because there was no budget for lavish imagery, the initial schema was built on the name alone. As the collection grew, however, the Revlon campaigns also used the endorsements of fashion designers (all of them female), much as tribal or religious leaders endorse trades in nonindustrial societies. By the late 1930s Charles Revson had distribution in department stores and was timing his nail polish introductions to the fashion "seasons." Each season he held press conferences and parties to announce the season's shades. Store stylists were invited and their cooperation solicited for promoting the new colors. Joint displays featuring the "new season's colors" in both clothing and nail polish then would appear in store windows all over America. By the early 1940s, these "shade promotions" had become regular retail events—that is, ritual occasions for naming and categorizing a new group of goods to be exchanged.

Under this system, the names, rituals, and uses of cosmetics continued apace to ever more exotic combinations, saturated colors, and poetic names. Then, in 1940, Revlon introduced "Matching lips and fingertips." As with many other Revson inventions, the rhythm of the slogan and the presentation of the matching colors have become important moments in American fashion history. Over the next five years, the Revlon shade promotions included increasingly outlandish imagery and were coordinated with ever more outrageous publicity: 1945's "Fatal Apple" included not only a richly photographed magazine spread, but promotional giveaways of "golden" apples. The image of the Fatal Apple, with all its references to the Garden of Eden, Snow White, the first luxury, the first seduction, the first sin, is true to the multilayered tropes typically produced by ritual. Each window, each sale, each application, of Fatal Apple could now be fully understood only amid the thickest description, an instance of what anthropologist Clifford Geertz has called "deep play."[37]

Our tastes in objects are underpinned by cultural categories, narratives, and metaphors that have become attached to them by such rituals as these. Through the ages, images that have been ritually attached to various objects become accepted as "appropriate" for them. Thus, ads for a certain class of objects must be interpreted in the context of a particular thing's poetic history. For instance, in the long history of perfume making, a set of images has evolved that we now see as "appropriate" in the context of fragrance. Veils, fans, and birds have long been present in the poetics of perfume, probably because of its "airborne" properties. Oriental imagery is common because of the traditional eastern sources for many of the ingredients in perfume. Perfume has had a long association with both religion and drug usage; before modern processing developed, there were close chemical similarities among fragrance, poison, and drugs. Indeed, the European chemists who provided aristocrats with their perfumes also provided their poisons as well as love potions and spells. Thus, the ads for Opium and Poison perfumes have identifiable imagistic roots. The same substances, furthermore, often have been used in religious contexts as an aid in transforming consciousness in meditative experience. The associations with drug use, death, or transcendent consciousness often evoked in today's perfume advertising are not necessarily expressions of misogyny, as feminists often claim, but refer legitimately to the historical language of fragrance.

We should not make the mistake of assuming that readers take literally much of the "magic" of cosmetics advertising. Even the Trobriand islanders, who indulged in elaborate fetishizing for purposes of trade, were rationalists of a sort. Similarly, today's buyer is unlikely to think she can fly because she uses Wings, nor that taking the stopper from a bottle of Gigli's Genie will release a spirit to do her bidding. For all the play at magic and spells, there is always a willing suspension of disbelief and a purposeful approach to the lure of metaphor.

Every culture has its notions about what things are pleasing: what combinations of colors are complementary, what is excessive ornamentation or beautiful simplicity. Nevertheless, putting things together in ways that are fresh is usually a highly valued talent, a kind of material artistry. The poetics of objects also are affected by current practices in other artistic realms. Perhaps the most famous fragrance campaign of the 1930s, for Elsa Schiaparelli's Shocking, used illustrations that married fashion imagery and the art of surrealism. Modernist trends in sculpture, dance, and theater were reflected in the fashion photographs of the 1930s, particularly those taken by Edward Steichen, Horst P. Horst, and George Hoyningen-Huene.

Much of this cross-fertilization was the handiwork of Carmel Snow, who created an articulate link between the fashion world and the art world. Over the course of her career at *Harper's Bazaar,* she published Evelyn Waugh, Colette, Virginia Woolf, Gertrude Stein, W. H. Auden, Marianne Moore, e. e. cummings, and Dylan Thomas. Eudora Welty, Truman Capote, and Carson McCullers were all first published in *Bazaar.* Snow reproduced paintings by Picasso, Matisse, Braque, and drawings by Chagall, Cocteau, Dufy, and Dalí. Carmel Snow's most important contribution, however, was the expressive outlet she gave photographers, including Louise Dahl-Wolfe, Man Ray, Henri Cartier-Bresson, and Richard Avedon, as well as those just mentioned. In Snow's hands, fashion became allied to art more than to aristocracy.[38]

Another actor in this trend was Diana Vreeland, who would become the leading figure in the fashion/art revolution of the 1960s. Carmel Snow met Vreeland (who was dressed in an outfit that vaguely resembled a toreador's) at a party in 1934, and, acting completely on impulse, asked her to come to the office the next morning. Soon thereafter appeared Vreeland's column, "Why Don't You . . . ?," one of the most incongruous texts of the era. In the face of bread lines and dust bowls, this column would ask: "Why don't you . . . Have a yellow satin bed entirely quilted in butterflies . . . ?" Each month brought a slew of imaginative but excessive ideas. Some are cheap do-it-yourself projects or just unusual uses for ordinary objects: "Cover a big cork bulletin board in bright pink felt, banded with bamboo, and pin with colored thumb-tacks all your various enthusiasms as your life varies from week to week."[39] Vreeland herself was later embarrassed by the column, but under these suggestions is a spirit in keeping with the trends toward color and artifice. That spirit is an indefatigably playful one, a seeker after beauty, an optimist at all times.

Even in times of crisis, it is necessary to create little interludes of play, momentary glimpses of beauty, in order to go on. Many of the world's cultures believe that sensual experiences—certain colors, scents, textures, sounds—have the power to uplift and renew the spirit as well as inspire the imagination. Unfortunately, our own ideas of economic rationality and necessity discredit such acts, so the use of objects to cheer oneself at a time of scarcity becomes almost obscene. We dignify our bodily needs by calling them "necessities," while demoting all other needs into false, even immoral, cravings for luxury. Few would suggest that books and music should be considered immoral on the basis of their lacking connection to our purely biological needs. Yet any scheme for thinking about economics that affords legitimacy only to the physical would necessarily exclude both. Indeed, many things that are uniquely human would fall into that category, as would the preparation and presentation of many "basic" objects, such as food.

To imagine a material life without any elements of cognitive significance, spiritual sustenance, or social convention is difficult to do. Under such a scheme, we could eat but could not use spices or forks. We could seek shelter but not architecture, leaving caves as one of the few housing alternatives. Clearly, this scenario quickly devolves into something beastlike. Schudson cautions that the "human being, to be human, must show that he or she is not just an animal or brute, not just biological, and must in some manner make that nonanimal nature visible."[40] So, people build, make, eat, and display themselves in ways that make their nonanimal nature visible, in the process signifying not only an array of traditions and values but the uniqueness of their own spirit.

## A SIGNAL TO THE WORLD; A SIGNAL TO YOURSELF

In a short story that appeared in the *Ladies' Home Journal* in 1930, Christel Duncan is a young woman who offers no surprises to herself or anyone else. Although she and her husband, Bradley, are well-to-do and part of a sociable set, Christel never looks forward to going out. As she dresses for a dinner party, Christel comes across an unused lipstick someone had given her: "Christel never used rouge at all. Bradley didn't like it. But she picked this lipstick out and pulled off its little metal top. It was very red. She rubbed it across her lips rather awkwardly and then continued to experiment with more interest."[41]

Christel's husband commands her to remove the lipstick, saying "I don't want my wife to look like that." She reluctantly takes the lipstick off and "when she finished, her mouth was small and obedient." Christel finds herself resenting Bradley's attitude: "It sometimes seemed to Christel that Bradley never thought of her except as his wife. That should perhaps be a compliment and tribute. She thought he meant it that way. But the compliment and tribute always seemed to return to him like a boomerang, as if her great success was in belonging to him and not in being herself." She tucks the lipstick into her purse.[42]

At the party, Christel feels ignored by the others. In the ladies' room, she overhears two other women. One is applying lipstick: "it's kind of a signal to the world that you aren't dead yet. Or a signal to yourself. I tell you. I get a lipstick mood. It gives me a kind of nerve." When they leave, Christel takes the lipstick and "began carefully to destroy the line which seemed so characteristic of acceptance and reserve. It changed from the mouth which marriage and life with Bradley had been forming. It became a free-lance mouth, red, confident and just a little insolent."[43]

Christel returns to the party knowing she is pretty, fashionable, and worth noticing, but unaccustomed to her new appearance and uncertain how she will behave. With a sense of detachment, she observes people gaze at her with mild puzzlement and fresh interest. She watches the crowd make her the center of attention. She pretends not to notice her husband's fury. She marvels as the men address her as if she were a different person and the women treat her with new respect. Christel chats animatedly, all the while experiencing an epiphany of self-realization. She likes the way others respond to the lipstick's message.

On the way home, Bradley, still fuming, shows Christel more consideration. When he asks her to remove the lipstick, it is a request rather than a command. "She rubbed it obediently away. For after all it had done its work and there was plenty more where it came from."[44] Although the story ends here, we are clearly to infer that the relationship has changed forever. He seems humbled. Christel will no longer be predictably obedient, but will satisfy her own needs and desires. The appearance of the lipstick is the sign that Christel is living a few moments for herself.

This story, called "The Lipstick Mood," gives us an opportunity to observe the way women use cosmetics to mediate their experiences, to conceptualize their own internal view, and to express their intentions to others. Christel's inner experience is described as a vague dissatisfaction with herself, a growing awareness of her husband's dominance, a sudden feeling of rebelliousness, a detached observation of others' responses to her, and, finally, a new resolve. As these feelings first come on her, she picks up a lipstick—not a habitual act for her but a conscious transgression. She puts it on, wipes it off, puts it on again, wipes it off. Each time the changing emotional status of her inner self is not just being expressed by the action with the lipstick but is being worked out through it, as if each surge of the self's assertion erupts in a red paste on her lips and then, cowed, disappears. As she watches the changes in the mirror, her own characterization of the lipstick ("insolent," "free-lance") and her bare lips ("meek," "obedient") is a reflexive commentary on the process of realization.

Christel's action is structured by her cultural knowledge of lipsticks worn by independent women and colors described as "daring." Her experience of wifely passivity and personal boredom thus lead her to express rebellion by picking up a lipstick. Christel is not doing this in a dumb belief that it will change her life, but the action can't be separated from its associations with personalities very different from her own. Putting on the lipstick does not merely release some animistic property. Instead, the act of applying (or removing) the lipstick is constitutive of the meaning of her experience.

Many feminist essays complain that makeup and other grooming practices are "lies" because they cover up the "true self." This argument is flawed by the supposition that the self is an authentic essence prior to experience—thus preexisting, already made, but knowable at will. Today many psychologists prefer the notion of a self that is created, or at least cultivated, by the focus of attention and conscious actions that seek to realize it. In this model, there would be no possibility of peeling off a false mask to reveal the "real me" inside. Instead, the self is created through a trial-and-adjustment process in which some goals are expressed, some rejected, some refined. The path that bridged inner feelings and outer experience would be cultural signs including words and pictures, but also objects such as dress and cosmetics. Just as the story says, a mark of grooming is both "a sign to the world" and "a sign to yourself."

## DRESS, KINSHIP, IDENTITY

In Louise Armstrong's Michigan jurisdiction, there was a young woman "who was at war with life, probably more intensely, violently, and still quite wholesomely so, than anyone I have ever known." Something in her basic makeup or something in her past, Armstrong speculated, had made this girl cast aside anything feminine: "She called herself Jim, she dressed like a man, had her hair cut like a man's, and in every way possible lived the life of a man, and yet with all this eccentricity there was nothing in the least unbalanced or unwholesome about her, and she was very bright and exceedingly likeable." Jim lived with a widow, for whom she played the role of both son and daughter: "When she was ill, no daughter could have given her gentler or more tender care, and on the other hand Jim was able to do, and did, all the work about the place which would ordinarily have required a man."[45]

Like other manifestations of human culture, kinship rules vary wildly from place to place, but they generally govern who may marry whom, who may (or may not) have sex with whom, rules of inheritance, terms of lineage, and membership in clans. Kinship rules also govern both labor specialization and consumption ethics and thus have profound economic implications. Every society divides labor by sex, although what tasks are considered "women's work" varies. The resulting gender specializations usually make the combination of a man and a woman the smallest economically viable unit. For example, if men hunt and women gather, then a woman must exchange what she has gathered with a man to assemble a complete diet. And a man must do the same. Thus, the arrangement between Jim and the widow allowed them to survive by putting together the two essential economic functions: the "man's work" and the "woman's work."[46]

When a society is so fundamentally organized along lines of biological sex (and this is a characteristic of every known society, not just the capitalist ones) there arises a practical need to mark the differences between the sexes. Thus is created biology's social manifestation, "gender," in which women are expected to have, wear, and exhibit certain "feminine" attributes, while men are expected to show "masculine" characteristics along the same dimensions.

The combination of male and female economic functions is made both formal and permanent through an exchange ritual we call "a wedding." Although most of us shy away from reducing matrimony to an economic behavior in today's American culture, until recently, marriage has been used primarily to improve and guarantee the material security of entire families, not just the two who actually "tie the knot." Around the world, marriage still often occurs as an extended negotiation between two clans, in which the exchanges of bride and dowry are reciprocated by promises of support that extend far into the future. Women are traded as commodities in return for long-term economic promises.

Marital ties involve obligations of the husband to the wife's kin, so men are as implicated in the marital exchange as are women. Men, too, are commodities. However, they are usually in control of the exchange process, which means they get to *choose* when and with whom they will exchange themselves. Consider, for instance, that Charles Revson exchanged sex for nail polish distribution frequently during the early years of the Depression. A skilled lover, he apparently could trade his sexual services for a manicurist's agreement to carry Revlon. This fact is unremarkable in that it carries no threat of censure or shame for Revson; indeed, many would consider it a compliment to his masculinity that he was able to do business like this. In contrast, the Depression press is full of concern that women in hardship will be forced to trade sex in order to survive. Women exchanging themselves for any material consideration is prostitution and, by 1930, that was not only a sin, but a crime.[47]

The male, as the one who traditionally controls the exchange of persons in matrimony (even under the romantic ethic, he is the one who proposes, she is the one who waits), can assert rights over the woman's body. He not only has exclusive rights to her sexually, but, as in the case of Brad's wish to control Christel's use of lipstick, he may also try to dictate her appearance, her behavior, and her whereabouts, in a kind of assertion of ownership. Such arrangements may produce the feeling, even in a modern American marriage like Christel's, that a woman's "greatest success was in belonging to him and not in being herself." Thus, some anthropologists have argued that the oppression of women stems not from the fact that they *are* exchanged, but from kinship systems that award men the rights to exchange women but do not allow women *the right to give themselves.*

What is "feminine" or "masculine" takes varied form, but femininity *nearly always* requires sexual passivity. Obviously, if the system demands heterosexual unions and gives males the right to control matrimony, then the female libido becomes a potential threat to the entire order. Sexually aggressive women, women who insist on choosing their own mates, women who are lesbians, or who exhibit any sexual behavior except that sanctioned for females (that is, heterosexual marriage as permitted by male kin) are a far more direct threat to the system than women who do men's work or wear men's clothes. This is why most societies have strong mechanisms to control female sexual behavior.

Because appearance is a marker of the gender system at work—but can also be used to announce the intention to subvert it—dress is often assiduously policed. In a sexually-stratified society, both Christel's use of lipstick without her husband's permission and Jim's aggressively masculine appearance are fists in the face of the system. Women expropriating men's clothing, women doing men's work, women engaging in market behavior in a traditionally "masculine" way, and women consuming "masculine" goods (smoking cigars, buying pornography) destabilize the marks of gender and so are a potential threat to the system's continuance. This is why cross-dressing and other "gender-bending" activities often are harshly punished.

One day Jim and the widow went to Armstrong's sewing project, which was under the supervision of a capable but self-righteous evangelist who called herself the Reverend Sarah.

> As was her custom with any newcomer, the Reverend Sarah asked what kind of garments they wished to make. Jim said that they would like to make some overalls. "Who do you want to make them for?" inquired the Reverend Sarah, eyeing Jim with suspicion. "For myself," answered Jim, and I can imagine her fixing the evangelist with a steely look. . . ."If you want to make a dress for yourself, you're welcome to it," she announced, "but you'll get no overalls here." Jim replied that she had no use for dresses, since she was doing man's work, and that she saw no reason why she did not have just as good a right to have a pair of overalls if she wanted them as any other person did to have a dress. A few more barbed remarks were exchanged, with the temperature rapidly rising. Then the Reverend Sarah came out with, "Well, what are you anyway, I'd like to know—a man or a woman?" To which Jim very aptly replied, "It's none of your God-damn business!"

When the Reverend Sarah came looking for approval for her censure, Louise Armstrong gave her no comfort. Instead, she tried to make amends with Jim, advised her not to return to the sewing circle, and gave her a relief order for overalls. The other sewing project members, having put up with the Reverend Sarah's religious preachments for longer than they would have liked, felt no particular loyalty toward their "leader." At the next meeting, the women expressed their disapproval of the reverend's behavior and threw her out. As for Jim, "She was a gentleman in this affair, as she was on numerous other occasions."[48]

The support that this seemingly traditional group of women showed toward Jim's chosen way of presenting herself is a parable for what, in my mind, should be the feminist ideal. We should strive to be tolerant and supportive of our "daughters'" (and sisters') choices of self-presentation, and we should not stand for leaders who harangue and exclude them for the way they wish to look. No evangelizing of this sort should be allowed at the sewing circle.

As with Jim's overalls (or Christel's lipstick), any object that is a sign of inclusion can also be a sign of differentiation and opposition. Thus, the idea that, just because a certain mode of dress is conventional, it is by definition conservative or oppressive is in error. Furthermore, all signs of the self must be intelligible to others to be meaningful even as opposition. The pipe dream so often presented by feminist critics that we should somehow devise ways of dressing that are totally independent of social convention is impossible and undesirable. Such an order is like asking a woman to form a sentence independent of language. Even the attempt to do such a thing would necessarily be "read" by others within the framework of past experience and so could never be *received* as a culture-free statement. Utter uniqueness for everyone, even if it could be achieved, would result in the kind of perceptual chaos in which human consciousness cannot operate—and a collection of completely singular individuals could in no way be called a community.

Total homogeneity is no more practicable. Here, too, we must have balance between sameness and difference: "People are so different from each other genetically and experientially that, in order to reflect such differences accurately, individuals must structure their attention differently, thus building selves that diverge from each other in a variety of ways." A truly vital community allows individuals to pursue the common goals while adding their own unique perspectives, creating a community of plurality, not homogeneity. Feminists often have called for a notion of "naturalness" that, if actually followed, results in a kind of dress code. The more desirable alternative would be a feminist community of plurality. Women would be free to choose from among the available signs in the way that they cultivated and expressed themselves. If that meant overalls and short hair, fine, but if it meant high heels and silk stockings, so be it.[49]

Like Jim, Shirley Abbott felt like a misfit in her hometown. Although she had been taken to the beauty parlor at an early age, although she had stood at her mother's elbow and watched with fascination as she "made up," and although she had attended as many "escapist" movies as her mother would take her to see, Shirley became a feminist when she grew up. As is often the practice with converts to feminism, Shirley changed her style. Then she left home to be among women who understood. Years later she returned to Arkansas to help care for her ailing mother: "Her right hand was faltering that day; for a reason that she claimed not to understand, her fingers could not quite handle the stoppers and lids and paraphernalia. Once again, I helped a bit, undid the caps, snapped the little containers shut. I knew, although she did not quite yet realize it, that she was dying." One day, while attempting to get dressed, Shirley's mother suffered a frightening seizure, "an intimation of mortality, a fast and vicious dress rehearsal for her death throes six months later." Velma Abbott realized then that death was near. "After that day, there was no more frivolity. She never opened the dresser drawer again."[50] For Velma, the cessation of grooming was the sign that she recognized the coming of the last passage. To stop grooming is to stop cultivating the self, to give up on life, to call an end to all the experiences that have made a person who she is.

## MARX FOR WOMEN

At the request of Helen Resor, Margaret Bourke-White spoke to a meeting of the J. Walter Thompson staff on February 1, 1933. Bourke-White, who had just returned from Russia, was at JWT to show her recent photographs. Although she was invited to display her photographic skills, she made some interesting observations about the status of Russian women fifteen years after the revolution.

Russian women, Bourke-White noted, worked alongside men at the factories, operating big machinery and using heavy industrial materials. But she also reported a change of attitude among Russian women since the early postrevolutionary years: "Right after the revolution all the women wanted to go around as much like boys as they possibly could. But lately they have become more feminine and the government has let down the bars a little in recognition of this and is allowing those women who can get them to wear silk stockings." As was the case throughout the Soviet Union's existence, however, inattention to consumer culture made such products hard to buy: "The women are beginning to be very eager to use cosmetics. It is hard for them to get them. The government imports a small amount of French face powder and you can see the women going into the stores, sometimes paying a ruble for a grain of powder." A powerful articulation of the scarcity of "the elements to be a person" in the Soviet Union was that any retail display of attractive clothing items became a major event, drawing people to gaze in admiration—and to stand in long queues hoping to buy.[51]

This presentation at JWT raises several issues important to us. First, the characterization of Russian women's desires runs counter to the dearest hopes of feminist dress reformers: even when working alongside men in "nontraditional jobs" and even in a socialist society, women continued to want cosmetics and stylish clothing. Second, these desires were strong enough to have political impact even when the society had no advertising and no fashion industry. Third, the prices such objects commanded were clearly unrelated to any objective notion of "use value." In Marxist thought, the true value of an object is its "use value," which is the cost of labor and material, and is supposed to be also the equivalent of the cost of maintaining a worker's family. When products are sold for a profit—that is, some amount over their use value—it is because of the "commodity fetishizing" that is typical of capitalist society, particularly its advertising. Yet no institutional mechanism existed to manipulate Russians into buying such things; indeed, the system discouraged such behavior.

The whole complex of meanings called Fatal Apple make a little bottle full of red polish into what anthropologists call a "fetish," an inanimate object imbued with animate properties. As we have seen, the fetish is not arbitrarily magical or religious, but helps to accomplish a variety of cultural tasks. Today the word "fetish" has a negative connotation. Much of this is attributable to Sigmund Freud's use of the word to describe people who are sexually attached to things, but among intellectual feminists, the term often refers to Marx's notion of the "commodity fetish." Thus, taking their cues from Marx, today's feminists often criticize advertising for creating a "fetish" out of objects they believe should be kept free of animate properties.

Although the concept of "use value" may be satisfying in an abstract sense, it is less impressive when used to analyze concrete instances. In the case of Revlon nail polish, for example, there was a factory with women in it who filled and labeled bottles. Even before that, though, there were colorists, designers, chemists, and marketing people who conceived of the product, its color, its name, its package, and so on. Then there were all sorts of people, from salesmen to truck drivers, whose labor was necessary to bring the bottles of nail polish to their final purchase point. At the end, a manicurist labored to paint a fingernail. However, the manicure itself, as we have seen, is a central part of the consumption experience. In this case, much of the product's value is added by its circumstances of consumption, as opposed to the conditions of its production, and therefore its value cannot be attributed entirely to the bare bones of its ingredients or use value. The manicurist's receipt is not just an hourly wage plus tips, but a commission for selling Revlon. When, thanks to the labor of colorists, designers, chemists, and marketing people, a customer walks in and says, "Have you gotten Fatal Apple in yet?" the manicurist benefits. In fact, at each point along the way, somebody benefits: The distributor, salesperson, and so on, each take some portion of what is finally the cost to the consumer. At the end, the manufacturer does profit, but he is not the only one to do so.

At what point in this trajectory does the genuine "use value" stop and the "fetishizing" begin? The only way to answer that is to identify a single worker's action as *the* point of production and drop out all the rest as "magic." Not only does this devalue all the other labor that went into making the product, it artificially removes the moment of production from its complex social milieu. Once this is done, it's easy to see how Marxist critics can talk about the impersonal nature of capitalism and the worker's alienation from the product; however, their perception of impersonal exchange is a function of the superficiality of analysis.

Feminists, following Marxist rhetoric, often also complain of the excessive "commoditization" that characterizes postindustrial capitalist society. Some scholars argue, however, that the reason for the explosion in the number of items traded by postindustrial cultures is not capitalism but monetization. The ability to "translate" homespun fabric into money, which can be saved for later purchases or used for immediate needs (rather than turned into cases of molasses), greatly facilitates exchange. Thus, wherever money—literally a medium for exchange—is introduced, the traffic in trade goes up precipitously. Centrally planned economies have been no less inclined toward commoditization than free market economies.

The price of a commodity also reflects the process of exchange. The price of a bottle of nail polish in Depression-era America included the commissions, tips, favors, rebates, and advertising that went into making it available. Like her capitalist counterpart, the Russian woman who pays a ruble for a grain of powder is paying for the service provided in making the product available, which, because the product is "difficult to get," commands a substantial premium. The powder was imported from France because the Soviet Union forbade its manufacture. Because Soviet society did not allow advertising or any other form of "commodity fetish," prices should have reflected only the costs of production. But the difficulty in obtaining cosmetics had removed face powder so far from the circumstances of production that the price was thoroughly in the control of the final seller. Certainly these prices cannot be said to be proportional to the living expenses of a Soviet worker. Yet the system did not hold down the price, protect the worker, keep someone from making a profit, or suffocate the demand for a luxury product. This imbalanced transaction occurred precisely *because* the ideology refused to recognize the full range of objects people need.

Another continuing complaint in the feminist critique of consumer culture is that advertising doesn't just sell us goods, it sells us culture—as if it were possible to separate a culture from its objects. Commodities are consumed for reasons that go far beyond the reach of production-based estimates of value—they are used to mark rites of passage, to provide excuses to see friends, to repay favors, to have a little fun, and so on. Commodities are used in this way regardless of the existence of advertising and independently of the mode of production.

A grain of powder worth a ruble is a fetish whether it has a brand name or not. By declaring cosmetics taboo, the Soviets gave them a powerfully fetishlike quality. Furthermore, the very fact that women wanted powder—rather than, say, bear grease—

points to previous cultural practices in which powdering already figured. How would we propose to take the cultural value out of a product that exists only because of the culture it's in?

The wonder about our society is not that we imbue our things with spirits—this is common human behavior—but that we believe so fervently that we should be "better" than that. Ironically, it is not our distance from the "natural" circumstances of trade to which cultural critics object, but our very proximity. The literature on nonindustrial societies, most of it written after Marx's death, has consistently shown that exchange practices are embedded in ritual, emotion, social approval, and folklore in a way that makes trying to study the economy of a society apart from its religion, kinship, and art an impossibility. Conversely, trying to analyze spiritual, familial, and aesthetic life without reference to economics is an empty exercise. The frequent complaints by feminists that advertising tries to sell us cultural values along with material goods is a naive demand for impossibly mute objects and an inhumanly desolate system of exchange.

## WEARING THE COLORS

At the outbreak of war in 1941, the U.S. government declared the production of lipstick a wartime necessity.[52] This fun fact from midcentury, outrageous as it may seem, makes more sense now that we have a better understanding of the immediate meaning of colored makeup in this period. The cultural association of face paint with strong, autonomous, industrious, even courageous women would have made lipstick an intelligible priority when American females were asked to transgress the roles normally stipulated by gender in a more challenging way than ever in their history. As women labored in factories, lived on military bases, managed charitable organizations, led government agencies, and headed families, the restrictions normally placed on their consumption and even their sexual behavior were somewhat loosened. They discovered new strengths but also new desires.

Men, after fulfilling an obligation to the tribe stipulated for their sex—killing and being killed for the group—returned, perhaps unawares, to a changed homeland. Advertisements, movies, and magazines were suddenly full of imagery encouraging marriage and family. The whole society seemed intent on pushing the traditional kinship system—along with its control over labor, sex, and exchange—back into place. Dress for both women and men—tight waists and big skirts versus buzzed hair and colorless clothes—were restyled into exaggerated statements of gender, as if to enforce through appearance the traditional restrictions on working and loving. Conformity was in the air. But, in fact, things would never be the same.

# CHAPTER 8

# FREUDIAN FEMINISM AND COMMERCIAL CONSPIRACY

IN 1957 AN UNEMPLOYED MARKET RESEARCHER NAMED JAMES VICARY ANNOUNCED TO the press that he had influenced the purchase behavior of a movie audience by messages spliced into film in a manner too rapid to be perceived. Vicary's intention, as it turned out, was not to hoodwink the public but to fleece the nation's advertisers. Over the next ten months he held press conferences and collected retainers from major manufacturers. Then the owner of the theater announced to the press that there had been no test. A demonstration demanded by the Federal Communications Commission failed to produce any effect on the commission members and congressmen assembled. Various members of the government, the press, and the marketing community began to ask difficult questions, and Vicary began to backpedal. Suddenly, in June 1958, Vicary disappeared without a trace. He left no clothes in his closet or money in his bank account. The millions in today's dollars he had taken from advertisers went with him too. James Vicary was never heard from again.[1]

During the 1950s, fears about brainwashing and mass control were at a high pitch, and the fashionable sciences of the mind, Freudian psychoanalysis and Skinnerian behaviorism, gave credibility to popular anxieties. Films, plays, and books, ranging from *The Crucible* to *The Invasion of the Body Snatchers,* also focused public consciousness on the ways in which witches, communists, space aliens, mad scientists, and even unconscious desires could steal into ordinary Americans' lives unnoticed and destroy them from within. A particularly intense anxiety about sexual manipulation runs through this material, a theme that perhaps reflects the reassertion of traditional kinship and gender roles after the war. The belief that citizens were being controlled by unconscious means through advertising was widespread, fears that were substantially fanned by the publication of Vance Packard's *The Hidden Persuaders* in 1957.[2] Perhaps, then, the general aura of fearfulness made people continue to believe in Vicary's subliminal advertising even after his dishonesty was evident.

Two canonical feminist books of this era, Simone de Beauvoir's *The Second Sex* and Betty Friedan's *The Feminine Mystique,* drew heavily upon then-fashionable theories of sexuality and unconscious control. Friedan, writing during the 1950s, gave considerable credence to theories of psychological control through advertising popularized by Vicary and others. Both books had long-term effects on the way feminists think about fashion, beauty, and commercial culture—spawning a generalized concern with being looked at and a special fear of commercial images, particularly those with allegedly sexual messages or implications. For this reason, a close, contextualized look at the arguments made by Beauvoir and Friedan can help us understand the feminist critique of advertising today.

## FEMINISM AND FREUD IN THE FIFTIES

Both Beauvoir and Friedan open their books with long critiques of Freudian psychoanalysis. The two authors point out, quite rightly, that Freud's theories were too culturally and historically specific to merit the literal and generalized applications being claimed for them in postwar western culture. They agree that the notion of "penis envy," interpreted in the concrete way popular in the 1950s, was unsupported by anything but male arrogance. They are both eloquent in rejecting the idea that the crux of human life is sexuality—which is something they both accuse Freud, his disciples, and his popularizers of saying. These two writers are merciless in their charges that empirical evidence for Freudian theory was lacking, arguing that the psychoanalytical perspective often depended on an almost occult reading of signs. After having thoroughly devastated the bases for Freud's approach to the psychology of women, however, both writers proceed to build their arguments about personal grooming and commercial culture on a Freudian foundation. Thus, in spite of their skepticism, each contributed substantially to the power that Freud would have over feminist thinking for the next fifty years.[3]

Beauvoir spends several early chapters of *The Second Sex* outlining the historical antecedents of women's oppression, to show that the specific, material circumstances of women's condition in any given time or place are crucial in understanding their status. Yet when she addresses the status of women in the 1950s, she resorts to a highly Freudian, ahistorical account. Beginning with infancy and moving through childhood and adolescence into maturity, Beauvoir's developmental explanation of women's psychology considers *only* the influence of sexuality.

Beauvoir argues that penis envy is the root cause of the narcissism, passivity, and self-hatred she claims all women suffer. Boys, she argues, have an advantage over girls because their genitalia hang on the outside, thus giving them a body part on which they project their subjectivity, their autonomy—indeed, their complete sense of being a separate self. Beauvoir does not address *why* little boys should need to project themselves on one of their body parts in order to develop a sense of their own subjectivity. She just relies on the reader's prior acceptance of the centrality of the penis in psychic development—that is, she counts on readers having already adopted a very literal interpretation of basic Freudian theory.

Girls, in Beauvoir's account, have a similar need to project themselves on a body part. As they are lacking the only part that will do for the purpose, they are offered a doll as a substitute. If you accept the argument that boys *are* their penises, then Beauvoir's next step is plausible: Having been asked to accept "a human statuette" instead of the more "natural plaything," the girl begins to think of herself as a doll, to be coddled and dressed up. Within a few lines, Beauvoir turns out a blanket theory of female narcissism: "This narcissism appears so precociously in the little girl, it will play so fundamental a part in her life as a woman that it is easy to regard it as arising from a mysterious feminine instinct."[4]

Added to the extreme vanity that Beauvoir says characterizes the female condition is the extreme fear of sexual intercourse. Beauvoir alleges that terror of intercourse regularly manifests itself in self-destructive behavior among teenage girls. Paradoxically, she claims that the certain knowledge of rape in her future also causes the adolescent girl to begin taking a perverse pride in her body, to view it as both a "weapon" and a "treasure," and therefore to cultivate its appearance: "She tries different make-ups, ways of doing her hair; instead of hiding her breasts, she massages them to make them grow, she studies her smile in the mirror." Again, Beauvoir characterizes attention to appearance as the direct outgrowth of fear and inadequacy.[5]

Beauvoir extends her argument into the imagined girl's maturity by arguing that sexual intercourse is a horrible event from which ordinary women shrink into a complex of pathologies. The first coition is presented as a life trauma, and although Beauvoir admits that some women like sex, she insists on characterizing the sexual experience as irreducibly humiliating. She awards men a sexual power and freedom that is grossly overstated and unrealistically oversimplified. Beauvoir then uses her counterposed caricatures of male and female sexuality to formulate very different orientations to self-decoration.

Because Beauvoir's man can use his preternaturally conscious penis to defile the prey of his desire, he is saved the necessity of vanity and self-decoration. Throughout history men have given a good deal of thought to their clothes, ranging in execution from the exquisitely elegant to the outrageously provocative; thus this theory of dress would run aground of contradictory evidence—if questions of evidence were a concern. However, Beauvoir seems unwilling to admit the existence of male vanity, and remains insistent on pathologizing self-decoration by the female. She does admit, in an all-too-brief aside, that pride in appearance is a necessary indicator of physical, mental, and sexual health in both sexes. But because the vanity of women arises from the absence of a penis and the perpetual fear of rape, what is mental health in a man becomes neurosis in a woman.

Because a woman's future lies in "becoming prey," Beauvoir argues, she learns to see herself as an object viewed from the outside; she begins to dress in such a way as to attract a lover, which involves imagining how one might appear to the desired male. Feminism has yet to resolve the question of whether it should be permissible for a woman—or a man—to dress in a way that signals sexual desire and availability. Please realize, however, that when we dress in what we believe is an appropriate manner for *any* occasion, we are invoking the expectations of others—thus, we are in some sense imagining ourselves as seen "from the outside." The "others" may be our bosses, our mothers, our friends, or our lovers. The motivation to dress, therefore, is better described as directed toward the "social gaze" rather than just the "male gaze" or even the "female gaze."

Dressing in response to an internalized "social gaze" would be consistent with the normal behavior of a fundamentally social creature, regardless of sex. Throughout *The Second Sex,* however, the most salient signs of woman's oppression are her attention to grooming and pleasure in her appearance. Beauvior traced this "neurosis of narcissism" directly from two sexual starting points: that a woman has no penis and that sex for her is painful, humiliating, and fearsome. Beauvoir makes no accommodation for any other factors—historical, economic, social, or aesthetic—and entertains no alternative explanations. The pageantry of human adornment through a thousand years is reduced to sex in its basest incarnation.

From Beauvoir's bizarre account of how penis envy becomes female narcissicism, feminist thought progressed to a place where beauty in general was repudiated and the sight of one's own face in the mirror an image to be despised. Central themes have been that women have no subjectivity, that women can only see themselves as objects posed to please a male gaze, that physical beauty is a sign of mental instability, and that the sex act is something done *to* women, not *with* them.

Although the American reception to Beauvoir's book was generally positive, reviewers noted that the cultural distance between the women of France and America, as well as the substantial distance between Beauvoir herself and most other women, French or American, undercut the generalizability of her point of view.[6] Beauvoir was a professor of philosophy at the Sorbonne during a time when most French women didn't attend college. She had lived unmarried with Jean-Paul Sartre for many years and, although birth control was still illegal in France, they had no children. They also had no religion and no nine-to-five jobs. They were alienated from their families and their countrymen. They were communists. American women, in contrast, were considerably better educated than French women, had ready access to birth control, and had quite a bit more choice in the workplace (although it was still limited compared to men). American women should have been far ahead of French women in their progress toward freedom. Yet Americans were having babies at a record-breaking pace and were going through a time in history when family, community, church, and country were second only to the demands of corporate employers in their influence over private life. In sum, the material and historical circumstances of American women in the 1950s were substantially different from French women generally and from Simone de Beauvoir in particular.

*The Feminine Mystique,* although as radical in its feminism as *The Second Sex,* is a different kind of book. Betty Friedan, trained as a psychologist, wrote while a housewife, sitting at her dining room table as the demands of home and children tugged away. Beauvoir's tools were theory and interpretation; Friedan's were investigative reporting and piles of statistics. Beauvoir attempted to construct a model that captured the essence of modern woman's predicament, but Friedan did not try to speak for anyone but middle-class American women of the 1950s. And these were not good times for that group.

Although the decline in the female labor force that occurred just after the war had reversed and completely recovered by 1950, matrimony and fertility rates rose precipitously throughout the next decade. The primary impact of this demographic shift was upon educational and professional achievement rather than on employment as such. Middle-class women, who would have been the most likely group to seek advanced degrees, break into the professions, and acquire other measurable modes of distinction, chose more often to marry, stay home, and have children. The negative impact on women's salaries and educational attainments was devastating.[7]

Friedan proposes that a belief system she names "the feminine mystique" arose during the early postwar years to assert that the only appropriate roles for a woman were those related to her reproductive system: her sexual and her maternal performance. The feminine mystique, according to Friedan, led millions of women to reject careers or community affairs to concentrate on pleasing their husbands and mothering their children. But, she argued, the narrowed expectations of this feminine mystique were causing many women to feel useless, depressed, and even suicidal. Friedan called the housewife's vague sense of her own pointlessness "the problem that had no name."

At the heart of the unnamed problem, according to Friedan, was the contradiction between the upbringing of American women and the ideology that greeted them at adulthood. Her subjects were educated women who had been given advantages and encouraged to excel, then pressured to throw away their accomplishments by marrying and becoming full-time mothers. The quandary haunting them sprouted from the fact that their situation was *discontinuous with,* rather than an outgrowth of, their upbringing. So Friedan's view was, in some ways, antithetical to Beauvoir's. "My thesis is," she wrote, "that the core of the problem for women today is not sexual but a problem of identity—a stunting or evasion of growth that is perpetuated by the feminine mystique."[8]

Friedan's first target is Freud. Friedan's argument demonstrates compellingly how the influence of Freudian thought on the unique circumstances of 1950s American culture had led to the proliferation of the feminine mystique. Although therapists already recognized many weaknesses in Freudian theory, the popular take on Freud was heavy-handed and overly literal, in Friedan's opinion. She bemoans the consensus often expressed in the popular media that full sexual expression for both males and females was the main measure of mental health. Friedan reports that Freudian theory was being widely used to explain what was then seen as "the demise of the American male." Claiming that American males were weaker, more cowardly, and less potent than previous generations, popular commentators were blaming the sexual gluttony of American women. The data Friedan presents does suggest that American men of the 1950s were less interested in sex than were their women and that this lack of ardor had become a common source of female complaints. Friedan reports—with apparent seriousness—that extramarital affairs and orgies had become common practice for middle-class women yearning for more sexual fulfillment than their husbands could provide. Such a development would be *impossible* to explain from Beauvoir's perspective. Further blame for this allegedly effeminate, infantile cohort of men was being dumped on the mothers of the Depression years. Friedan suggests that the sudden selfless dedication to children among young women of the 1950s was a response to charges that the previous generation of mothers had failed their sons. The problem with American women at this time, at least in Friedan's estimation, was that they were sublimating all intellectual and creative energy, aggressively redirecting it into an exclusively sexual role—as sexual partners and also as bearers of children—in response to the criticisms from a popularized Freudianism.

Friedan argues that the women's service magazines were major perpetrators of the feminine mystique. Under the female editors who managed the women's magazines before the war, she claims, women had been encouraged to excel. But, she said, a shift to male editors after the war produced a remarkable change in the magazines' content. Not only did fiction and nonfiction suddenly change emphasis to romance and motherhood, Friedan argued, but attention to world events, government, and other more important concerns had dwindled. Friedan's assertion that most of the women's magazine editors were female before the war is quite correct and her characterization of women's press involvement in significant issues is also accurate. It is furthermore true that, although the staffs of the women's magazines remained mostly female during the 1950s and early 1960s, many editorships were suddenly given to males. Many cultural analysts since the postwar period have noted the sudden ideological shift toward matrimony and motherhood that seems aimed at getting women back into prewartime kinship roles.

Friedan also blames American business for its contribution to the feminine mystique. Initially her discussion of the ideological bent evident in the ads of her day is quite persuasive. Today, any casual perusal of ads directed to women of the 1950s supports Friedan's charge that advertising contributed mightily to the feminine mystique. It is when she starts to posit a more subtle, invisible mechanism behind these ads that she gets into trouble.

Friedan was puzzled and concerned by what she saw as an inexplicable rise in the consumption of household goods. As the kinship system slammed back into place with the return of the soldiers from war, the first inclination of many young people was to marry and procreate. The production capacity and technologies of the war years were put to use in making consumer products with features and benefits not previously available: the superior cleaning power of laundry detergent over soap, the ease of instant cake mixes, the wonders of frozen food, new and affordable household appliances, and so on. These "wonder" goods arrived on the market just as years of pent-up demand from the war and Depression years were released. With household formation on the rise and the increase in disposable income that came with postwar prosperity, a steep upturn in consumption logically occurred. So, although the consumer goods explosion mystified many people at the time, causing them to imagine dark forces behind it, today we can easily identify the precipitating factors that created it. No conspiracy theorists need apply.

Friedan did not have this long-term perspective, so she points to the postwar growth in consumer goods production as a puzzle that required a radical, possibly immoral solution. She infers that increased postwar production would require the creation of "new" or "false" demand to find a market of sufficient size to absorb the additional output. Friedan works from a basic assumption that needs are fixed, natural, and obvious—and that any consumption above the "necessities" must be explained by some intervention or moral failure. Her explanation accommodates both hypotheses: She posits advertising as an exogenous variable causing Americans to purchase by preying on their inner vulnerabilities (a.k.a., their "moral weaknesses").

For evidence, Friedan draws quite heavily on Vance Packard's *The Hidden Persuaders,* a bestseller while she was writing her book. Packard claimed that advertisers were using "mass psychoanalysis" to delve deep into the consumer's unconscious and appeal to "hidden needs."[9] The very idea of "mass psychoanalysis" is a contradiction in terms, but Friedan's normally healthy skepticism appears to have failed her here. *The Feminine Mystique* was the first of many less well-considered feminist works that claimed advertisements control women by beaming messages directly to the id. Unfortunately, therefore, this classic text put the likes of James Vicary into the grounding of feminist theory.

Friedan's basic strategy throughout *The Feminine Mystique* is to attack the notion that women are merely bodies, driven by libido and deeply rooted desires to reproduce, insisting instead on their autonomy, intelligence, and productive (rather than reproductive) potential. Yet when it comes to women's response to advertising, Friedan can no longer see women's critical faculties, and women are left vulnerable to subliminal messages involving either sex or motherhood. Ironically, she undercuts her overall argument by suggesting that, underneath their apparent education and rationality, women are quivering masses of desire and maternal sentiment.

The idea that psychoanalysis could be conducted on a mass scale and in a manipulative manner involves substantial perversion of psychic processes as understood by Freud, as well as of the specific technique, hypnosis, that had come to be associated in the popular mind with psychoanalysis. However, in cultural classrooms from Las Vegas to Looney Tunes, Americans had learned that people could be made to do all kinds of things—bark like dogs, cry like babies, and so on—without knowing why they were doing them and without being able to stop themselves. So, when Vance Packard told his readers that one James Vicary was using hypnosis to make housewives buy, the prospect was not only frightening but believable. Yet within six months of *The Hidden Persuaders*' publication, Vicary had disappeared. Friedan appears to have drawn liberally from Packard's book without sorting through the question of source credibility, because Vicary's stories appear in *The Feminine Mystique* also.

Another of the very few named sources in Packard's book was Dr. Ernest Dichter, who trained as a psychoanalyst in Austria before World War II. This same Dr. Dichter is almost certainly the nameless "expert" on advertising interviewed and quoted extensively by Betty Friedan in *The Feminine Mystique.* Dichter advocated "motivation research," a technique that consists of a long interview, known as a "depth interview," during which the market researcher (or psychoanalyst, in the case of Dichter) asks a number of questions about the uses of, purposes for buying, feelings about, and beliefs about a particular product. Consumer comments were then analyzed for the unconscious reasons people consume—to increase self-esteem, to express creativity, to win affection, and so on. We can now recognize that these reasons for consuming are all normal, explicable features of social and material life, as demonstrated in chapter 7. But in the 1950s, people still believed in a model of economic morality that was stripped of anything but physical "necessity." Thus, the vaguely sexual image of a psychiatrist manipulating consumers "on the couch" was quite offensive to readers of the 1950s, as silly as it may seem today.

Both Vicary and Dichter were vulgarizing a Freudian concept that, with additions from Marx, has since become central to feminist writing on advertising: the idea of the fetish. The human libido, according to Freud, had an "adhesiveness" that could connect to other people or to objects. The attraction of a "pervert" to inappropriate objects—which Freud called a "fetish"—could be caused by even a random exposure. The idea that one could be made a "sexual deviant" by unconscious, unsought, or accidental exposure to an object or image had unnerving power in a culture already fearful of such unwelcome "manipulation" and highly uncomfortable with sexual "deviance" in general. Thus, the notion that an ad could somehow cause an "unnatural" or "perverted" attachment to a product by an appeal to the libido was an appalling possibility.[10]

## DRESSING FOR SEX

Intense anxiety over sexual deviation was also evident in another arena of the culture where the postwar return to traditional family and gender roles was being vigorously policed. Historians of the gay and lesbian community have documented the emergence of sexual preference subcultures during the war. It appears that, under the duress of worldwide conflict society allowed a distinct loosening in traditional gender and kinship roles across the board. Not only were women encouraged to put on pants and do men's work to support the war effort, but lesbians in factory towns and in the military were tolerated to a degree never seen before.[11]

Both the defense plants and the military services attracted large numbers of lesbians. In the port cities and factory towns, cohesive lesbian communities developed, each with a coherent pattern of dress and behavior. However, once the conflict was over, efforts to police both gays and lesbians resumed at a level of viciousness unseen before the war. Thus, the same ideological imperative that sent women back to the home in the 1950s was applied with hateful fervor to sending lesbians and gays back undercover. Yet, once formed, their communities showed courageous resistance to the forces of traditional kinship.

The most publicly visible sign of the lesbian subculture was the appearance of the masculine-identified lesbian, or "butch." Several discrete symbols were part of the adult butch look: very short hair; either blue jeans or a man-tailored suit; boots, loafers, or sneakers. Butches claimed the desire to wear these items came from within, an expression of self and sexual desire. As one butch described it: "Dress for yourself. I like me butch, I know me butch, I know how to act butch. Be butch and dress for sex."[12]

The butch look was designed specifically to signal to a feminine-identified lesbian, the "femme," and was often a conscious attempt to attract or seduce. Femmes dressed in a way that was not only hyperfeminine and sexy but often rather formal. Silks and satins, spaghetti straps and high heels: These symbols appear repeatedly in the accounts of the early femmes. The femmes wore makeup, something that attracted and intrigued the butches. Femme lesbians did embrace the feminine aesthetic of appearance, but, in their choice of sex partners, refused to accept the culture's restrictions on sexual behavior. Thus, the butch's counterpart, the femme, was also a transgressive persona.

The femme finely tuned her display of self into an image of the feminine that, while recognizable as a stereotype, was aimed straight and specifically for the butch. She intended to be recognizable as a femme, not just as feminine. This necessitates a subtle difference in the cues, much like the one that can make a woman in pants a butch rather than a man. The ethic of this display is to give what has previously been forbidden or elusive for the butch—the experience of being *with* a feminine woman. Femmes also became sensitive to the signals of butches, whose characteristic smells, sights, and touches became highly eroticized in their imaginations: "I was thinking about Bobby, remembering her sitting, smoking, squint-eyed, and me looking down at the way her thighs shaped in her jeans."[13]

"Butch," too, was a highly cultivated look, an expression of identity and desire in which the slightest mistake could result in exclusion and disappointment. "Baby butches" who got lucky found a mentor, like Leslie Feinberg's Butch Al, who took Leslie "under her wing and taught me all the things she thought were most important for a baby butch like me to know." Al taught Leslie to tie her tie, how to treat women, and even how to use a dildo. So being butch, like being feminine, required an array of dress items, cut in a certain way and put together in a certain way, as well as a particular temperament to be expressed through manner and speech. Doing it well required focus, effort, and a sense of style. It also could inspire a very energizing vanity.

> I want to cut a clean straight line. I want a suit, a nice tailored sharp man's suit, and a smooth pair of boots that I can see my face in. I want a crisp shirt that feels like it crackles when I move. Listen to me: sharp, cut, bristle, crisp, crackle; like breakfast cereal, I'll make so much noise that they'll hear me coming before I arrive. I want to cut a clean straight line. I want to cut a broad swath through the fallow field.[14]

Having established cues for signaling each other, both parties enjoyed recognition and seduction.

> I remember years ago, the day I started working at the plant and you had already been there a few months, and how your eyes caught mine and played with me before you set me free. . . .
>
> I couldn't believe it the night I went to that new club on the West Side (a new bar almost every other week). There you were, leaning up against the bar, your jeans too tight for words and your hair, your hair all loose and free.
>
> And I remember that look in your eyes again. You didn't just know me; you liked what you saw. And this time, ooh, woman, we were on our own turf. I could move the way you wanted me to, and I was glad I'd gotten all dressed up.[15]

In this courting ritual, the grooming and showing of oneself to the other is stimulation and stimulating, buildup and denouement. The mating dance the lovers choreograph is a complex putting on and taking off of masks, of asserted power and revealed vulnerability: "There was a woman once for whom I danced my butch's dance. . . . And she initiated me, as surely as any high priestess, into the wonders of women's power. Hidden strength, deceptive power, always beneath the tranquil surface, a mask of apparent vulnerability and powerlessness. But with one swift movement women's power lashes out of the soft curves and slaps you in the face with startling muscularity, a punishment for simplistically and impudently believing that the looked-at have no power." It's ironic that this butch, who put together her own appearance with constant awareness of how she would look to the femmes, would think of *them* as the ones who are "looked-at" and implicitly *exclude herself* from that category. A consistent feminist objection (inspired by Beauvoir) to erotic representations of women is that a woman, by becoming something "looked at," is reduced to an object and thus rendered powerless. The butch and the femme, like a man and a woman, both show themselves to each other and look at each other in the course of seduction. Part of the butch's role is to be "the one who looks." The femme certainly *is* looking (and her partners know it), so she feigns the affect of being only looked *at.* Yet it is clear that femmes exerted power over butches through all the orchestration and display. "Tonight all the jokes will be funny I will be the entertaining, laugh-a-minute, woman-of-the-world butch. I will be the writer with the funny anecdotes, the witty comments. I will be barbed and bristling, busy, busy, with my butch performance. I will stand at that bar and select my femme, who picked me out moments beforehand anyway, and I will dance my butch's dance for her. I will be dapper and aching to please this woman, who spied the shark and reeled her in with a hand line."[16]

The harassment stories lesbians of this period tell are horrifying, involving police brutality and civilian violence. Yet butches also took chances that seem almost to invite disaster. There was a rule in New York, for example, that if a woman wasn't wearing at least three items of "woman's clothing," she could be arrested for impersonating a man. An easy way to deal with such a rule would be to dress like a butch, but wear some kind of women's underwear—not a bra, but maybe panties or a garter or stockings or *something.* But butches insisted on "dressing butch" right down to the skin. The police would strip them, humiliating in itself, and find BVDs. Then they were likely to be jailed, which often led to beatings.

Three things explain the butches' insistence on wearing men's underwear, even under such threatening circumstances. If the objective was to "dress for sex" and the climax of this mating ritual was the butch and femme undressing for each other (a situation also deemed important in heterosexual encounters), then the effect would be substantially dampened by the sudden appearance under the butch's carefully groomed exterior of, say, a garter belt. A lot of effortful seduction could go down the drain. Furthermore, if we apply the discussion of the use of material objects to *realize* the self as well as express it, then underwear was important to the butch's whole construction of herself as a sexual *subject.* Wearing frilly lingerie under the jeans, the starchy shirt, the boots, would have felt like a cheat, whether anyone else knew or not. Finally, as stories from both butches and femmes repeatedly show, getting dressed was itself part of the sexual encounter: the anticipation of attracting a partner and the gratification of observing their pleasure was all part of the buildup. Anticipating harassment by donning inconsistent underwear would have quashed anyone's ardor.

Today's feminists would not begrudge the expression of sexual orientation and desire through dress within the lesbian community, but the attitudes that pathologize the same behavior from a heterosexual female are still powerful. In the spirit of Simone de Beauvoir, they consider the effort to "dress for sex" with a man a pathetic, self-demeaning behavior—as if the human need for affection and erotic experience were less legitimate in a heterosexual situation. Presenting oneself in a way that expresses availability and desire is the way humans, male or female, gay or straight, get the love that they need. Nevertheless, one segment of the sexual spectrum is still precluded from expressing itself without condemnation from feminists: The feminine, heterosexual woman is still presumed to have no agency in the performance of gender, regardless of her transgressions in work, sexuality, or politics.

## IN THE BELLY OF THE BEAST

Although the intense pressures and fears characteristic of the 1950s have long since softened, the feminist belief in an advertising conspiracy against women has mushroomed into a cottage industry. The resulting literature has gone far beyond the notion that ads create perverse attachments to goods by talking straight to our unconscious sexuality. From Friedan's argument that the postwar economy needed women to become a class of consumers, feminist theory has proceeded to a point where the existence of markets *require* the oppression of women. Thus, in feminist criticism, it is not uncommon to read that the whole of postwar consumer culture was a conspiracy organized for the specific purpose of keeping women down. Feminists writing on media, advertising, or the market frequently claim that women, because they are excluded from the ranks of labor, are intrinsically separate from the life of the market and thus are wholly victimized by it.

Betty Friedan told us that women were suddenly excluded from the economy under the feminine mystique; Simone de Beauvoir told us that the postwar modern woman could think of herself only as an inert object. The decline in PhD's awarded and the number of women in managerial or professional jobs during the 1950s seems to lend statistical support to these claims. Yet the statistics also show that the upward trend in women's overall employment continued, which means women still were part of the market, as they had been for generations.[17]

Many of those women were employed by advertising agencies, which, in spite of the alleged conspiracy, were still widely believed to be good places for women to advance. Two of the most famous cosmetics campaigns of the 1950s were created by women. Both used sex as a basis for their appeal, so both campaigns have come under fire from feminist critics, but they have never been studied for the intentions behind the production. Indeed, to do that type of study is unknown in the feminist community. For this reason, the very existence of large numbers of women in advertising remains mostly unrecognized by feminist scholarship.

## The Sheitel and the Fardeener

When George took Shirley to meet his family in 1933, everyone was charmed except his mother. Shirley, sensing the matriarch's disapproval, waited until the car ride back to New York to ask what was wrong. George tried to avoid the question, but when pressed, he blurted: "She says you paint your hair. Do you?" Shirley "scrunched down on my side of the car" and kept silent. She had been lightening her hair since she was fifteen.[18]

Both George and Shirley were the children of Jews who had emigrated from Russia at the turn of the century. The "respectable" women of that culture shaved their heads and wore a wig, called a *sheitel,* in the belief that a woman's hair was an immoral decoration. Shirley's own mother announced her new status in America by cooking "American style," smoking cigarettes, learning to read, and being the first in their Brooklyn neighborhood to bob her hair. Other women were more conservative: "George's mother, on the other hand, was a rather silent, old-fashioned lady who wore a severe, pulled-back, tight haircomb, one step away from the *sheitel.*" All the way back to New York, Shirley imagined George's mother standing over the dishes and muttering obsessively to herself in Yiddish: "*Zee paint dos huer? Odder zee paint dos nicht? Zee paint dos huer? Odder zee paint dos nicht?*" George married Shirley anyway. They had a happy, companionable marriage, and for years their favorite private joke was *"Zee paint dos huer?"*[19]

Perhaps it was the influence of her mother's example, but there were other causes for Shirley Polykoff's own grooming practices. As a child, Shirley had worn boys' clothes and played boys' games, but her biggest ambition was to be the one thing only a boy could be, a *fardeener,* or money-earner. Shirley got her first job at age eleven, selling coats. She went home with her first pay, clutching the paper and coins in her fist until they were wet, and carefully put the money down on the kitchen table like an offering to her mother: "'See, Mom,' I said, 'even a girl can be a *fardeener.*'" Dyeing her hair at fifteen was consistent with her ambition—in the 1920s and 1930s when Shirley was getting her start, it was "career girls" who wore colored hair, just as it was "career girls" who wore colored nails. The nation's leading manufacturer of hair dyes, Clairol, furthered this attribution with its advertising campaign, which, from the mid-1930s to the mid-1950s, featured famous career women who dyed their hair.[20]

Like the "businesswomen" at J. Walter Thompson, Shirley sought a career in advertising. She began by working for many years writing ads for department stores, shoe stores, and other clothing and fashion retailers. Her career track was typical of many advertising women, particularly those from immigrant communities. Unlike many middle-class women, Shirley continued working even after she married, not because of financial need but out of her own need for challenge and autonomy.

Shirley worked her way up in her chosen profession, landed a job at one of the nation's most prestigious agencies in the early 1950s. Her first assignment, ironically, was for hair dye. The prevailing morality still held that "good" women—that is, middle class married women—didn't color their hair. Women who used hair color were considered glamorous but of dubious morality: "Who were these women? They were models, actresses in the tradition begun by Jean Harlow, members of the jet set then called café society, a few brave career girls like me, and a select group known as 'fast women.'" "Respectable" women kept their hair in its original shade; when it began to gray, they pulled it out.[21]

Shirley mulled over the problem for weeks, walking aimlessly in the streets talking to herself, discussing the problem with her husband, thinking about hair dye as she watched other women at parties. She decided to produce a campaign that pictured respectable women and spoke in an elegant but intimate manner. Every ad would exude middle-class morality, from typeface to photographs. Except for the headline. For that, she was going to use a loose English translation of her mother-in-law's old worry: "Does she . . . or doesn't she?"

"You wouldn't dare!" said her husband as she dressed for work. "Why not?" said Shirley, "Does she . . . or doesn't she? Or perhaps you prefer it in the original Yiddish?"[22]

Here we see a process of ideation that is typical of advertising campaign creation. Nearly always there is a "brief," an assignment, that gives the writer his or her instructions. The brief includes whatever has already been learned from market research, such as information about usage (how much of the product is used, when, and by whom) as well as attitudes (how consumers feel about the product and about the people who use it), and how it fits in with the array of other products available (its competitors, its complements, its potential substitutes). The research is nearly always distilled into a strategy statement. When the copywriter finally comes up with a campaign, however, she also makes use of things she already knows just by being a member of the same culture in which the ad is to be placed: the language, the most familiar pictures, the heroines, the best-known narratives, the prejudices, the habits. Necessarily, however, every advertising copywriter is a product of his or her upbringing, so it is not unusual to see some personal experience reflected in the ad.

The images were selected to communicate "respectability" and "naturalness." Polykoff's first memo instructed: "No slick overly made-up fashion types. . . . Shirtwaist types instead of glamor gowns. Cashmere-sweater-over-the-shoulder types. . . . This, in itself, will be a new twist. All very P. T. A.-ish and ladylike, if you'll pardon the expression. Very avant garde, you must admit, to have a 'lady' in a hair-coloring ad." Early in the campaign, client and agency also settled on the requirement that the woman would be shown with a child whose hair matched hers. This picture warranted the natural look produced by the hair coloring and said "mother" because of the perfect match with the child's hair. The woman wore a wedding ring, to be visible in all pictures. The new Clairol woman was no longer the career girl, with her enviable autonomy and questionable morality, but the epitome of middle class respectability, the mother.[23]

Why, with all this conscious effort to represent a squeaky-clean image, would Shirley Polykoff use an off-color headline? She claims that she intended the headline to be an "arresting" question, meaning it would catch the attention of the magazine's reader and thus stop her from turning pages. "Stopping the reader" is, even now, the primary goal of any print ad. Polykoff explains what was supposed to happen next: "And smack in the middle of all this understanding and middle-class morality, we placed the arresting question, the bombshell—'Does she . . . or doesn't she?' Then quickly to answer the question and bring the mind back from wherever it went, we followed with our second line, 'Hair color so natural only her hairdresser knows for sure.'"[24]

With a double entendre, Polykoff's ad reminded the reader that, as Friedan reported, married women were sexual creatures, too, and were widely reported to be demanding sex both in and out of the marital bed. In this sense, it was not unlike "The Skin You Love to Touch" Woodbury Soap ad of the 1910s. If the reader was interested in looking sexy to her husband (or to others), then the line might win her interest in the product. At the same time, the mask of the double meaning satisfied the need to *appear* chaste.

Shirley had an opportunity to test whether women with aspirations to respectability would hide behind her double entendre when *Life* magazine refused to run the Clairol campaign. Because media habits studies of the mid-1950s showed that more women were reading general interest magazines, such as *Life, Reader's Digest,* and the *Saturday Evening Post* than were reading any of the women's service magazines, placing ads in the general interest magazines allowed Clairol to reach more women. The all-male executive staff at *Life* balked at running a headline they saw as "suggestive." Shirley challenged them to take an informal survey of all their employees and see whether anyone else thought the headline was "dirty." She was confident of what they would find. Sure enough, the *Life* executives found that nearly all the men read the headline as "suggestive," but not a single woman in their organization had "gotten it." The women at *Life* brushed off the query with an air of injured innocence: "The dirt is in your own mind, boys. The ad simply asks a woman does she or doesn't she use hair coloring." Taken in by this false morality, the "boys" at *Life* ran the ads.[25]

The question of the "suggestive" headline did not even come up at the women's magazines. Again, this is testimony to the cleverness with which the ad was constructed: The "suggestiveness" issue arises only when male readers are potentially present; as long as the readers are mostly female, they can claim to read the ad as a message about hair coloring. From the point of view of feminist theory, then, the campaign presents a paradox: It is purposively constructed to work in a certain way for a *female* reader (or "gaze"). Although the presumed reader is admittedly considering "dressing for sex," she is willing to do so only in a way that is acceptable to the larger "social gaze." Thus, this case complicates, if not contradicts, theories that tell us all pictures in this culture are produced for a male gaze.

Before this famous Clairol campaign, the percentage of American women who used hair dye had been steady at seven percent. Within a few years, the number had spiraled to 50 percent.[26] Feminists would explain this phenomenon as the effect of "sexualizing" women with promises that hair color will turn them into sex objects for their men. From the point of view of the advertisers, however, the "Does she or doesn't she?" campaign was taking away the stigma of the "fast woman"—that is, the advertisers were trying to *de*sexualize hair coloring. Given the "position" of hair dye prior to the campaign—as something used by "sexualized" women—it seems that the advertisers' viewpoint is more culturally and historically informed and, therefore, probably provides the better explanation for the campaign's persuasiveness.

## Fire and Ice

The Revlon Fire and Ice campaign of 1952 was based on the assumption that even respectable women had secret sexy thoughts, but instead of playing on fear of discovery with a double entendre, the Revlon campaign forthrightly glamorized inner lust (see figure 8.1). A woman in a slinky, sequined dress with a bright red wrap has a streak of silver running through the front of her dark, seductively arranged hair. The copy claims American women are no longer "sugar and spice and everything nice," but something quite a bit sexier and offers a questionnaire for finding out whether the reader is, in fact, a Fire and Ice girl.

The Fire and Ice campaign seems made to order as an example of an ad constructed around Beauvoir's theory of the all-important male gaze. Later critics have built on Beauvoir's ideas by insisting that, because photographers are mostly male, photographs of women are all exercises in male desire. Indeed, critics have argued that it is in the nature of photography to turn women into objects because of the essentially male gaze of the camera.[27] Here we take a closer look at how the theory of the male gaze falls apart when the actual production of such campaigns is examined.

The first problem with the theory is the way that it excludes the role of the model in the creation of the photograph. The fashion model's role has evolved over time from a passive to an active one. Two of the key players in this change were the model and photographer of the Fire and Ice campaign, Dorian Leigh and Richard Avedon. Leigh was hardly the "flat image" that feminist critics insist fashion models are, but had been trained as an engineer, had quit her wartime job in protest of sex discrimination, had taken over her new career as a model by opening her own agency, and had flaunted traditional gender roles by having multiple affairs with men who were economically dependent on her, rather than vice versa. By the time Leigh was photographed for Fire and Ice, she was a leading figure in the fashion world, as both a face and a force. The power relationship between Leigh and the photographer of this ad was, therefore, also quite different from what feminist theory would lead us to believe. Dorian Leigh helped Dick Avedon get this job. She had modeled for the Revlon ads since the 1946 Ultraviolet campaign and had won enough credibility with Revlon management to recommend Avedon as a photographer. By the time of the Fire and Ice campaign, the two had been collaborating for two years. Indeed, anyone who worked with Leigh had to learn to collaborate, because she had clear ideas about how she, as a professional, liked to operate. She was also fiery-tempered and famous—if she stalked off the set, it was the photographer's loss.[28]

Another person on the set that day was Kay Daly, the author of the Fire and Ice campaign. Daly had written advertising copy at Revlon for many years and at the time was the highest-paid woman executive in the United States. It was Daly who invented the name "Fire and Ice" and orchestrated the entire campaign. The only advertising instructions Charles Revson had given her were: "I would like to see an ad that would be an answer to all the publicity going on that Italian women are the most exciting women in the world." Daly spent the following weekend working on the assignment, ending up with a "kind of *Time-Life* essay" on American women. Thinking the essay was too dull, she decided late on Sunday night to try doing the ad as a questionnaire. Monday morning Daly nervously showed Revson the questionnaire: "Charles sauntered in as he does, and he sat down at the end of the table reading this thing. He was very intent on it, and then he looked up with a grin on his face—which was very unusual—and he looked right around the table to me and said, "Who wrote this crap?"

Figure 8.1. Revlon's famous Fire and Ice advertisement of 1952

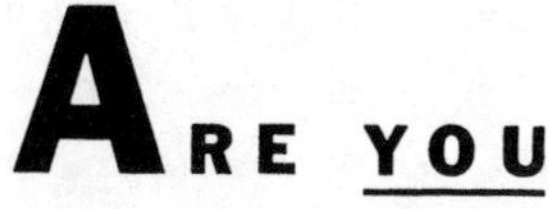

# ARE YOU MADE FOR 'FIRE AND ICE?'

**Try this quiz and see!**

What is the American girl made of? Sugar and spice and everything nice? Not since the days of the Gibson Girl! There's a *new* American beauty . . . she's tease and temptress, siren and gamin, dynamic and demure. Men find her slightly, delightfully baffling. Sometimes a little maddening. Yet they admit she's *easily* the most exciting woman in all the world! She's the 1952 American beauty, with a foolproof formula for melting a male! She's the "Fire and Ice" girl. (Are *you?*)

| | | |
|---|---|---|
| Have you ever danced with your shoes off? | *yes* ☐ | *no* ☐ |
| Did you ever wish on a new moon? | *yes* ☐ | *no* ☐ |
| Do you blush when you find yourself flirting? | *yes* ☐ | *no* ☐ |
| When a recipe calls for *one* dash of bitters, do you think it's better with *two?* | *yes* ☐ | *no* ☐ |
| Do you secretly hope the next man you meet will be a psychiatrist? | *yes* ☐ | *no* ☐ |
| Do you sometimes feel that other women resent you? | *yes* ☐ | *no* ☐ |
| Have you ever wanted to wear an ankle bracelet? | *yes* ☐ | *no* ☐ |
| Do sables excite you, even on other women? | *yes* ☐ | *no* ☐ |
| Do you love to look *up* at a man? | *yes* ☐ | *no* ☐ |
| Do you face crowded parties with panic—then wind up having a wonderful time? | *yes* ☐ | *no* ☐ |
| Does gypsy music make you sad? | *yes* ☐ | *no* ☐ |
| Do you think any man *really* understands you? | *yes* ☐ | *no* ☐ |
| Would you streak your hair with platinum without consulting your husband? | *yes* ☐ | *no* ☐ |
| If tourist flights were running, would you take a trip to Mars? | *yes* ☐ | *no* ☐ |
| Do you close your eyes when you're kissed? | *yes* ☐ | *no* ☐ |

Can you honestly answer "yes" to at least eight of these questions? Then *you're* made of "Fire and Ice!" And Revlon's lush-and-passionate scarlet was made just for you—a daring projection of your *own* hidden personality! Wear it tonight. It may be the night of your lifetime!

And that's the only compliment I ever considered he paid me." Daly also designed the ad's overall look, including Dorian's costume, which she made herself. Daly felt she could not ask Revlon's house designer, Norman Norell, to sew the rhinestones on a full-length evening gown, so she called "a strange little man I knew who designed G-strings and clothes for strippers." He didn't have enough help to create such an elaborate costume, so Daly, her assistant, and the G-string designer sat for hours sewing on sequins. The work was so slow and tedious that they only made the front of the dress. When Daly showed Avedon her idea, however, he cautioned that she needed more contrast. So she had a red Balenciaga cape copied to provide color and cover the back.[29]

Thus the initial photograph was a highly collaborative affair that included Avedon, Leigh, and Daly, as well as Daly's assistant and the G-string man. Importantly, the "boss" at the photo shoot would have been Daly, not Avedon, because she was the one who hired everyone and would pay for the picture. Although Avedon would want to be pleased with the view through the camera, it wouldn't matter unless Daly, too, was happy with the result. Ultimately Charles Revson, as Daly's employer, would also have to approve. Leigh and Avedon, however, were not employees of Revlon, but of other companies, where they had other "bosses." In 1952 Leigh worked for Eileen Ford's modeling agency and Avedon worked for *Harper's Bazaar,* where he reported to Carmel Snow. Both Ford and Snow had as much power over those present at this shoot as did Charles Revson. Carmel Snow would have to approve the ad to run in *Bazaar,* and Revlon hoped her magazine would support the campaign with publicity. By 1952 Eileen Ford was the most powerful woman in the modeling business. If a photographer or a model got on her bad side, she could *and would* fix it so they never worked again. Ford had discretion over which models went to which clients, so it was even in Revlon's interest to keep her happy. Therefore, at least six "gazes" had to be pleased by this photograph, two male (Avedon, Revson) and four female (Daly, Leigh, Snow, and Ford). Notice, too, that none of these people have a sexual interest in this shoot, but everyone has their particular business or creative interest.

When the photograph was taken to Charles Revson for his approval, the cosmetics magnate demanded that the shot be taken over because the position of Leigh's hands—spread across her breasts—was something "no woman would do." Leigh and Avedon disagreed, so Revson grabbed the cleaning lady, who was the only one left in the office.

> "Now," he said to the woman, who was quite puzzled by his behavior, "look at this picture and tell me if you see anything wrong with it."
>
> She looked at it carefully, bending close to get a better look. Then she shook her head. "I don't see anything wrong." Dick smiled triumphantly.
>
> "Wait." Charles held the picture up in front of the woman. "If there's nothing wrong with this, then let me see you do the same thing. Do what the model is doing with her hands."

> The woman's face clouded with suspicion. She shook her head. "No. No. I can't do that."
>
> "There, you see?" Charles shouted to Dick. "Take the shot over again!"[30]

Now we have both the male "gazes" involved in this shoot redoing the work because of the imagined "gazes" of several million females as represented by one cleaning lady.

When Daly took the final photograph to Revson, the cosmetics tycoon immediately asked Bea Castle, Revlon's publicist, her opinion. She answered: "I think she looks like a little tootsie whom the Aga Khan would have spotted on the Riviera." Revson, still afraid of making a mistake, made Daly go show the piece to Jessica Daves, then the editor of *Vogue.* Daves pronounced it "classy," so the ad ran and *Vogue* devoted a special issue to Fire and Ice.[31]

Revson's deferral, first to Castle and then to Daves, was indicative of the powers involved in the next part of the process. If the press and the trade did not like the advertising, Bea Castle would have trouble pulling off a successful publicity effort. Bea Castle was no token female in the publicity department; most of the leading publicists in cosmetics and fashion at this time were female, including "big names" such as Bernice Fitz-Gibbons, Helen Nash, Eleanor Lambert, and Muriel Fox.

The audience that Castle played to was also predominantly female. At the top were influential fashion writers such as Patricia Peterson and Eugenia Sheppard, and department store managers such as Geraldine Stutz, president of Henri Bendel, and Dorothy Shaver, head of Lord & Taylor. At the grassroots level, buyers, sales clerks, and window dressers in local stores would have to support and push the promotional theme in order to continue the appeal from the magazines. In 1955 buyers, sales clerks, and window dressers were still usually women. So when Revson asked Bea Castle about the ad, he asked a woman whose judgment was predicated on her ability to anticipate the reactions of hundreds of women in jobs around the country—all of them with a business, not a sexual interest.

The Fire and Ice campaign was an enormous success. It was featured in nine thousand window displays. Preview parties were held at twenty-two hotels, including the Plaza in New York. Across the nation, Fire and Ice beauty contests were held. On television, Arthur Godfrey, Jimmy Durante, and Steve Allen joked about the promotion. Dave Garroway even gave the Fire and Ice quiz to a woman on the *Today* show. At the end of the year, *Advertising Age* picked the Fire and Ice ad created by Daly, Avedon, and Leigh (as well as Revson, a cleaning lady, and a guy who made G-strings) was picked as the best ad of 1952.

Many of the commentators of the day thought the campaign sold lipstick as a tool for "glamour," which they insisted was a trade euphemism for "sex." It is true that the essential idea was that every woman harbored a secret desire to sin: "there's a little bit of bad in every good woman," suggested the ad's copy. Daly allows that she was trying to give women "a little immoral support," but insists that "it wasn't that serious, I think women had a lot more humor about themselves at that time than advertisers gave them credit for. The things that I did for Revlon I always did sort of tongue-in-cheek, feeling that women would be amused."[32] In imagining that the readers of her ad would be chuckle, Daly was attributing abilities to American women that feminist theories of commercial images do not allow. For a woman to be amused by this ad, she must have the ability to step back from the claim and see its silliness. She would certainly know that she wasn't going to win a man with a lipstick. And yet she might play along, even buy the lipstick—but in the spirit of fun rather than as desperate posturing for the male gaze.

Shirley Polykoff and Kay Daly, as well as thousands of publicists, buyers, models, artists, window-dressers, and other women working in marketing, would certainly have been participants, had there been an ad conspiracy during the 1950s. It has become fashionable to deal with the "problem" of women in the market by treating them as traitors to feminism. And yet feminism measures its progress by how many women hold certain kinds of jobs, achieve certain levels of education, and make a certain amount of income. By definition, then, much of what feminism counts as its own success is caused by the achievements of women as participants in the market economy.

Feminists of the 1950s had their own market stake. The movement likes to position its literature as "outside" the market, so we forget that *The Second Sex* and *The Feminine Mystique* were best-sellers in their time, as were many feminist tracts that followed. These books have been ordered repeatedly by college bookstores for over three decades, selling millions of copies for their publishers and authors. Here, too, the idea that feminism operates outside the market fails to match with the facts.

Women in the marketplace of the 1950s surely had a different view of their work from today's feminist critics. This divergence of values regarding sex, beauty, and the market marks a rift in the movement and has, as we have seen, long-standing precedents. The women's movement has made concrete progress only when it could enlist the support of middle-class married women and working women, yet its tendency over time has been to disparage the values held by both these groups. One of the stickiest examples of this conflict is another book with roots in the 1950s. Its author, Helen Gurley Brown, has been a front-line feminist activist throughout her long and productive life. Her book, *Sex and the Single Girl,* was also a best-seller in its day and, perhaps, has some claim to the feminist canon itself.

## SEX, WORK, AND THE SINGLE GIRL

*The Feminine Mystique* was a wake-up call for the housewife, and *The Second Sex* a manifesto for the intellectual. *Sex and the Single Girl* was a how-to guide for the working girl, a road map to having it all—men in bed and success at work—without falling into the indignity and parasitism of housewifery. Although it is written in a light style and uses simple vocabulary, *Sex and the Single Girl* was as threatening to the status quo as either of the other two books, because of its direct attack on marriage and the sexual hypocrisy of the 1950s, accompanied throughout by unapologetic market ambition.

The "problem that had no name" had little relevance to the "career girls" of the 1950s; nor would the sexual fears described in *The Second Sex* have resonated with them. Brown herself was one of these "girls." Never having had the advantages Friedan and Beauvoir enjoyed, she went to work after high school because she had to support her mother and sister. Unlike the subjects of *The Feminine Mystique,* Brown had no choice about whether she was going to work nor much flexibility about what she did. Brown worked for seventeen years as a secretary until one day someone let her write an ad. She then became a successful copywriter until, at the age of thirty-seven, she married a famous film producer, who encouraged her to write a book about her years as a working, unmarried woman.[33]

Within a year of its appearance, *Sex and the Single Girl* had earned Brown about $2 million in today's dollars. In less than two years, the book "went paperback" with an unheard-of first run of 1 million copies. Then a Hollywood producer paid Brown $200,000 for the film rights—the largest amount of money ever paid for the film rights to a nonfiction book.

The critical reception of *Sex and the Single Girl* was quite different from that of either *The Second Sex* or *The Feminine Mystique.* Even those who disagreed with the Beauvoir and Friedan books treated them respectfully, as if the authors' pedigrees required polite discussion, even if their politics inspired anger. Helen Gurley Brown had no such pedigree, nor did the readers of her book, and so reviews frequently were full of ridicule. Although all three books were commercially successful, only Brown's book was openly and frequently discussed in terms of its market impact. And, though one might expect otherwise, only *Sex and the Single Girl* resulted in anger and open animosity among reviewers. The reason for the vituperative response was the same whether the reviewer was male or female, conservative or liberal: Helen Gurley Brown openly encouraged single working girls to have affairs with married men.

With the publication of *Sex and the Single Girl* hit the press, Helen Gurley Brown candidly admitted that American working girls have sex, emphasized that they should have sex, encouraged them to go after good sex, and said that married men were fair game. She therefore drew fire from those who sought to protect the interests of the middle-class matron. Consider, however, that the willingness to breach the taboo against extramarital sex is as transgressive an act against the prevailing kinship system as dressing like a butch lesbian.

Brown's philosophy has its own pragmatically feminist ethos. She exhorted her readers to "do your own work. Don't live off of anybody else, don't be a parasite, make your own money, use your talent, live up to your potential." Brown imagined readers to be like herself as a young woman—not particularly pretty, not extremely intelligent, not educated, but determined to make it anyway: "Use your own guts and energy to improve yourself, your job, your intellect, and every other possible thing. You can't sleep your way to the top or even to the middle, and there is no free lunch. You have to do it yourself, so you might as well get started."[34]

Brown averred that there were two important things in life, work and love. She always emphasized work as being the more primary of the two, if only because you got a crack at better men from good jobs. She gave readers ideas for promoting themselves, competing (with men) for jobs, getting raises, and so on. Although she encouraged women to go after men aggressively, her avowed purpose was not to help girls get married, but to teach them "how to stay single in superlative style."[35]

There seems no doubt that *Sex and the Single Girl* found an audience—single working women who wanted to get ahead in their careers and sleep with some interesting men while they were at it. This is a group unimagined by Beauvoir and apparently unnoticed by Friedan, but one as easily identifiable in the ads and movies of the 1950s as they were in the labor statistics of the day. In advertising, magazines, and film often deified the housewife of the 1950s, but the purveyors of popular culture sometimes cast the traditional housewife as a stupid stay-at-home who looked like a loser compared to the worldly and sophisticated single career woman. For instance, one ad for a collection of "Great Books," opened: "The Women Your Husband Works With—Are You as Interesting as They?" The copy goes on to explain that the buyer of the collection will be better prepared to compete with "the gals at the office" who are "in the swim of things, while you wrestle with diapers and diced carrots." The subtext here was a common threat: The housewife, no matter how moral, maternal, and respectable, could always lose her man to the "pretty, lascivious and undignified" working girl.[36]

Beauvoir and Friedan assert that working women of the 1950s were seen as masculine, castrating bitches. As we have seen time and again, however, the "working girl" in American cultural history is not only feminine but vivacious, resourceful, and likeable. If she is threatening, it is more because her attractiveness puts pressure on the security of marriage than because she is a challenge to the masculinity of her coworkers. How do we account for this difference in viewpoint?

In the 1950s, working women were still referred to as "career women," "businesswomen," and "business girls," as well as the traditional "working girl" and the more contemporary "career gals." The usage can be confusing because the term "career woman" also was used to refer to a subgroup we can now see was quite different: the highly educated, often unmarried, professional woman with whom feminists traditionally had been identified. Both of these groups were identified with women's emancipation, but for different reasons. The educated professional was seen as a feminist mostly because the public leaders who spoke for feminism came from this class. The working girl was identified with "women's emancipation" because of what she did: work every day and see men on her own terms.

These two groups—the professional daughter of the upper class and the scramble-to-the-top "working girl"—have always presented themselves quite differently, the first dressing conservatively and rather like a man and the second dressing flamboyantly and, often, seductively. Feminist literature usually omits this distinction and simply breaks women's dress styles into two groups, the feminine and the masculine, with the latter being strongly favored. So, when Friedan and Beauvoir (and many other feminist writers) talk about the masculine career woman, they are not talking about the single working girl so beloved of popular culture. That very large group of women seems not to exist in the minds of feminist writers, because they are neither silly nor intellectual, neither passive nor masculine, neither "slavish little sisters" nor "women of education and refinement." Yet their very existence has presented a concrete rebuttal to the claims of feminists that "a woman couldn't work and still be considered feminine."

Within a few years of the publication of *Sex and the Single Girl,* Brown was offered the chance to run her own magazine. The male editors of the 1950s and early 1960s were unsuccessful, as a group, at maintaining their magazines' circulations. The decline in subscriptions among the leading women's service books was a frequent news story by the end of the decade.[37] In 1965 the circulation of *Cosmopolitan* had fallen below 800,000 and was still dropping. Predictably, Brown as the new editor of *Cosmo,* turned it into a vehicle that disseminated the philosophy she had first espoused in *Sex and the Single Girl.* The response was dramatic: circulation increased 16 percent in the first three years, and advertising revenue more than doubled.[38]

From the viewpoint of feminist orthodoxy, *Cosmo*'s success is hard to explain. The magazine's unabashed libertinism and its flagrant disrespect for the middle-class married woman continued to threaten the status quo. At the same time, it devoted considerable space to telling women how to compete with men for jobs. Yet American advertisers exhibited no queasiness about running ads in *Cosmo*—in fact, the ad revenue outstripped the subscription income. Further, in spite of the supposed power of the feminine mystique over both the media and its advertisers, *Cosmo*'s revenue went up, at the same time the revenue of the women's service magazines went into a steep decline.

Another phenomenon that is, to this day, unrecognized by feminist critics, affected circulation softness in women's media. Women have constituted a significant readership of general-interest magazines and books throughout the life of the modern media. By the 1950s, regularly published readership research showed that women not only read more than men but read more widely. By the mid-twentieth century, in fact, women were more likely to read the so-called general interest magazines than they were to read the women's press, a trend that had already affected the placement of campaigns such as Clairol. Thus, Friedan's concern that women were not being exposed to world events simply because male editors of women's magazines were focusing on the feminine mystique was unwarranted. Women of the 1950s read about these issues, but in other vehicles.[39]

During the 1970s, when *Cosmopolitan*'s circulation passed 3 million, Brown's unwavering support of feminism in her magazine undoubtedly brought many otherwise skeptical "working girls" into the fold. As an early member of the National Organization for Women, as one who marched in the 1970 Strike for Equality, as friend and ally to Betty Friedan, and as a frequent commentator on feminism in the national press, Brown was prominent among the first ranks of the Second Wave. Yet her interest in sex, her commercial success, and her personal appearance have made her an outsider in contemporary feminism.

Within the market economy of the 1950s therefore, there continued to be a form of feminism suited to the needs and sights of the "working girl." This brand of feminism can be viewed as the inheritance of Victoria Woodhull or Margaret Sanger; the intellectual feminism of Simone de Beauvoir appealed to the great-granddaughters of the Anthony New Woman; and Betty Friedan's focus worked in the tradition of the women's club movement. Thus in the 1950s and early 1960s, the key distinctions among these three streams were still holding. The intellectual stream tended to be more abstract, more theoretically "trendy," somewhat high-handed toward women of lower status, and generally negative toward pleasure, sex, and self-decoration. The middle-class stream, although educated, tended to focus on practicalities, continued to be reformist in spirit, and even while objecting to exclusive focus on the home was not particularly antisex or antidecoration. The working woman's feminism was somewhat adversarial in relation to both of the other streams, due to differences in values and interests as well as to real or imagined slights from those other classes of women. Although the intellectual woman disdained the market and the media, and the middle class woman distrusted both, the working woman sought refuge and power in the economic success she could find in the market economy, particularly in employment that involved media and fashion.

This latter group of women appears also to have had very different attitudes toward sex. Perhaps because their material circumstances were different from the intellectual Frenchwoman who wrote *The Second Sex,* the working women did not see sex as an irreducibly humiliating act but as an earthly pleasure to be sampled at will by the successful, independent female of the postwar age. In this light, the threat of subliminal manipulation through sexual images becomes suddenly impotent. If the sex act is not something to be feared and avoided, but an experience to be chosen with delight, then the mere presentation of sexual imagery would not be particularly threatening to the integrity of the individual or, by extension, to the social fabric.

An ideology glorifying passive, home-oriented women was salient in the 1950s. The ads, the TV shows, the movies are all still there to be seen. But what was their effect? Friedan speculated that exposure to this ideology would make the next generation, who had not known the prewar feminist perspective, into a cohort of superfeminine, ultra-passive consumers. But that is not what happened.

## CHILDREN OF CONSPIRACY

The young girl growing into adolescence, wrote Simone de Beauvoir, "simply submits; the world is defined without reference to her, and its aspect is immutable as far as she is concerned." This universal victim "does not dare to be enterprising, to revolt, to invent; doomed to docility, to resignation, she can take in society only a place already made for her. She regards the existing state of affairs as something fixed."[40] In two hundred years, the American Girl has *never* been someone who "regards the existing state of affairs as something fixed." The girls of the baby boom proved to be no exception to that tradition.

In fact, one of the most important bits of evidence against the idea that the commercial media simply force their oppressive will into the heads of unsuspecting women is the response of millions of little girls all across America to the culture of the 1950s. The substantial majority of these children did not become stay-at-home housewives, as they had been "conditioned" to do. Indeed, the efforts of this single generation not only recovered but exceeded the educational and economic setbacks caused by the feminine mystique. In terms of degrees acquired, nontraditional jobs entered, honors awarded, and any other measure of secular achievement, the generation weaned on the feminine mystique and the postwar consumer culture contributed more to the advancement of women than any other of the twentieth century. If these women had been "brainwashed" from birth, this momentous social achievement could never have occurred.

The banner under which these achievements were made was a renaissance of feminism now known as the Second Wave. It is important to understand that the Second Wave was no dim echo of the suffrage movement. On the contrary, the women's movement of the 1970s, peopled largely by young women born between 1948 and 1954, was far more radical, much more explicitly feminist in orientation, substantially broader based, and considerably more far-reaching in impact than was the First Wave had been. Indeed, historians of global feminism deem the Second Wave to have been the most widespread, successful, and effective women's uprising in *world history.*[41]

It is important also to remember that the "college girl" feminists of 1970 were participating in at least the third radical movement of their generation. The civil rights and antiwar movements drew substantial support from young women. The environmentalist initiative and the sexual revolution were also typical of that generation's breakthrough thinking and lifestyle. Thus, the daughters of the feminine mystique challenged conventional thinking, subverted accepted ways of living, and upset politics as usual on many levels. So perhaps it's time to take a fresh look at the formative experiences that gave rise to such a widespread challenge. Perhaps we should ask what things these little girls used from the conservative landscape of the 1950s to begin exploring the parameters of resistance.

CHAPTER 9

# SOMETHING DIFFERENT

THE FASHION EDITOR TOOK ONE LOOK AT THE GAWKY GIRL HUNCHED OVER IN THE doorway of the studio and thought Diana Vreeland had finally made a mistake. This "gangly little urchin" had stringy hair and was wearing black bell bottoms. Her strange face paint made her look like a rag doll, a cat, and Jiminy Cricket, all rolled into one. But before the editor could throw the creature out, the photographer held up his hand. "She's perfect," he said. "Don't touch her."[1]

In the next issue of *Vogue,* Richard Avedon's photos introduced the odd-looking teenager as "The Girl of 1967." Penelope Tree, insisted the commentary, projected the spirit of the hour. She was "a walking fantasy, an elongated exaggeratedly huge-eye beautiful doodle drawn by a wistful couturier searching for the ideal girl." Although this freshman at Smith was as "marvellous" to talk to as she was to look at, wrote *Vogue,* it was her fantastic face paint that first intrigued. Tree explained that she had started her makeup habit at thirteen as a way to annoy her friends' parents. Over the next year, Tree appeared on the pages of *Vogue* in many fantastic guises. Avedon, her constant collaborator, enthused that she "invents every moment a new little role for herself which she plays with devastating humour."[2]

With the support of Vreeland and Avedon, this unlikely young woman became, along with a herd of others, the Face of the 1960s. Many of those other Faces of the Year were designed to shock, too. Everywhere, in fact, designers, photographers, editors, and models were engaging in a mode of rebellion that, although charming and whimsical on the surface, challenged expectations of class, race, and gender right down to the bedrock. What gave rise to the attack on American beauty standards, however, was a sea change among the ranks of potential fashion followers: the entry of millions of teenage girls with a playful attitude toward fashion and a serious taste for annoying everyone's parents, especially their own.

In 1960 the huge cohort born after World War II was between five and twelve years of age. By the end of that decade, the baby boom children were moving into early adulthood. In between, the explosion of their teenage years made history. The intensity of the "generation gap" between these young people and their parents is now legendary. However, it is essential to understand that the rift was caused by more than sheer numbers: Between these two generations opened up an enormous gulf of differing values.

## MOMS OF THE MYSTIQUE

One of the ironies of the feminist critique of fashion is that its exclusive emphasis on pleasing the male gaze so obviously overlooks what many of us experience as the primary power relationship in dress: mothers versus daughters. "It has taken years for most of the women I know well, including my sister and me, to get over dressing to please or displease our mothers," wrote an eminent scholar, Elizabeth Fox-Genovese, in 1996. "I know successful, independent women who can still be reduced to anxious girls—or even to tears—when their mothers disapprove of something they wear or, worse, suggest that maybe it does not do much for their figure. It is as if mothers unconsciously see clothes as a way of retaining control of their daughters—of keeping them girls rather than facing them as independent women."[3] As we have seen, the record of American popular culture documents this dynamic often, from the Gibson Girl to the flapper. But the friction that traditionally attends the relationships between mothers and daughters—and that is consistently expressed in a struggle over dress and sex—was perhaps more threatening in the 1960s than at any other time in the century.

The new attitudes toward dress displayed open sensuality and often blurred the distinctions between genders. Although the "sexual revolution" has become a catchphrase of American popular history, often forgotten is that this phenomenon occurred largely in the shift between generations, causing even more tension between mothers and daughters over emergent sexuality than is already characteristic of this developmental relationship. Because the expression of sexuality is so often the subtext of struggles over daughters' dress, the sexual revolution was played out in thousands of arguments over the short skirts, long bangs, and fantastic makeup that typified the outrageously theatrical look of the 1960s.

The initial appearance of this confrontational strategy—in which play, dress, sex, and rebellion are fused into one unsettling challenge—is, I believe, behind the success of the 1959 introduction of the Barbie doll. To understand how that could be the case—after years of seeing Barbie as a conservative force—we need to bear in mind the intense intergenerational tension between the Boomer Girls and their mothers. As the parents Dr. Spock advised, the middle-class mothers of the baby boom were infamous for their perceived permissiveness. Yet what their daughters remember is extreme conservatism when it came to sexuality and femininity. Fearful of any sign of sexuality from their daughters, these mothers were ruthless in their efforts to quash childhood masturbation, vigilant to ensure little girls always sat with their knees together. They were extremely family oriented and encouraged the same values in their daughters by buying them "appropriate" toys, a never-ending parade of baby dolls and toy kitchens. These mothers, after all, were the women about whom Betty Friedan wrote: matrons imprisoned in an ideology that undervalued their brains and overvalued their wombs. Disinclined to rebellion themselves, however, the feminine mystique cohort trained their daughters to adhere to the mind-set of the 1950s.[4]

## TROJAN TOY BOX

Barbie was the first fashion doll ever made available to the mass of American children. Before mass production, the dolls owned by most American children were homemade, rather crude in design, and often of indeterminate sex. Mass-produced baby dolls became popular in the 1850s; "little girl" dolls with flat chests and stocky legs were introduced in the 1920s. Both types of doll were thought to be "healthy" toys because they encouraged mothering as play.[5]

By the mid-twentieth century, adult dolls had virtually disappeared. So, as an adult doll with an extensive, up-to-date, and beautifully crafted wardrobe, the Barbie doll presented a possibility for play new to Americans of that time. The brainchild of Ruth Handler, founder and chief executive officer of Mattel Toys, Barbie was inspired by the hours of play Handler saw her own daughter devote to paper dolls. She wanted to produce a three-dimensional doll that could wear stylish outfits, but the engineers at Mattel insisted such a doll could not be made. On a 1957 trip to Europe, Handler saw an adult doll modeled on a "naughty" German cartoon character. Handler brought it back to show the doubters in engineering. Barbie was a replica of that German doll.[6]

Barbie's shape is attributable to the erotic nature of that cartoon, but also to practical limitations posed by her clothes. The original Barbie clothes were miniatures of outfits that a grown woman would love to have as her own. The clothes were made of the same fabrics as life-size prototypes and were sewn in exquisite detail: finished seams, linings, buttons and buttonholes, real zippers, and the like. The designs were in the current style, with narrow waists and either straight or wide, circular skirts. Because the fabrics were the same as in the adult-size versions of the clothes, Barbie's body had to be produced in a disproportionate shape—the waist had to be extra small to allow for the gathering of fabric at the base of the bodice. Often the clothes had special trims, such as ribbons or fur, and intricate work, such as fine pleating or tiny appliqués. Each outfit came accessorized with the shoes, bag, hat, and other props needed to complete the appearance of a fashionable young woman engaged in a variety of activities.

A group of young women recruited from fashion design worked on producing Barbie's wardrobe, which proved to be as much of a challenge as producing the doll itself.

The team was led by Charlotte Johnson, who had worked in the garment industry since she was seventeen. Johnson, tall and blonde, bore an uncanny resemblance to Barbie herself. She was also single, sexually aggressive, a perfectionist, and a tough negotiator. She not only designed the first clothes for Barbie, she supervised their production in Japan—no small achievement for a woman in the late 1950s. Johnson was assisted by textile consultant Lawanna Adams. Another woman, Hiroe Okubo-Wolf, designed Barbie's makeup, while Jean Ann Burger styled Barbie's hair.

Barbie and her wardrobe have always suggested a range of imaginative situations, but initially many of the scenarios were fashion work-related. Barbie had clothes and props to be a fashion designer ("Fashion Designer" 1960–61, "Busy Gal" 1960–61), a dress shop owner ("Barbie Fashion Shop" 1960–61), a fashion editor ("Fashion Editor" 1965), and a fashion photographer ("Photo Fashion" 1965). It seems as if the women who produced and marketed Barbie—all successful fashion professionals—groomed, dressed, and packaged their doll as a miniature version of themselves.

Although Barbie was outfitted with the clothes and accoutrements to be a designer or editor, it is notable that she was sold with the explicit description, "teen-age fashion model." In the late 1950s, modeling was only just emerging from disrepute. Like chorus girls, models had been stereotyped as the illicit playmates of prosperous married men since at least the turn of the twentieth century. The most successful model of the 1950s, Dorian Leigh, did not use her real last name for fear of bringing shame on her family. By the end of the decade Dorian's sister, Suzy Parker, could use the family name, but the new respectability was still fresh and middle-class matrons still attached a stigma to the profession. The old model's immorality probably clung to Barbie in the early days, a fact that was undoubtedly emphasized, in the eyes of the Mystique Moms, by her heavy make-up and exaggerated breasts.

In Mattel's consumer testing, Handler found out what the Barbie generation soon learned: kids loved Barbie, but mothers absolutely *hated* her. To mothers, Barbie was too sexy, too grown-up, too flamboyant. Mothers wanted their daughters to have dolls that were either babies or little girls, not adults. This prudish reaction, symptomatic of the typical discomfort mothers feel about their own daughters' sexuality, is usually overlooked in the many critical essays that have been written about Barbie. Right from the first, however, Ruth Handler was advised that little girls might see owning a Barbie as a way of rebelling against their mothers.[7]

Retailers also did not accept Barbie. Sears, one of Mattel's biggest customers, publicly refused to stock the doll because she was too sexy. Most of the trade followed Sears' lead. When the Barbie ad campaign broke in March 1959, it had little effect on sales. Barbie dolls stood on toy store shelves collecting dust. Then summer came and, without apparent reason, those dolls seemed to walk out the door. Within months, sales of Barbie dolls exploded and an unprecedented phenomenon was on the scene.

My theory: It took about three months for little girls to wear down their mothers' resistance. I base this hypothesis on personal experience.

As my mother repeatedly informed me, Barbie was "not the kind of woman that nice little girls grew up to be." The old doll did not have the wide-eyed, puff-brained innocence of today's Barbie. She had slitty, slanty eyes that never met your gaze. She wore heavy eyeliner, lascivious shoes, and dangling earrings. And her breasts—well, I had to beg for a Barbie from my Southern Baptist family because of those boobs. My sister and I didn't know the word for it, but we could tell from the reaction of our parents that Barbie was a slut. Nobody ever told me I "had to look like Barbie," as feminists often claim. Instead, the message came through loud and clear that I was never to show up anywhere looking like Barbie.

I remember the arguments with my mother over whether we could have this wicked new doll. Aunts, grandmothers: all of them closed ranks on us. We dug in our heels, and we won. I can *still* feel the triumph. I don't remember how long it took, but three months sounds about right.

Even when competitive dolls appeared, they were either much shorter or much taller than Barbie and their proportions fat and babylike, rather than fine and detailed like Barbie's. If you and your playmates tried to play with Barbie and with those other dolls, the proportions were wrong. On the other hand, if you played with friends, sisters, and cousins who had their own Barbies, everything was the right size, clothes could be shared, and the overall scale of the playspace was consistent. Ultimately, that meant any little girl who was going to participate *had* to have a Barbie or be frozen out. So, once Barbie reached a critical threshold of popularity, it was only a matter of time before the doll diffused throughout neighborhoods—and throughout the country.

"Playing Barbie" was a very different social experience from playing with baby dolls—more like a grand adventure you made up in spontaneous collaboration with a small group of playmates. Each girl provided the voice for her doll, moved her about in response to the action, and helped spin the narrative as the group went along. You could play your Barbie as a witch, starlet, mermaid, angel, criminal, or wicked stepsister, just as you could pretend to be another character when you played dress-up. The claims of today's feminists that children were indoctrinated to *be* Barbie underestimates both the imaginative range of doll-playing and the rebelliousness of the Baby Boomer girls.

The success of Barbie rested on a triangulation of the tension among Mystique Moms, Boomer Girls, and the "sexy single girls" of the late 1950s. There was considerable pressure, as you might imagine, to turn Barbie into a wife and mother by providing her the appropriate clothes and props. Ruth Handler resisted. That's why Barbie had sisters but no children, and why she was begrudgingly given a boyfriend and a wedding dress, but no clothes for the PTA meeting. It is particularly interesting that Ken, reluctantly introduced by the Barbie ladies in 1961, has never been very successful. My own recollection—and I have confirmed this with several first-generation owners among my current friends—is that Ken was not considered particularly desirable as either a man or a toy. In the social world of playing Barbies, the fashion doll's boyfriend was little more than another accessory. Only one of my playmates had Ken and the car—the entire group passed both around, just as we did the clothes. In this attitude toward men, the Barbie ethos was much like Helen Gurley Brown's: men were nice to have, but they were not the main show. Yet for the Feminine Mystique crowd, the necessity of being married was unquestionable.

First-generation Barbie owners experienced vicariously the discomfort a teenage girl's appearance could cause their own mothers, as well as the upset that could be produced by their own playful practices. For the Boomer girls, then, fashion was first experienced as play *and* as resistance. Importantly, the catalyst was a toy made in the image of a single working woman, a concept that was anathema to the postwar ethic of middle-class motherhood. Just as the Barbie owners were learning this lesson, real working girls in fashion were bringing about another revolution, a vehicle that the younger generation would eventually ride to their own rebellion.

## OUR MOTHER'S SKIRTS

As in other domains of culture during the 1950s, trends in the fashion world had been rather conservative. In the pages of *Vogue* and *Bazaar,* socialites modeled ballgowns for the cameras of famous photographers. Entire features were devoted to the life, home, and garden of a single socially prominent woman, usually a woman of some age. The prevailing look at home was self-consciously understated: man-tailored British tweed suits, circle pins, Shetland sweaters, and monochromatic faces. Society tastes were inclined toward mature women with dignified, worldly wise beauty. The big "stars" were two socialites, Babe Paley and Gloria Guinness, both in their fifties. Their thoughts on fashion, as well as their photographs, were the gold of the fashion pages. When Jacqueline Kennedy became First Lady in 1960, she commanded *some* of the attention away from Paley and Guinness. Magazine articles also frequently featured Jackie's older sister, Princess Stanislaus Radziwill. In an article exemplary of the times, *Vogue* ran a feature honoring "The Face of the Hour: The Strong Face," in which Lee Bouvier Radziwill is shown in an extreme close-up. The accompanying text is a rhapsody to aging faces. Aristocratic daughters, such as Arabella Churchill and the Cushing sisters, were duly introduced to the world, but with the attitude of condescension generally reserved for young wine. Actresses, too, were appreciated for mature beauty. Elizabeth Taylor, at 32, modeled fur coats for *Bazaar,* as did Carol Channing, who was 43, and Bea Lillie, who was 70. When Marilyn Monroe died at the age of 36, Bert Stern had just photographed her for the next issue of *Bazaar.* The pictures ran, with a short eulogy that included this evaluation of her beauty: "For these were perhaps the only pictures of a new Marilyn Monroe—a Marilyn who showed outwardly the elegance and taste which we learned that she had instinctively; an indication of her lovely maturity, an emerging from the hoyden's shell into a profoundly beautiful, profoundly moving young woman."[8]

In contrast, the emergent fashion trends of the 1960s reflected the class loyalties of a new generation of designers, as well as the early influence of the youthquake. The conventional wisdom gives credit for the first blow to London designer Mary Quant, who invented the miniskirt and popularized the Sassoon haircut. Remembered Quant of these early years, "I came in wanting to create for people like me and for a life that was very real: women who had a job and a fantasy life that took that job into account."[9] A group of British designers followed Quant, all of them inspired by young working-class dress and all of them insistent on creating clothing affordable by that group.

Similar forces were at work in Paris. Emmanuelle Khanh began her fashion career as a model at Balenciaga. Feeling that her employer designed clothes for women as if they were furniture rather than people, she began making her own. Her designs were endorsed in the French magazine *Elle* by two young fashion editors, and soon Khanh became known as "the French Mary Quant." Another model from Balenciaga, Christianne Bailly, followed a similar route, as did Michele Rosier and Sonia Rykiel. This group of young women "intended their clothes not for the grand salon but for the street. By this they meant that they would be worn by active young women whose plane of existence was the office and the walk-up apartment, the Metro and the bistro."[10]

The designers in both London and Paris contracted with American ready-to-wear manufacturers in order to make their clothes available and affordable to working women. Thus, Penney's, Macy's, and other well-known retailers came to carry the revolutionary new fashions very early. Even in the couture, however, new designers began to take their cues from the young and employed. André Courrèges, Emmanuel Ungaro, and Paco Rabanne objected to the elitism of the couture system, with its concentration on older women, which they saw as emblematic of its inherent snobbery and sexism. All three disparaged couture's traditional focus on expensive evening gowns. Ungaro produced an evening gown covered in white Styrofoam balls by which he "meant to destroy the idea of evening clothes." Rabanne made gowns from sheets of plastic discs and from chain mail. Courrèges's first collection shocked couture by emphasizing pants when many restaurants and most offices would not allow women in trousers. The next year, 1965, this irreverent Frenchman showed his disapproval of spiked heels by showing only white glacé boots (soon to be known as go-go boots) and Mary Jane flats. As *New York Times* fashion critic Marilyn Bender wrote about the

Courrèges look: "The woman who adopted it, becoming or not, served notice that she had cut her ties with the past."[11]

The revolution continued at retail. Biba in London and Paraphernalia in New York were both central to pop fashion. These stores promoted clothes in surroundings designed to stimulate the spirit of playing dress-up. One shopper remembered Biba as "jumbled clothes, feathers, beads and lurex spilling out over the counters like treasure in a cave." Customers were allowed—even encouraged—to spend hours playing with the clothes and accessories. This playtime atmosphere became typical of boutiques everywhere—even those that were installed within department stores by the end of the decade. At Paraphernalia, an integrated design, production, and retailing concept, an improvisational, use-whatever's-in-the-box-today playfulness prevailed. Designer Elisa Stone recalls of her dresses: "I thought of them as toys." One group of Stone's dresses were made of soft brown paper, decorated with strips of construction paper that dangled like giant bugle beads. Betsey Johnson, perhaps the most famous Paraphernalia designer, produced a do-it-yourself dress: a shell of clear plastic with a small kit of adhesive numbers, letters, and squiggles that consumers could arrange and attach as they pleased. (As any Boomer could tell you, this was a sartorial adaptation of a popular toy called Colorforms.) "Noise dresses," also by Johnson, came with shower curtain rings attached. In their own laughing, imaginative way, these designers were determined to break every convention of fashion: "We were all protesting one way or the other."[12]

Throughout the mid-1960s, the new fashions were closely associated with music and models. After the Beatles were introduced in America in 1964, British working-class youth culture became the hottest thing there was, in fashion as well as music. A model named Jean Shrimpton epitomized the "Young London Look," and became all the rage. Everywhere, the new fashion was also associated a new kind of dance club, the discothèque. Cheetah, the quintessential disco, even included a boutique of discowear on the premises. People came in, bought new clothes, changed into them, and went dancing.

When the toybox attitudes toward dress that were to characterize the 1960s began to appear within the dignified, formal, mature aesthetic of the Mystique Moms, the reigning socialites surmised that the influence was the younger generation. Gloria Guinness wrote an article for *Bazaar* in 1964: "You asked me to report to you on the new super world of the young. Well, I have bad news. We are being licked. They are invading our territories, stealing our pleasures and destroying our illusions."[13] The ground must have rumbled as she wrote.

## LIVING DOLL

Leslie Hornby was only fifteen years old when she arrived in the United States from London as "Twiggy." Crowds of young girls swarmed in for her appearances, just as they had for the Beatles. *Newsweek* called Twiggy "the first child star in the history of high fashion, crowned queen of the mod by the same adolescent army of teen-spenders that has already seized and conquered pop music."[14]

In the glare of Twiggy's popularity, particularly among very young girls, Mattel decided it was time to offer an updated doll. So, it introduced a Twiggy doll the same year as the British model's epic trip. With her shorter stature and flatter shape—the very thing that distinguished Twiggy from Suzy Parker—the new dolls were "more boyish than bovine" so that they could wear the new Mod clothes. The connection back to play from fashion was thus made almost immediately—and with the connection to the Mod movement, it still had its rebellious element.[15]

For Twiggy's young fans, a distinguishing aspect of their idol's appearance was her makeup. The Mod's face emphasized the eyes. For this look, girls wore very light-colored lipstick, often frosted, which minimized the lips. The skin was even and matte in finish, but eyelids were elaborately painted. Usually different colors were used on the lid, in the crease, and below the eyebrow. The darkest color went in the crease of the lid and was sometimes arched higher than its natural line to achieve the illusion of roundness. Not only were Twiggy's eyes big and circular, she devised a way of painting them that made them even more emphatic. She used the same basic strategy I have just described, but painted a dark line in the crease of the lid with eyeliner and short lines under the lower lids. She added two pair of false eyelashes on her upper lids and one on her lower lids. Her eyes looked enormous. Soon, around the world, other teenage girls were gluing false eyelashes on, too.

Twiggy was the same age as girls who had been eight when Barbie was introduced. These girls extended their play years by emulating her—and an affordably-priced line of "Twiggy" designs was quickly introduced to help them do it. Young girls wrote to Twiggy with practical questions ("When you put on and take off mascara every day don't your eyelashes fall out?") and declarations of admiration like this one:

> Dear Twiggy,
> Much like yourself I am skinny and shapeless and flat. I have a scrapbook on you, my hair is styled like yours and my big brown eyes are accented like yours. Many of the boys in my neighborhood call me Twiggy. I hope that you will keep on modeling because teenagers will never grow tired of you.
>
> Yours truly, C. S.

Twiggy's followers were girls who had yet to reach a point where curves were either a blessing or a curse. Like many her age, Twiggy's metabolism allowed her to eat massive amounts of fat, sugar, and starch without getting heavier.[16]

Twiggy has been chastised endlessly for setting a beauty standard that most women had to starve themselves to achieve. If older women did starve themselves to look like

Twiggy, they chose her from among recognized mature beauties—they were not "forced" into it. The fashion press, as late as 1967, still provided many images of mature women, beautifully coiffed and dressed, accompanied by columns of lavish praise. My mother and her friends were not impressed with Twiggy—they were all still trying to look like Jackie Kennedy, who was thirty-eight in 1967. Even that late, in some months the high-fashion magazines look like publicity organs for Radziwill, Guinness, and Paley. Because Twiggy was so solidly identified with youth, I doubt there were that many grown women who even tried to look like her.

Instead, Twiggy became a standard-bearer for the younger generation. *Newsweek* described Twiggy's body in explicitly childlike terms: "Her figure belongs to the youngest of Venus's handmaidens, not to Venus herself; four straight limbs in search of a woman's body, a mini-bosom trapped in perpetual puberty, the frail torso of the teen-age choirboy." Sometimes the commentary was downright insulting. An *Elle* editor delivered the kind of backhand that was often used to describe Twiggy and her fans: "With that underdeveloped, boyish figure, she is an idol to the 14- and 15-year-old kids. She makes a virtue of all the terrible things of gawky, miserable adolescence." In response to the criticism, Twiggy, like many of the young at that time, was bluntly patronizing in her rejection of age for youth: "Sometimes I cry at those old films on telly on Sunday afternoon, with stars like Ava Gardner or Greta Garbo. They were so beautiful weren't they, and now they're old. Attractive, I s'pose, but older. I think that's sad."[17]

With that kind of flat declaration, the war between the Boomer Girls and their moms was officially on. Two competing aesthetics clashed. On one side was a waistless, breastless silhouette and a very short skirt. One the other side were big skirts and small waists. One face had big eyes and disappearing lips; the other had bright red lips and unremarkable eyes. One wore flat, childlike boots or Mary Janes; the other, spiked heels. One peeked out from long, shiny bangs; the other swept her hair back and up from her face. Mothers' reactions to the long bangs typical of the Mod look is now a shared memory among those who were young girls at the time. Diane Ackerman recalls: "I know so many women whose mothers would greet them—sometimes before even saying hello—by pushing their hair straight back and exclaiming, 'You'd look so much better with the hair off your face,' and it's always accompanied by yanking the hair back severely, as if it should be held by an Ace bandage."[18]

Throughout their teenage years, the Boomer girls used the clothes, songs, and texts of popular culture to disturb their mothers' notions of propriety. Whether it was miniskirts or long bangs, the music of the "girl groups" (think: "Leader of the Pack") or the Rolling Stones, the female children of the baby boom were well known long before they went to college for rubbing their mother's noses in a rebellious aesthetic.[19]

## SOMETHING DIFFERENT

When Twiggy landed in New York, a reporter asked, "Do you think you're beautiful?" She answered, "No, I don't think I'm beautiful. Jean Shrimpton's beautiful, I'm something different."[20]

"Something different" had become the grail of the two most influential figures in 1960s fashion, Diana Vreeland and Richard Avedon. When Vreeland was given the helm of *Vogue* in 1962, everything changed. "From the moment she came to *Vogue*, she created a revolution. Diana Vreeland shook up years of tradition that needed to be reexamined. She brought iconoclastic daring. She encouraged the breaking of rules and taboos." Between 1934 and 1962 *Vogue* had struggled along behind the leadership of Carmel Snow's highly imaginative *Bazaar*, where Vreeland had been fashion editor. Both Edna Woolman Chase and her successor, Jessica Daves, were rather stodgy in comparison to Snow, and it showed in their magazine. But after Vreeland moved over, *Vogue* became the epicenter of a fashion earthquake.[21]

In the 1960s, Vreeland was wearing her hair lacquered black, her face painted white with bright red cheeks. She surrounded herself with the color red. Her clothes were red, her office was red, her home was red ("a garden in hell," she called it). She created the drama of herself purposefully: When she finished dressing each morning, she would ask "Do I look Kabuki enough?" Although Vreeland was pushing seventy—and though she was the titular guardian of high society—she became a sought-after member of the emerging pop fashion subculture. "Unleashed at last, Vreeland's fevered imagination was in perfect harmony with the wild hedonism of the era. Rock music, the Pill, the Warhol Factory—all, to use one of her pet phrases, thrilled her to madness."[22]

The fashion spreads in *Vogue* under Vreeland's leadership are really outlandish. The clothes, the makeup, the scenes, the postures—all is sheer theater. Vreeland did not expect anyone to dress like that, but she did expect to broaden the scope of who was considered beautiful. To a large degree she achieved that goal. In one of the many articles that appeared after her death, she was remembered for her contribution: "Convinced, to paraphrase Francis Bacon, that there is no beauty without strangeness, Vreeland brought in quirky-looking girls with curious genealogies—Veruschka, Tree, Twiggy, Anjelica Huston, Marisa Berenson, Edie Sedgwick—who redefined the era's standard of attractiveness."[23]

As with everything in her aesthetic view, Vreeland selected models impetuously, dramatically, but always by working against the grain of convention. Some of the models "discovered" by Vreeland were grateful and felt affectionately toward her; others were scared of her. One of her "odd" favorites, Anjelica Huston, recalls: "I first met her when I was sent to see her by Dick Avedon when I'd just arrived in New York. I was about 17 years old. She always terrified me somewhat. She had a kind of gilded presence . . . a wondrous thing, a strange bird of paradise." Lauren Hutton was caught watching Vreeland dress down her editors during a fashion shoot: "We were just scurrying around. Nobody ever noticed models. . . . I completely forgot myself. I thought I was hidden by the racks and these other girls were marching around. Vreeland was in the middle of a sentence, talking about the dress. . . . I remember this glove, this long finger in the glove, pointing to me in the middle of a sentence. I said, 'Me?' And she said, 'Yes, you have quite a *presence.*' I didn't quite know what that meant. But I said, 'Boy, so do you.'"[24]

The selection of the photographer, however, was as important to Vreeland's agenda as the choice of model. She used many of the top photographers of her day, but her favorite, Richard Avedon, was ultimately her true collaborator in developing what they saw as the "image of a new kind of woman." After Vreeland hired Avedon away from *Bazaar,* many at Condé Nast were sure that a dangerous combination had been born. Even the publisher confessed that he did not have the strength to control them. Perhaps justifying the fears of conservative onlookers, Vreeland gave Avedon tremendous latitude, under which he feels he experienced a creative rebirth. "Being with Dick was like being with another kid in the playground," Lauren Hutton remembers. "*Vogue* would put out these huge tables with two hundred pairs of shoes and another table just piled with jewelry. *Vogue* was a huge, serious operation, but the studio was a wonderland of make-believe. Dick and I would plow through all these things and dress me up and tell each other stories."[25]

The models, therefore, entered into a three-way collaborative relationship with Vreeland and Avedon, producing remarkable results. Soon the highest-paid models were willing to work for *Vogue* for a tiny fee (perhaps $50) just to spend the day with Avedon. It is not surprising that when Twiggy came to New York, she insisted that all she wanted to do was to meet Betsey Johnson and shoot with Richard Avedon. She said working with the *Vogue* photographer was more like "playing Barbies" than work.[26]

Other models were also adding their own distinctive thinking to the production of these outlandish pictures. At the forefront were two other remarkable Faces of the 1960s, Rudi Gernreich's model, Peggy Moffitt, and a fantastically creative newcomer, "Veruschka." Moffitt designed painted faces that echoed the spirit of the clothes and created scenarios for the photographs in which she wore them. She was imaginative and erudite, using a range of inspirational sources from Nijinsky to Pagliacci. Her most famous face was completely white with eyes, peeking out from under deep bangs, that were painted Kabuki-style. Moffitt brought a new philosophy to modeling: "I saw something else in it. The possibility of its being a new art form."[27]

The emerging artistry of modeling was dramatically evident in the pictures of a young German named Vera von Lehndorff. With her huge frame and oblong face, von

Lehndorff was hardly a conventional beauty, but she consciously created a persona that became a distinctive mark of the 1960s: "I had no doubts about myself. I knew I had something which was interesting and I wanted to work with that. So I said, 'OK, now we have to find a way to make sure that others see it too.'" Her solution was pure theater: "I'm just going to invent a new person; I'm going to be Veruschka."[28]

Many of the photographs of Veruschka that appeared in *Vogue* involve elaborate makeups and hairdos so blatantly unlifelike they look more like sculpture than fashion. Vreeland and Veruschka developed a relationship unique among models and magazine editors. Veruschka would come up with ideas for features, call Vreeland to get approval, then take a photographer and manage the shoot herself. Staging the photograph was both direction and performance, a way of doing things that Veruschka found creatively satisfying: "Of course I was a model, but I didn't see myself as typical. Maybe I'm a frustrated actress. I did it more like a big theater play."

The experimentation among Vreeland, Avedon, and the models themselves often resulted in pictures that were different from "the look" for which the model was known. Jean Shrimpton would be transformed from the "dollybird" of swinging London into a Jane Austen heroine or a space-age cowgirl. Twiggy would appear with masses of hair. So, although their faces and names were known by many, their looks were not really "imposed" on the audience as a single standard; they changed too much from picture to picture for that to have occurred. Instead, the ultimate representation was like an invitation to play. And play is exactly what readers did.

## MAKING FACES

The aesthetics of beauty represented by Peggy Moffitt, Twiggy, Penelope Tree, and Veruschka were not concerned with fidelity to reality, any more than were the graphics of 1960s artist Peter Max. Everyone knew that these women were engaging in a form of dramatic play. No one labored under the impression that Peggy Moffitt (or Twiggy or Penelope Tree) "really looked like" their pictures in the magazines. In fact, features from *Vogue* to *Seventeen* showed the makeup procedures of Peggy Moffitt and Twiggy in diagram form with step-by-step instructions. You could try these faces on, like a mask for Halloween, and then adopt, reject, or adapt them to your own desires. Trying these ideas out on your own face was not pathetic or oppressive, but fun.

Although the magazines presented the readers with beautiful and often elaborate images, they did not try to deceive viewers into thinking the photographs were casual snapshots of models as they were. In the May 1967 issue of *Vogue,* for example, a full-page picture of a model with a huge head of hair has another picture of the same model on the reverse side. The overleaf, however, shows the model from the back while she was being photographed—with a huge piece of cardboard clipped to the back of her head to make the hair stand up "big."

Even as consumers, readers seem to have been quite aware that the use of a product was not going to turn them into Twiggy or "the Shrimp." Just as they could see the joke in a pop art dress, consumers of the 1960s could laugh at the suggestion of a "magical transformation" coming from a lipstick. The idea that a woman would simply transfer the poses and attitudes of fashion model directly to her daily life was the subject for jokes. Viewers of fashion pictures, therefore, were not duped by these outrageous images, but often became adept themselves at all kinds of sartorial subterfuge.

Ads of the period show cosmetics and clothes that were boldly artificial: green lipsticks and gold lipsticks and two-tone lipsticks; false eyelashes, plastic jewelry, and paper dresses. Makeup produced in palette form and in little pots further encouraged the association with art and drama. Consumers were even encouraged to re-create old shoes by painting them bright colors and to mix their own nail polish. Yet alongside the playful mood was an in-your-face attitude about the sexuality of young females.

The emphasis on individual creativity and experience—"doing your own thing"—was central to the aesthetic. As Penelope Tree explained to the press in 1968: "You can't look like *Vogue.* It doesn't want you to. . . . It just wants to show you what individuality is."[29] Individuality was conceptualized in the way I described in the chapter on the Depression—as a kind of plumage, donned and cultivated. Perhaps it is worth drawing the distinction again between "individuality" and "naturalness." Today, feminist criticism equates "the true self" with a face unaltered by artifice. Such a concept paradoxically defines the presence of self by the absence of its expression. The self is thus imagined as passive and preexisting rather than processual and consciously spoken. An "expressive self" seems as valid and liberating a concept as the pared-down notion of unvarnished selfhood advocated by feminism. From an "expressive" viewpoint, valuing individuality is not inconsistent with the unabashedly artificial self-adornment practices of the 1960s.

## GIRLS OF THE YEAR

Full as they were of exaggerated makeup and flamboyant clothing, the 1960s were also a time of exaggerated naming and flamboyant terminology. Journalists from Diana Vreeland, to Tom Wolfe, to Gloria Steinem coined phrases like "Youthquake" and "Jet Set," but also employed the convention of capitalizing otherwise ordinary words in order to communicate Something Important. As part of this propensity to overstatement, the media bestowed descriptions like "The Face" or "The Girl of the Year" or "The Look of '66" or some other equally hyperbolic title on a young woman, making her into an overnight celebrity and propelling her into a new class.

Models in fashion magazines were identified by name for the first time in the 1960s, reversing the long-standing practice of naming only the social elite and leaving the pictures of models anonymous. Jean Shrimpton, who epitomized the London Look, first appeared in American *Vogue* in November 1962. She was featured prominently in four of the eight fashion features, but, although her name was well known in the fashion world, she was unnamed in every one of these first photos. Soon thereafter, however, Vera von Lehndorff insisted on having her name printed in *Vogue* features. Von Lehndorff was a working girl, but she was *also* a countess. Her father had been part of the plan to assassinate Hitler during World War II. He was killed and the rest of the family barely escaped with their lives. So, young Vera grew up in the postwar era with a title but no wealth to go with it. When Diana Vreeland wanted to publish her picture in *Vogue,* therefore, Vera had a perfect right to ask that, according to custom, her name be printed as a member of the international aristocracy. Vreeland agreed. The name that was published, however, was not "Countess Vera von Lehndorff," but the self-created model's trade name, "Veruschka." In one stroke, the clear line between the working girl who modeled for a living and the socialite who modeled for prestige was erased.

Soon thereafter, Shrimpton's name also began to appear. Then in 1965 her face appeared on the cover of *Newsweek* as "the template from which the face of Western beauty will be cast until further notice." That cover article reported that fashion had declared her "The Face." *Glamour* magazine said, "This Is the Girl That Is."[30] Within a short time frame, Vreeland started referring to Shrimpton by her typically 1960s sobriquet, "the Shrimp," even in headlines.

Twiggy arrived in the United States in the same year that "The Girl of 1967," Penelope Tree, made her first appearance in *Vogue.* Twiggy came from working-class British roots; Tree was the daughter of a multimillionaire. Tree's mother, Marietta Peabody Tree, was "the reigning goddess and salon-keeper of the intellectual wing of the Democratic party." When Penelope took a year off from Smith to try modeling, it was purely as a lark, a balance for the "humdrum life of schooling." The feature profiling her first appearance was in keeping with Vogue's penchant for introducing society's daughters to readers.[31]

But in March 1968 Twiggy and Penelope Tree danced through the pages of *Vogue together,* looking like a couple of toys from Mattel, while wearing the clothes that had always distinguished the elite from the rest of society. Although their social backgrounds could not have been any more different, they look rather like sisters, almost twins, and Vreeland emphasized the effect by using nicknames: no longer do we have Penelope Tree, daughter of old American money, and Lesley Hornby, daughter of London's East End, but "The Tree" and "The Twig."

The likes of "The Twig" and "The Tree" were increasingly likely to mix socially, which sometimes led to a clash of values and manners. As the "mini-queen of the new social aristocracy," for example, Twiggy was invited into places that contrasted strongly with her own working-class background: "I remember a dinner party I went to a few months ago at a house in Paris, given by some French nobleman. His wife was very young, about the same age as me. And they had all these servants waiting on us, about one servant to each guest at dinner, bowing and scraping they were. And the young wife was talking to these servants as if they were nothing, ordering them about in a bossy way. They were old enough to be her mother or father! It was degrading. I was humiliated for them—and for her."[32]

The influences also went the other direction, causing different kinds of conflict. Penelope Tree, after being photographed by Avedon for several years, became the model and lover of British photographer David Bailey, who had struggled up from the working class by shooting and being the lover of Jean Shrimpton. Tree moved into Bailey's London house, painted the rooms black and purple, and brought in a cacophony of people Bailey didn't like: Black Panthers, hippies, Tibetan monks. Tree's radical friends incensed Bailey's working-class sensibilities: "I'd be getting into my Rolls and there would be three of them in the back smoking joints that I had paid for and calling me a capitalist pig!"[33]

By decade's end, the "Popocracy" from fashion (and music) was not only dominating the pages of fashion books, it was also partying with the Jet Set. The working class as a source of fashion standards was suddenly present, not only in the magazines but in the social whirl formerly reserved for elites. The only antecedent needed was beauty. Vreeland dubbed the new elite "The Beautiful People." In the exuberance of the 1960s, therefore, the definition of "fashionable society" was changed once again. Fashion models, in particular, rose in social standing in a moment as dramatic as the rise of actresses. The old Yankee Protestant elite continued to hold its debutante balls and have its "reigning beauty" each year. Among the Beautiful People, there was also a kind of reigning beauty, but she was chosen by the media. Tom Wolfe called her "the Girl of the Year."[34]

As editor of a magazine that was both the bible of the international Jet Set and the most creative of fashion books, Vreeland was in a particularly good position to declare someone "The Girl of the Year." So, when she commented that Jane Holzer was "the most contemporary girl I know" in 1964, it was incontrovertible evidence of Holzer's currency. Holzer's first big splash occurred in early 1964, when she traveled to Paris for the spring shows. All the designers were predicting (or "dictating") a "small head" that year. A "small head" simply meant that the appropriate way to wear one's hair with the next season's clothes was to keep it close to the head, either by cutting it short or pulling it back into a knot. But Jane Holzer showed up wearing Big Hair. Not just her own hair long and bushy, but a hairpiece, too. *Huge* hair. Independence in this matter impressed DianaVreeland (who was wearing her own very weird hair). So, when the

Paris shows were reported in the next *Vogue,* Jane Holzer's hair became A Statement. Soon thereafter Holzer appeared in *Life* magazine. Tom Wolfe described her sudden fame: "Jane Holzer—well, there is no easy term available. . . . The magazines have used her as a kind of combination of model, celebrity and socialite. And yet none of them have been able to do much more than, in effect, set down her name, Baby Jane Holzer, and surround it with a few asterisks and exploding stars, as if to say, well, here we have . . . What's Happening."[35]

The Girl of the Year usually had a distinctive look about her. She might be glamorous or eccentric or polished, but she was not usually a conventional beauty. Holzer, for instance, had a long nose and was said to have a distinctively "New York" look—she was not, in the idiom of the moment, "A Beauty." Whether the Girl of the Year was beautiful in a classical sense or not, she was emulated by others. Lots of people did Big Hair, for example, after Jane Holzer.

When Barbra Streisand appeared on the scene, there were endless discussions about whether she was A Beauty. Yet she was photographed by Avedon for *Vogue* and her distinctive style was widely emulated. A young reporter who interviewed Streisand for *Seventeen* in 1966 wrote: "She came into her dressing room wearing a black and white monkey fur jacket, a black sweater, black stretch pants and high black leather boots. Her hair was smooth and backswept and her eyes were made up; she looked like half the girls in New York City. Or rather, half the girls in New York City now look like her."[36]

Unlike Holzer and Streisand, Gloria Steinem was, in everybody's book, A Beauty. Not "the pretty one," the modest phrase she now uses to play down her looks, but a knock-down, drop-dead, honest-to-god Beauty. Gloria's fame was not as hard to explain as Holzer's, since she was a writer for some of the most prestigious national journals. Steinem wrote profiles of James Baldwin, Barbra Streisand, Paul Newman, and Lee Radziwill. She evaluated fashions, such as textured stockings, for the *New York Times* and covered popular designers. She wrote a fluff piece for the *Ladies' Home Journal* on Zsa Zsa Gabor's bed. There were her witty articles for *Esquire.* She published a whimsical and funny work called *The Beach Book* with an introduction by one of her famous friends, John Kenneth Galbraith. At super-hip *New York* magazine, Steinem wrote the popular personal shopping column.[37]

Gloria Steinem had grown up in poverty, but by the 1960s she was earning $30,000 a year as a writer, then an large income. Like other working women of the 1960s, she had discovered that looks and knowledge of fashion could be used to gain an entrée into the nation's most elite circles. Marilyn Bender reported in *The Beautiful People:* "Although she sounded offhand about the labels in her dresses, Miss Steinem is knowledgeable about fashion. She dropped two of the right names, Pucci and Bendel's. In the fall of 1964, she had the wit to turn up at the LBJ Discotheque—a temporary dance hall improvised by Democratic fashion society on the premises of El Morocco to raise money for the campaign—in a clingy, jersey dress that revealed her long-legged curviness, even in the nearly total darkness. It was just an old Gernreich, she said as the photographer took her picture."[38]

As a contributing beauty editor of *Glamour* in the early 1960s, Steinem had also appeared as a fashion model. She was the *Glamour* girl for February 1964 and was photographed having her hair cut by Sassoon. She was featured on a date in *McCall's*. Magazines ran stories on the decoration of her apartment (done by Jane Holzer), the way she entertained, and her beauty regimen. Steinem appeared at the right parties, wearing the latest fashions, pursued by paparazzi, and in the company of Jackie Kennedy, Norman Mailer, and Andy Warhol. By the mid-1960s, "Gloria had become an almost legendary figure on the New York 'pop' scene." She even got fan mail. To be seen with her was a social achievement. It was (often) said that Gloria Steinem could get through in one phone call to anyone in the United States, save (perhaps) the president. Julie Andrews, then starring in three major motion pictures at once, told a journalist that if she weren't herself, she would be Gloria Steinem. Steinem appeared on Walter Cronkite's television coverage of the moon shot in 1968—for no readily discernible reason. In a later decade *Newsweek,* writing on Steinem for a new reason, remarked: "As far back as 1963 or 1964, long before she had more than hinted at her best work, Steinem was a Beautiful Person and pop celebrity around town—a phase that she would now like to think lasted about two weeks."[39]

Part of Steinem's appeal was keeping up with the men she dated. By the late 1960s, Gloria had been linked to director Mike Nichols, jazz musician Paul Desmond, comedy writer Herb Sargent, decathlete Rafer Johnson, and presidential advisor Ted Sorenson—all of them, as they say, "very eligible." Columnist Liz Smith gossiped: "Ted Sorenson didn't want her to drink or smoke. He wanted her to wear her hair in a bun. He said it was more feminine. Imagine, what could be more feminine than Gloria?" It was well known that these confirmed bachelors were inevitably anxious to tie the knot with Steinem, who, just as inevitably, refused every one of them. Talk show host Dick Cavett said Gloria Steinem was "the Ideal Girl." She was called "the thinking man's Jean Shrimpton" and "Goldie Hawn with brains" and "a counterculture Barbie doll." She was said to have, like Daisy Buchanan in *The Great Gatsbv,* "a voice that sounded like money." A reporter from her home town of Toledo described her as "the sweet belle of success . . . queen of the slicks and the sweetheart of the slickers."[40]

After the British era of the pop fashion movement shifted into the more politically articulate California years, the Beautiful People shifted first into cocktails with the Black Panthers and then into parties for the Second Wave of feminism. This new alignment between Beautiful People and leftist politics was christened "Radical Chic" by writer Tom Wolfe.[41] The parties of the Radically Chic were a hodgepodge of wealthy aristocrats, liberal Hollywood types, intellectuals and artists, Black Panthers and farm-workers, and assorted hangers-on. Radical Chic had its Girl of the Year, too, and certainly Gloria Steinem was one of them. Being Beautiful in the 1960s didn't keep you out of politics. In fact, one of the most important political initiatives of the day was about the politics of getting into Beauty.

## BEAUTY, POWER, AND PROTEST

"Black Is Beautiful" signaled the African American community's demand to be included in the arena of beauty, as well as the culture of commerce, and—by extension—in the sharing of power in the society. The "Black Is Beautiful" sentiment was manifest in the dress of both men and women—as in "Afro" hairdos and dashikis. It was also evident in pressure from activist groups, such as the Congress for Racial Equality (CORE) and the National Association for the Advancement of Colored People (NAACP), to include images of blacks in the national media.

At the beginning of the 1960s, the American media, like other American institutions, was segregated. There were black newspapers, magazines, and radio stations. The white press, often referred to as the "general," "mainstream," or "national" press, had no black writers or photographers and covered black affairs only insofar as events such as race riots impinged on the news. The black press was so clearly separate from the white press that it even had its own wire service. There were only three television networks, all of them owned and run by whites. No black faces were allowed to appear on television in either the regular programming or the advertising. Consequently, integrating black faces into the national media, including the fashion press, was as important as integrating any other public facility. It is for this reason that the history of black women as exemplars of beauty is substantively different from the history of white women or of any other group. As discussed in previous chapters, pictures of Native American, Hispanic, and Asian beauties have been part of the discourse of fashion in America from the beginning. Although feminists often claim that the American aesthetic included only white women, the actual record simply does not support this argument. Instead, only the Africans have been completely absent as ideals of appearance. Thus, the emergence of beautiful black women during the 1960s is a significant historical event.

Designer Oleg Cassini first used black runway models in the mid-1950s. By the mid-1960s, two all-black model agencies were operating in New York. The first black woman to appear in one of the high fashion magazines was Donyale Luna, photographed by Richard Avedon for *Harper's Bazaar* in 1964. In March 1968 the *Ladies' Home Journal* became the first of the women's magazines to put a black woman on its cover. Advertisers integrated fashion ads at about the same time. The earliest "integrated" fashion ad I have found is a 1965 ad for Ship N' Shore blouses from the March issue of *Seventeen.* By 1970 black models were appearing frequently in the national women's magazines. Both *Glamour* and *Mademoiselle* put black women on their covers in 1968. *Vogue,* however, did not show a black model on its cover until 1974, when it presented Beverly Johnson there. Johnson had begun modeling for *Glamour* in 1971 and, from the beginning, her popularity among *Glamour* readers, as measured by regular polls, was striking. Her popularity was often attributed to her casual, accessible looks; however, two other models of the period, Iman and Naomi Sims, were quite exotic in appearance and were also very popular.[42]

Johnson's acceptance among young college and professional women suggests something important about the reasons behind the sudden integration of fashion imagery after over a hundred years of excluding African Americans. Growth in the numbers of young women made *Seventeen, Glamour,* and *Mademoiselle* into publishing powerhouses in the late 1960s and early 1970s. Those same numbers had propelled certain "youth" brands and designers to prominence and profitability. Like the flappers, the "flower children" of the 1960s were recognized as a powerful market, in spite of their differences from the genteel mainstream. Historians and pollsters have shown repeatedly that these young women had values on issues from work to race that differed as dramatically from their mothers' as did their dress habits. The fashion powers of the 1960s, therefore, were responding to the pressures of the Civil Rights leadership to be sure, but they were also responding to a known market force: the diametrically different politics of the heavy-spending youth audience.

It has become a commonplace in the feminist literature to criticize the images of black women in the media on three counts: (1) black women appear only if they are light-skinned; (2) black women are portrayed only as either Aunt Jemimas or "bad girls"; and (3) black women, like other women of color, are treated as exotics. Most of the black models who first broke into the American fashion industry were not light-skinned, nor did they have Caucasian features. None of them was represented as an Aunt Jemima. Neither were they presented as sultry sex toys. Although Iman and Naomi Sims (and sometimes Donyale Luna) were treated as exotics, black women are most frequently pictured in clothing, settings, and poses that are indistinguishable from those of whites.

Thus arguments about the representation of black women are not only inaccurate, they create a smoke screen for a troublesome contradiction. White feminists have staked a great deal on the assertion that their disempowerment is predicated on their exploitation as objects of beauty. Yet black women, having been excluded from those same images, clearly saw breaking into *Vogue* and *Glamour* as major victories. And, in the overall trajectory of the Civil Rights movement, the "Black Is Beautiful" campaign seems perfectly aimed at the connection between having power and being considered beautiful. For white women to see beauty a barrier to power and for black women to see it as a bridge to power reflects another contradiction inherent in the antibeauty ideology.

Magazines of the 1960s also show many other ethnic minorities. Particularly with the international Jet Set in focus, there existed many opportunities to show high-born Hispanics, such as the Duquesa de Cadaval modeling Balenciaga in the April 15, 1967, issue of *Vogue.* Gloria Guinness was a native of Mexico. *Vogue* published a multipage feature on one of the biggest celebrities of the 1960s, Raquel Welch (born Raquel Tejada), who also did ads for Coke, Coppertone, and Foster Grant.

Because of the trend toward "ethnic" clothing, especially among the counterculture, Native American clothes, jewelry, and imagery appear often in the fashion books. *Mademoiselle* showed Native American college girls dressed in updated traditional clothing in a college feature in the August 1968 issue. The August 15, 1970, issue of *Vogue* included a six-page fashion feature on Native American clothing, showing singer/actress Cher (who is part Cherokee) in various examples of traditional face paint. The Revlon theme of 1971 was "Canyon Colors," showing Evelyn Kuhn dressed as a Native American.

Because of the late 1960s preference for long, straight hair, Asian women appear often in ads for shampoos and conditioners. The straight hair fad, however, had more salient political connections to the protest movement: "among the rebels who yearned to be like Judy Collins and Joan Baez, [straight hair] expressed a sincerity based on contempt for society, hand-me-down values, and the coifed generation's ideals."[43] The long, straight hair of the young women of the late 1960s was the counterpart to the controversial long hairstyles of the young men. These were acts of rebellion against the highly constructed female hairdos and very short male haircuts of the previous generation. This is why, after all, one of the key cultural events of the generation was a musical called *Hair* and why one of the most inflammatory remarks of the time was "Get a haircut!"

Famed for its free sexual attitudes, casual drug culture, "acid rock," "psychedelic" graphics, and pleasure ethic, the colorful, defiant neighborhood of Haight-Ashbury in San Francisco was the mecca for the hippie culture of the late 1960s, distilling as it did the attitudes of the young across America toward the morals and dress codes of their elders. The frequent dances held in the Haight provided throngs of hippies with an occasion to dress up. But their dress up clothes were more like those worn by children at play than adults out for an evening: "They were in Mod clothes, Victorian suits, and granny gowns, Old West outfits, pirate costumes, free-form costumes." New designers coming from California by 1967 were often counterculture members themselves. San Francisco's Linda Gravenites lived in the Haight; Los Angeles' Holly Harp had a shop right on the Strip. Both used beads or paint on unlikely fabrics, such as chiffon and jersey—even denim—and found a ready clientele among female rock stars. By the end of the decade, counterculture designs had made it all the way to the pages of *Vogue,* often modeled by the likes of rock stars Janis Joplin or Grace Slick.[44]

One of the most fascinating practices of the hippie culture was its love of old, cast-off clothing. There was also a distinct taste for ethnic costumes, which could be purchased inexpensively from import shops. If cheap dresses and throwaway evening wear were a challenge to the old couture, recycling old clothes was even worse. Yet the fashion magazines all ran features on boutiques, thrift shops, and import stores.

Haight-Ashbury was full of runaways and improvised communal living arrangements. The dress ethic of San Francisco also created new identities for daily life: "Haight-Ashbury's orgiastic and egalitarian utopia asked its participants to sever old loyalties and prior identities. New clothes were essential to this rite of passage. Divesting themselves of the uniforms of the prevailing hierarchies, these dissidents devised masquerades that were incomprehensible to the noninitiated." The fantastic dress among the hippies, both male and female, was thus an intentional statement of rebellion against traditional morality, sex roles, politics, and consumption. Members of the older generation, by and large, got the message. They didn't like it.[45]

Although the culture of the Haight was rebellious in a lifestyle sense more than an explicitly political sense, the overall counterculture was definitely tied to the emergent "New Left" (see figure 9.1). The street theater tactics often adopted by the Left were formally similar to the sensual expressions of the Aquarian Age—it was hard sometimes to distinguish "love-ins" and "happenings" from "sit-ins" and protest rallies. In either case, the dress, music, and, often, the participants were the same.

## THE GIRL NEXT DOOR

Diane Ackerman recalls that, "In the late sixties, a white woman was nowhere if she didn't have straight hair. Straight hair suggested a nonethnic (and therefore upper-class) bloodline; the cheerleaders all wore their blond hair straight." The association with straight hair was not, as I have described, exclusively "white" or upper class. By 1970, however, the image of a blond woman with long, straight hair did appear in the fashion images with increasing frequency. A belief in the preponderance of blondes in the fashion magazines, particularly the advertising, was to become a key issue for the feminists of the early 1970s—and today the complaint is still made that advertisers "tell us we all have to be blue-eyed blondes."[46]

In fact, however, dark-haired models have outnumbered blondes in advertising images through most of the twentieth century (see figure 9.2).[47] The perception that there are more blondes appears to be the artifact of an anomaly that took place between 1965 and 1975, when there was a noticeable increase in the number of blondes

Figure 9.1. Youth fashion becomes associated with the protest movement and the New Left. *Vogue,* December 1967.

presented in the advertisements of the women's and fashion magazines. By 1975, however, the situation had reversed, returning to the traditional proportions where dark hair outnumbered light hair two to one, a mix that has held to this today. Nevertheless, the anomalous upsurge of blondes around 1970 supported the careers of several new models, including Cheryl Tiegs, Christie Brinkley, and Cybill Shepherd.

Three identifiable factors contributed to the increase in images of blond women in the ads of this time. One was the surfing subculture, with its ideal of the "California Girl," which arose in the mid-1960s. The Beach Boys, Jan and Dean, and the Ventures produced a style of music that was distinctively different from the British bands, the protest singers, and the "head" bands of San Francisco. Along came beach movies and surfing posters, as well as ads for tanning products and bathing suits. The California Girl in these images was almost always a tanned blonde.

The biggest category of ads with blond women were those touting the introduction of the first safe, reliable blond hair dyes. Beginning in the mid-1960s, these products were marketed by Clairol, Revlon, L'Oreal, and Max Factor. When these products were new, they had a major effect on the number of blondes in the ads at that time. Once the newness wore off, however, the number of these ads declined, causing the percentage of blondes to fall back to what it had been for the previous twenty-five years.

A third factor was the rising popularity of the "natural" aesthetic. Demand for "natural" products in categories ranging from household cleansers to processed food was attributable to consumer concerns about the environmental and medical risks of chemical additives. Also influential were the turn of the youth culture toward a back-to-nature ethic, the emergence of the environmental movement, and the revival of the feminist movement.

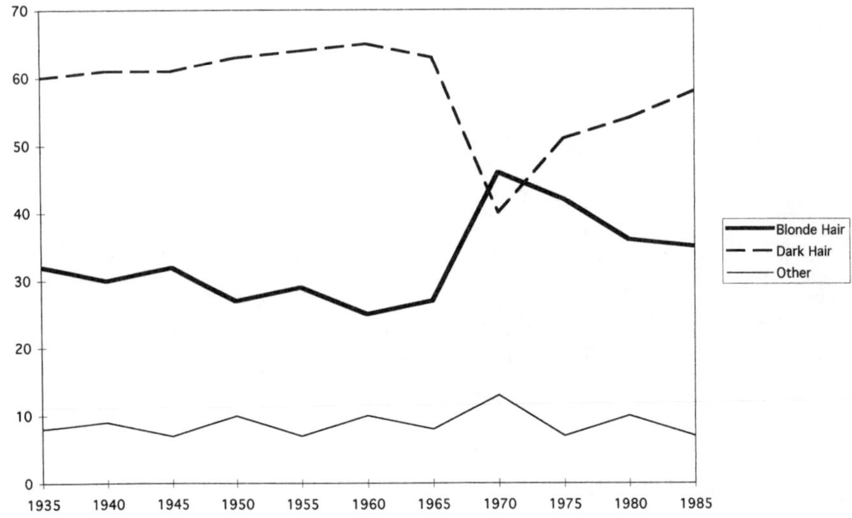


Figure 9.2. Incidence of blondes versus females with other hair colors in the advertisements from 1935 to 1985. Based on a large sample drawn from *Vouge, Glamour, Mademoiselle,* and *Bazaar.*

In the cosmetics and fashion arenas, the craze for the "natural" was evident in a return to all-natural fibers, the popularity of denim blue jeans, fragrances based on pure essences, and a sudden shift toward less theatrical makeup in the late decade. There was also an emphasis on "clean," "simple," and "good for you" products. Except for Revlon, which sometimes used dark-haired models for its "natural" line, the models for these products were blond.

Cover Girl's "Clean Makeup" campaign provides a case in point. In 1967 hexachlorophine, the "miracle ingredient" in Cover Girl, was banned. Cover Girl had to change its campaign, although it could still use the word "medicated" and "clean" because the product contained Noxzema face cream. In February 1968, a new campaign for Cover Girl, called "Clean Makeup," was introduced. The creative director recalled: "Once we did 'Clean Make-up,' we had to get a look for it. Clean, clean, clean, that operative word ran through everything we did, everything we touched, everything we wrote. Models dressed all in white were shown boating, running, swimming. The . . . color scheme is white and blue." The art director expands their thinking on hair color: "It's like on a wonderful summer day if you're out at the beach or you're looking up and the sky is blue and the air is clean and all. And it goes so well with the look, which is the blonde, blue-eyed All-American girl." The producer describes their choices of settings, props, and models as a conscious decision to communicate "clean": "The girls always had that kind of fresh, clean look. They didn't have to be blondes, but they had *to feel* blonde, in a way."[48] The campaign theme song was sung by a male vocal group with a clear, rather high-pitched sound and close harmonies like the Beach Boys. So the Clean Makeup campaign drew on the current California Girl imagery, but it also tapped long-standing American prejudices about light people being cleaner than dark people.

The outdoor scenes and "natural look" were very much in tune with the youth culture by the late 1960s as well as with the embryonic feminist movement, which demanded that women look "natural." Apparently, many women who wanted to be feminists, but who didn't want to give up their makeup, switched to Cover Girl during this time. Lynn Giordano was a journalism major at the University of Wisconsin in the late 1960s. Years later, when she was the creative director on Cover Girl, she remembered: "No woman, no matter how radical her politics—this is the real truth, I mean, you'll never get women to admit this but no matter how left of center they stood, they wanted to look good when they were standing there. . . . And one of the reasons Cover Girl went through the roof was that they were selling a no-makeup look right when it was great to be a no-makeup look."[49]

By the 1980s, Cover Girl was the leading makeup among women under forty. According to those who managed the campaign, the keys to its success were the "natural" appeal and feminist pressure to look more "real." Thus, ironically, the "no make-up" dictum of the Second Wave was a determining factor in the long-term success of one of America's leading cosmetics brands. And this occurred in the context of many ad campaigns that equated "natural" and "clean" with "blonde."

## GET REAL

"I went home one day," remembered the fashion editor. "And the next, Diana's red office, the leopard rug, her Rigaud candles, her scent, her being were gone. The walls were beige."[50] In 1971 Diana Vreeland was abruptly fired and replaced by her assistant, Grace Mirabella.

Vreeland's innovative fashion spreads, once the pride of the industry, were now said to be showing "clothes that most women wouldn't wear on Halloween." Her philosophy suddenly was not commercial enough. She was accused of photographing clothes that weren't even available for purchase! As those who worked with her knew, such concerns had never been central to Vreeland's mission, but in the wake of the 1971 recession, *Newsweek* suggested, "Fantasies suddenly became *de trop* . . . retailers complained that *Vogue* magazine's arty layouts no longer showed their clothes to advantage. In the first three months of 1971, *Vogue* lost 38 percent of its advertising pages (*Harper's Bazaar* dropped 37 percent) and Mrs. Vreeland, then 71, stepped down in favor of her 40-year-old assistant Grace Mirabella." Mirabella's philosophy, said Condé Nast management, was more congenial to fashion as a business.[51]

Mirabella's mission was to "update *Vogue* for an era of antifashion and women's liberation" *and* to increase the advertising interest in the magazine. Mirabella explained to the press that her strategy would be to make *Vogue* more "realistic" by using more "natural" models in more "typical" environments. So, in the name of a more "realistic" and "natural" look, the variety of faces appearing in *Vogue* was suddenly gone. The connection between the new "realism" and commercial appeal was borne out. After Mirabella replaced Vreeland at *Vogue,* circulation rose from 400,000 in 1971 to 1,245,000 in 1987, when she left to start her own magazine. The demand for a "natural," more "realistic" look and, ironically, for a clearer link between image and purchase had finally killed the rebellious playfulness of the 1960s.[52]

## FAST FORWARD

The feminist critique of beauty that emerged in the early 1970s came on the heels of the fast-changing, paradoxical milieu that made Cheryl Tiegs and Lauren Hutton as well as Twiggy and Iman. As a consequence, the critique is based on several assumptions peculiar to the conditions of its time. Although these observations have not held up over the decades, they have continued to be believed as myth.

One is the belief that the beauties in the media are predominantly blond. As we have seen, the early years of the Second Wave coincided with an anomalous increase in the number of blond images that were attributable to concrete events, such as new hair dyes and the surfing craze. Today the argument is still made, although it is no longer accurate.

Then there is the myth of The Face. From Una Stannard in 1971 to Naomi Wolfe in 1995, we were told that fashion presents us with one standard of beauty at any time.[53] We must all conform to The Face, they say. I hope readers have noticed the number of times in this chapter that a different woman was declared "The Face" or "The Girl of the Hour." At any time, there was an array of faces being loudly proclaimed "The Face" in one way or another. In truth, "The Face" existed in the minds of feminist critics and media pundits, but it doesn't describe what is observable in the discourse.

A third is the one in which the "youth worship" of the culture is condemned for rendering older women useless and unappealing. This, too, is an artifact of the 1960s experience from which the Second Wave feminists came. As we have seen, the young faces and styles of the 1960s were consciously put forward against a backdrop dominated by society matrons, old movie stars, crusty designers, and haughty models. The youth movement was aimed at upending an entrenched worldview that favored mature adults, including its beauty aesthetic and dress standards. Thus, the negative attitude toward the "old" in the 1960s context was more than a blind glorification of youth. It was a rejection of past hierarchies, norms, snobberies, and values. The movement was successful largely because its ranks were drawn from the single largest demographic cohort in American history. The "youth worship" that some have read into that moment is not a universal or necessary factor, but a variable dependent upon demographics, history, and social structure.

In the faces of popular culture today, we see many who survived the youth movement of the 1960s as beautiful celebrities, thus giving the lie to claims that the culture can only recognize the young as beautiful. At sixty-one, Gloria Steinem was chosen as *People* magazine's 1995 Fifty Most Beautiful People in the World. Although Jean Shrimpton retired long ago, she was still getting modeling offers throughout her 40s. Now in her sixties, Lauren Hutton is still one of the highest-paid models in the world. Anjelica Huston is more actress than model, but she still appears in the fashion features. Christie Brinkley was still commanding $500,000 for a television commercial into her late forties. Cybill Shepherd and Candice Bergen both had success in their forties as television actresses—and made commercial endorsements for beauty products. Cheryl Tiegs has her own lines of eyewear, hosiery, socks, jewelry, fashion watches, and shoes. Isabella Rossellini, "discovered" by Diana Vreeland when she was seventeen, was the spokesperson for Lancôme for at least a decade, until she was nearly fifty. Elizabeth Taylor introduced two of the most successful perfumes of the last decade of the twentieth century—and she appeared in the ads herself. Jackie Kennedy was considered to be one of the most beautiful and glamorous women in the world right up until her death in 1995 at the age of sixty-five.[54]

Although modeling is now a lucrative and a prestigious occupation, however, feminists would still prefer that everyone go to law school or medical school. The class differences once expressed in the division of "working with your head" versus "working with your hands" have combined with the feminist ideal of the "heroine of the mind" to exclude models and other "heroines of the body."

Barbie is still taking the brunt of these kinds of criticisms, in spite of the wide range of responses that four decades of play have evoked among Barbie owners. For many of us, Barbie, being the stuff of the imagination, is as much a heroine of the mind as of the body. She has been painted by Andy Warhol and Kenny Scharf, photographed by William Wegman and Francesco Scavullo. Calvin Klein, Liz Claiborne, Betsey Johnson, Yves Saint Laurent, and Frederick's of Hollywood have all designed clothes for her. Vidal Sassoon has done her hair. The book *Mondo Barbie* contains poems and stories by forty-two different authors, male and female, and *The Art of Barbie* drew works from leading artists. Many people, it seems, like the idea of "playing Barbie."[55]

Yet Barbie remains the symbol against which feminism sets its anchor. It has not been enough for Barbie to be a doctor, a lawyer, a pilot, or an executive. It has not been enough that she has remained single and childless all these years. It has not been enough that she is now available in every hair color, skin tone, and ethnic dress imaginable. For decades now, feminist critics have been telling us that playing Barbie is damaging, because her hair is too blond and her breasts too big. Barbie, they tell us, is "unrealistic" and thus encourages little girls to create fantasy worlds when they play—an odd criticism to make of a toy.

The last myth is the one says that the Second Wave "liberated" women by insisting on a more "natural" look, a more "real" presentation. Yet the antibeauty crusade interrupted a moment when people were wearing a variety of ethnic clothes, recycling "antique" dress, blurring the lines of gender, and playing the "natural" against the "artificial" with true abandon. In *The Beauty Myth,* Naomi Wolf wrote of a utopian vision, in which "young girls could find a thousand wild and tantalizing visions of possible futures."[56] If the "anything goes" aesthetic of the 1960s doesn't constitute "wild and tantalizing visions," then I'm not sure what would.

Second Wave feminism emerged with a handicap when it came to play and a blind spot where the love of beauty was supposed to be. *Ms.* ran an article on Diana Vreeland in the mid-1970s that demonstrates this point to a painful degree. The writer enthuses about Vreeland's success and outrageousness, but then condescends in a way that is pathetic in its self-conscious seriousness, its utter lack of confidence or joy: "One feminist asks: 'How can anyone devote a lifetime to fashion?' But that this woman worked in fashion is beside the point, and then again, exactly the point after all. Vreeland in fashion is like Golda Meier running the Girl Scouts. She's a brilliant woman who did the best within the confines of what was allowed her. It is sobering to think of what Diana Vreeland might have accomplished, had she been able to change reality instead of creating escape." That this feminist cannot conceive of a reality in which play, color, and fantasy have a legitimate place says more about her own shortcomings than about Vreeland's accomplishments.[57]

Feminism's insistence on a predetermined "natural" appearance, although aimed at destroying fashion, only created a change in styles in the 1970s. There was no death blow to the commercial patriarchy. On the contrary, a culture of dress that had recently become diverse, fantastic, androgynous, democratic, and expressive was suddenly brought to heel under the directive to "be natural" instead. The fashion establishment took back its control—and its profits.

Since the 1970s, feminist essays on fashion and beauty have consistently assumed that decoration is oppressive and an unadorned look is more politically radical. But the costumery of the 1960s expressed an explicit critique of mid-twentieth-century American life—a potentially subversive reference it still holds today (see figure 9.3).

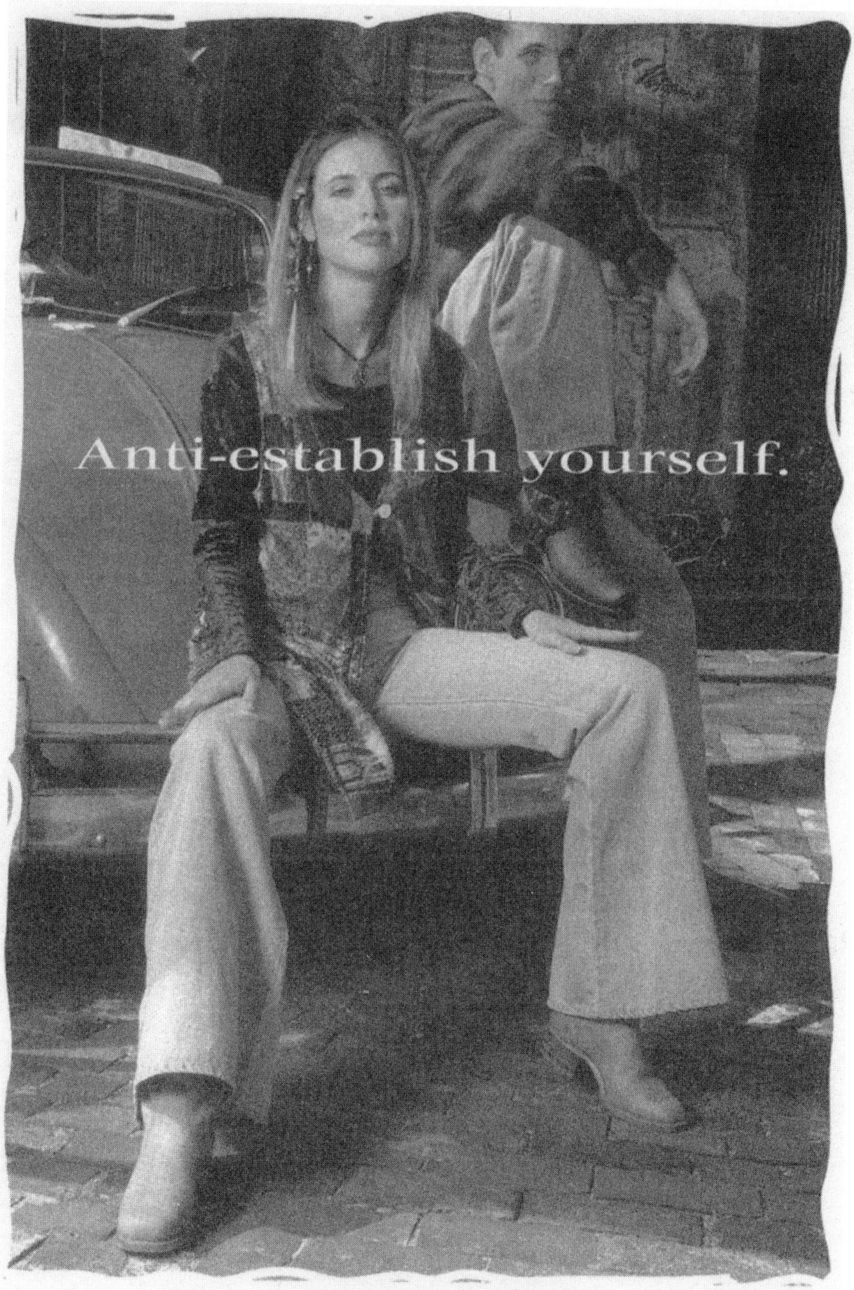
Anti-establish yourself.
CODE WEST
FOOTWEAR

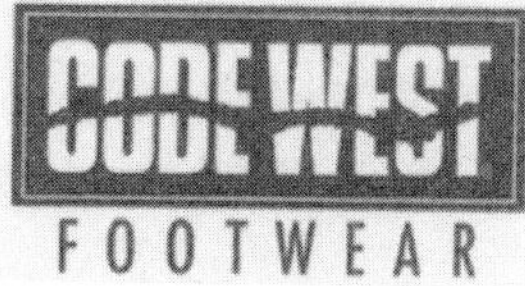

Figure 9.3. The costumes of the 1960s could still evoke the spirit of rebellion thirty years later, as in this ad from the mid-1990s.

As we'll see in the next chapter, when the New Feminists of the early 1970s advocated a certain style of appearance as "natural," they in fact signified their political alliances. Complete conformity was demanded within the group to demonstrate compliance with the preferred ideology. Only at risk of exclusion could you do Something Different.

## Chapter 10

# STYLE AND SUBSTANCE IN THE SECOND WAVE

Susan Brownmiller stood on the curb of Lexington Avenue at East 54th Street in the expensive, Jackie Kennedy–style dress she thought was appropriate for the occasion. Behind her, a bewildered group of feminist protesters huddled in the scattered snow, too frightened to go into the gleaming skyscraper across the street. Exasperated, Susan stepped off the curb and began walking toward the doorway. Familiar with the territory and confident in her own readiness, she strode into the lobby and pressed the elevator button. The jittery group followed.[1]

When the elevator doors opened on the offices of the *Ladies' Home Journal,* the perfectly groomed Brownmiller led the group two by two down the corridor, past the executive secretaries, and into the office of the editor-in-chief, John Mack Carter. Looking up expectantly when they entered the room, Carter appeared to be waiting for them. A reporter, it seems, had tipped him off that the "women's liberationists" were about to stage a "sit-in" in his office.

The group crowded into the small room, as did a television crew that had followed them from the street. Brownmiller stood before Carter's desk and read their demands: "an immediate stop to the publication of articles that are irrelevant, unstimulating, and demeaning to the women of America," that Carter resign and a woman be put in his place, that all the male staff members at the *Journal* be replaced with women, that objectionable advertisements be barred from the pages of the magazine, that free day care be provided for *Journal* employees, that the focus on home and family be dropped, and that the feminists themselves be allowed to edit an issue of the magazine. An ABC reporter with a bright smile shoved a mike in his face and asked what he had to say. The editor said only that he would not negotiate under pressure. Determined, the group settled in to wait him out.

After about two hours at this impasse, more women's voices were heard coming down the hallway. The new arrivals were tougher, scruffier, and more defiant than the first group. They smoked the editor's cigars and openly discussed throwing him out the window. Brownmiller objected, "Sisters, sisters! This is not the way!" The tough crowd's leader, a tall, delicately beautiful woman with blond hair and a southern drawl, warned, "If you don't deal with them"—pointing to Brownmiller and her more peaceful group—"you get us." The stand-off continued another eight hours. In the end, Carter agreed to allow the group to write a supplement for the *Journal,* for which they would be paid $10,000.[2]

The March 1970 occupation of the *Ladies' Home Journal* is now a high moment in feminist legend. The story, however, also distills a number of conflicts that plagued the Second Wave: its problematic relationship with the national press, its distance from ordinary women, and its internal disagreements. The protest action itself, for instance, illustrates the movement's habit of placing the blame for women's oppression on the media, particularly the women's magazines, despite the group's privileged ties to the national press. Susan Brownmiller, like several others involved in the movement, had an established career in the media, having worked for ABC-TV and NBC-TV, the *New York Times,* and even the *Journal* itself. Marlene Sanders, the ABC reporter who shoved the mike in Carter's face, was a respected television journalist and also a charter member of the National Organization for Women. Several other women in the room that day had jobs with leading media institutions or contracts with major publishers.

During the earliest years of the 1970s, the emergent "women's liberation" movement was described, reported, and analyzed repeatedly by *Time, Newsweek,* the *Atlantic, Saturday Review,* the *New York Times, U.S. News & World Report,* and many other national magazines, as well as *McCall's, Glamour, Vogue,* and all the other women's magazines. Contrary to what is usually claimed, nearly all of this coverage was respectful and even supportive. Although feminists of the time were constantly complaining about the male reporters' derogation of the movement, most of the journalists sent to cover the "New Feminism" were women and, in fact, a substantial number were active in the movement. Looking back now at the by-lines, there is a remarkable overlap with those names prominent in the history of the Second Wave: Susan Brownmiller, Betty Friedan, Germaine Greer, Alice Rossi, Lucy Komisar, Gloria Steinem, Sally Kempton, Vivian Gornick, and others appear in both places.[3]

One of the big sins of the women's service and fashion magazines in the eyes of the Second Wave radicals was that they were edited by men. True, in the 1950s and early 1960s most editors of the women's service magazines were male. But by the time Brownmiller and her friends camped out at the *Ladies' Home Journal,* females edited several of the other magazines aimed at the women's audience: Shana Alexander at *McCall's,* Edith Raymond Locke at *Mademoiselle,* Ruth Whitney at *Glamour,* Helen Gurley Brown at *Cosmopolitan,* Diana Vreeland at *Vogue,* Enid A. Haupt at *Seventeen,* and

Nancy White at *Bazaar.* Although other reasons have been given for choosing the *Journal* as the target for this sit-in, it is pretty obvious that the whole event would have looked pretty pointless if the feminists had camped out in the *McCall's* office of Shana Alexander, who was an active member of NOW, or any of the other strongly feminist editors.

The movement's penchant for imposing ideas on less radical or educated women was also detectable in the microcosm of the *Journal* occupation. The feminists who occupied John Mack Carter's office simply assumed that they were equipped to speak to and for the readers of the *Journal* by virtue of shared sex. This group's presumption that no meaningful differences existed between themselves and this readership is a harbinger of the movement's most devastating tactical mistake: treating its own audience too casually. The condescension implicit in the way these feminists thought the *Journal's* readers did whatever their magazine told them was equally present in the assumption that, once the feminists were publishing in the *Journal,* readers would simply follow whatever "women's lib" told them, too. The persistent belief that the subscribers of the women's magazines *read nothing else* would also become a frequently made mistake. The few attempts made by the press to see what women outside New York thought about feminism were viewed with suspicion by the feminist movement. So the decade rolled forward with a growing distance between the small feminist groups described in the press and the large subgroups of women who read about them. Feminist activists appear to have been either unaware or unconcerned about the danger this gulf posed.

The contrast between the first and the second group arriving at the *Journal* that morning illustrates the different tactics, standards of behavior, and appearance that were symptomatic of factions already forming within the movement itself. NOW, which had been founded in 1966, had thus far dominated the Second Wave. Ti-Grace Atkinson, the leader of the second installment of feminists arriving at the *Ladies' Home Journal* that morning, was among a growing group of disaffected radicals who found NOW's efforts too conservative. Atkinson, a former president of the New York NOW chapter, was a protégée of Betty Freidan. Having been chosen to lead the New York group because of her patrician manners and aristocratic looks, Atkinson surprised the mother movement by making increasingly extreme statements to the press. In 1968 she had resigned from NOW, under some pressure, and formed her own group, the Feminists, which was the first of several cadres of feminists with loyalties to the far Left, such as the Redstockings and WITCH (Women's International Terrorist Conspiracy from Hell). The media were fascinated with the theatrics of the new groups and seemed determined to turn Atkinson into a "star" because she was pretty, articulate, and dramatic.

Atkinson's emerging radicalism foreshadowed the heavy theorizing to follow: She told the press that western societies set their laws, ordered their educational systems, designed their technology, and formed their family structures around the imperative to control women as domestic serfs and breeders. She described marriage as an institution of slavery and institutionalized rape, love as a matter of dependency that women would have to learn to live without. In one speech, this charming southerner trashed the Virgin Mary until a woman from the audience climbed to the podium and tried to hit her. Atkinson was among the first to suggest that women eschew the company of men as a feminist statement: "The basic issue is consistency between belief and acts. A woman saying men are the enemy with a boyfriend sitting next to her is both humiliating and tragic." Such statements shocked and infuriated NOW members as well as other, more distant watchers.[4]

The Second Wave feminists, therefore, were not a monolithic front, as they were often perceived by the public, but were instead a heterogeneous lot of varying constituencies, divergent philosophies, and different attitudes toward hierarchy and leadership. Betty Friedan, Gloria Steinem, Germaine Greer, Kate Millett, and others who were prominent in the movement differed from each other, often dramatically, in their dress, grooming, and manners. Their styles of self-presentation were visible statements of philosophy, identity, and past history that connected them to other women who shared similar beliefs, loyalties, and experiences. Therefore, attitudes about "looking like them" versus "looking like us" marked battle lines on highly charged issues.

The most radical groups developed a philosophy of dress that reduced appearance to sex appeal and attributed all control over personal presentation to men. By treating self-presentation as a purely gender-determined issue and by refusing to recognize that differences among women, as well as personal identities and private desires, were visibly expressed in ways far more subtle than was allowed by this thinking, the movement side-stepped several issues that left them vulnerable to an ambush in the mid-decade.

## DRESS FOR SUCCESS

The activists who formed the National Organization for Women were a handpicked membership of a hundred successful professional women who wore trim suits, discreet jewelry, and well-managed coiffures. They came from all over the country and many had been working against sex discrimination from within "the system" for some time. The first president of the new group, Betty Friedan, was chosen because her best-selling book, *The Feminine Mystique,* had given her a national presence and because, as a freelance writer, she was the one among them who could not be fired, demoted, or reassigned because of her activities on behalf of women.

The choice was made with reservations, however. Friedan was bossy, unkempt, and emotionally volatile. One woman involved in the early organization decisions said she hesitated to support Friedan: "All Nancy Knaak could see in this would-be leader was a distinctly unattractive woman in outlandish clothes, wearing a flowing, brightly colored cape when everybody else was wearing navy-blue tailored suits, an incoherent speaker who, Nancy was convinced, was 'not all there.'" Throughout the Second Wave, women behind the scenes at NOW managed Friedan's appearance: They took her shopping, chose her clothes for public appearances, encouraged her to have her hair done.[5]

As a group, the women of NOW were good-looking, well connected, and adept in the ways of the world. They had assembled an advisory board of twenty-eight members that included professors, executives, ministers, and labor leaders who were respectable, attractive people. In this way, NOW hoped to avoid becoming stereotyped in the public eye: "The last thing in the world you wanted was an image of a sad-sack group of disgruntled women who needed either a man or a job."[6]

Their strategy served them well. By 1970, NOW had already accomplished a great deal. By filing lawsuits, petitioning government, and demonstrating, this well-managed organization had made the Equal Employment Opportunity Commission (EEOC) enforce the antisex discrimination provision of the 1964 Civil Rights Act, achieved the liberalization of abortion laws in New York state, successfully fought for the elimination of separate male and female employment ads, registered complaints against over three hundred corporations and colleges for unfair employment practices, and pressured the Equal Rights Amendment (ERA) out of the House Judiciary Committee, where it had been gathering dust for twenty years.

The image of feminists as attractive, well-dressed, feminine women was also being protected successfully. Public opinion polls taken at the opening of the 1970s showed that only 12 percent of American women and only 9 percent of men thought "women's lib" groups were composed of "a bunch of frustrated, insecure, ugly, hysterical, masculine-type women." Furthermore, a huge majority of American adults saw no contradiction between political activism and femininity, nor between femininity and professional ambition. The substance of the NOW agenda was also surprisingly uncontroversial. For example, a 1970 Harris poll showed that the phrase "women's liberation" was most strongly associated with equal rights and employment opportunities, principles that were widely accepted by then. Even some issues that were considered potentially volatile, such as abortion and day care, had surprising support among average Americans. In 1970 about half of both American women and men believed that abortion laws should be repealed. Further, 64 percent of women and 50 percent of men supported increased day care for working mothers.[7]

NOW also had the support of most Americans in their objections to the portrayals of women in the media, particularly in advertising. The depiction of women as creatures who "had orgasms at the sight of a waxed floor" was a recurring theme in NOW rhetoric, particularly from Betty Friedan. NOW staged demonstrations at the corporate offices of major packaged goods manufacturers, pasted stickers on sexy ads that said "This ad exploits women," and gave out "Barefoot and Pregnant" awards for offensive advertising.[8]

A study published in the February 1971 issue of the *Journal of Marketing Research* reviewed 729 advertisements drawn from *Look, Life, Newsweek. The New Yorker, Saturday Review, Time,* and *U. S. News & World Report.* Only 12 percent of the workers shown in ads were female, though 33 percent of full-time workers were women. No woman appeared as a professional or executive. Most ads that showed women were in ads for household items—food, cleaning products, drugs, household appliances, and furniture—and cosmetics. Men, on the other hand, appeared most often in ads for cars, travel, liquor, cigarettes, industrial products, and financial or institutional ads. About half the time women appeared in ads for "male" products, they were portrayed as decorations.[9]

A group of powerful women at J. Walter Thompson, led by market research specialist Rena Bartos (also a member of NOW), conducted a series of studies of demographic changes among women, with particular attention to labor force participation and the impact of these changes on attitudes toward family life and consumption behaviors. In 1971, when this study began, 58 percent of American women were not in the labor force, while 42 percent worked. At the end of the decade, the proportions were almost reversed: 48 percent were not working, 52 percent were. And, although sixty percent of married women did not work in 1970, by 1980 the proportion had shifted until fully half of all wives were active in the labor force.[10]

Bartos found that the breakdown of "working" versus "stay-at-home" was insufficiently sensitive, so she grouped women into four categories: career women, women to whom work was "just a job," housewives who planned to go back to work, and housewives who planned to stay at home. The oldest, least affluent, and less educated group was the stay-at-home housewives, while career women were both highly educated and very affluent. Neither stay-at-home housewives nor just-a-job workers were particularly fashion conscious, and both groups ranked low on their readership of women's magazines. Housewives who planned to go back to work were as fashionable as they could afford to be, but they seldom had money to spend on themselves. In fact, their hopes about returning to the workplace were focused on having the money to spend on their own appearance. Some reported being jealous of their husband's ability to afford stylish clothes for himself; others said getting money for clothes from their husband was a source of conflict.

Career women were, by far, the most fashion conscious and the heaviest readers of women's and fashion magazines. However, this segment read broadly, scoring very high on national news and political commentary. Career women dressed more for professional performance than romance; however, their dress habits were mostly motivated by self-expression. Interestingly, the other three groups viewed career women, not men or movie stars, as the source of fashion standards.

As the result of such studies and the growing chorus of objections, many advertisers changed their representations of women during the 1970s. For example, although ads for grooming products had focused on promises of romance for decades, new appeals to career ambition and personal empowerment began to show up in the pages of the women's magazines. The most successful fragrance introduction of the decade, Charlie, played on the character of a newly liberated woman. The number of ads for employment opportunities in the women's magazines, for both traditional and non-traditional jobs, increased. Interestingly, after NOW succeeded in knocking down the rule that women could not advance past the level of colonel in the U.S. military, one of the biggest categories of advertising in the young women's fashion magazines became military recruitment. More ads also recognized women's political involvement, sometimes when the connection between product and politics was fairly tenuous. And, most ominously, special interest groups, such as oil companies, began lobbying in the pages of the women's press. Over the decade, some advertisers that had traditionally aimed at men produced ads specifically for women and placed them in the women's and fashion magazines.

The women's magazines themselves also responded to the new imperatives. As ambitious young women took full advantage of the new opportunities won by NOW, the women's press advised them on the manners, clothing, and behavior that would help them to feel confident working in uncharted territory. Beauty features focused on professional grooming ("What to Wear When You're Doing the Talking: How to Present a Confident Image"). *Glamour* even ran a fashion spread, "For the Girl Who Hasn't Much Time to Think About Fashion," starring Brenda Fasteau, legal counsel for NOW. In his best-selling book, *Dress for Success,* John Molloy codified the look of the successful professional woman epitomized by the NOW membership. Molloy claimed to have done extensive research on the clothing that would make women most successful in a business environment: skirt suits, plain shirts, sensible shoes, ties or scarves at the neck, and expensive accessories. The fashion magazines picked up the approach, running spreads with titles like "Clothes that Work." *Glamour* expanded a regular column called "How to Get More from Your Job" and ran features encouraging readers in new endeavors of all sorts: "Working for Yourself: Is It for You?"; "How to Start Doing What You Are Too Scared to Do"; "What You Should Know about Business Travel." Ambitious female executives scooped up other how-to books, such as *The Managerial Woman* and *Games Mother Never Taught You,* and propelled them to the bestseller lists. As the 1970s drew to a close, the figure of the young female professional was as much a cliché as the big-skirted housewife had ever been.[11]

Throughout the decade, the women's service magazines covered the ERA, put women in nontraditional roles on covers, and informed their readers of a variety of life options, including divorce, childlessness, and careers—and with a supportive, not a denigrating attitude. *Redbook,* for example, did a series on the feminist movement in 1972, which opened with the following declaration of position: "What does *Redbook* think about the Women's Liberation Movement? We believe that every human being should have the right and the opportunity to make her or his own choices in every area of life. This seems to be a very simple and obvious point of view. But, of course, it is not, and it may not ever be a popular one. Yet we do not see how freedom can be defined otherwise. The Editors." Profeminist fiction appeared, such as "The Meeting" by Joel Stone, published by *Redbook* in March 1975. The cover of that same issue of *Redbook* features Christene Gonzales, the first female engineer for the Atchison, Topeka and Santa Fe Railroad. Inside are features on women in the war in Northern Ireland and the "second shift" problem faced by working women. *McCall's,* too, was in full support of the women's movement from day one. As early as 1971, *McCall's* sniffed that the only people who opposed day care were those who had been brainwashed into a blind love of motherhood. This magazine gave prominent space to job discrimination stories and kept housewives informed of ways to retrain themselves. By 1973 well-known feminist Letty Cottin Pogrebin was writing a monthly column called "The Working Woman" for the *Ladies' Home Journal.*[12]

The fashion magazines were even more vocally feminist. *Vogue* had been haranguing its readership about the need for a resurgence of feminism before the Second Wave got started. Anthony West's brilliant, angry "Who Takes Advantage of American Women? Men" appeared in the May 1968 issue (while *Vogue* was still under Diana Vreeland). The opening: "Fifty years after the apparently complete triumph of feminism of the type associated with such names as Victoria Woodhull, Lucy Stone, and the formidable Carrie Chapman Catt, a startling feature of life in the United States is the extent of the survival of the large numbers of disabilities affecting women as women, and the virtual disappearance from the social scene of influential organized groups of feminists campaigning for their removal." Mrs. Josephine Redding would have been proud. In the September 1970 issue *Vogue* celebrated the return of organized feminism: "The first time Women's Liberation (as opposed to its older, weaker sister, Women's Emancipation) hit the news was 1968. A group of protesting women turned up at the Miss America finals in Atlantic City, New Jersey, and . . . burned their bras. The symbol of male tyranny and oppression of Woman-as-Object: ban *Playboy,* cosmetics, Little Woman-oriented advertising: reform, radicalize—it was heady stuff. Now there are numerous organizations: Redstockings, NOW (National Organization for Women), Women's Liberation Front, WITCH (Women's International Terrorist

Conspiracy from Hell)." *Vogue* even introduced a rating system for a woman's feminist/femininity quotient and offered a "Ten-Point Manifesto for the New Woman."[13]

*Glamour* and *Mademoiselle* had always devoted substantial attention to employment and education. During the 1970s, these magazines focused intensely upon the new interest in feminism, careers, and politics. *Glamour,* for example, informed readers of the May 1971 issue "Where to Find a Women's Lib Group Wherever You Are." In both magazines, articles warning against anorexia appeared, as well as features on "fat power" and self-defense, and feminist books were positively reviewed. Features explained important political issues, such as the 1977 Supreme Court ruling on pregnancy benefits, as well as social problems, including wife-beating. *Glamour*'s editor, Ruth Whitney, encouraged readers to write key senators and representatives in support of the Women's Educational Equity Act, providing names and addresses of the congressmen involved. *Mademoiselle*'s regular column, "The Intelligent Woman's Guide to Sex," openly warned against dependence on men and took a vocal feminist stance.[14]

From the point of view of liberal feminism, the interaction between the movement and the women's media in the Second Wave appears to have been productive. Stereotypes were challenged, coverage expanded, images upgraded, women promoted, product choices widened, issues aired. Even so, feminist rhetoric continued to treat the women's press as the mouthpiece of the patriarchy.

## THE NEW FEMINISTS

The ranks of the "New Feminists," as they were called by the press, were composed primarily of recent college graduates who had been involved in leftist politics on campuses in the 1960s. These women were motivated to start a feminist movement by the shabby treatment they received from male leaders of the Left. However, many brought New Left tactics and philosophies to the movement, which meant that feminism, which had been fairly "ladylike" up to that time, would suddenly be the force behind all kinds of street theater, subversive acts, and outrageous statements. These radicals also brought an affinity with Marxism and a distrust of American capitalism that linked women's freedom inextricably to the destruction of the whole socioeconomic system.

These young feminists either wore their hair cut very short or let it go long, straight, and free. They wore blue jeans and T-shirts most of the time and often did not wear bras. Sturdy shoes rather than spiked heels were required, and handmade, imported clothing not contaminated by capitalist machinery was preferred. It was, in essence, the uniform of the peace movement of the late 1960s. Because both men and women of the youth movement dressed this way, you could say the ensemble was gender-neutral.

However, it was not in the least socially neutral, but instead was the sign of a particular age group, as well as a college education and leftist politics.

The new radicals saw the NOW group as matronly, suburban, and hopelessly bourgeois. The press often called Betty Freidan the "mother of women's liberation," but the new contingent saw Simone de Beauvoir as their revolutionary mother—and saw in NOW the image of their own mothers. Although they acted out of sympathy for their mothers' Feminine Mystique experience, the young radicals were determined not to be like the previous generation in any way. So, their politics involved a *rejection of the mother* as well as *retribution on her behalf.*[15]

With the broadscale tension between generations at this time, then, it's no wonder that the New Feminists rejected anything that looked, smelled, felt, or smacked of their mothers.The appearance of the radicals served to identify them with others of their own generation, but also to differentiate them from the mothers of the movement. They had no intention of following NOW's lead; they wanted to take the movement in a direction of their own. This direction included not only different ideas about power and resistance, but different views about grooming, dress, pleasure, and sex. Their concern was not to win practical legal and economic battles for women but to "theorize" the way that the culture itself enslaved women through pictures, text, and other cultural artifacts. Certainly their contribution was long overdue; many of the sexist slights we now consider odious would still be invisible to us if it were not for the ideas of this group.

The earliest statements of the New Feminist aesthetic were actually ritual acts. The first, held at the Miss America pageant in 1968, involved tossing a variety of grooming products and clothing into a "Freedom Trashcan." The media reported this action as "bra burning," but feminists stress that no one burned anything. Whether they actually burned bras or not, the ritual of discarding cosmetics, lingerie, and other grooming devices became a movement cliché, as did going braless. At the first Congress to Unite Women in New York in 1969, another ritual was performed. Twelve short-haired women climbed on the stage and formed a semicircle. A woman with long hair walked to the center and allowed them to cut off her tresses "as a symbol of her rejection of sexual lures." Marlene Sanders, who filmed the conference for ABC-TV, remembered: "People were screaming 'No!' and 'Yes!' from the audience, and we shot her whacking it all off." Then members of the audience were pressured to participate in the ritual. One woman, an actress, stood and tearfully explained that her hair was an essential prop in the way she earned a living. They reluctantly let her pass.[16]

Sanders had gone through tense negotiations with the Congress leadership in order to be allowed to tape the conference. Unlike the publicity-conscious members of NOW, the new wing was deeply suspicious of the press. Radical feminists complained when the media ignored them, but they also made it difficult for reporters to have access to meetings or even to conduct telephone interviews. The New Feminists were rude even to reporters with known ties to the feminist movement. In spite of Sanders's early NOW membership, for example, her clothes and camera crew identified her as a member of the "Male Establishment," which made the crowd wary and hostile. Before her crew left the scene, Sanders realized that the tape of the haircutting ritual was missing. She later found out that it had been dropped into the Hudson River, allegedly by writer Rita Mae Brown. Furious and embarrassed in front of her crew, Sanders recalled: "I hated the fact that the movement could be represented by these women."[17]

Crude underground newspapers dedicated to feminism began to appear that consistently advocated that women cut their hair, quit shaving, stop wearing makeup, and refrain from having sex with the enemy: "If we are going to be liberated, we must reject the false image that makes men love us, and this will make men cease to love us." In this rhetoric, a faceless ruling force controlled women through texts and pictures. "Women" as a class were depicted as extraordinarily gullible creatures chasing magical formulas in a demented quest for transmutation: "In every new jar of face cream, box of powder, tube of lipstick, mascara, eyeliner, she expects to find the magic formula that will transform her into a beauty. . . . She never gives up. Her blue hair waved, circles of rouge on her wrinkled cheeks, lipstick etching the lines around her mouth, still moisturizing her skin nightly, still corseted, she dies." With such grand strokes, every grooming practice was reduced to a foolish belief in magic and a desire to be attractive to men. The absolute power of fashion over women was overstated in nearly every case: "they obediently conform every time the fashion masters crack the whip. A woman conforms to all the whims of the cosmetic and fashion industries so that she will not be singled out from the mass of women, so that she will look like every other woman and thus manage to pass as one of the fair sex." Grooming practices were doggedly characterized as false or artificial. The practices forbidden by the new ideology were broad and various, but the acceptable appearance for the New Feminist was narrowly defined: The new radicals' idea of "true" and "natural" was their own appearance, just as the founding feminists' had been.[18]

For all their averred erudition in cultural theory, the New Feminists were putting together a politics of dress for the "liberated woman" that was not only naive but intolerant. They recognized but one dimension to self-presentation: sex appeal. Many of the practices advocated by this group therefore robbed the individual of her identity—as a unique personality at the crossroads of gender, age, nationality, occupation, and ethnicity. Their philosophy of dress bore a disquieting resemblance to Cold War stereotypes—China's Red Guard cut women's hair in the purge of 1966—an uncomfortable similarity to American Puritanism, and a disturbing analogy to institutions that depend upon obliteration of identity as a form of control—prisons, slavery, concentration camps, the military (see figure 10.1). As Joyce Carol Oates commented:

# "If I join the Women's Army Corps they'll cut off my hair."

Some girls believe the myth that the Women's Army Corps will try to make foot soldiers out of them. Cut their hair. And give them a baggy uniform.

Well, that's just plain nonsense.

Off duty or on, a girl can tint, tease, frost, iron her hair, or top it off with a new wig.

So there's never a hang-up with hair. There's even a place for your wig stand.

We know how special a girl's hair is to her total look. After all, we're girls, too. And we wouldn't dream of telling her how to wear it.

We do have one very practical rule that says hair should be kept above the collar while on duty. Just like any professional girl in uniform.

And there's one big regulation about the uniforms—that they make a girl look like one! It's her patriotic duty to stay looking trim and attractive.

A girl in the Women's Army Corps looks great because she feels great. About the world of travel, new friends, and job opportunities she's discovered.

Send the coupon, and we'll share it with you.

Or write: Army Opportunities, Department 400/450A, Hampton, Virginia 23369.

Please indicate education in your letter or coupon.

Your world is bigger in the Women's Army Corps.

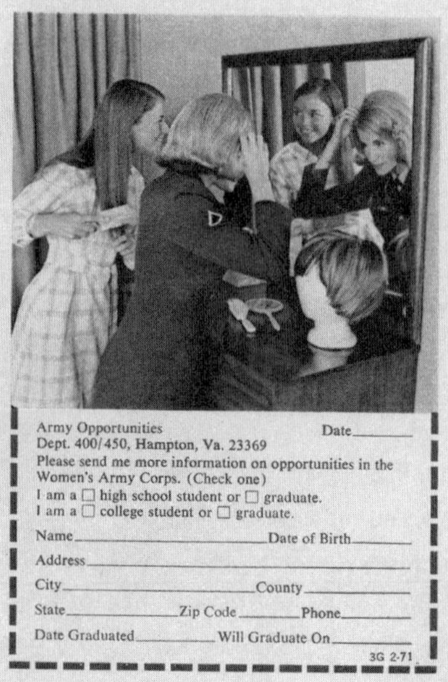

Army Opportunities Date______
Dept. 400/450, Hampton, Va. 23369
Please send me more information on opportunities in the Women's Army Corps. (Check one)
I am a ☐ high school student or ☐ graduate.
I am a ☐ college student or ☐ graduate.
Name______ Date of Birth______
Address______
City______ County______
State______ Zip Code______ Phone______
Date Graduated______ Will Graduate On______
3G 2-71

Figure 10.1. Forced hair-cutting was associated with the military and other coercive settings. *Glamour,* February 1971.

"The individual may be compartmentalized into any number of compartments, the absurd boxes of the poll-taker (the 'Irish Catholic,' the 'suburbanite, affluent,' the '35-year-old divorcee,' etc.). . . . No categories can contain or define us, and that is why we draw back from the female chauvinists who claim a biological sisterhood with us, just as we draw back from the male chauvinists who have attempted to define us in the past."[19]

The radicals showed a particularly outrageous insensitivity to the dress politics among lesbians. Often butches were summarily dismissed from movement meetings for being "male-identified." Femmes fell under equally strident, Beauvoir-inspired censure: "[Femmes] have wholly identified with the beauty ideal. . . . They want to continue to live in the one-sexed world of infancy, in the cocoon of their mother's or their own unconditional love. Lesbians are merely more unadulterated narcissists than heterosexual women." Although resentful of the unwillingness of the grim moralists of the Second Wave to understand the politics behind their dress, many lesbian feminists adopted the baggy jeans and plaid shirt uniform. After three decades of struggling for the right to express their sexual orientation in their appearance, lesbians were once again in disguise.[20]

Ironically, blue jeans, sturdy shoes, and handmade imports were the fashions of the decade. During the late 1960s and early 1970s, specialty stores sprouted up to meet the "wildfire proportions" of the jeans craze. Even though not a single jeans store existed in 1965, there were more than five thousand by 1971, some of which, such as Jeans West, the Gap, and Miller's Outpost, became national chains. Far from being a nonconformist dress statement, wearing jeans was, in the terms of the times, "groupthink." Furthermore, the assumption that wearing "just jeans" kept a woman from being a sex object was made ludicrous by the overtly sexual trend in jeans advertising, exemplified by Jordache and, soon, Calvin Klein. The preference for sturdy, comfortable shoes was most strongly expressed in the popularity of Earth Shoes and Roots. Both advertising and fashion features supported tie-dyeing and other craft approaches. Even the practice of going braless, supposed to shake the establishment to its foundations, simply became another "look." By 1971 the *Ladies' Home Journal, Glamour,* and *Vogue* had published stories endorsing the "no-bra look," and department store manikins had nipples.[21] Radical feminists continually asserted the dominant culture's fear of women who wouldn't conform to their dictates of dress, but the fashion machinery seems to have adapted easily to the new circumstances. Wearing a bra was not a crucial ingredient of sex appeal, as it turned out, and neither was it necessary to industrial capitalism.

The leaders of the New Feminism also benefited financially from media interest in their movement. Most coverage was probably an honest reflection of feminism's newsworthiness. Some, however, was engineered by publicity agents representing feminists who had signed contracts with major publishing houses. In 1970 alone the new wing produced three books—Kate Millett's *Sexual Politics,* Shulamith Firestone's *Dialectic of Sex,* and Robin Morgan's *Sisterhood Is Powerful*—that were published not by radical underground presses but by Doubleday, Random House, and William Morrow, respectively. Other publishers brought out still more feminist books. Basic Books published Vivian Gornick's *Woman in Sexist Society* in 1971, followed in the same year by Karen Decrowe's *The Young Woman's Guide to Liberation* and Lucy Komisar's *The New Feminism.* Apparently, feminist books, no matter how radical, must have been good business. Book-of-the-Month Club, the Literary Guild, Time-Life Books, and many other book-buying outlets, from which feminist books could be purchased advertised heavily in the women's magazines. By the time *Sisterhood Is Powerful* appeared with the woman sign prominently displayed on the cover, the same symbol had already been "co-opted" by a pantyhose package (see figure 10.2). Both were popular commodities.

The first and most impactful of these books was Kate Millett's *Sexual Politics,* which debuted in 1970 and quickly found a place on the best-seller list, making its author, in her own words, "shamefully, pointlessly rich." The book was positively reviewed, particularly by *Time* magazine, which put Millett's picture on the cover of the August 31, 1970, issue, anointed her the new "high priestess" of feminism, and called her the Karl Marx and the Mao Tse-tung of the movement, all in a manner connoting lavish praise. During the next six months the "priestess" appeared on the *Dick Cavett Show* and *David Susskind* as well as the *Today Show.*[22]

In February 1971 Millett was the subject of a feature interview called "A Day in the Life of Kate Millett" in *Mademoiselle.* The fashion magazine's praise of Millett's book was effusive: "*Sexual Politics* is one of those books that change irrevocably and forever one's way of seeing things." The reporter recounts that she interviewed Millett running to a luncheon given by Doubleday to promote her book. Kate couldn't decide what to wear, a striped pants outfit or an embroidered Mexican dress she had bought to appear on *Dick Cavett.* Millett called Doubleday, where they settled the question by telling her to wear the dress. This was a sensible solution because it allowed Kate to express her individuality and her immunity to fashion while wearing a style of clothing that the *New York Times* had recently endorsed as the look of the year. *Mademoiselle* itself had admired embroidered "peasant shirts" for their imaginative versatility: In one recent feature, the editors had suggested that these shirts could be "an elegant are-there-any-more-ice-cubes-please shirt" or "a funky where-are-my-Che-Guevara-peace-beads shirt" or "a brooding he-is-my-man-Sofia shirt," even though they were pictured as a "we-must-get-the-harvest-in-by-Monday shirt."[23] Obviously the "ethnic look" was adaptable to a "going-to-Garden-City-for-a-Doubleday-luncheon" occasion. By the mid-1970s, even the Breck Girl was wearing it.

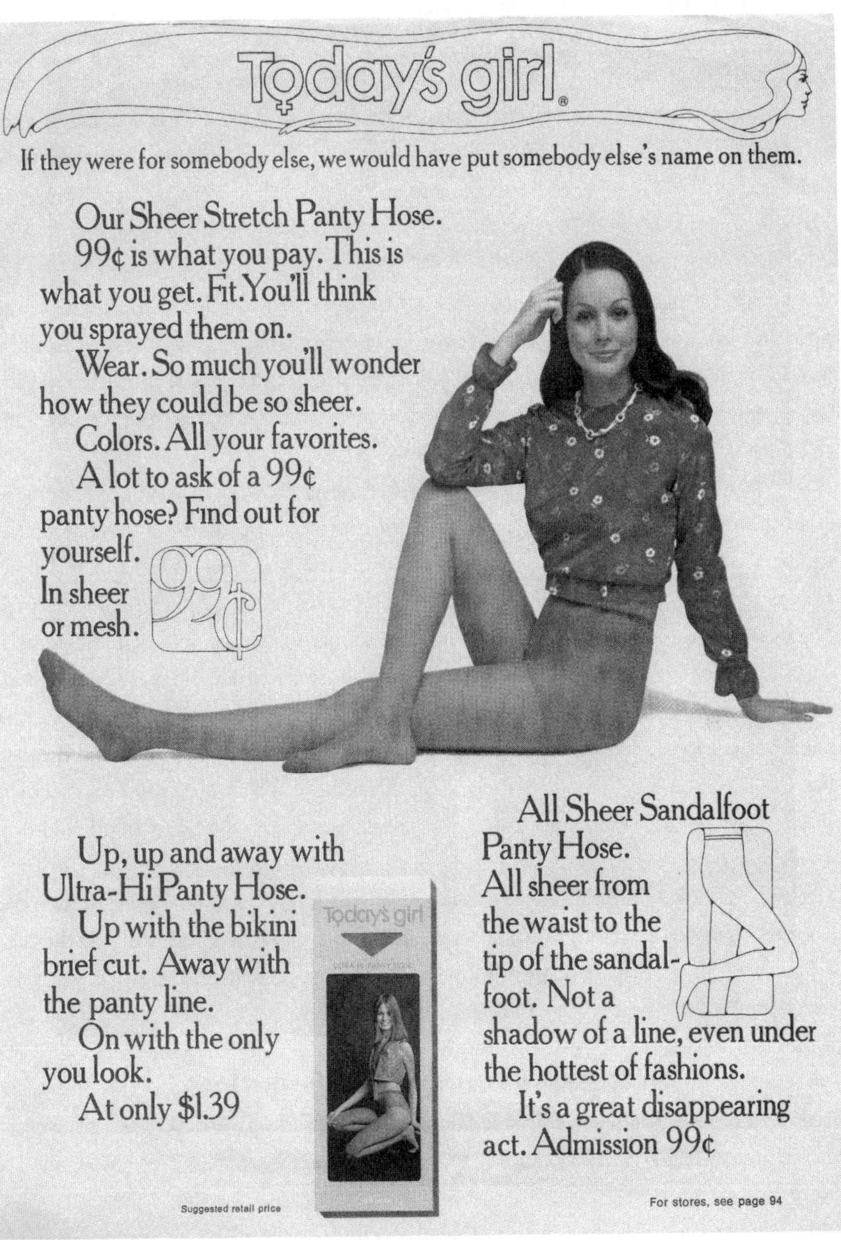


Figure 10.2. The woman sign, already strongly associated with the feminist movement, was incorporated into a pantyhose logo. *Mademoiselle,* August 1971.

In spite of all this interplay among publishing, marketing, fashion, and radical politics, feminists continued to complain that they did not see themselves or their friends in the ads. However, one young radical, Lucy Komisar, was among those consulted by Diane Daley and Ellen Levy of BBDO during long interviews to investigate feminist objections to advertising. Komisar subsequently wrote up her views on advertising for publication in an anthology of New Feminist writings. She offered specific suggestions on how ads could be made more acceptable to feminism: "For example, why not an ad showing men and women rushing out to work after leaving the dishes soaking in some wonderful pink liquid that eats away at the grease while they are poring over their accounts? Or stumbling home wearily from the office, throwing their briefcases on the table, and exuding praise for some jiffy convenience food that lets them eat without an hour's preparation?" By the mid-1970s scenarios just like these were appearing. At the end of the decade, however, such briefcase toting women would become the new "antifeminist stereotype" in the minds of radicals.[24]

The Marxist ideology embraced by New Feminists dictated that no advertisement could be acceptable to feminism anyway—not because of its effect on women per se, but because of its relationship to industrial capitalism. One essay, called "Consumerism and Women," which appeared in *Notes from the Second Year,* took issue with the Freudian/Marxist theory of consumption espoused by the feminist movement. This "Redstocking Sister" pointed out that nobody really believes that a cigarette will make you sexy, that people were not psychically incapable of resisting ads, and that the makers of ads were unlikely to have the kind of superpowerful diabolical intelligence that such theories implied. Nevertheless, in this author's words, the belief that women were hypnotized into consumption by advertisements already had "the invulnerability of religious dogma."[25]

The New Feminist philosophers were under no obligation to test their theories or to see if other women thought them true. The only important thing was that the theory be in keeping with the extant body of left-wing social thought, such as was provided then by the Frankfurt School or Simone de Beauvoir. So the New Feminists conducted no surveys of attitudes toward cosmetics. Nor did they undertake any actual investigation of the fashion industry or begin any ethnographies of contemporary dress. The question of whether the feelings they discussed in their own consciousness-raising groups really reflected other women's experiences never seems to have caused a doubt in their minds.

Had these young women even bothered to check the available secondary sources, they would have found information to suggest their own relationship to fashion was a function of other conditions besides gender. In 1970 only 65 percent of American women told pollsters that they tried to keep up with fashion at all. The reported desire (or pressure) to follow fashion was, furthermore, substantially skewed by age, income, and education. As young, college-educated adults from upper-income backgrounds, the radical feminists were in that segment of the population where a fashionable appearance was most highly valued. Since only 25 percent of American women went to college at that time and a minority of American households earned more than $15,000, it is doubtful that these young women's intense feelings were generalizable to the population at large. Indeed, these differences raise the possibility of subgroups having a considerably different relationship to fashion and therefore a quite different view of it. But, just as nineteenth-century feminists did not consider that slaves and Catholics might have a different view of the politics of appearance, New Feminists of the 1970s never tried to see beyond their own narrow scope.[26]

## RADICAL CHIC

"In hip-hugging raspberry Levis, two-inch wedgies and tight poor-boy T-shirt, her long, blond-streaked hair falling just so above each breast and her cheerleader-pretty face made wiser by the addition of blue-tinted glass, she is a chic apotheosis of with-it cool," observed *Newsweek* of Gloria Steinem in 1971. "Her cheekbones are broad and high, her teeth white and even; the fingernails on her tapered hands are as long and carefully tended as a tong chef's."[27] By joining the feminist movement, Steinem bestowed the ultimate honor on the New Feminism: She declared it radical and young and cool. Like the other Beautiful People who patronized the Black Panthers and farmworkers, Gloria now offered her glamorous aura to the fledgling movement.

The popular press was starry-eyed. Invariably, reporters noted that the new feminist leader was a beautiful woman who dressed in the height of the new pop fashions. Gloria had a career anyone would envy, and her smart, witty, handsome, rich, famous masculine suitors were living proof that she was not joining the feminist movement because she was hard up for dates. But the press would quickly caution that Steinem was more than a pretty face, she was also a "good person."

"At certain times the press is really looking for people to embody a trend the way fashion magazines look for women who actually wear the clothes they put out," said Tom Wolfe, adding, with characteristic tact, "And the press would rather have Gloria be Women's Liberation than the other trolls working under the bridge." Between 1971 and 1974 Steinem appeared on the covers of *People, McCall's, Newsweek, Redbook,* and *New Woman. McCall's* named her "Woman of the Year." Vehicles ranging from *Vogue* to *Today's Health* devoted long interviews and special sections to the new feminist star.[28]

Steinem had experienced her conversion to feminism—her "click" moment, in the language of the day—while covering a Redstockings meeting for *New York* magazine in 1968. Her article, "After Black Power, Women's Liberation," appeared in the April

7, 1969, issue. In it Steinem identified the movement with other radical groups and treated NOW as a completely separate phenomenon. She wrote that the real feminist movement was "in no way connected to the Bloomingdale-centered, ask-not-what-I-can-do-for-myself-ask-what-my-husband-can-do-for-me ladies of Manhattan, who are said by sociologists to be 'liberated.' Nor do the house-bound matriarchs of Queens and the Bronx get much satisfaction out of reading about feminist escapades. On the contrary, the whole thing alienates them by being a) radical and b) young."[29] It was clear where her sympathies were.

Steinem was soon traveling the country, speaking at colleges and in town halls and, much like Lucy Stone, converting even the most unlikely listeners wherever she went. She was so much in demand that her agency said it could book her twice a day, every day. Her fees were reported to be anywhere from $750 to $7,500 per engagement. After her talks, Steinem would sit up late with small groups of local people, male and female, listening to their stories and offering what advice she could. Each time, she left town having made lifelong friends and many, many dedicated followers. All who spoke with her observed her sincere, confident, yet somehow self-effacing loyalty to the cause.

University students pinned her photographs to their bulletin boards (my own college scrapbook contains her picture, now yellow and fragile, from the student newspaper). Young women all over America began to sport the distinctive Steinem "look"—long, straight, streaked hair, parted in the middle and held to the temples with tinted aviator glasses (see figure 10.3). A latter-day Gibson Girl, she had come to stand for the movement as a picture, an attractive icon, a cult figure. For many she was the "image" that made joining the feminist movement something to aspire to.

Those who rise to the top so quickly often draw unwelcome attention. Even inside the movement, Steinem was the target for criticism from both the conservative and radical members. Betty Friedan declared her a "phony" and, with unabashed cattiness, revealed that: "I used to catch her hiding behind a *Vogue* magazine at Kenneth's, having her hair streaked." Freidan denied being jealous, of course, but in unguarded moments let it slip that Gloria's beauty intimidated her: "All those reporters who suggested that I was jealous of Gloria because she was blonde and pretty and I was not. . . . Gloria is assuredly blonder, younger and prettier than I am—although I never thought of myself as quite so ugly as those pictures made me. . . . I was no match for her, not only because of that matter of looks—which somehow paralyzed me." Nora Ephron observed that "Betty Freidan, in her thoroughly irrational hatred of Steinem, has ceased caring whether or not the effects of that hatred are good or bad for the women's movement." When Gloria declared that any woman who spent more than fifteen minutes getting dressed in the morning was "getting screwed," even her friends came forward to reveal that she herself spent more than an hour just putting on her makeup.[30]

Figure 10.3. Young women of the 1970s modeled themselves on Gloria Steinem much as young women of the Gilded Age had imitated the Gibson Girl.

"Steinem's expressed attitude toward her own loveliness is that she just wishes everyone would just ignore it, yet she seems to ask for it," wrote a conservative female journalist. Did Steinem get support from feminists when she was accused of "asking for it"? No, apparently they saw the situation in a similar light. Steinem responded that she didn't buy into the new aesthetic being pushed by radical feminism: "If you don't want to be a sex object, you have to make yourself unattractive. But I'm not going to walk around in Army boots and cut off my hair. There is no reason for us to make ourselves look like men." With typical idealism, she told *Redbook:* "We mustn't be divided because of minor differences such as age, or whether one is married or not, or is of a special economic status, or has physical beauty or not." For all the insistence on the commonalities among women, however, radical feminism was not persuaded by appeals to inclusiveness when it came to beauty.[31]

When asked about how ordinary women could reconcile feminism with their desire for love, their attachment to the pleasures of femininity, or the fun they had decorating themselves, Steinem, like the New Feminists, responded with abstractions.

> *Liz.* Is it in the real interest of women to be for the Movement or is there some chance—and I believe this is a fear among some women—that they will lose their femininity or lose their men or lose their sexual satisfactions?

> *Gloria.* Well, there's no such thing as femininity—that's a cultural value. In some cultures it has been "feminine" to till the soil or "feminine" to take care of all the money. No woman can lose her *femaleness,* but "femininity" is just the enshrinement of cheap labor. It's being passive, doing what you're told.[32]

Telling women that femininity was a fiction that boiled down to economics was theoretically correct, as we have seen. But all cultures are essentially groupings of categories. The choice, therefore, is not between truth and falsehood but between one set of culturally constructed attributes and another. Most disturbing here, however, is the failure to recognize that cultural categories are things people actively use to live. Losing femininity meant that a significant building block of each woman's identity would somehow have to be reworked. Because feminism seemed to be offering nothing but an austere vacuum in its place, the prospect could be scary and confusing. But the movement, including Gloria, was determined to answer a central question of identity with a formula.

Another radically chic celebrity seemed to address this question directly, but nevertheless managed to miss the mark. Born in Australia and educated in England, Germaine Greer came to the United States in 1971 to promote her book, *The Female Eunuch,* an appeal to the power of the female libido. Throughout her tour, Greer dressed eclectically, flirted brazenly, and behaved outrageously. One of her first appearances was in a debate moderated by writer Norman Mailer and attended by the most well connected of New York's self-conscious avant garde. Greer appeared in a cheap, slinky dress with a huge, flashy stone hung around her neck and "a floozie kind of fox fur" boa that she dangled creatively throughout the event. Greer and Mailer's onstage flirtation was so obvious it was noticed by the audience and offensive to the other panel members. "Sensuous and attractive to men," declared *Life,* "Germaine Greer makes no secret of the fact that she enjoys their company, too." She commandeered a taxi driver in New York and took him with her for the rest of the trip. Greer explained coquettishly that if she took a lover who was her intellectual equal, he wouldn't be able to satisfy her physical needs. The press jubilantly reported the way Greer so confidently reversed the roles of sexual interactions. Predictably, Greer's image became "the feminist even men like," whose "easy charm distinguishes her from more militant members of the sisterhood." Her philosophy of dress was sexually oriented: "I don't go for that whole pants and battledress routine. It just puts men off."[33]

Although Greer's appearance was billed as offbeat and unconventional, it was fully in the spirit of 1970s fashion. In their cover story, *Life* reported: "Imposingly tall and attractive, she wears a long buckskin shirt, clogs on her feet, bangles and beads and other hippie accouterments around her neck." Fashion magazines were still showing fringed buckskins. Ads ran for clogs and slinky dresses; columns showed fox fur boas.[34]

In spite of the obvious fashionability of her own appearance, Greer was contemptuous of the American fashion magazines' endorsement of the dress-for-success look worn by NOW types: "If I have one more executive wardrobe described to me, I will go stark, staring insane. I'm not interested in executives of either sex. As far as I'm concerned, they're all male." Steinem echoed Greer's opinion by condemning "the antifeminist stereotype of Super Woman. The male-imitative, dress-for-success woman carrying a briefcase became the media image of a woman worker, even though a blue collar woman's salary was often higher than her glorified secretarial sister's, and though women at a real briefcase level are statistically rare." In response, Betty Friedan offered that the "radical chic" image perpetrated by the likes of Greer was bad for the movement because it encouraged people to associate feminism with sexy, "liberated" clothing and behavior.

Both Steinem and Greer objected to the dress-for-success look on the basis that it was too masculine, while vocally rejecting feminine dress—all the while presenting themselves in a very fashionable and alluring way. Furthermore, because the pictures of women with briefcases had been a response to feminist complaints that ads showed women either as housewives, sex objects, or in "pink-ghetto" jobs, the criticism of these ads seemed self-contradictory to some. The contradiction can be reconciled only by understanding the relationship between the critics and the role models for these ads—that is, the members of NOW.

At the Germaine Greer and Gloria Steinem level, therefore, feminism was hipper-than-thou. It was only appropriate then that supercool *New York* magazine would be the origin of the Second Wave's national periodical. Clay Felker, Gloria Steinem's editor, had the idea for a slick, commercial magazine devoted to the feminist movement. A prototype was produced and inserted in *New York.* The issue sold out in eight days, and 35,000 women mailed in requests for subscriptions. Warner Communications put up $1 million to publish *Ms.* magazine on a monthly basis. Felker chose Gloria for the editorship because he thought she would bring publicity to the magazine.[35]

Betty Friedan promptly accused Gloria of "ripping off the movement for private profit." This was an interesting statement coming from a woman who once quit her publisher because he wasn't prepared to market *The Feminine Mystique* aggressively enough: "I remember him pleading with me . . . and I remember looking him right in the eye and saying, 'George, you made me feel Jewish for trying to sell that book. Go fuck yourself.'"[36]

*Ms.* magazine was designed as an explicit response to the frivolous content of the women's magazines. But from the beginning, *Ms.* had its own type of frivolity. The covers, for example, were just as likely to feature celebrities such as actors Meryl Streep, Kate Jackson, and Alan Alda as were other popular magazines, but often were as provocative as those of tabloids. Actress Valerie Harper appeared nude behind a giant dollar bill on one cover; on another, a hairy-chested hunk flirted behind a mask of John Wayne.[37]

The new magazine had its own fashion and beauty commentary. The first issue included an article called "Body Hair: The Last Frontier." These authors tell us removing body hair is unnatural (although stating, in the same paragraph, that many other cultures do it). Then we are given an outrageously exaggerated discussion of leg-shaving (resulting in "a strong desire for Darvon," and "dainty dots of toilet paper when a tourniquet would have been more appropriate"). Finally, we get to the real message: "The Afro-coifed black and the un-shaven woman, regardless of her color, nationality, and class, make of their personal grooming a political statement. They reject an image of beauty and acceptability imposed by the society and risk the censure reserved for the rebel. . . . But more and more individual women are risking those stares to affirm their natural femaleness." This naive insistence on "naturalness" would be shelved, however, if the writer was dealing with a "primitive" practice like tattooing. The April 1976 issue treated the female "beard" tattoos of the lower Colorado Indians and the "abstract facial tattoos" worn by Maori women with reverence. *Ms.* reported a new interest in tattoos among American women, attributing "this rise in popularity in part to the new sense of freedom and rebellion against traditional gender identification which has been one result of the Women's Movement." The similarity of tattooing to two practices the magazine condemned as "unnatural"—colored makeup and cosmetic surgery—escaped the writer. What was supposed to further distinguish the *Ms.* attitude toward dress was its insistence on individuality. The constant refrain was a desire to "be me," punctuated by an abstract largesse for everyone else to "be them," too. We have already seen the limits of this freedom: If being yourself meant wearing St. John suits and Ferragamo shoes—or, heaven forbid, Frederick's of Hollywood with Candies—then, well, that couldn't possibly be the "real" you. And, even though writers for *Ms.* seemed intent on making every act of vanity a political litmus test, the dress suggestions given were hardly guerilla fashion. The ads that ran in these pages also reflected the widespread popularity of "individual style," yet all the images were within the realm of what was then considered fashionable.[38]

## TOTAL WOMEN

In late 1971, Vivian Cadden traveled across America trying to find out how feminism was playing in the heartland: "My plan was to wander around the country to see whether outside the big cities Women's Lib was having any effect on the thoughts and lives of young women. Was it catching on and becoming a grass-roots movement or was it only a publishing phenomenon?" Cadden went from New York to Cleveland, then to Warren and Hudson, Ohio; New Palestine and Bloomington, Indiana; Winnebago, Illinois; Iowa City, Iowa; and finally to Waco, Killeen, and Dallas, Texas, before returning to write her article for *McCall's.* She talked to married women, single women, mothers, lesbians, waitresses, farmer's wives, beauticians, factory workers, and nursing students. What she found surprised and deeply saddened her: "Except in the larger cities and on the campuses, liberation does not yet seem to be an aspiration for young women."[39]

Yet each Second Wave faction, including the most radical, claimed to represent the interests of women as a class. Ti-Grace Atkinson began most speeches with this statement, "I, Ti-Grace Atkinson, speaking for all the women of America. . . ." But neither she nor any of the other radical leaders appears to have been interested in what "all the women of America" really thought. A phenomenon erupted in mid-decade that demonstrated too poignantly how far the feminists were from understanding the needs of ordinary women, particularly the dependent housewife.

In 1974 a book called *The Total Woman,* written by a Florida housewife named Marabel Morgan, topped the best-seller list, outselling even the Watergate exposé, *All the President's Men.* Morgan's book, a silly mishmash of self-help manuals, born-again Christianity, and sex counseling, told housewives how the author had saved her own failing marriage. The idea at the heart of "Total Womanhood" was the wife's subjection of self to the husband—not exactly an original concept. What was new was the combination of a sexy attitude, a love of pleasure, and a focus on play within the framework of a traditional Christian marriage. The most famous aspect of the Total Woman strategy was its employment of provacative costumes for the purpose of sexual arousal. The idea was that "a man who 'chases skirts' might be cured of his wandering ways if his wife augmented her own skirt collection." Women were encouraged to use creative costumes to keep hubby interested: "Never let him know what to expect when he opens the front door; make it like a surprise package. Be a pixie or a pirate, a cowgirl or a show girl."[40]

The book was published by a religious press and issued with a minimum of promotion. And yet this unlikely volume sold 370,000 hardcover copies in 1974 and went on to sell 3 million paperbacks over the next four years. In response to a deluge of fan mail, Morgan started a national network of Total Woman courses, taught by teachers she trained herself. Based on the grassroots sales structure that characterized Avon and Madame C. J. Walker, the Total Woman courses quickly infiltrated households all over America. By 1975 there were 100 instructors in 28 states and 15,000 graduates of the Total Woman training. Some "students" took the course two and three times.[41]

What probably sold the book and the courses more than anything else were anecdotes of husbands' responses to the Total Woman technique. One man, arriving home to find his wife dressed only in fishnet stockings, high heels, and an apron, dropped his briefcase and shouted "Praise the Lord!" (A special irony: One husband, informed by a somewhat timid wife that she was "wearing the 'no-bra look,'" announced, "This is one of the happiest moments of my life. I just don't want it to end.") Another woman, following Morgan's advice to find something positive about her husband and compliment him on it, racked her brain for days. Finally she told him how much she had respected and appreciated his efforts to keep the family going during the Great Depression—and he immediately burst into tears. Hundreds of women reported that the submissive role was more than rewarded by the affection their mates suddenly showed them, although most conceded that the submission had been primarily symbolic, a kind of marital ice-breaker.[42]

Once the national media discovered this scourge in the heartland, it began its habitual manner of analysis. Experts in sociology, psychology, psychiatry, and other disciplines were called in to comment. Virtually all declared Total Womanhood "sick," a last-ditch effort by the truly desperate, and, having dismissed this disturbing groundswell, they moved on. One freelance writer, Joyce Maynard, actually went out and observed housewives in the process of embracing Total Womanhood. What she found was far more disturbing than what Vivian Cadwell had observed on her cross-country trek four years earlier.[43]

In the makeshift classrooms of the Total Woman courses—usually in churches—women of all ages gathered. Most of the Total Woman neophytes were of modest means, uneducated, white, and employed as "just housewives." They had married young and sometimes lived in homes they had built with their own hands. They were extremely religious. These poor housewives were also living the kind of quietly desperate lives that feminists had said they were. But Total Women were afraid of the feminist movement because it seemed to threaten the only security they had—their husband's income. Even more frightening, apparently, was the haunting fear that their security would be ripped from them by a miniskirted working woman who seduced their spouses and left them desolate. Although feminists claimed that working women were thought to be ugly or unfeminine, the sexy working girl was alive and well in the nightmares of American housewives.

Maynard observed that the small-group association of the Total Woman courses engendered the same deep sisterhood experience that consciousness-raising sessions encouraged, but she concluded that the kind of liberation these women wanted was very different from what feminism had offered. In response to the famed sexual revolution of the late 1960s, traditional religious strictures against permissive sexuality had actually tightened, having the unfortunate—but hardly surprising—result of bringing repression home. What Marabel Morgan accomplished was to make sex something Christian people should enjoy within the confines of marriage. In a few cases, however, the lingering resistance to sex shocked even the Total Woman teachers. Some students were still undressing in the closet, too modest for their husbands to see them naked. A thin woman without makeup, wearing homemade clothes and self-barbered hair, embarrassed an entire classroom by asking: "What I'd like to know is what do you do if your mother raised you believing sex was bad. I want to change, but I've been married 28 years. My mother told me never to call my husband by his first name. I call him Daddy. He calls me Mommy." Cutting her own hair, going without makeup, staying away from mass-produced fashion, and believing sex was bad had clearly not gone far toward liberating this woman.[44]

Morgan's ideology trumped feminism on the valuation of pleasure. Not only was this born-again Christian woman promoting sex, she was also recognizing a fundamental need for sensual experience and playfulness. Bubble baths, candlelight, lacey lingerie, and wine were all required elements of the Total Woman's seductive setting. The encouragement to indulge in such pleasures tapped into something the New Feminists must have known but ignored: Many of the accoutrements of femininity are pursued for their own intrinsic pleasure.

Radicals had focused on (and exaggerated) the pains of self-adornment. Years later Susan Brownmiller wrote a book called *Femininity* that recognized the pleasurable aspects of the "exquisite aesthetic" of femininity and noted the strategic error of having taken the opposing position: "In past centuries and present totalitarian regimes, those who have harangued against cosmetics have been grim moralists who have sought to control or crush the sexuality of women, equating the age-old tools of feminine decoration with worldly decadence, immodest pride, and the devil's lure."[45] The New Feminists, living in relative sexual freedom, saw only oppression in having to "play like" sexy women. For a spirit so imprisoned by fundamentalism it cannot experience sexual pleasure or fantasy, is it really so retrograde to explore the forbidden thrills of being a "sex object"?

Joyce Maynard's Total Woman story appeared in the *New York Times Magazine.* Sarcastic, amused, outraged letters appeared: "I can think of innumerable ways to please my husband (and he, me) during short mental breaks while doing something professionally and socially creative. . . . However, our respective mental fulfillments are other—and equally important—'turn-ons' which have enriched our fourteen years together. In short, I found Marabel Morgan's ideology pathetic." Another reader chastised the *Times* for running the story at all: "considering the enormous strides that have been made in the past decade within the women's movement, the counterrevolution—i.e., Total Woman—seems all the more insipid and stupid." This readers could not believe there was reader interest in "witless housewives . . . in the most outlying, rural parts of the land." She concluded: "There is no time in the world today for these halfwits, who shouldn't be called women in the first place."[46]

Halfwits who shouldn't be called women in the first place? Our respective mental fulfillments? Witless rural housewives? Unfortunately, this kind of rhetoric was fairly common for feminists. Gloria Steinem was particularly inclined to such phrases as "nothing but a housewife" and could sometimes pack a whole string of them into one sentence. Her promise about the benefits of Women's Liberation to men was: "Fewer boring women, childlike wives; no more unearned alimony (think of the votes for that issue): no more responsibility for the identity of a semi-adult human being; fewer lady parasites attached to rich and gifted men." When asked why she didn't marry, Steinem could be harsh: "The role of 'wife' is so inhuman and unattractive to men." And one of her most famous "Steinemisms": "Marriage makes you legally half a person and what man wants to live with half a person?" Housewives read such rhetoric as disparagement. Steinem's call to eliminate alimony—coming as it did from a glamorous career woman who was running about with many men—must have exacerbated Total Women's fears about losing their husbands to someone at the office.[47]

The insults were also characteristic of the sexiest single girl of them all, Helen Gurley Brown. Although radical feminists did not see Brown as one of their own, she identified herself as a feminist, and she appeared often in the press on behalf of "women's lib." She was happy, as always, to slam housewives: "I know wives you couldn't drive out of the house with a poisoned, pointed stick (except to go shopping, lunching, bridging, or maybe fashion-showing). . . . (And don't get me started on alimony and how women exploit men!)."[48] So it was not entirely without reason that new recruits to Total Womanhood felt the women's movement saw them as second-class citizens and threatened their security. Is it really that they didn't listen? Or did they listen too well?

Many interpreted the Total Woman phenomenon as a response to the proliferation of career woman imagery. *Time* wrote: "Marabel's books are significant as a kind of cartoon version of genuine problems that confront millions of American housewives today, including those who may sneer at her preachings as silly. Some of those problems are as old as the Fall. . . . Others spring from the new writ that women should find work and fulfillment outside the home." One woman wrote to the *Washington Post:* "Traditionally, the role of a woman was that of wife and mother, homemaker and nurturer. If that stereotype was oppressive to many, its antithesis today is no less tyrannical. . . . I do not consider all working women (having been one myself) to be child-neglecting, emasculating, selfish vipers. It would be nice if I in turn were not regarded as a mindless, cookie-baking, gingham-clad nitwit."[49]

The Total Woman concept was also situated in personal political issues that feminism was finding hard to solve. Writer Sally Kempton, in her soul-rending piece called "Cutting Loose," examined the real difficulties that the anger released by feminism posed for daily living with a spouse. We can see in Kempton's story the scenario Total Women feared: Once the charade was over, there was an uncontrollable anger to be confronted, as well as loneliness, boredom, and poverty. Feminism's failure to reach out to its constituency with compassion rather than condescension is sad. But the Total Woman phenomenon was just the ludicrous tip of a serious political iceberg.[50]

## SILENT MAJORITY

Phyllis Schlafly had published nine books, run for Congress twice, and established a power base among right-wing groups all over America. She had also raised six children, all of them breast-fed and home-schooled. "Though she is hardly one of them," remarked Morton Kondracke of the *New Republic,* "Schlafly represents the stay-at-homes who look at women's liberation and the working lifestyle as a threat and a rebuke. The old rules decreed that women got married and had babies, and millions of women dutifully followed the pattern. Now the rules are suddenly being changed, and these women are being told they have wasted their lives. They won't sit for it. They are taking it out on ERA, and Schlafly is leading the way."[51]

An anti-ERA essay in her conservative newsletter, *The Phyllis Schlafly Report,* struck a nerve among its readers. Quick to spot an advantage to be taken, Schlafly put together an small but well-organized and blindly obedient organization called StopERA. A consummate rhetorician, she appropriated "hot buttons" in the speeches she began making around the country, leading her audiences to believe that the amendment would end marriage, force women to work even if they didn't want to, abolish alimony and child support, as well as a lot of other preposterous things, such as making unisex toilets mandatory and putting pornographic pictures in school textbooks. Her skill at twisting other people's statements, of drawing insane conclusions from tenuous premises, made her almost impossible to debate. Unfortunately, she often was able to make these accusations by *quoting someone* from within the feminist movement.

The Equal Rights Amendment had shot through thirty of the thirty-eight state legislatures needed for ratification within twelve months after being passed by Congress. By 1975 four more states had ratified and there were only four more to go. Schlafly and her organization got involved at that point. The ERA did not win another ratification.

The women's magazines attempted to rescue the amendment. Thirty-four women's magazines joined together to publish a report on the ERA in their July 1976 issue, a gesture that was repeated again in 1979. *McCall's* explained the intention:

> As of the month of July, 1976, the Equal Rights Amendment to the Constitution of the United States has been ratified by 34 states. In order for the Amendment to become part of the basic law of the nation, four more states must ratify the Amendment by March, 1979. There has been much discussion of the ERA—pro and con. And in recognition of the importance and urgency of well-informed discussion, the editors of 34 women's magazines published in the U.S. have joined together to discuss the Equal Rights

> Amendment in their July issues. While each magazine will approach the subject matter in its own way, we are unanimous in our opinion that discussion is of primary importance.
>
> —The Editors[52]

In an exemplary piece, *McCall's* writer Marilyn Mercer took each of Schlafly's objections one by one and, in a most dispassionate tone, proceeded to destroy every one. The *McCall's* editors had been vocally pro-ERA from the beginning of the decade, and they remained so to the bitter end. So, too, were the editors of *Redbook. Glamour* kept readers informed with a monthly update on the status of the ERA, complete with action steps to take in each state to further the progress of the amendment. In response to an article called "Actively Supporting the ERA," a reader wrote: "I hope articles such as yours will get men and women to actively support the Equal Rights Amendment. I recently quit being an 'armchair supporter' myself and joined the ninety thousand who marched in Washington in July."[53] But it was too late already. The ERA was dead.

But Schlafly did not stop there. Her goal was to destroy the movement entirely. When Congress granted funding for the International Women's Year conference to be held in Houston in 1977, the Schlafly organization took advantage of the requirement that the conference be ethnically and politically diverse. A coalition of Baptists, Catholics, and Mormon churchwomen ("thousands of housewives who feel neglected by the feminists," said *Newsweek*) eventually dominated the delegations from many states in the South. In Utah, they took over the process until the feminists who had organized the effort were reduced to picketing outside. When these groups arrived at the national convention, Schlafly told the press, "Houston will finish off the movement."[54]

"She has clearly tapped elemental currents of resentment, fear, and anger," remarked one essayist on Schlafly. Certainly these emotions were largely centered on gender roles; however, once again, the interaction of class and ethnicity had been largely overlooked. Many women found the feminists' religious attitudes disquieting. For all their Marxist rhetoric, feminists' insensitivity to class experience had been devastating. Throughout the early 1970s the support for feminism among working-class women had dragged behind other groups; now the difference widened. One reason was that working-class women did not have the kinds of career choices that the feminists did. If going to work meant they had to do the kind of boring, dehumanizing, and sometimes dangerous work their husbands did, they preferred to stay home. Women like this depended heavily on their husband's income for whatever financial security they had. Feminist rhetoric simply did not address that difference. Gloria Steinem's suggestion that the unpaid housework problem be solved by requiring husbands to pay their wives a legally determined percentage of their salary must have seemed ridiculous in households where the husband's income was stretched to cover the barest necessities. From the working-class housewife's point of view, the prospect of well-to-do women trying to liberate them had a class subtext that was, at best, ambiguous.[55]

In homes like these, pleasures were dear and infrequent. One way middle American women experienced sex discrimination, in fact, was being left home when their husbands went out to play; they were more angry about that than about "sex objects" in magazines. None of them had money just to "spend on myself." Now they were being told nice clothes and bubble baths shouldn't matter by people who could afford to think so. Some women who were making these arguments, such as Steinem or Greer, were visibly not following their own advice. Were less privileged women to give up the small pleasures of femininity for a liberation that did not include them? One angry woman demanded: "Women's liberation cannot possibly be just for unmarried women, it can't be just for university women. It has got to be for every woman. . . . Involve all women. Right from the top to the bottom, you've got to start with the biggest group available—and that's the ones at the bottom.[56]

The perceived callousness of feminism to the importance of family was also alienating. The working class was concentrated in urban neighborhoods where the extended family was the basic social structure. The people who lived in these neighborhoods were predominantly second- and third-generation Italian, Irish, German, or Polish immigrants and, therefore, heavily Catholic. Insults to the Virgin Mary did not go down well in those neighborhoods. New Feminism's affected dalliances with Marxism didn't either. Eastern European immigrants and their descendants had given asylum those escaping the pogroms of communism—or had lost loved ones. Many still had relatives living behind "the Iron Curtain." How cavalier Vassar graduates spouting Mao must have seemed to them! The similarity between the appearance politics of feminism and those of the "communist bloc" would have been of more than casual concern.

Instead of trying to bridge the gap between itself and the audience, instead of trying to make a reality—rather than a slogan—out of sisterhood, the movement just condemned anyone's discomfort with its positions on dress, grooming, religion. The arrogance and elitism of feminism was unflattering, certainly, but at this point in the game, the sheer strategic stupidity was to be fatal. The New Feminists' painstaking efforts not to be associated with the bourgeoisie had cost them the support of the very person they were supposedly liberating: the American housewife. Their strategy could not have been better suited to alienating middle America had it been designed and planted by "the enemy." And so, although the struggle continued in magazines and classrooms, in prayer meetings and political conventions, the Second Wave lost its lead. The movement was beaten not by media, money, or men, but by women who should have been in its ranks.

## Chapter 11

# EXCLUSIVE RIGHTS

M. G. Lord, a cultural critic, sat in a beautiful office with an expansive view, talking to Jill Barad, the chief executive officer of Mattel. Lord was writing a book about Barbie, a doll that, by September 1992, when this interview took place, was being purchased around the world at a rate of two per second. Yet having secured an interview with the strong, capable woman who ruled the world's largest toy manufacturer, all Lord could think about was her companion's appearance: "I had, of course, seen photos of her, but that did not prepare me for the perfect hair, seamless manicure, and makeup striking enough for television. She made the Barbies look unkempt."[1]

Barad, confesses Lord, made her feel like Midge, Barbie's not-so-beautiful and never-as-commercially-viable best friend. Looking perhaps to level things a little, Lord shoots Barad the "impossible" question: Does Barad consider herself a feminist?

It's a tense moment. Barad, "in a cool voice," answers no. "The fact is," explains the executive, "I really don't know what that means."[2]

Later, when Lord writes up the interview for her book, she explains to readers that this admittedly intelligent, confident, diplomatic corporate leader is a "homeovestite," a woman who exaggerates her femininity to disguise her "masculine" ability, in essence "cloaking one's cross-gender strivings by disguising oneself as a parody of one's own sex." Homeovestism is the inverse of transvestism, she tells us, placing Barad's beauty and elegance squarely in the domain of deviance.[3]

Yet within months of *Forever Barbie*'s release, a feature appears in *Elle,* a leading fashion magazine, chronicling Lord's own decision to hire a personal image consultant. In the glare of publicity surrounding her book, she confides, the need to look right on *The Today Show* and other venues demanded professional advice.[4]

Lord and Barad, as historical creatures, are representative of different subgroups of women, both of which have its own traditions with regard to the politics of appearance. Barad, an exemplar of the Modern Woman tradition, is beautifully dressed and well mannered, in addition to being successful and powerful. Lord, heir to the scholastic suffragists of the 1910s and the campus radicals of the 1970s, feels the need (and the right) to criticize Barad's clothing, to question her commitment to feminism, and to assume for herself the neutral dress position.

But two important factors, new in the late twentieth century, have been added. The first is the celebrity created to market feminist books on popular culture, which leads Lord to cultivate her own "look" for the camera. The aura of this celebrity is so powerful that Lord can even appear in a fashion magazine confessing her contract with an image consultant without fear of enduring the kind of criticism she has leveled at Barad. This leads us to the second factor, which is the power assumed by intellectual feminists to claim exclusive rights to what is or is not feminist, primarily by surrounding the definition with a fog of dense prose. The privilege of inclusion has been repeatedly denied to anyone who dresses as Barad does—but more important, it is denied to anyone who has reached a position of corporate leadership within the market economy. So, when Barad answers Lord's "impossible" question, "Do you consider yourself a feminist?" her negative answer is correct, regardless of her commitment to the equality of women. Barad *is* excluded from feminism as defined by women like Lord.

## SECOND WAVE AFTERMATH

After the defeat of the ERA, the uneasy Second Wave coalition parted company. Many entered or returned to the private and government sectors, becoming lawyers, doctors, corporate executives, and public officials, in the process breaking down barriers that had only been weakened by previous generations. Another group went back to the universities and became scholars. Some went home to start families. In each sector, significant political changes occurred: Children were raised differently, boardrooms were opened, and fields of research were recast. But the old divisions continued and so, too, the dress habits that marked them.

University professors researching their topics from a feminist perspective produced a remarkable body of work, contributing vastly to our knowledge of women in several fields. With the power of print behind them, however, the new scholastics also assumed control over the movement. A large literature was produced delimiting which political positions, actions, and living choices were legitimately feminist. Sadly, the arrogance manifest in asserting the right to define, codify, and direct a preexisting social movement sometimes spilled over into excluding by definition the grassroots members of the movement itself.[5]

Far from dimming in the progress of years, the dress prerogative of the Second Wave radicals was elaborated and strengthened, becoming a tool for making visible the status difference between academic feminists and other women. The commercial viability of books and magazine articles focusing on the beauty critique gave feminists a forum, powered by the publicists of the major publishing houses, from which to continue to impose their dress aesthetic as a prerequisite for membership in the ever-shrinking circle of "true feminism." The arguments made in support of the critique were thin on evidence and heavy on "theory." The history used in these treatises is distorted (as we have already seen), but the examples used were also highly selective (rather than representative), and the empirical evidence for the effects claimed was either nonexistent or contradictory. The result was a polemical, poorly researched collection of work that, not coincidentally, relied for its power on the presumption that the author had interpretive powers beyond what an ordinary woman could muster. Thus, the critique not only alerted the reader to be fearful of a conspiracy against her, but engendered dependence on "experts" to enlighten and protect her. The dress critique thus functioned effectively to cement the leadership of the academics and celebrities who brought the antifashion ideology to market. The feminist dress stance also served to discredit the most viable alternative leadership, nonacademic professional women, who continued to distinguish themselves not only by their substantial accomplishments but by good grooming and feminine dress, as they had done for more than a century.

"Dress correctness" became a litmus test on campuses in the 1990s. Loyal young followers of the Second Wave radicals emerged at the end of the decade with the notion that their central issue should be "body image." The famously ambivalent majority dressed more like the professional women likely to be their role models in life. The moments of rudeness between these two groups were legendary. Elsewhere in the culture, the divisiveness of the feminist position on dress was also evident. Among lesbians, friction over whether a more masculine appearance (presumed to be more feminist) would be the ticket to respect and inclusion briefly produced in the 1990s a rebellious subset known as lipstick lesbians. Issues related to ethnicity and class remained unassimilated into the discourse on appearance. A wonderful literature on the aesthetics and politics of black women's appearance has been written in the past five years, but it exists on a plane utterly parallel to the "mainstream" dress critique. The dress of Latinas, which historically has been more flamboyant and decorative than the traditional ruling class Yankee Protestant look, also produces tensions at the local level. And so it goes.[6]

Despite its corrosive contradictions, the fashion critique's tenets have become second nature to many American women, due in no small part to the commercial forces that make the critique ubiquitous.

## SELLING US BACK OUR INSECURITIES

Since the end of the 1970s, the number of popular books produced that take the criticism of fashion and beauty as their primary topic has vastly overshadowed publications on what we might see as more pressing feminist issues, such as economic advancement, job discrimination, family support, poverty, and rape. This heavily promoted and commercially successful corpus contributed substantially to the creation of an elite among feminists, a group of recognizable faces from never-ending talk shows and magazine features. Membership in this elite flows between the world of the media (Susan Faludi, Naomi Wolf, Gloria Steinem, Susan Brownmiller) and the academy (Susan Bordo, Camille Paglia) as well as parts along the path in between (Jean Kilbourne).

Two key factors supported this literature and made possible the emergence of their authors as feminist gatekeepers: (1) the participation of the major publishing houses, which used their publicity machines to get these authors on television and into the magazines; and (2) the existence of a ready-made market for this material among college women in the burgeoning women's studies programs. The adroit publicity behind this phenomenon has produced at least three best-sellers, a few acclaimed academic texts, as well as a deluge of less stellar but probably profitable wannabes. A particularly vivid stream alleged the negative effects of fashion on teenage girls and the presumed role of thin models in reducing self-esteem, producing eating disorders, and creating other dangerous behaviors. Other spinoffs include books on products critiqued by feminism, such as Lord's book on Barbie.[7]

Anyone who visited the chain bookstores of the 1990s can remember these books in the displays and crowding the shelves. However, the fantastic popularity of women's studies programs virtually guaranteed a university market regardless of what the retail sector could move. (Between the time women's studies was first established in the mid-1970s and the end of the century, more than 670 undergraduate and 111 graduate programs were established at 250 colleges nationwide.) Such programs not only provided a ready outlet in the form of required reading lists, they also supported the purchase of expensive videotapes for classroom use and provided paying venues for traveling lecturers associated with the beauty critique. One prominent beneficiary of the commercialized beauty critique, for instance, was Jean Kilbourne, who produced four videotapes on the topic between 1979 and 2000. A popular speaker on college campuses, she commands fees of about $10,000 per lecture.[8]

In spite of her charges that the publishing industry was stoking the fires of antifeminism, Susan Faludi's *Backlash* appeared in Borders' windows from coast to coast, and she herself was on the cover of *Time. The Beauty Myth,* too, propelled pretty Naomi Wolf to celebrity status, from which she could display herself in classic Hollywood glamour style in the pages of *Esquire* and win a stint promoting No Nonsense pantyhose. (Interestingly, although Wolf's books have done much to promote the antibeauty agenda, her personal appearance brings sorority-girl snipes from professors. For instance, Jennifer Wicke writes: "Wolf is somewhat hard to take at face value (as it were) if you happened to have known her when she was a Yale undergraduate; the subtitle for her first book could have been that irritating Pantene advertising line: 'Don't hate me because I'm beautiful. . . . ' My tart criticisms are meant for the insufficiencies of her book and of her politics, not for celebrityhood itself, much as the Scavullo photograph of Wolf on her book jacket annoys me—such big hair!"[9])

The blatant commercialism evident in the promotion of these texts was enough to shame a lipstick manufacturer. Jean Kilbourne's *Killing Us Softly* was casually reissued in almost identical form as *Still Killing Us Softly,* then followed up within a few years as *Killing Us Softy 3.* Having been the main purveyor of antibeauty, antiadvertising videos for two decades, Kilbourne finally published a book in the late 1990s. She published the exact same text under two different covers and titles. *Can't Buy Me Love: How Advertising Changes The Way We Think and Feel* is identical to *Deadly Persuasion,* but if you order them online, you probably won't figure that out until they both arrive.[10]

The entrance of Camille Paglia into the fray successfully sold three books within five years. The icy response of Second Wave feminists and Paglia's own melodrama gave the whole discourse a carnivalesque aspect. Exchanges of insults between famous feminists took on all the dignity of those wrestling matches where each fighter roars incoherent threats and insults to his opponent for the benefit of the TV audience. This circus makes good television: *Larry King, 60 Minutes,* even *Letterman* have been hosts to the feminist celebrities.

There have also been a few attempts to argue directly with the beauty critique (Karen Lehrman's *The Lipstick Proviso,* Ellen Zetzel Lambert's *The Face of Love*) or engage it as part of a larger critique of feminism's growing exclusivity (Christina Hoff Sommer's *Who Stole Feminism?* and Elizabeth Fox-Genovese's *Feminism Is Not the Story of My Life*). In each case, the response from gatekeepers was an emphatic door-slamming, accompanied by disingenuous protests that no one in feminist groups really judges others on the basis of their appearance and that there are many "feminisms" from which the dissenters have merely assembled a "straw woman." In *Ms.*, the response to these challenges was worthy of the most misogynist media. For years feminist criticism has claimed all kinds of violent intentions behind the images in the media, but *Ms.* magazine and Susan Faludi didn't hesitate to employ caricature and symbolic violence when depicting the women they dubbed "Pod Feminists." Clearly not above "symbolic violence against women" when it serves their purposes, *Ms.* allowed the artist to use push pins where Paglia's breasts should be. Perfectly capable of creating caricatures that "unrealistically distort" what women really look like, *Ms.* shows writer Katie Roiphe with a huge nose and lips seated at a computer wearing blinders. Less than squeamish about symbolic dismemberment, the article shows author Rene Denfeld wearing boxing gloves, about to attack a punching bag that is a Victorian lady's head. It's hard to know whether this vituperative attitude is motivated by "true feminism" or by the desire to keep profits coming and power intact.[11]

## THE BEDROCK

*Decoding Advertisements,* a book by Judith Williamson, and *Killing Us Softly,* the first video by Jean Kilbourne, were important late 1970s works that extended Second Wave essays on beauty and commercial culture into a basic theoretical framework (Williamson) and a popular articulation (Kilbourne). Both concentrate specifically on advertisements—because both works carry, as do most feminist texts of the post-Second Wave, hostility to market-based societies as a first premise. (Today, both authors' books are sold, "bundled" together, at Barnes & Noble online.) Williamson's and Kilbourne's footprints can be discerned beneath scholarly works such as Susan Bordo's *Unbearable Weight,* middle-brow books such as Diane Barthel's *Putting on Appearances,* and bestsellers such as *The Beauty Myth* and *Backlash,* not to mention innumerable articles in journals from the *Media Studies Journal* to *Bitch.*[12] Their influence, therefore, reached well beyond the early 1980s to help produce the phenomenon of feminist beauty books of the 1990s.

The *Killing Us Softly* videos are each alarmingly casual with statistics and offer no substantiation—other than the ads shown—for any of the sweeping claims made. Like many feminist critics who followed, Kilbourne asserts that advertising presents a single ideal of beauty to which women must conform. She also condemns ads for leading women to artifice, but she doesn't attempt to define what is natural for human grooming. Kilbourne further protests that contemporary grooming practices ignore "who we are; what comes from within the mask." Her position relies on the notion that the self is a preexisting essence, rather than on the more current ideas explored herein, where the self is cultivated, performed, and realized using objects as signs.

Kilbourne's visual analysis is as untutored as her approach to "nature" and "self." She shows images ranging from the simple cropping typical of western representation to surrealistic pictures of disembodied legs, claiming that in all of them women are hacked apart. In the 1987 version of the video, she asserts the increasing frequency of violent images, but she uses the very same ads used in the first video to make her point. If the frequency was increasing, it should have been simple to find some new ones for the videotape. The doubt raised here points to an issue that plagues the entire critique: How representative are the images under discussion?

Kilbourne also asserts in the 1979 version that advertisements present women only as sex objects or as housewives. However, like other critics of the late 1970s, she also excoriates the advertising industry for foisting a new "superwoman" executive on American women—but she does it in the same speech where she complains that ads only show women as housewives or sex objects. Kilbourne also charges advertisers with presenting an unrealistic ideal in the new "superwoman" images—most working women, she says, work at low-end jobs for little pay. Yet Second Wave feminists originally demanded the new professional woman image as a more positive ideal for female viewers, not as a request for realism.

Kilbourne's primary tactic is to prey on extant audience fears of advertising by alluding to powerful secret weapons, much as her predecessors, Vance Packard and James Vicary, did. She never substantiates either the practice or the effect.[13] I have tried to show through examples strewn from the beginning to the end of this book that advertising campaigns are not produced through magic. Successful campaigns result from some fairly straightforward market research as well as rhetorical techniques as old as Aristotle (or Lucy Stone). The effects of advertisements are pretty unpredictable, even to the people who make them. Although advertising people certainly can be charged with looking for more foolproof ways of influencing audiences, the most fabled schemes—subliminal advertising, motivation research—have not panned out. Even wildly successful advertising campaigns, such as the one for Woodbury Soap, can suddenly, inexplicably, fail.

The mistrust of advertising, however, is the most distinctive feature of the entire post-Second Wave critique. Judith Williamson's *Decoding Advertisements* articulates a Marxist position on the topic of imagery and commerce, and thus represents an application of the pronounced swing to a socialist perspective.[14] Williamson asserts that the function of advertising in contemporary society is to obscure the true "use value" of objects with the illusionary "exchange value." (Recall the problems with this idea discussed in chapter 7 on the Depression.) She accuses advertising of selling social values along with products, creating "structures of meaning" around objects that they would not otherwise have. Williamson asserts that the phenomena she describes are unique to industrial capitalism; she seems unaware that other types of economies also attach social meaning to goods.

Williamson finds phallic symbols and sexual innuendo in everything—and assumes their mere appearance would be sufficient to motivate purchase behavior. She construes the power of each image as total and uniform—and her own point of view on each picture as the final truth from an expert. As we saw in chapter 4 on the Gibson Girl, this approach to imagery is fatally flawed because it underestimates the active involvement of the viewer, not to mention the importance of context, the impact of style, and the range of uses to be made of the image.

Williamson never indicates how representative the ads are or what their place is in the overall commercial discourse. She never makes comparisons, never explains a product's competitors or substitutes, never tells who the users are. Because Williamson fails to address why someone should choose Revlon over Clinique or to spend money on perfume instead of pantyhose, she seems to say that all ads work the same way—that is, they work perfectly. Thus, the readers this theoretical perspective implicitly constructs would go broke pretty quickly from trying to buy literally everything that appeared in the magazine.

As we have seen, the whole phenomenon of brand differentiation in toiletries stems from the existence of multiple, competing ideals of beauty within the same discourse. Readers will select one thing—say, the clothes—about a particular ideal and then combine it with something from a different ideal—perhaps a hairdo—to produce a unique statement about themselves. That process—much more sophisticated in its implications for human cognition than either the Kilbourne or the Williamson argument—necessarily requires imagination, judgment, and creativity.

To the extent feminists ever admit that multiple ideals of beauty exist, these are immediately turned into negative forces that "pull women in opposite directions" and cause them undue cognitive stress.[15] However, as I have explained, the differentiation among products is an essential part of consumption from both a cognitive and cultural standpoint, so any theory ultimately will have to address the fact that people deal with it every day in thousands of minute ways. The failure to acknowledge the agility and adaptability of human beings in the context of exchange is the weakest point about this literature. It is also the most politically damning part of the critique.

True to the spirit of the founding feminists, the critique of fashion and beauty continues to presume the stupidity and spiritual unworthiness of those who dress in style. The average reader's ability to interpret messages and make decisions for herself is mercilessly denigrated. In spite of all the data showing that women read more and read more broadly than men, feminists still presume that their sisters read nothing but fashion magazines. In Naomi Wolf's words: "Women are deeply affected by what their magazines tell them (or what they believe they tell them) because they are all most women have as a window on their own mass sensibility." That little aside—"or what they believe they tell them"—represents perhaps the most pernicious part of all this—that women need the feminist expert to tell them what the magazines are "really" telling them.

Diane Barthel, for example, introduces *Putting on Appearances* by telling her readers: "Instead of assimilating advertisements semiconsciously, as a consumer, I have sought to apply insights from a wide reading in social and feminist theory." The first major insight she offers is something most of us have figured out on our own: "[Advertisers] speak as though they had expert knowledge; more significantly, they imply that this knowledge of theirs is disinterested. But of course it is not. It is very much in their interest, the interest of the advertisers and the manufacturers, that women accept it unquestioningly and buy the advertised product unthinkingly." I suppose if you were fool enough not to know that advertisements were interested messages, you might accept "unquestioningly" and buy "unthinkingly." Yet it is typical of this critique to grossly overstate people's urge to buy and their inability to resist. One feminist claims that the fashion magazine "elicits in their readers a raving, itching, parching product lust. . . ."[16]

If women were as gullible as this critique suggests (and obviously *they are not*), then females should never be allowed into positions in which decisions of serious consequence have to be made. By what rationale should a creature this incapable of thinking for herself be given political leadership, management power, or even the right to choose an abortion? If we hold sincerely to the belief that women have the ability (and the right) to think for themselves, to lead, to create, to work for change, then the repeated construction of an idiot reader by these critiques is itself an antifeminist act. Indeed, it would seem like madness for a feminist to suggest such a thing. But there is method in it.

The critic who constructs such a weak reader inevitably asserts her own ability to discern things that cannot be accessed through ordinary reading by ordinary women. To the degree that the actual reader buys into the notion that the author can see and reveal things that she herself cannot discern, then she has accepted the authority of the critic to determine her reality. From there, power belongs to the critic, not the reader.

## SUPERWOMEN

During the Second Wave, the feminist demand that media imagery show more working professionals (as an ideal for women to aspire toward) resulted in a noticeable rise in the number of such images, in both commercial messages and other popular forms. The political agenda of the Second Wave also influenced a number of communications researchers to track and count the appearances of such figures in advertising, especially as compared to the housewife figure. These studies show that the "superwoman" of the 1970s and 1980s was not the dominant figure in ads but that such representations grew from near zero to a substantial presence (10 to 20 percent, depending on what magazines you look at) in a very short period of time. In addition, historical and anecdotal evidence suggests that the material surrounding the ads (TV programs, magazine editorial) showed the professional woman figure prominently.[17] So the perception that this image had become dominant in advertising is probably the result of both a novelty effect and the reflection in other cultural forms.

In any case, it is clear that the career woman became the popular articulation of feminism in the media of the 1970s and the '80s. As we have seen, a positive image of the career woman had roots in popular culture at least a hundred years long. But this heroine resurged with noticeable strength in the years immediately following the heyday of the Second Wave. And this time the media representations were paralleled by major changes in the labor profile of females.

Survey data, employment trends, and statistics of all sorts document an enormous, abrupt, and nationwide shift in the educational and professional activities of women since 1970. Most of us are familiar with the broader trends involved here: the increase in the number of working women, in the number of female-headed households, and so on. It is instructive to look a little more closely at some of the details. For instance, the number of bachelor's and master's degrees awarded to women has indeed steadily increased since 1970, but the trend is a recovery from the dramatic downturn during the Feminine Mystique years, and only recently have the numbers risen beyond the pre–World War II level. The increase in the number of professional degrees from 1970 to 1990, however, verges on the apocalyptic. Whether you look at law schools, business schools, medical schools, or dental schools, the rise is from roughly 5 percent of degrees awarded to nearly 50 percent—in only twenty years. As a result of this change in educational accomplishment, the representation of women in several professional fields previously hostile to them has risen a great deal. In 1970 only 5 percent of lawyers were female. Now 29 percent are women. In 1970 only 10 percent of physicians were women. In 1998 the figure was 27 percent. Women accounted for 12 percent of pharmacists before the Second Wave; by the end of the century, they were 44 percent. Eleven percent of systems analysts were women at the beginning of this period, now 42 percent are female.[18]

Women have been filtering into the business world since the early 1970s, sometimes enduring outrageous indignities (sexual harassment being only one). But the gains have been substantial and pervasive. In 1970 there were virtually no women on corporate boards. Today more than 70 percent of all boards have a female presence. On the other end of the scale, women have financed, begun, developed, and led small firms in large numbers. Today, women start businesses at twice the rate of men. In order for all this to occur, a number of sexist practices, from segregated classified ads to discriminatory lending decisions, had to be challenged and struck down. So, not surprisingly, many Americans see these gains as an outcome of "women's lib." And, by and large, they view these changes positively.[19]

Those kinds of broadly supported initiatives constitute what academic feminists call "liberal feminism." That term is unambiguously negative in the academic discourse—a pejorative, an epithet. Instead, all the "feminisms" seen as legitimate by the academy share one common thread: They are all hostile to market activities. Thus, none would see the female corporate leaders of the twenty-first century as feminists, regardless of what those women might *say* when asked "the impossible question."

Let's now step back and consider the situation as an extension of the power conflict within the Second Wave. Remember, the New Feminists and the NOW feminists represented different groups: broadly, young radicals versus accomplished professionals. Remember that they were engaged, particularly from the radicals' point of view, in a bitter struggle for leadership of the movement. And, finally, remember that their political differences were expressed not only in appearance (the "natural" blue jean look versus the well-groomed and tailored suit look) but in *the desire to control the appearance of others.*

Much of the discourse surrounding the career woman *was* focused on her appearance. From "dress for success" to "power dressing," the look of the Modern Woman was put forward as an ideal even more prominently than it had been before World War II. Part of the explanation for this lies in a the actual shift in the aspirations of women, especially among the Boomer Girls. "Power dressing,'" writes dress historian Joan Entwhistle, "marked a new development in the history of women and work; it addressed a new kind of female worker. It was a discourse that did not speak to all women; it did not address the cleaning lady or the manual worker or even the female white-collar worker, but a new breed of working woman who emerged in the 1970s, the university-educated, professional middle-class career woman entering into career structures previously the preserve of men."[20]

With the professional woman becoming the apparent favorite of popular culture and with social trends showing a distinct shift toward the NOW model of success, the New Feminists (many of whom were actually back on campuses) must have felt they were losing the competition for leadership of the movement. Since the academics' political theory was explicitly antimarket, their sense of social status insecurity would have been bolstered by the same conviction of moral superiority that characterized the "ultras" of nineteenth century feminism. And, indeed, efforts to delegitimize the professional woman on a "theoretical" basis appear early. For instance, Elizabeth Cagan, writing for the journal *Social Policy* in 1978, made the argument that the professional woman images were, at base, antifeminist because they were coming from (and, in her view, facilitating) capitalism. And being anticapitalist, she makes clear, is a prerequisite for being a true feminist. Further, she says, the ambition that was motivating women to adopt power-dressing was also contrary to true feminist objectives: "The logic of a feminism which is not explicitly anti-capitalist leads to the demand that men at the top share their positions of power and privilege with women, not the rejection of those positions altogether."[21] Thus the ground was laid to belittle or ignore the accomplishments of thousands of women who, thinking they were supporting the movement, endured the painful process of breaking into schools, jobs, and fields where females emphatically weren't welcome.

To attack a popular and increasingly powerful subgroup directly was not, perhaps, the best strategy for staying in control of the movement. Maybe this was why the critique shifted to a focus on matters of dress. In her 1983 book *Femininity* Susan Brownmiller complained about the dress behavior of her professional acquaintances: "My made-up friends are defiantly pleased with their feminine tricks of beautification. They are in step with the Eighties, brave and chic, women on the go, and I am the one who feels defensive and left behind, suffering from self-doubt." Like so many others, however, Brownmiller expresses a self-doubt she doesn't really feel. Throughout her book, she chastises other women, especially these "friends," for wasting their time and weakening the movement by their dress. Rita Freedman, in *Beauty Bound,* characterizes the feminine touches of the successful professional woman as "a chimp presenting her rump" to the men she works with. The example she gives, in a staggering show of disrespect, is the ruffled collar that Supreme Court Justice Sandra Day O'Connor wore with her robe.[22]

These writers consistently devalued women who attend to dress as silly or frivolous: "Serious women have a difficult time with clothes, not necessarily because they lack a developed sense of style, but because feminine clothes are not designed to project a serious demeanor."[23] Looming large across such statements today, however, is the shadow of a huge group of American females who, although they are more powerful, even on men's terms, than they have ever been before, continue to dress fashionably, groom immaculately, and project a feminine aesthetic—millions of highly accomplished Barbies casting darkness over feminism's Midge.

## ANTIBEAUTY IDEOLOGY AND THE THIRD WAVE

Given the history of this movement, we should not be particularly surprised at this latest development. The "ugly feminist" has real historical roots in the past of the movement's leadership and its internal politics. We see her first in the New Woman espoused by Susan Anthony, last in the forcible hair-cutting of the Second Wave. Notice that whenever this ugly feminist has appeared, it has been in the face of pressure from a more attractive ideal: the Steel-Engraving Feminist of Lucy Stone, the social feminists of the suffrage years, the NOW women of the Second Wave. This, too, should suggest to us that what is at stake is not really the political correctness of a "natural" appearance but leadership, control, and loyalty. On the college campuses of the late twentieth century, this struggle took center stage.

The prevalence of books, tapes, and speakers representing the feminist critique of beauty has had unfortunate consequences in university culture. First, it has given "true" feminists, young and old, a sense that they are entitled to exclusive behavior toward those who may be equally committed to eliminating the oppression of women but who dress differently. This permission is shored up by the debates about "true" and "false" feminism on more lofty planes—to the degree that differences in dress are symptomatic of different visions of feminism, many seem to feel that they are justified in freezing out those who are less clearly in line with approved ideologies. Second, the obsession with personal appearance has focused the energies of feminism on a relatively trivial issue at a time when the challenges of globalization seem poised to demand more of the next generation than a politics of body fat: It has created a vocal cohort of young feminists who actually center their vision of feminism on their own appearance.[24]

The first few books from the Third Wave had been hopeful signs. Katie Roiphe and Rene Denfeld took on their movement mothers with the critical eye and feisty attitude appropriate to a new generation stepping up to claim their place. Not only were they slammed down by established older feminists, they were attacked by members of their own generation unable to contemplate that there could be something better. In *Bitch,* a young feminists' magazine on popular culture, Julie Craig wrote an essay called "I Can't Believe It's Not Feminism" that attacked Camille Paglia, Christina Hoff Sommers, Elizabeth Fox-Genovese, and Katie Roiphe for raising criticisms. The essay appeared in 2002, but it is virtually a rewind-and-replay of Susan Faludi's 1993 *Ms.* essay on the same topic. The article focuses on marking off feminism in such a way as to shut out dissident authors. For the most part Craig relies, as did Faludi, on personal attacks to achieve her desire to exclude: Elizabeth Fox-Genovese, despite her impeccable credentials, is merely a childless hypocrite for suggesting there needs to be a "family feminism" that addresses the needs of young mothers and their children (to Craig, a feminism that takes family questions seriously "doesn't sound much like feminism at all"). Daphne Patai, who wrote a book questioning the feminist orthodoxy that constrains debate in women's studies departments, is rudely dismissed. No possibility of reform can be considered. Instead, Craig wants the lines drawn tighter: "If nothing else, these authors force feminists to take a serious look at how we identify ourselves and how we define participation in the feminist movement. They stretch the limits of whom we include under the rubric of feminism." Craig takes for granted the right to announce who is included and who is excluded.[25]

Jennifer Baumgardner and Amy Richards have strong ties to Gloria Steinem and *Ms.* magazine, and are thus heirs to the good media connections of the Second Wave. Nevertheless, they do better than Julie Craig in their book, *Manifesta: Young Women, Feminism, and the Future,* in considering "out-of-the-box" possibilities for feminism's future. Although they give all credit for the achievements of the Second Wave to campus radicals (more on that later), at least they do call for today's feminists to make a distinction between those within the movement making sincere criticisms and actual antifeminists. Baumgardner and Richards also make interesting comments about a group of young feminists emerging outside the in crowd of feminism, the Girlies. "Although I wish the Girlie feminists in this book would organize as well as they onanize, they have created a joyful culture that makes being an adult woman who calls herself a feminist seem thrilling, sexy, and creative (rather than scary, backbiting, or a one-way ticket to bitterness and the poorhouse). I think Girlie-style feminists are unfairly maligned for this act."[26]

Notice that these two bright young women, although they have assumed the mantle of feminism for their generation, seem unaware of a previously existing tradition that "makes being an adult woman who calls herself a feminist seem thrilling, sexy, and creative." There is no Victoria Woodhull in that sentence, nor Jane Croly, nor Margaret Sanger, nor even Helen Gurley Brown. The reason for this omission is something we've seen before: the exclusive viewpoint behind the histories. Not only do the histories of the movement written since 1970 almost completely ignore any but the Anthony-Stanton dynasty, the new works emerging to document the history of the Second Wave often leave out the original NOW women entirely. Although Marcia Cohen's *Sisterhood* is admirably even-handed and full in scope, Susan Brownmiller's *In Our Time: Memoirs of a Revolution* tells the history of the Second Wave as if it were the story of the New Feminists in New York. From Baumgardner and Richard's comments, we can tell which version is making it into the classroom. And, frankly, much of what is now coming out of the Third Wave sounds as if it were written by their professors.

Young women today do generally support the erstwhile goals of Second Wave feminism now dismissed under the "liberal" rubric. Among my own students, the haunting worry is how they will balance career and motherhood. A look at the demographics quickly shows that the concern is important. In 1972, only 15 percent of females with college degrees were trying to handle work and family both. Today most young women expect to juggle the two. Yet the gender gap in incomes is consistently associated with motherhood—it is not a straightforward connection to gender. Women under forty who are childless make 98 percent of men's salaries—nearly equal. Once children are present, the gender difference emerges: Mothers make 75 percent of men's salaries. And this is not just a problem of would-be wealthy career women. Women between the ages of eighteen and twenty-four are 60 percent more likely to live in poverty than men. The presence of children, once again, is the key.[27] Yet the new gatekeepers of feminism like Julie Craig can't see a feminism that is concerned with family as "any kind of feminism at all." Although fewer women were trying to work and raise children then, this motherhood-or-career issue was center stage at the opening of the Second Wave. Little or nothing has since been solved—instead the very idea of motherhood got subsumed under the antisex umbrella and treated to the same kind of shunning as the idea of lipstick. Feminism may well be "in the water" today's young women swim in, as Baumgardner and Richards aver, but a good bit of detritus is still floating around in it unsolved. Most of it is about sex and reproduction.

We are at a point ominously like the 1920s. The apparent areas of distinction between this generation's concerns and the dictates of today's academic feminists are spookily similar to those between the flappers and the old suffragists: dress, pleasure, sex, and family. Today, as then, the concerns of the young are dismissed ("false consciousness," "private desires," "individualism") by the feminists of the previous cohort. The Old Feminists were asexual, bent on women concerning themselves only with "important" things, leaving sex, family, and the marketplace to "less serious" women. Like the academic feminists today, the scholastic suffragists were the ones teaching the college classes and writing the books. As historians have noted, they were not prepared for the challenges that faced them in the second half of their lives as feminists. As for the Jazz Age New Girls, it seems they saw the Old Feminists as a bunch of crusty old babes who didn't know how to have a good time, who didn't care enough about love and family, and who really weren't interested in listening to women who weren't like them. The New Girls were right.

I fear that the New Girls of today are right, too. The next generation will make its own choices, of course. It would be good, however, if the historians of the future didn't have to write that, once again, feminism failed to formulate livable answers to questions of pleasure, love, and family—except to "rise above" those issues—and so sent the next generation scrambling back into the jaws of an oppressive kinship system.

The younger generation also has a market orientation similar to the New Girls of the Roaring Twenties and appears to be continuing the aspirations that increased the number of professional women of the last thirty years. Marketing courses are increasingly peopled with women. More than two-thirds of the college students majoring in advertising today are women. Women in public relations outnumber men ten to one.[28] The women in these programs are smart and, in my experience, committed to the principle of equality for women (and often think of themselves as "feminists," even though they know *never* to say this to the campus groups). The dissonance between what they are doing with their lives and the Jean Kilbourne sound bites you can get from any of them suggests they are finding little in feminism to help them where they are going: out to market goods in a planetary economy.

Introducing consumer goods into a culture is not a politically neutral or abstract act. As I have tried to show, every little grooming innovation, every new technique in dress, adds up quickly to a revolution in daily life—and these efforts are not managed by a nameless, faceless machine, but by identifiable groups of people, many of them female. The feminist sensibilities of the women who do this work have mattered in the past and *they will matter in the future.* Of necessity, corporations are going to be sending thousands of Modern Women out to manage the global marketplace. These women will have chances to affect the culture of a place and the position of women in it to a degree that academic writers can only imagine. Instead of pretending these women don't exist—or reviling them for being involved with the market at all—feminists on college campuses should be trying to prepare them for meeting the reality of women's oppression they are going to find.

If the Old Feminists of today are to engage meaningfully with this next generation of Modern Women, they are going to have to find more to say than "wait for the revolution." Feminism has been slow to develop a real understanding of economics.[29] The fashionability of a brand of "political economy" in which knowledge of language theory is more important than understanding price dynamics has led to the false assertion of economic sophistication by an entire generation of academic feminists. Muttering references to Marx and roundly condemning anything that can be stretched to define as "commoditization," many feminists have lulled themselves into thinking they are dealing with the challenges of global capitalism. In fact, they are missing the entire moment, even as it passes under their noses.

CHAPTER 12

# FRESH LIPSTICK

> To see ourselves as others see us can be eye-opening. To see others as sharing a nature with ourselves is the merest decency. But it is from the far more difficult achievement of seeing ourselves amongst others, as a local example of the forms human life has locally taken, a case among cases, a world among worlds, that the largeness of mind, without which objectivity is self-congratulation and tolerance a sham, comes.
>
> —*Clifford Geertz*

AMERICA SAT TRANSFIXED. THE IMAGES OF THE WORLD NEWS NETWORKS BROKE, REarranged themselves, and repeated, like pieces of glass in a kaleidoscope. Over and again two towers crumbled in smoke, dark-skinned people danced in a faraway street, and tense men in ties tried to explain. For the first few days, citizens of a wealthy, educated but insular nation learned about conditions in parts of the planet many had never even thought about. At the center of the lesson was the tragic state of Afghanistan. There religious fundamentalists, having imposed their retrograde will on their own people, had now turned toward the West to avenge fear of a changing world.

Life under the Taliban, as glimpsed through the lens of CNN, was brutal. Most salient among the intolerable conditions was the treatment of women. Covered and cloistered, adult females were kept from interacting with the world in any way—and were horrifically punished if they broke through the wall of custom and law that held them. Denied education or employment, they were trapped in the despair of an elaborate system that, like many traditional patriarchies, was designed specifically to keep their sexuality contained so their bodies could be controlled and traded by men.

Within the framework of these shocking images, however, were two vignettes of resistance, two poignant gestures of courage and hope. On one hand were videos showing educated women secretly teaching girls. And on the other were films of women grooming other women in the styles of the West. Whether learning to read or learning to apply lipstick, these women, through these acts, were resisting their oppression and, in the process, risking their safety. None of these actions, however, was as dangerous as transgressing this order at its center—by giving your own self sexually to a man of your choosing. For that kind of resistance, the punishment was public execution.

Globally oriented feminists have tried for decades to shake America into awareness about the unspeakable circumstances of women around the world. Suddenly those conditions had literally hit home. Yet the high-relief illustration these clips provided of how limited American feminist thought was when it came to dress seemed to go unnoticed.

A tube of lipstick as an instrument of revolution? A love affair as an act of resistance? A traditional economy more oppressive to women than any industrialized nation? There is nothing in the feminist ideology on grooming, kinship, or economics to account for these contradictions. And indeed, the more you look at it, the more contradictions there are: a culture where women are held in place by being "desexualized," not "sexualized"; a place where women are oppressed by *not* allowing men to ogle them. But in Afghanistan there is no fashion industry, no advertising.

There was also no advertising in the former Soviet Union. Yet the women coming forward from the ruins of that socialist state over the past decade have not reported their lives as a feminist utopia. In fact, the writings of newly emerged eastern European and Russian feminists often have clashed with the received view, causing those Americans who care to engage in the dialog to rethink some of their most basic assumptions about the nature of women's oppression.

The globalization of the western economy, like the imperialism of the past, threatens tribal cultures in Africa and South America and in pockets all over the globe. In these small civilizations, we still see suggestions of the full extent of variation in human dress and grooming. And, as is often the case with cultures very different from our own, the practices still observable often turn our own assumptions upside down. The men of the Dinka tribe in Africa, for instance, wear elaborately beaded corsets (and little else) every day from puberty to old age. A few wealthy women are also allowed to wear them. To a Western eye, the tight, bright corsets look extremely uncomfortable and definitely "sexualizing." Yet they are clearly a mark of power and outline a stratification system only partly accounted for by gender.[1] With the help of museum exhibitions, such as the one on body decoration held at the American Museum of Natural History in New York during 1999, Americans learn to look at the shaping and painting of the human body in other cultures as an art form. Yet even with glossy exhibition catalogs at our disposal, few of us can accord our own body decoration practices the same status.

Across the board, in fact, we seem to be unable to view our own dress practices for what they are: "a local example of the forms human life has locally taken." We paint our faces, pour ourselves into tight clothes, even undergo plastic surgery, as part of a long-standing and universal tradition in human behavior. As one anthropologist wrote: "There is no known culture in which people do not paint, pierce, tattoo, reshape or simply adorn their bodies." Yet feminist ideology expects us to be different—and in this way, *better*—than the rest of humanity. By taking this position, the self-declared leaders of this movement push us into a way of dealing with life that is fundamentally inhumane. By ignoring the way that self-decoration expresses the human force of creative expression—the song of the self to come into being—and by denying the strength these practices can bring at moments of depression, dislocation, and even death, the antibeauty critique engages in cultural cruelty.[2]

And this happens by way of an intellectual hoax. One of my strategies in researching and writing this book was to take the sacred cows of the critique one by one and check them out against the historical record. A lot of the evidence I turned up directly contradicted what feminists were saying. As it turns out, blondes did *not* dominate the discourse on beauty, the fashion industry was *never* a patriarchy, the editors of the fashion magazines have *not* been mostly men, the most effective feminists in history have *not* all looked like clones of Susan B. Anthony. The ideas that feminists writing on this topic have advanced about the way pictures work, or the way people "naturally" dress, or the way advertising-free economies operate do *not* square with cross-cultural or historical evidence. In fact, the more I poked around at the feminist critique of fashion, the more aware I became that it has been constructed mostly of unsubstantiated assertions, many of which are flatly untrue but which get repeated, each feminist citing the other, until they take on lives of their own. What I also found, consistently, were phenomena considerably more complex, problematic, and intelligent than the critique allowed.

Perhaps the most dishonest aspect of this critique is the way it asserts the "natural" position, the philosophical "God's eye view." A woman in a pair of blue jeans and a T-shirt arriving in Taliban-controlled Afghanistan (or any number of other places around the world) is not "natural" and certainly not politically neutral, regardless of how little makeup she may wear on her face. The same woman is no more natural at home in the United States just because we are accustomed to looking at her. And she occupies no less interested a position here than abroad. All human dress speaks of social order and therefore is *never* politically neutral.

The feminists' preemption of a "natural" position on dress is, as I expect my readers to recognize now, possible *only* because of their superior status vis-à-vis other women (those whose dress they try to control). The impulse to reform the dress of others is an extension of the historical trajectory of appearance in America. In this sartorial history, higher moral value has been given to certain modes of dress—simple, colorless, asexual—largely because of their associations with certain groups: the Puritans of the colonial period, Yankee Protestants of the early Industrial Revolution, scholastic suffragists from the turn of the century, neo-Puritans of the Jazz Age, and neo-Marxists of the Second Wave. Other groups have had more colorful ways of dressing and have been just as important to the feminist movement, but histories of American feminism have overlooked them. Still in the shadows are the penny capitalists of the early fashion and beauty industry, actresses of both stage and screen, lesbians, women of the old West, witches, the "flower children" of the 1960s, and a substantial variety of "ethnic" women. Without a doubt, these women had a different viewpoint on the politics of dress than did the Puritan feminists. Are we prepared to say their views were, categorically, less valid?

The continuing refusal by feminists writing on this topic to consider other viewpoints suggests that they don't believe another legitimate opinion or experience exists. Thus they claim for themselves the "view from nowhere": a philosophical position that is absolutely true and objective, the single viewpoint from which all is clear, all is known, and nothing is assailable. Ironically, feminists once used this phrase to describe the viewpoint asserted by white, prosperous males (a.k.a. "the patriarchy"). One of the most difficult and important tasks of early Second Wave intellectual feminism was to argue against the notion that the male view was the only right, objective way to look at the world. Feminists had to show—and *did* show—that gender makes a difference in a person's experience and therefore constructs another viewpoint that, although equally legitimate, affects estimations of what is rational, good, fair, moral, or even true.

By the 1990s, white intellectual feminists were being criticized for having asserted their own view from nowhere. In response, Susan Bordo wrote that people who propose to focus attention on the particularities of dress, rather than admitting to the obvious reality of the matter in general terms (that is to say, the truth as viewed from nowhere), are merely indulging in a fantasy she dubs "the dream of everywhere."[3] The problem with the view from everywhere, she argues, is that it fragments the feminist critique, degenerating into facile "celebrations" of diversity and leaving the movement weakened.

This book *is* intended as an attack on the true feminist's "God's eye view" of dress. But it is *not* some sloppy dream of seeing "from everywhere." Instead, my proposal is more modest: I am simply suggesting that true feminists consider the possibility of a view from *elsewhere.* The politics of dress that I have described in this book is one with which we can recognize multiple strategies, differing origins, and various aspirations, and thus has a sharper edge for analyzing the power relations expressed through dress than simply breaking the world down into a false, self-interested idea of "natural" versus everything else. By explaining this, I hope I have convinced some true feminists to show a little more humility and lot more compassion toward the dress of other women. By demonstrating how much the meaning of dress and grooming habits varies according to each woman's place in race, class, and history, I hoped to sensitize all my readers to the need to reserve judgment on such matters until they have considered them thoughtfully and with the benefit of a reasonable amount of evidence to support their theories.

In the end, I hope I have encouraged others who are dedicated to the equality of women, but who do not wish to give up the pleasures of self-decoration, to renew their commitment to the project of feminism. Voices from around the world report a variety of conditions and systems under which only one thing holds constant: the universal second-class status of females. If there was ever a moment when the women of one culture had a responsibility toward their sisters in other nations, this is it. We should not waste time quibbling over what to wear to the conflict. Instead, I would hope that, armed with a new perspective, a rejuvenated resolve, and, yes, even a little fresh lipstick, American feminism could venture out into the world to meet the challenge.

# NOTES

## INTRODUCTION

1. Susan Faludi, *Backlash* (New York: Crown, 1991). Naomi Wolf, *The Beauty Myth* (New York: Doubleday, 1992). Lois W. Banner, *American Beauty* (Chicago: University of Chicago Press, 1983). Susan Bordo, *Unbearable Weight* (Berkeley: University of California Press, 1993).
2. Nancy F. Cott, *The Grounding of Modern Feminism* (New Haven, CT: Yale University Press, 1987), 48–49. A flagrant, and extended, application of the heroine of the mind/body concept is Rachel Brownstein, *Becoming a Heroine* (New York: Viking Press, 1982).
3. Sherna Berger Gluck, *Rosie the Riveter Revisited* (Boston: Twayne, 1987), ii-iii. Elisabeth Griffith, *In Her Own Right* (New York: Oxford University Press, 1984), 146–147.
4. Simone de Beauvoir, *The Second Sex,* trans. and ed., H. M. Parshley (New York: Knopf, 1953). Betty Friedan, *The Feminine Mystique* (New York: Norton, 1963).
5. Ann J. Simonton, "Women for Sale," in *Women and Media,* ed. Cynthia M. Lont (New York: Wadworth, 1995). Jean Kilbourne, *Killing Us Softly,* videotape (Cambridge: Cambridge Documentary Films, 1979). Christina Hoff Sommers, *Who Stole Feminism? How Women Have Betrayed Women* (New York: Simon & Schuster, 1994), 111.
6. Mary Pipher, *Reviving Ophelia* (New York: Ballantine, 1994). Ophira Edut, ed., *Adiós Barbie* (Seattle: Seal Press, 1998).
7. The major histories of American feminism definitely show this bias. Eleanor Flexner, *Century of Struggle* (Cambridge, MA: Harvard University Press, 1975). William L. O'Neill, *Everyone Was Brave* (Chicago: Quadrangle Books, 1969). For the way the prejudice gets perpetuated, see how Sheila Tobias tells the story of feminism in *Faces of Feminism* (Boulder, CO: Westview Press, 1997).
8. Banner 13–14.

## CHAPTER ONE

1. Among many other sources for my statements on personal adornment throughout this book, I have consulted the following historical, anthropological, sociological, and psychological works. Maggie Angeloglou, *A History of Makeup* (London: Studio Vista, 1970). Quentin Bell, *On Human Finery* (New York: A. A. Wyn, Inc., 1949). Roland Barthes, *The Fashion System.* Trans. Matthew Ward and Richard Howard (New York: Hill and Wang, 1983). Robert Brain, *The Decorated Body* (New York: Harper & Row, 1979). Christopher Breward, *The Culture of Fashion: A New History of Dress* (New York: Manchester University Press, 1995). Justine M. Cordwell and Ronald A. Schwartz, *The Fabrics of Culture: The Anthropology of Clothing and Adornment* (New York: Mouton, 1979). Richard Corson, *Fashions in Makeup* (New York: Universe Books, 1975). Arnold J. Cooley, *The Toilet in Ancient and Modern Times* (New York: Burt Franklin, 1866). Ernest Crawley, *Dress, Drinks, and Drums: Further Studies of Savages and Sex* (London: Methuen & Co., 1931). Fred Davis, *Fashion, Culture, and Identity* (Chicago: University of Chicago Press, 1992). Elizabeth Ewing, *History of Twentieth Century Fashion* (London: B. T. Batsford, 1986). Erving Goffman, *The Presentation of Self in Everyday Life* (Garden City, NY: Doubleday, 1959). Lois M. Gurel and Marianne S. Beeson, *Dimensions of Dress and Adornment* (Dubuque, IA: Kendall Hunt Publishing Co., 1975). Anne Hollander, *Seeing Through Clothes* (New York: Penguin, 1975). Elizabeth B. Hurlock, *The Psychology of Dress* (New York: Ronald Press Company, 1929). Claudia Brush Kidwell and Valerie Steele, *Men and Women* (Washington, D.C.: Smithsonian, 1989). Renne Konig, *The Restless Image: A Sociology of Fashion* (London: George Allen & Unwin, 1973). Arline and John Liggett, *The Tyranny of Beauty* (London: Victor Gollancz, 1989).

Arthur Marwick, *Beauty in History* (London: Thames and Hudson, 1988). Doris Langley Moore, *The Woman in Fashion* (New York: B. T. Batsford, 1949). Paul H. Nystrom, *Economics of Fashion* (New York: Ronald Press Co., 1928). Frank Alvah Parsons, *The Psychology of Dress* (Garden City: Doubleday, 1920). Mary Ellen Roach and Joanne Bubolz Eicher, *Dress, Adornment, and the Social Order* (New York: John Wiley & Sons, 1965). Mary Lou Rosencranz, *Clothing Concepts* (New York: Macmillan, 1972). Ruth P. Rubinstein, *Dress Codes* (San Francisco: Westview Press, 1995). Michael R. Solomon, *The Psychology of Fashion* (Lexington: D. C. Heath, 1985). Valerie Steele, *Fashion and Eroticism* (New York: Oxford, 1985). Thorstein Veblen, *The Theory of the Leisure Class* (New York: New American Library, 1953; first published in 1899). Olivia Vlahos, *Body: The Ultimate Symbol* (New York: J. B. Lippincott, 1979). André Virel, *Decorated Man* (New York: Harry N. Abrams, 1979). John Woodforde, *The History of Vanity* (New York: St. Martin's Press, 1992). Max Wyckes-Joyce, *Cosmetics and Adornment* (New York: Philosophical Library, 1961). Agatha Young, *Recurring Cycles of Fashion* (New York: Cooper Square, 1966).

2. Sources on American ethnicity: James Hennesey, *American Catholics* (New York: Oxford University Press, 1981). Matthew Frye Jacobson, *European Immigrants and the Alchemy of Race* (Cambridge, MA: Harvard University Press, 1998). Jack Larkin, *The Reshaping of Everyday Life 1790–1840* (New York: Harper & Row, 1988). Ronald Takaki, *A Different Mirror* (New York: Little, Brown & Co., 1993). Thomas Sowell, *Ethnic America* (New York: Basic Books, 1981). Stephan Thernstrom, *The Other Bostonians* (Cambridge, MA: Harvard University Press, 1973). Edward K. Spann, *The New Metropolis* (New York: Columbia University Press, 1981).
3. Sources on the New England tradition were: Alice Morse Earle, *Customs and Fashions in Old New England* (Detroit: Singing Tree Press, 1968). John Putnam Demos, *Entertaining Satan* (New York: Oxford University Press, 1982). Carol F. Karlsen, *The Devil in the Shape of a Woman* (New York: Norton, 1987). Lyle Koehler, *A Search for Power* (Urbana: University of Illinois Press, 1980). David Freeman Hawke, *Everyday Life in Early America* (New York: Perennial Library, 1989). On the preferences of the "founding feminists," see Blanche Hersh, *The Slavery of Sex* (Urbana: University of Illinois Press, 1978), 159–160. Andrea Moore Kerr, *Lucy Stone* (New Brunswick, NJ: Rutgers University Press, 1992), 36.
4. Carol Devens, *Countering Colonization* (Berkeley: University of California Press, 1992).
5. Sources on slave life: Eugene Genovese, *Roll, Jordan, Roll* (New York: Random House, 1976). Paula Giddings, *When and Where I Enter* (New York: W. Morrow, 1984). Jacqueline Jones, *Labor of Love, Labor of Sorrow* (New York: Vintage Books, 1986). Harriet Ann Jacobs, *Incident in the Life of a Slave Girl* (Cambridge, MA: Harvard University Press, 1987). Elizabeth Keckley, *Behind the Scenes* (New York: Arno Press, 1968). Dorothy Sterlin, ed., *We Are Your Sisters* (New York: Norton, 1984).
6. Shirley Abbott, *Womenfolks* (New Haven, CT: Ticknor & Fields, 1983), 41, 40.
7. Sources on the pioneer women: Martha Mitten Allen, *Traveling West* (El Paso, TX: Texas Western Press, University of Texas at El Paso, 1987). Dee Alexander Brown, *The Gentle Tamers* (New York: Putnam, 1958). Christiane Fisher, ed., *Let Them Speak for Themselves* (Hamden, CT: Archon Books, 1977). Dorothy Gray, *Women of the West* (Millbrae, CA: Les Femmes, 1976). Julie Roy Jeffrey, *Frontier Women* (New York: Hill and Wang, 1979). Cathy Luchetti and Carol Olwell, *Women of the West* (New York: Orion Books, 1982). Elinor Richey, *Eminent Women of the West* (Berkeley, CA: Howell-North Books, 1975). William Forrest Sprague, *Women and the West* (New York: Arno Press, 1972). Ross Nancy Wilson, *Westward the Women* (Freeport, NY: Books for Libraries Press, 1944).
8. Lillian Schlissel, "Diaries of Frontier Women: On Learning to Read the Obscured Patterns," in *Women's Being, Women's Place,* ed. Mary Kelly (Boston: G. K. Hall, 1979) 26–52, quote on p. 60. See also Mary Ryan, *Womanhood in America* (New York: New Viewpoints, 1979), 140.
9. Glenda Riley, *The Life and Legacy of Annie Oakley* (Norman: University of Oklahoma, 1994).
10. Gray 61–74. See also Takaki and Sowell. Some fashion historians have erroneously asserted that all Chinese women bound their feet. It is quite clear, however, that the peasant/prostitute girls did not, at least in the nineteenth-century American experience. Histories and firsthand accounts of Chinese immigrants of this period note a specific class of "small foot" women, who were the wives of prosperous men (and also kept virtual prisoners in their homes). Further, U.S. immigration authorities used the size of Chinese females' feet to judge whether the woman was "respectable" or

likely to be a prostitute. "Small foot" women were allowed in, while the peasants with big feet were deported because they were assumed to be "lewd women." See, for instance, Judy Yung, *Unbound Feet: A Social History of Chinese Women in San Francisco* (Berkeley: University of California Press, 1995), 6–7, 16, 19, 24, 41.

11. John D'Emilio, *Sexual Politics, Sexual Communities* (Chicago: University of Chicago Press, 1983), 9–22. Carroll Smith-Rosenberg, *Disorderly Conduct* (New York: Knopf, 1985), 272–273.
12. Gae Whitney Canfield, *Sarah Winnemucca of the Northern Paiutes,* 1st ed. (Norman: University of Oklahoma Press, 1983). Dorothy Clarke Wilson, *Bright Eyes* (New York: McGraw-Hill, 1974).
13. Joel Willams, *The Crucible of Race* (New York: Oxford University Press, 1984).
14. Lynn M. Hudson, *The Making of "Mammy Pleasant"* (Urbana: University of Illinois Press, 2003). Raymond J. Martinez, *Folk Tales along the Mississippi* (New Orleans: Hope Publications, 1956). Robert Tallant, *Voodoo in New Orleans* (Gretna, LA: Pelican, 1983).

## Chapter Two

1. Sources for Elizabeth Oakes Smith and Paulina Wright Davis include: Kathleen Barry, *Susan B. Anthony* (New York: New York University Press, 1988) 72. Paulina Wright Davis, *A History of the National Woman's Rights Movement* (New York: Kraus Reprint Co., 1971; first published in 1871), 4. Eleanor Flexner, *Century of Struggle* (Cambridge, MA: Harvard University Press, 1975), 81. Elisabeth Griffith, *In Her Own Right* (New York: Oxford, 1984), 44, 75. Ida H. Harper, *The Life and Work of Susan B. Anthony* (Indianapolis: Bowen-Merrill Co., 1899), 72. Blanche Hersh, *The Slavery of Sex* (Urbana: University of Illinois Press, 1978), 54, 59. Keith E. Melder, *Beginnings of Sisterhood* (New York: Schocken, 1977) 152–153, 123, 137, 143. Mary Ann B. Oakley, *Elizabeth Cady Stanton* (Long Island, NY: Feminist Press, 1972). Elizabeth Oakes Smith, *Selections from the Autobiography of Elizabeth Oakes Smith,* ed. Mary Alice Wyman (New York: Columbia, 1924), 97, 151–153. Andrew Sinclair, *The Emancipation of the American Woman* (New York: Harper, 1965), 8–9. Elizabeth Cady Stanton, *Eighty Years and More* (London: T. Fisher Unwin, 1898), 194. Mary Alice Wyman, *Two American Pioneers* (New York: Columbia University Press, 1927), 190. Entry for "Paulina Wright Davis," *The National Cyclopedia of American Biography* (Clifton, NJ: J. T. White, 1984), 327–328. Linda Steiner, "Evolving Rhetorical Strategies/Evolving Identities," in *A Voice of Their Own,* ed. Martha M. Solomon (Tuscaloosa: University of Alabama Press, 1991). Mari Boor Tonn, "The *Una,* 1853–1855: The Premiere of the Woman's Rights Press," in *A Voice of Their Own.*
2. Harper 72. Barry 72. Hersh 111.
3. In addition to the biographies of the early feminists I have already cited, I have used: Lois W. Banner, *Elizabeth Cady Stanton* (Boston: Little, Brown, 1980). Ellen Carol Du Bois, ed., *Elizabeth Cady Stanton and Susan B. Anthony* (New York: Schocken, 1981). Andrea Moore Kerr, *Lucy Stone* (New Brunswick, NJ: Rutgers University Press, 1992). Alma Lutz, *Created Equal* (New York: John Day Co., 1940). Sources for the history of feminism in this period: Ellen Carol DuBois, *Feminism and Suffrage* (Ithaca, NY: Cornell University Press, 1978). William L. O'Neill, *Everyone Was Brave* (Chicago: Quadrangle Books, 1969). William L. O'Neill, *The Woman Movement* (New York: Barnes & Noble, 1969). Ross Paulson, *Women's Suffrage and Prohibition* (Glenview, IL: Scott Foresman, 1973). Alice S. Rossi, *The Feminist Papers* (New York: Bantam, 1973).
4. Sources on dress in New England: Alice Morse Earle, *Customs and Fashions in Old New England* (Detroit: Singing Tree Press, 1968). John Putnam Demos, *Entertaining Satan* (New York: Oxford University Press, 1982). Carol F. Karlsen *The Devil in the Shape of a Woman* (New York: Norton, 1987).
5. Sources on anti-Catholicism: Ray Allen Billington, *The Protestant Crusade, 1800–1860* (New York: Rinehart & Company, 1938). James J. Hennesey, *American Catholics* (New York: Oxford University Press, 1981). Ronald Takaki, *A Different Mirror:* (New York: Little, Brown & Co., 1993) 26, 139–165. Thomas Sowell, *Ethnic America* (New York: Basic Books, 1981) 17–68, 100–132.
6. Main sources on the pre-Revolutionary aristocracy, their attitudes, dress, and grooming habits: Richard L. Bushman, *The Refinement of America* (New York: Knopf, 1992). Gordon S. Wood, *The Radicalism of the American Revolution* (New York: Knopf, 1992). Hersh 125.

7. Main sources on the everyday lives and dress habits of the commonfolk: Jack Larkin, *The Reshaping of Everyday Life 1790–1840* (New York: Harper & Row, 1988). David Freeman Hawke, *Everyday Life in Early America* (New York: Perennial Library, 1989). Suellen Hoy, *Chasing Dirt* (New York: Oxford University Press, 1995). Stuart Blumin, "Black Coats to White Collars," in *Social Structure in Industrializing America,* ed. Stuart Bruchey (New York: Columbia University Press, 1980), 100–121.
8. C. Willett and Phillis Cunnington, *The History of Underclothes* (New York: Dover, 1992).
9. Bushman 66. Sandra Bartky, *Femininity and Domination* (New York: Routledge, 1990). Susan Brownmiller, *Femininity* (New York: Linden Press, 1984).
10. Bushman 44, 81.
11. Lois W. Banner, *American Beauty* (Chicago: University of Chicago Press, 1983). Barbara Welter, "The Cult of True Womanhood," *American Quarterly* 18 (Summer): 151–175.
12. This story of the post-Revolutionary struggle for cultural control is Wood's thesis in *Radicalism.* Hersh 121–123. Rossi 241–281.
13. Abba Gould Woolson, *Dress Reform* (Boston: Roberts Brothers, 1874), 7. Banner, *American Beauty,* 18, 20, 29–31.
14. Richard Hofstadter, *The Age of Reform* (New York: Vintage Books, 1955). Edward Spann, *The New* Metropolis (New York: Columbia University Press, 1981). Richard Sennett, *Families Against the* City (Cambridge, MA: Harvard University Press, 1984). Stephan Thernstrom, *The Other Bostonians* (Cambridge, MA: Harvard University Press, 1993). Stephan Thernstrom and Richard Sennett, *Nineteenth-Century Cities* (New Haven, CT: Yale University Press, 1969). Banner, *American Beauty,* 26. Hersh 132. See also Bushman, Larkin, Hawke.
15. Sources on the rise of the nouveau riche and their interaction with elites, especially in the cities: Bushman, Spann, Hofstadter, Banner, *American Beauty.* Sennett, and Frederick T. Martin, *The Passing of the Idle Rich* (New York: Doubleday, 1975).
16. "Editorial," *Vogue* 6 (November 14, 1895): 312.
17. "William Leach, *True Love and Perfect Union* (New York: Basic Books, 1980), 122–129.
18. "The Delsarte System of Physical Culture," *Delineator* (July 1893): 100–101. Also "The Delsarte System of Physical Culture," *Delineator* (June 1893): 657–659.
19. Bushman 60.
20. Spann 263. Other sources on working girls and women: Lucy Larcom, *A New England Girlhood* (Boston, MA: Northeastern University Press, 1986). Lillian Williams Betts, *The Leaven in a Great City* (New York: Dodd, Mead & Co., 1902), 141. Leslie Woodcock Tentler, *Wage-Earning Women: Industrial Work and Family Life in the United States, 1900–1930* (New York: Oxford University Press, 1979). Susan Strasser, *Never Done: A History of American Housework* (New York: Pantheon, 1982), 125–144. Helen Campbell, *Prisoners of Poverty* (Cambridge, MA: John Wilson and Son, 1887). Susan Potter Benson, *Counter Cultures* (Urbana: University of Illinois Press, 1986). Nancy F. Cott, *The Bonds of Womanhood* (New Haven, CT: Yale University Press, 1997). Joanne J. Meyrowitz, *Women Adrift* (Chicago: University of Chicago Press, 1988). Kathy Peiss, *Cheap Amusements* (Philadelphia: Temple University Press, 1986). See also Bushman, Larkin, Hawke. Sarah Eisenstein, *Give Us Bread But Give Us Roses* (Boston: Routledge & Kegan Paul, 1983), 72.
21. Main sources on urban life and immigrants: Takaki; Sowell; Spann; Sennett; and Thernstrom. Main source on Irish immigrant women: Hasiah Diner, *Erin's Daughters in America* (Baltimore: Johns Hopkins University, 1983) 77.
22. Takaki 288–289, 293. Sowell 85.
23. Robert Hendrickson, *The Grand Emporiums* (New York: Stein and Day, 1979).
24. Caroline Bird, *Enterprising Women* (New York: Norton, 1976).
25. Takaki 298.
26. See Billington, Hofstadter, and Lee Benson, *The Concept of Jacksonian Democracy* (Princeton, NJ: Princeton University Press, 1961).
27. Dixon Ryan Fox, *Yankees and Yorkers* (New York: New York University Press, 1940).
28. Benson 212.
29. Barry and Kerr both discuss the association of the feminists with the ultras.

30. Joseph R. Gusfield, *Symbolic Crusade,* 2nd ed. (Urbana: University of Illinois Press, 1963, 1986). Sowell 17–42, 59–61. Takaki 139–165.
31. Sources on social purity and the relationship between feminism and these reforms: Gusfeld; Paulson; Rossi; Paul S. Boyer, *Purity in Print* (New York: Charles Scribner's Sons, 1968). Barbara Meil Hobson, *Uneasy Virtue* (New York: Basic Books, 1987). David J. Pivar, *Purity Crusade* (Westport, CT: Greenwood Press, 1973).
32. Richardson Wright, *Hawkers and Walkers in Early America* (New York: Arno Press, 1976 [1927]), 178, 198. Peter Benes, "Itinerant Entertainers in New England and New York, 1687–1830," in *Itinerancy in New England and New York,* ed. Peter Benes (Boston: Boston University Press, 1984) 113.
33. Pivar 288, Appendix B, "Topics for Study and Discussion at Mothers' Meetings."
34. Sources on servants include Campbell, Diner, as well as Lucy Maynard Salmon, *Domestic Service* (London: Macmillan, 1897), 151–166. Carol Lasser, "'The World's Dread Laugh': Singlehood and Service in Nineteenth-Century Boston," in *The New England Working Class and the New Labor History* ed. Herbert G. Gutman and Donald H. Bell, (Urbana: University of Illinois Press, 1987), 72–89.
35. Campbell 228–229.
36. Hersh 126–128. Griffith 70.
37. Banner 25. Diner 141–142.
38. Caroll Davidson Wright, *The Working Girls of Boston* (New York: Arno Press, 1969 [1889]), 120, 126, 118.
39. Ryan 85–97. Susan Hirsch, "From Artisan to Manufacturer: Industrialization and the Small Producer in Newark," in *Small Business in American Life,* ed. Stuart W. Bruchey (New York: Columbia University Press, 1980), 80–99. Caroline Reynolds Milbank, *New York Fashion* (New York: Harry N. Abrams, 1989), 16–45. See also Blumin 100–121.
40. O'Neill, *Everyone Was Brave,* 72.
41. Glenna Matthews, *The Rise of Public Woman* (New York: Oxford University Press, 1992).
42. Arthur Marwick, *Beauty in History* (London: Thames and Hudson, 1988), 272–287.
43. Barbara Belford, *Brilliant Bylines in America* (New York: Columbia University Press, 1986), 54–69, 99–113, 114–149.
44. Rossi 86–99. Celia Morris, *Fanny Wright* (Urbana: University of Illinois Press, 1992). Rossi 97. Hersh 67, 120.
45. Neither woman is mentioned in Berg. DuBois's *Feminism and Suffrage* doesn't mention Smith at all, but gives Davis three brief mentions, including one in a footnote. Flexner does mention Smith in a list of attendees at the 1850 convention and mentions Davis three times, all of them one sentence or less. Melder mentions Davis as organizer of the 1850 convention and as a teacher of anatomy, and gives Smith two mentions, each in a list of names. Neither of O'Neill's books mention either Smith or Davis, nor does Paulson's. Sinclair mentions Smith but says nothing of her feminist activities. He gives Davis only three brief mentions, one of which implies that she was a dilettante as a feminist.

## Chapter Three

1. Linda Steiner, "Evolving Rhetorical Strategies/Evolving Identities," in *A Voice of Their Own: The Woman Suffrage Press, 1840–1910,* ed. Martha M. Solomon (Tuscaloosa: University of Alabama Press, 1991), 183–197. Quotations on 190, 187, 189. In this exceptionally astute essay, Steiner herself uses extremely pejorative language to describe more traditional women ("driveling, dependent imbeciles," 190). This kind of implicit editorializing is pervasive throughout feminist literature on a variety of topics, thus adding, even when the thesis is not explicitly anti-beauty, to the general perception that being "a good feminist" necessarily precludes participation in the fashion and beauty culture. A main source for commentary on the early woman movement journalist is Solomon's *A Voice of Their Own,* including: Bonnie J. Dow, "The Revolution," 171–186, and Edward A. Hinck, "The Lily," 40–53.
2. Sources for the bloomer issue: Jules Archer, *Breaking Barriers* (New York: Viking, 1991), 35–38. Lois Banner, *American Beauty* (Chicago: University of Chicago Press, 1983), 86–105. Kathleen

Barry, *Susan B. Anthony* (New York: New York University Press, 1988), 67–78, 71–72, 81–83. Alice Stone Blackwell, *Lucy Stone* (Norwood, MA: Plimpton, 1930), 105–111. Rheta Childe Dorr, *Susan B. Anthony* (New York: Frederick A. Stokes, 1928), 90–93. Eleanor Flexner, *Century of Struggle* (Cambridge, MA: Harvard University Press, 1975), 83–84. Charles Neilson Gattey, *The Bloomer Girls* (New York, Coward-McCann, 1968). Elisabeth Griffith, *In Her Own Right* (New York: Oxford University Press, 1984), 71–72. Elinor Rice Hays, *Morning Star* (New York: Octagon Books, 1978). Blanche Hersh, *The Slavery of Sex* (Urbana: University of Illinois Press, 1978), 50–51. Andrea Moore Kerr, *Lucy Stone* (New Brunswick, NJ: Rutgers University Press, 1992), 62–65, 94. Alma Lutz, *Created Equal* (New York: John Day Co., 1940), 63–80. Alma Lutz, *Susan B. Anthony* (Boston: Beacon Press, 1959). Louise R. Noun, *Strong-Minded Women* (Ames: Iowa State University Press, 1969), 14–19. Elizabeth Cady Stanton, *Eighty Years and More* (London: T. Fisher Unwin, 1898), 201–204. See also Susan Brownmiller, *Femininity* (New York: Linden Press, 1984), 88–91. Rita Jackaway Freedman, *Beauty Bound* (Lexington, MA: Lexington Books, 1986), 229.

3. Griffith 72.
4. Gattey 47, 82. Griffith 70–71.
5. Gattey 62–65. Lutz 68–69.
6. Lutz 70, 69.
7. Barry 71. Hinck 41.
8. Kerr 65.
9. Gattey discusses the Anti-Slavery Society meeting on page 97 and says that Lucy addressed the Women's Rights meeting on September 7, 1853, wearing bloomers. Barry says that Susan arrived home on November 8, having been on the road since August. Anthony started wearing bloomers in December 1852 and stopped wearing them after only a year. Stone, who also had been on the road prior to the convention, started wearing the bloomer between June and December 1852. So the event had to take place when both women were still wearing bloomers and were in New York City at the same time. That means it had to be between January and December of 1853.
10. The source for the discussion of Anthony's childhood, dress, and feminist awakening is Barry. Quotation is from Glenna Matthews, *The Rise of Public Woman* (New York: Oxford University Press, 1992), 37.
11. Barry 46–47, 51.
12. Sandra Bartky, *Femininity and Domination* (New York: Routledge, 1990) 11.
13. Griffith 71. Gattey 53–54. William Leach, *True Love and Perfect Union* (New York: Basic Books, 1980), 256–257.
14. Rachel M. Brownstein, *Becoming a Heroine* (New York: Viking Press, 1982).
15. William L. O'Neill, *Feminism in America,* 2nd rev. ed. (New Brunswick, NJ: Transaction Books, 1989), 20.
16. Kerr 65, 74.
17. Mary P. Ryan, *Womanhood in America* (New York: New Viewpoints, 1979), 259.
18. The ideal I am calling the "Modern Woman," is very close to the "Fashionable" as described by Lois Banner in *American Beauty* 17–27.
19. Sources for Sarah Hale's life: Maurine H. Beasley and Sheila J. Silver, *Taking Their Place* (Lanham, MD: American University Press, 1993). Caroline Bird, *Enterprising Women* (New York: Norton, 1976), 57–66. Isabelle Webb Entrikin, *Sarah Josepha Hale and Godey's Lady's Book* (Philadelphia: University of Pennsylvania, 1946). Ruth E. Finley, *The Lady of Godey's* (Philadelphia: Lippincott, 1931). Sherbrooke Rogers, *Sarah Josepha Hale* (Grantham, NH: Tompson & Rutter, 1985). Helen Woodward, *The Lady Persuaders* (New York: I. Oboloensky, 1960). Richardson Little Wright, *Forgotten Ladies* (Philadelphia: Lippincott, 1928), 187–219.
20. Gloria Steinem, "Sex, Lies, and Advertising," *Ms.* (July/August 1990): 18–27. Quotation on 25.
21. Finley 22. Flexner 65
22. Melder 133.
23. Kerr 79.
24. Wendy Kaminer, "Feminism's Identity Crisis," *Atlantic Monthly* (October 1993): 51–68.
25. Sources on Demorest: Caroline Rennolds Millbank, *New York Fashion* (New York: Abrams, 1989). Ishbel Ross, *Crusades and Crinolines* (New York: Harper & Row, 1963).

26. Valerie Steele, *Corset* (New Haven, CT: Yale University Press, 2001).
27. *Madame Demorest's Mirror of Fashion* (November 1885).
28. Harriet Prescott Spofford, "Evolution of the Hired Girl." *Ladies' Home Journal* (September 1892).
29. O'Neill 47–50. Other sources on Jane Croly: Barbara Belford, *Brilliant Bylines* (New York: Columbia University Press, 1986), 38–43. Mrs. J. C. Croly, *The History of the Woman's Club Movement in America* (New York: Henry G. Allen, 1898). Ross.
30. Belford 43.
31. Ross 100. Croly 23.
32. Sources on Harriet Hubbard Ayer: Margaret Hubbard Ayer and Isabella Taves, *The Three Lives of Harriet Hubbard Ayer* (Philadelphia: Lippincott, 1957). Margaret Hubbard Ayer and Isabella Taves, "The Mystery of Harriet Hubbard Ayer," (three-part series). *McCall's* (September–November 1955).
33. Ayer and Taves (October 1955): 157.
34. John Burke, *Duet in Diamonds* (New York: G. P. Putnam's Sons, 1972), 211–223. Parker Morell, *Lillian Russell* (Garden City, NY: Garden City Publishing, 1943). Amanda Darling, *Lola Montez* (New York: Stein and Day, 1972).
35. Ross 163–164. Belford 115. Budd Leslie Gambee Jr., *Frank Leslie and His Illustrated Newspaper 1855–1860* (Ann Arbor: University of Michigan, 1964), 24. Robert Booth Fowler, *Carrie Chapman Catt* (Boston: Northeastern University Press, 1986), 116–119.
36. Sources specifically on Woodhull: Johanna Johnston, *Mrs. Satan* (New York: G. P. Putnam's Sons, 1967). M. Marion Marberry, *Vicky* (New York, Funk & Wagnalls, 1967). Emanie Sachs, *The Terrible Siren* (New York, Arno Press, 1978). Lois Beachy Underhill, *The Woman Who Ran for President* (Bridgehampton, NY: Bridge Works, 1995).
37. Lutz 211.
38. Johnston 66, 67.
39. Johnston 84, 86, 91.
40. Johnston 86.
41. Kerr 169. Johnston 133. Barry 246
42. Gatty 89.
43. Ross 92. Patricia Marks, *Bicycles, Bangs, and Bloomers* (Lexington, KY: University Press of Kentucky, 1990), 170.

## Chapter 4

1. Charlotte Perkins Gilman, *Women and Economics* (New York: Harper & Row, 1966), 148.
2. Commentaries on the Gibson girl and the "American Girl": Charles Belmont, "Mr. Charles Dana Gibson and His Art," *Critic* 34 (January 1899): 50. J. M. Bulloch, "Charles Dana Gibson," *Studio I* (June 8, 1896): 75–81. Spencer Coon, "Gibson's American Girl," *Metropolitan Magazine* 7 (December 1896): 345–350. Richard Harding Davis, "The Origin of a Type of the American Girl," *Quarterly Illustrator* (January/March 1895): 3–8. Winfield Moody, "Daisy Miller and the Gibson Girl," *Ladies' Home Journal* 21 (September 1904): 17. Frederick Morton, "Charles Dana Gibson, Illustrator," *Brush and Pen* 7 (February 1901): 282–284. Cora Potter, *Beauty and Health* (New York: Paul Elder, 1908), 242–243. Caroline Ticknor, "The Steel-Engraving Lady and the Gibson Girl," *Atlantic Monthly*, LXXXVIII (July 1901): 105–108. Howard Chandler Christy, *The American Girl* (New York: Da Capo Press, 1976). "The Growth of Greatness XIX. Charles Dana Gibson." *Life* (Nov. 7, 1895): 313.
3. Lois Banner, *American Beauty* (Chicago: University of Chicago Press, 1983) 154–174. Patricia Marks, *Bicycles, Bangs, and Bloomers* (Lexington: University Press of Kentucky, 1990). Martha Patterson, "'Survival of the Best Fitted': Selling the American New Woman as Gibson Girl, 1895–1910," *American Transcendental Quarterly* (June 1995): 73–85.
4. In addition to the contemporary commentary and feminist analyses already given sources on Dana Gibson and on the Gibson Girl's history include: "Charles Dana Gibson," *Biographical Sketches of American Artists* (Lansing: Michigan State Library, 1924), 131. Robert Koch, "Gibson Girl Revisited," *Art in America* 53:1 (1965): 70–73. Loring Homes Dodd, *A Generation of Illustrators and*

*Etchers* (Boston: Chapman & Grimes, 1960), 54–64. "Charles Dana Gibson," *The National Cyclopedia of American Biography,* vol. 11, 1901, p. 290. "Charles D. Gibson Dead at Age of 77," *New York Times* (December 24, 1944): 26. Fairfax Downey, *Portrait of an Era* (New York: Scribner's, 1936).

5. The characterization of Gibson's illustrated characters is based on the novels that Gibson illustrated for Richard Harding Davis and Constance Harrison as well as stories published in *Life.* Richard Harding Davis, *The Princess Aline* (New York: Scribners, 1895). Constance C. (Mrs. Burton) Harrison, *The Anglomaniacs* (New York: Arno Press, 1977 [1890]). Constance C. (Mrs. Burton) Harrison, *Sweet Bells Out of Tune* (New York: Scribner's, 1893).
6. *Life* (October 9, 1913): 645.
7. Kate Gannett Wells, "Transitional American Woman," *Atlantic Monthly* (December 1880): 817–823. Anne Warner, "The New Woman and the Old," *Century* (November 1909): 85–92.
8. Coon 345.
9. Christy 24. Finley Peter Dunne, "On the New Woman," *Mr. Dooley in Peace and in War* (Urbana: University of Illinois Press, 1988), 80–82. Finley Peter Dunne, "The Divided Skirt," *In the Hearts of His Countrymen* (Boston: Small, Maynard & Co., 1914), 154–157.
10. "Editorial," *Vogue* 6 (December 12, 1895): 402. Moody 17.
11. Linda Gertner Zatlin, *Aubrey Beardsley and Victorian Sexual Politics* (New York: Oxford University Press, 1990), 84.
12. In addition to the cartoons appearing in old issues of *Life,* I have examined all the available book-length collections of Gibson's drawings including those published at the time and more recently. Two examples: Charles Dana Gibson, *The Best of Charles Dana Gibson* (New York: Bounty Books,1969). Charles Dana Gibson, *The Gibson Book,* vols. 1 & 2 (New York: C. Scribner's Sons, 1907).
13. Ellen Gruber Garvey, "Reframing the Bicycle: Advertising Supported Magazines and Scorching Women," *American Quarterly* 47, 1 (March 1995): 66–101.
14. L. Coy Ludwig, *Maxfield Parrish* (New York: Watson-Guptill Publications,1973). Edna Woolman Chase, *Always in Vogue* (Garden City, NY: Doubleday, 1954), 85–87.
15. Florence Heath, "Ladies How Does Your Figure Correspond with the Measurements of Charmion," *Denver Post* (October 9, 1904): 2
16. Michael Schau, *All-American Girl* (New York: Watson-Guptill, 1975). E. H. Gombrich, *Art and Illusion* (Princeton, NJ: Princeton University Press, 1969).
17. Main sources on vision, enculturation, and learning: E. H. Gombrich, Julian Hochberg, and Max Black, *Art, Perception, and Reality* (Baltimore: Johns Hopkins University Press, 1972). Bill Nichols, *Ideology and the Image* (Bloomington: Indiana University Press, 1981). Ned Block, ed., *Imagery* (Cambridge, Mass: MIT Press, 1981). Lorisa DeLorenzo and Robert John DeLorenzo, *Total Child Care: From Birth to Age Five* (Garden City, NY: Doubleday, 1982).
18. Kenneth Burke, "Literature as Equipment for Living," in *The Philosophy of Literary Form* (Berkeley: University of California Press, 1973), 293–304.
19. Mark Sullivan, *Our Times* (New York: Scribner's, 1926), 195. Banner 170.
20. Inez Haynes Irwin, *Angels and Amazons* (Garden City, NY: Doubleday, 1934), 267–278. [Need footnote on ads.] O'Neill, *Everyone was Brave* 43–45.
21. Ticknor 106, 108.
22. Moody 17.
23. "Notes for Spring," *Vogue* 3 (June 1894): 294. *Vogue* 6 (1895): 187. *Delineator* (April 1890): 275. Ross, *Crusades and Crinolines* 144.
24. Jane Grey Swisshelm in *St. Cloud (Minnesota) Democrat,* November 13, 1865, reprinted in Barbara Bedford, *Brilliant Bylines,* 20–37.
25. Irwin 270.
26. Helen Woodward, *Through Many Windows* (New York: Harper and Brothers, 1926), 119–120, 147–8, 125.
27. Sources on Madame Walker: Deborah Stone, *Madame C. J. Walker* (Englewood Cliffs, NJ: Quercus, 1990). A'Lelia Bundles, "Madam C. J. Walker—Cosmetics Tycoon," *Ms.* (July 1983): 91–94. George S. Schuyler, "Madam C. J. Walker," *The Messenger* 6 (1924): 251–257. Penny Colman,

*Madame C. J. Walker* (Brookfield, CT: Millbrook Press, 1994). Ayana D. Byrd and Lori L. Tharps, *Hair Story: Untangling the Roots of Black Hair in America* (New York: St. Martin's Press, 2001). Della A. Yannuzzi, *Madame C. J. Walker: Self Made Businesswoman* (Berkeley Heights, NJ: Enslow Publishers, 2000). A'Lelia Bundles, *On Her Own Ground* (New York: Scribner, 2001). Kathy Peiss, *Hope in a Jar* (New York: Henry Holt 1998), 61–96.

28. Bethune quoted in Stone 31.
29. Suellen Hoy, *Chasing Dirt* (New York: Oxford University Press, 1995), 89–92, 117–121. Rooks 51–74.
30. Rooks 1–5.
31. Belle Livingstone, *Belle Out of Order* (New York: Holt, 1959), 22, 30.
32. Livingstone 40.
33. Livingstone 40.
34. Brown 127. Livingstone 45, 48.
35. Livingstone 194.
36. Livingstone 41–42, 42.
37. Livingstone 45.
38. Livingstone ix.

## Chapter Five

1. Michael Strange, *Who Tells Me True* (New York: Scribner's, 1940), 122–125.
2. "As Seen by Him," *Vogue* (March 22, 1894): 4. Supplement.
3. "Editorial," *Vogue* (July 11, 1895): 18. "Editorial," *Vogue* (August 15, 1895): 82. "Editorial," *Vogue* (July 18, 1895): 34. "Editorial," *Vogue* (October 3, 1895): 210.
4. As Seen By Him," *Vogue* (January 25, 1894): 6. Caroline Seebohm, *The Man Who Was* Vogue (New York: Viking Press,1982), 46.
5. Main sources on Nast, Edna Woolman Chase, and *Vogue:* Seebohm; Edna Woolman Chase, *Always in Vogue* (Garden City, NY: Doubleday, 1954).
6. "Twenty-two True Stories of Success," *Vogue* (September 1, 1912): 13. Seebohm 120.
7. Seebohm 82. Sources on Mrs. Chase also include: "Edna Woolman Chase," *Current Biography* (1940): 160–161. "Vogue: France Awards the High Priestess of Fashion a Ribbon," *Newsweek* (August 24, 1935): 25–26.
8. Helen Rosen Woodward, *The Lady Persuaders* (New York: I. Oboloensky, 1960), 95.
9. Chase 122.
10. Carmel Snow with Mary Louise Sewell, *The World of Carmel Snow* (New York: McGraw-Hill, 1962), 30. Other sources on Carmel Snow: Calvin Tompkins, "Profile: The World of Carmel Snow," *The New Yorker* (November 7, 1994): 148–158. "Carmel Snow," *International Celebrity Register,* U. S. edition, ed. Cleveland Amory (New York: Celebrity Register Ltd., 1959), 707–708.
11. Strange 122–123.
12. Maorilanda, "The March of the Suffragists," *Vogue* (September 1, 1910): 56.
13. Alfred Allen Lewis and Constance Woodworth, *Miss Elizabeth Arden* (New York: Coward, McCann & Geoghegan, 1972), 60–61. Other sources on Elizabeth Arden: "I Am a Famous Woman in This Industry," *Fortune* 18 (October 1938): 58+. Richard Gehman, "Elizabeth Arden—the Woman," *Cosmopolitan* 140, 6 (June 1956): 68–73. Hambla Bauer, "High Priestess of Beauty," *Saturday Evening Post* 220 (April 24, 1948): 26–27. "Elizabeth Arden," *Current Biography* (New York: H. W. Wilson, 1957), 19–21. Kathy Peiss, *Hope in a Jar* (New York: Henry Holt, 1998), 61–97.
14. Helen Woodward, *It's an Art* (New York: Harcourt, Brace, 1938).
15. Gehman 70–72.
16. Lewis and Woodworth 60–61. "I Am a Famous Woman" 60.
17. Sources on Helena Rubinstein: "Helena Rubinstein," *Current Biography* (New York: H. W. Wilson, 1943), 642. Elaine Brown Keiffer, "Madame Rubinstein," *Life* 11 (July 21, 1941): 36–45. Patrick O'Higgins, *Madame* (New York: Viking Press, 1971). Maxene Fabe, *Beauty Millionaire* (New York: Thomas Y. Crowell, 1972). Also Kathy Peiss's chapter on "Beauty Culture and Women's Commerce."

18. Keiffer 45.
19. Lewis and Woodworth 121–133.
20. William L. O'Neill, *Everyone was Brave* (Chicago: Quadrangle Books, 1969), 110, 114, 73, 142, 111. Karen J. Blair, *The Clubwoman as Feminist.*
21. Nancy Cott, *The Grounding of American Feminism* (New Haven, CT: Yale University Press, 1987).
22. Vincent Vinikas, *Soft Soap, Hard Sell* (Ames: Iowa State University Press, 1992), 13.
23. Sources on the *Ladies' Home Journal* and Edward Bok: Salme Harju Steinberg, *Reformer in the Marketplace* (Baton Rouge: Louisiana State University Press, 1979). John Tebbel and Mary Ellen Zukerman, *The Magazine in America* (New York: Oxford University Press, 1991), 92–107, 170–176. Jan Cohn, *Creating America* (Pittsburgh: University of Pittsburgh Press, 1989). Theodore Peterson, *Magazines in the Twentieth Century* (Urbana: University of Illinois Press, 1956). James Playstead Wood, *The Curtis Magazines* (New York: Ronald Press, 1971). James Playstead Wood, *Magazines in the United States* (New York: Ronald Press, 1949). John Tebbel, *The American Magazine* (New York: Hawthorn Books, 1969). Jennifer Scanlon, *Inarticulate Longings* (New York: Routledge, 1995). Edward Bok, *The Americanization of Edward Bok* (New York: Charles Scribner's Sons, 1930). Mary Ellen Zuckerman, *A History of Popular Women's Magazines in the United States, 1792–1995* (Westport, CT: Greenwood Press, 1998), 1–100.
24. *Pictorial Review* from "Account Histories: *Pictorial Review,*" February 13, 1926. Account Files, Box 1, Folder P, J. Walter Thompson Archive, Duke University Special Collections. Peterson 167. Tebbel 102.
25. In "The Curtain," *McCall's* (June 1919): 80, the editors write "Do you notice how they call us Sir! They always do, and here we are with the largest circulation of any magazine in the country edited solely by women, for women, and they continued to address us, Sir." Inez Haynes Irwin, "The Vamp," *McCall's* (April 1919): 13. Mary Heaton Vorse, "Ma and the World," *McCall's* (April 1919): 8. Mary Heaton Vorse, "Abandoned Lands and Patchwork Quilts," *McCall's* (June 1919): 16.
26. Sources on Helen Resor in addition to the materials in the J. Walter Thompson Archives: Scanlon. Edd Applegate, *The Advertising Men and Women* (Westport, CT: Greenview Press, nd). Stephen Fox, *The Mirror-Makers* (New York: Random House, 1984).
27. Scanlon 169–196. Quote on 176.
28. The source materials for Pond's, except for the ads themselves, come from the J. Walter Thompson Archives at Duke University: "Account Histories: The Pond's Extract Company." J. Walter Thompson Information Center Account Files, Box 4, Chesebrough-Ponds, Inc., 1923, 1926. "Pond's Account History," Account Files.
29. "Account Histories: The Pond's Extract Company," 2.
30. "An Interview with Mrs. O. H. P. Belmont on the Care of the Skin," advertisement for Pond's Cream, *Ladies' Home Journal* (February 1924): 65.
31. "Margot Asquith Writes on Woman's Instinct to Make Herself Attractive," advertisement for Pond's Creams, *Ladies' Home Journal* (May 1927): 51. "Miss Anne Morgan Points the Way to the Business Women of America," advertisement for Pond's Cream, *Woman's Home Companion* (February 1926): 43.
32. Source on saleswomen: Susan Porter Benson, *Counter Cultures* (Urbana: University of Illinois Press, 1988).
33. Eleanor Flexner, *Century of Struggle* (Cambridge, MA: Harvard University Press, 1975), 213–214.
34. O'Neill 16, 17.
35. O'Neill 136–137.
36. Woodward, *Lady Persuaders,* 106
37. Roland Marchand, *Advertising the American Dream* (Berkeley: University of California Press, 1985), 54.
38. Vinikas 13.
39. Mary Louise Williams, "The Negro Working Woman: What She Faces in Making a Living," *The Messenger* 5 (July 1923): 763.
40. Madam F. Madison, "What They Are Wearing," *Half-Century* (April 1917): 7. Madison, "What They Are Wearing," *Half-Century* (October 1916): 7.

41. Inez Haynes Irwin, *The Story of Alice Paul and the National Women's Party* (Fairfax, VA: Denlinger's Publishers, 1964), 256–296, quote on 299.
42. Paula Giddings, *When and Where I Enter* (New York: Morrow, 1984), 85–131. Darlene Clark Hine, Wilma King, and Linda Reed, ed., *"We Specialize in the Wholly Impossible"* (Brooklyn, NY: Carlson, 1995). Jacqueline Jones, *Labor of Love, Labor of Sorrow* (New York: Vintage, 1986). Dorothy Sterling, ed. *We Are Your Sisters* (New York: W. W. Norton, 1984). Cott, 30–31, 69–72.

## CHAPTER 6

1. See especially Sumiko Higashi, "Cinderella vs. Statistics: The Silent Movie Heroine as a Jazz-Age Working Girl," in *Woman's Being, Woman's Place,* ed. Mary Kelley (Boston: Hall, 1979), 109–125.
2. John R. McMahon, "Unspeakable Jazz Must Go!" *Ladies' Home Journal* (December 1921): 34, quotes on 34 and 115. Judge William McAdoo, "The Frightful Pace of Modern Jazz," *Ladies' Home Journal* (October 1927): 22, quote on 152.
3. MacAdoo 152.
4. Mary Ryan, *Womanhood in America* (New York: New Viewpoints, 1975), 253–303. Sara Evans, *Born to Liberty* (New York: Free Press, 1989) 175- 195. Victor Rousseau, "Peggy Roche: Saleslady," *Photoplay* 11, 4 (March 1917): 19–28. Advertisement, *Photoplay* (February 1917): 118.
5. Joseph P. Collins, "Woman's Morality in Transition," *Current History* (October 1927): 33–40.
6. Sources on feminism in this period: William O'Neill, *The Woman Movement* (New York: Barnes & Noble, 1969). Nancy Cott, *The Grounding of American Feminism* (New Haven, CT: Yale University Press, 1987). Eleanor Flexner, *Century of Struggle* (Cambridge, MA: Harvard University Press, 1975).
7. Ellen Carol DuBois and Linda Gordon, "Seeking Ecstasy on the Battlefield: Danger and Pleasure in Nineteenth-century Feminist Sexual Thought," in *Pleasure and Danger,* ed. Carole S. Vance (Boston: Routledge and Kegan Paul, 1984), 41. Ryan 268. Cott 48, 165–167. Robert S. Lynd and Helen Merrell Lynd, *Middletown* (New York: Harcourt Brace, 1929), 123–125. Linda Gordon, *Woman's Body, Woman's Right* (New York: Grossman, 1976), 186–300.
8. Ethel Puffer Howes, "The Meaning of Progress in the Woman Movement," reprinted in O'Neill, *Woman Movement* 196–204.
9. McAdoo 22. Emma Goldman, "The Hypocrisy of Puritanism," in *Red Emma Speaks,* ed. Alix Kates Shulman (New York: Schocken Books, 1982), 150–157, quote on 150–153. Goldman, "Tragedy of Women's Emancipation" 166–167.
10. Carrie Chapman Catt, "Woman Suffrage Only an Episode in Age-Old Movement," *Current History* 27, 1 (October 1927): 1–6. Charlotte Perkins Gilman, "Woman's Achievements Since the Franchise," *Current History* 27, 1 (October 1927): 7–14. Collins 35–36. Martha Bensley Bruère, "The Highway to Woman's Happiness" *Current History* (October 1927): 26–29.
11. Ida M. Tarbell, "The Housework Boycott," *Woman's Home Companion* (February 1916): 20.
12. Winifred Raushenbush, "The Idiot God Fashion," in *Woman's Coming of Age,* ed. Samuel D. Schmalhausen and V. F. Calverton (New York: H. Liveright, 1931), 424–425.
13. "Bachelors—Why? Part 1," *Good Housekeeping* (March 1910): 335–340. Bachelors—Why? Part 2," *Good Housekeeping* (April 1910): 461–465.
14. "Bachelors—Why? Part 1" 340; "Bachelors—Why? Part 2" 462.
15. "Fiancees—Why Not?" *Good Housekeeping* (May 1910): 588–594.
16. Raushenbush 425.
17. Jerry Robinson, *The Comics* (New York: G. P. Putnam's Sons, 1974).
18. Leslie Carbaga, *The Fleischer Story* (New York: DaCapo Press, 1976). "The Betty Boop Collection," video, Republic Pictures, January 20, 1998.
19. Robert Sklar, *Movie-Made America* (New York: Random House, 1975), 18, 90.
20. M. H. Abrams, "Comedy," *A Glossary of Literary Terms,* 6th ed. (New York: Harcourt Brace Jovanovich, 1993), 29. Sklar 105.
21. Helen Duey, "Better Movies Department," *Woman's Home Companion* (December 1916): 24.
22. Marjorie Rosen, *Popcorn Venus* (New York: Coward, McCann & Geoghegan, 1973), 21. Ryan 265.
23. David Stenn, *Clara Bow* (New York: Doubleday, 1988) 35.

24. Biographical sources: William M. Drew, *Speaking of Silents* (Vestal, New York: Vestal Press, 1989). Edward Wagenknecht, *Stars of the Silents* (Metuchen, NJ: Scarecrow Press, 1987). J. G. Ellrod, *Hollywood Greats of the Golden Years* (Jefferson, NC: McFarland & Co., 1989). Anthony Slide, *The Idols of Silence* (New York: A. S. Barnes and Co., 1976). Scott Eyman, *Mary Pickford* (New York: Donald I. Fine, Inc. 1990). Joe Morella and Edward Z. Epstein, *The "It" Girl* (New York: Delacorte Press, 1976). Mary Astor, *My Story: An Autobiography* (Garden City, NY: Doubleday, 1959). Fay Wray, *On the Other Hand* (New York: St. Martin's Press, 1989). Anthony Slide, *The Griffith Actresses* (New York: A. S. Barnes and Co., 1973). James Robert Parish with Gregory W. Mank and Don E. Stanke, *The Hollywood Beauties* (New Rochelle, NY: Arlington House, 1978). Ethan Mordden, *Movie Star* (New York: St. Martin's Press, 1983). Lillian Gish with Ann Pinchot, *The Movies, Mr. Griffith and Me* (Englewood Cliffs, NJ: Prentice-Hall, 1969). Esther Ralston, *Some Day We'll Laugh* (Metuchen, NJ: Scarecrow Press, 1985). Curtis Nunn, *Marguerite Clark* (Fort Worth: Texas Christian University Press, 1981). James Robert Parish, *The Leading Ladies* (New Rochelle, NY: Arlington House, 1977). "A Vamp with a Goulash Name," *Photoplay* (February 1917): 73. David Ragan, *Who's Who in Hollywood, 1900–1976* (New Rochelle, NY: Arlington House, 1976). "Blanche Sweet," *Photoplay* (August 1916): 18. "A Little Lesson in Spanish," *Photoplay* (April 1917): 81. Louise Scher, "A Flower of Japan," *Photoplay* (June 1916): 110–112. "Mabel Taliaferro," *Photoplay* (August 1916): 17. "Plays and Players," *Photoplay* (September 1917): 112. Clare P. Peerler, "The Career of an Opera Star: Geraldine Farrar—A Study," *McCall's* (February 1914): 16. Quote is from Stenn 13.
25. Stella Blum, *Everyday Fashions of the Twenties* (New York: Dover, 1981), 2.
26. "Man Crazy," *Life* (January 12, 1928): 28. Alev Lytle Croutier, *Taking the Waters* (New York: Abbeville Press, 1992), 188.
27. Stephen Fox, *The Mirror-Makers* (New York: Vintage Books, 1985), 86–87. Helen Resor was the author of this campaign according to these sources in the J. Walter Thompson Collection at the J. Hartman Center in Special Collections at Duke University: Howard Henderson, Letter to Mr. I. E. Lambert, April 22, 1940. R. V. Beucus, Letter to Howard Henderson, March 28, 1940. Howard Henderson, Letter to I. E. Lambert. March 28, 1940. R. V. Beucus, Letter Mr. I. E. Lambert, December 16, 1939. Letter to Mrs. Resor from Research Department at J. Walter Thompson, July 11, 1946. Sidney Bernstein, Interview with Henry Flowers, November 1963. Sidney Bernstein and Marianne Keating, Interview with Sam Meek, November 22, 1963. Memo from Research Department dated February 9, 1950, "Re: 'A Skin You Love to Touch.'" Sidney Bernstein, Interview with Mr. James W. Young, November 1963.
28. Fox 81, 86–89. Daniel Pope, *The Making of Modern Advertising* (New York: Basic Books, 1983), 221. Roland Marchand, *Advertising the American Dream* (Berkeley: University of California Press, 1985), 10, 87. Michael Schudson, *Advertising: The Uneasy Persuasion* (New York: Basic Books, 1986), 59.
29. Robert Jay, *The Trade Card in 19th-century America* (Columbia: University of Missouri Press, 1987).
30. Carl N. Degler, "What Ought to Be and What Was: Women's Sexuality in the Nineteenth Century," *The American Historical Review* 79, 5 (December 1974): 1467–1490.
31. Sources on the history of bathing, in addition to Croutier: Georges Vigarello, *Concepts of Cleanliness,* trans. Jean Birrel (New York: Cambridge University Press, 1988). Suellen Hoy, *Chasing Dirt* (New York: Oxford University Press, 1995). May N. Stone, "The Plumbing Paradox: American Attitudes toward Late Nineteenth-Century Domestic Sanitary Arrangements," *Winterthur Portfolio* 14 (Autumn 1979): 283–309.
32. "As Seen By Him," *Vogue* (January 4, 1894): 4. Suzanne Sheldon, "Summer's Beauty Base," *McCall's* (September 1919): 27.
33. Hoy 65 and plate between 86–87, 15. Frank Presbrey, *The History and Development of Advertising* (Garden City, NY: Doubleday, 1929), 426, 427.
34. Presbrey 396.
35. The story of Woodbury, unless otherwise noted, was assembled using the Andrew Jergens files on Woodbury in the J. Walter Thompson Collection at the Hartman Center, Duke University, Durham, North Carolina. The specific files and documents, all from Account Files, Box 12:

Speech by Stanley Resor; "The Story of Woodbury's Facial Soap"; Case Histories—1911, 1929, October 30, 1958; J. Walter Thompson "Consumer Investigation" October 1929; April 12, 1926 Account Histories: The Andrew Jergen's Company—Woodbury's Facial Soap. J. M. Manss, Letter to Stanley Resor dated February 1, 1928.

36. Marchand 52–56.
37. The story of Lux, unless otherwise noted, was assembled using the Lever Brothers files on Lux Toilet Soap in the J. Walter Thompson Collection at the Hartman Center, Duke University, Durham, North Carolina. Specific files and documents: "History of Lux Toilet Soap, 1925–1951." Information Center, Box 3, Lever Brothers—Lux Case History 1923–1973. Information Center, Box 3, Lever Brothers, 1916–1959.
38. "The Story of Woodbury's Facial Soap."
39. DuBois and Gordon 43.
40. See, for example, Higashi, Ryan, and Evans, as well as Carroll Smith-Rosenberg, *Disorderly Conduct* (New York: Knopf, 1985).

## Chapter 7

1. "Revlon after Revson," *Forbes* 116 (September 15, 1975): 26–30, 54. "Merchant of Glamour," *Time* (September 8, 1975): 62. Andrew Tobias, *Fire and Ice* (New York: Morrow, 1976). "Revlon's Revson dies; was demanding ad critic." *Advertising Age* (September 1, 1975): 35.
2. C. C. Concannon, "Drugs and Cosmetics in the Depression," *Drug and Cosmetic Industry* (March 1933): 209–210. Eleanor Gordon and Jean Nerenberg, "Everywoman's Jewelry: Early Plastics and Equality in Fashion," *Journal of Popular Culture* 13 (Spring 1980): 629–644.
3. Louise Armstrong, *We Too Are the People* (New York: Arno Press, 1971) 77.
4. Studs Terkel, *Hard Times* (New York: Pantheon Books, 1970), 387, 420.
5. Susan Ware, *Holding Their Own* (Boston: Twayne Publishers, 1982), p. 33. Other sources about women during the Depression: Lorine Pruette, *Women Workers Through the Depression* (New York: Macmillan, 1934). Winifred D. Wandersee, "The Economics of Middle-Income Family Life: Working Women During the Great Depression," in *Decades of Discontent,* ed. Lois Scharf and Joan M. Jensen (Boston: Northeastern University Press, 1983), 45–58. Armstrong 360.
6. The information on Cutex and much of the information on manicuring practices, as well as other cosmetics usage is from the Northam Warren files in the J. Walter Thompson Archives at Duke University, Durham, NC. Account Histories: Northam Warren Corporation-Cutex, February 23, 1926. Account Files Box 1, Folder W, Northam Warren. Ruth Field, "Extracts from Report, 'Two Week's Selling Experience in Toilet Articles Department at Lord & Taylor,'" December 1923, p. 1, reel 38 of microfilms. Creative Staff Meeting, February 1, 1933, Staff Meetings, Box 5, J. Walter Thompson Collection.
7. Dan Morgan, *Rising in the West* (New York: Knopf, 1992), 55.
8. Joan M. Crouse, *The Homeless Transient in the Great Depression* (New York: State University of New York Press, 1986), 111, 113. Armstrong 162–163.
9. Pruette 46–47.
10. David Matza, "The Disreputable Poor," *Class Status and Power: Social Stratification in Comparative Perspective,* in Reinhard Bendix and Seymour Martin Lipset, eds. (New York: Free Press, 1966), 289–302.
11. Michael Schudson, *Advertising, the Uneasy Persuasion* (New York: Basic Books, 1984), 132.
12. Marcel Mauss, *The Gift,* tr. W. D. Halls (London: Routledge, 1990), 21–29, quote on p. 22. Mary Douglas, "Foreword," in *The Gift,* vii-ix.
13. Elizabeth A. Perkins, "The Consumer Frontier: Household Consumption in Early Kentucky," *Journal of American History* (September 1991): 486–510.
14. Ole Salthe, "Beauty and the Beast" *Independent Woman* (January 1940): 9. Catherine Oglesby, "Women in Cosmetics," *Ladies' Home Journal* (November 1930): 28.
15. "Helene Curtis," *International Directory of Company Histories,* vol. 28, ed. Jay P. Pederson (Detroit, MI: St. James Press, 1999), 183–184. *50 Colorful Years: The Clairol Story,* p. 7, in author's collection. "The Two Mrs. Lauders," *Mirabella* (December 1994): 86.

16. Shirley Abbott, *Womenfolks* (New Haven, CT: Ticknor & Fields, 1983), 168–169.
17. Diane Ackerman, *A Natural History of Love* (New York: Random House, 1994), 195.
18. Ware 21–37. Bolin 296–311.
19. Abbott 158.
20. bell hooks, "Black Is a Woman's Color," in *Bearing Witness,* ed. Henry Louis Gates Jr. (New York: Pantheon, 1991), 338–349.
21. Cutex Account Histories, February 23, 1926, 4, 7. Abbott 155.
22. Hazel Rawson Cades, "Some Call It Nature, Some Call it Art," *Woman's Home Companion* (June 1935): 62.
23. Alfred Allen Lewis and Constance Woodworth, *Miss Elizabeth Arden* (New York: Coward, McCann & Geoghegan, 1972), 61. "Maybelline History," Maybelline historical materials provided by Maybelline, Inc. Mascara ads in *True Story* (February 1923): 113, 126. Yardley of London was offering lipstick, cream rouge, and eye shadow in the *Woman's Home Companion* in April 1938.
24. For mentions of the social biology theory of lipstick as well as the Egyptian theory, see: "Pow! Right on the Kisser" *Washington Post,* Sunday January 5, 1992, F1, F4. Brownmiller 179. Rita Jackaway Freedman, *Beauty Bound* (Lexington, MA: Lexington Books, 1986), 56.
25. "Pow, Right on the Kisser," F4.
26. Carmel Snow with Mary Louise Sewell, *The World of Carmel Snow* (New York: McGraw-Hill,1962), 30.
27. Lucius Beebe, "Glamour: 1937–38 Version," *Mademoiselle* (October 1937): 25. Quotes on l60.
28. Ruth Field, J. Walter Thompson Collection.
29. "Does the Society Woman Wear Painted Nails or Natural?" *Woman's Home Companion* (February 1932): 6. "Do Banker's Wives Wear the Bright Corla Cardinal Ruby Nails?" *Woman's Home Companion* (March 1934): 105. "Do Smart Businesswomen Wear Tinted Nails or Natural?" *Woman's Home Companion* (October 1932): 95.
30. Robert Brain, *The Decorated Body* (New York: Harper & Row, 1979).
31. "Make-up is a Cheap Make-Shift," *Woman's Home Companion* (September 1927): 103. "Must you hide your skin under a concealing coat of cosmetics?" *Woman's Home Companion* (October 1927): 133. "A Painted Face is Digusting," *Woman's Home Companion* (June 1927): 70.
32. Hazel Rawson Cades, "What Smart New York is Wearing on its Face," *Woman's Home Companion* (May 1928): 108. "Manual of Good Looks: On and Off with Makeup," *Woman's Home Companion,* (September 1936): 50.
33. Abbott 171.
34. Tibor Scitovsky, *Human Desire and Economic Satisfaction: Essays on the Frontiers of Economics* (New York: New York University Press, 1986).
35. Armstrong 322–323.
36. Igor Kopytoff, "The Cultural Biography of Things," in *The Social Life of Things,* ed. Arjun Appadurai (New York: Cambridge University Press, 1986), 64–91, quote on 64.
37. Clifford Geertz, *Interpretation of Cultures* (New York: Basic Books, 1973), 412–453.
38. See Snow with Sewell; also Calvin Tompkins, "Profile: The World of Carmel Snow," *New Yorker* (November 7, 1994): 148–158.
39. S. J. Perelman, "Frou-Frou, or the Future of Vertigo," reprinted in *The New Yorker* (November 7, 1994): 246 (first published 1938).
40. Schudson 133.
41. Margaret Culkin Banning, "The Lipstick Mood," *Ladies' Home Journal* (August 1930): 6. Quotes on 6, 7.
42. Banning 7.
43. Banning 7, 99.
44. Banning 101.
45. Armstrong 316.
46. Gayle Rubin, "The Traffic in Women: Notes on the Political Economy of Sex," in *Toward an Anthropology of Women,* ed. Rayna R. Reiter (New York: Monthly Review Press, 1975), 157–209. Peter Farb and George Armelagos, *Consuming Passions: The Anthropology of Eating* (Boston: Houghton Mifflin, 1980).

47. Rubin 173–174. Tobias 59.
48. Armstrong 317, 318.
49. Mihalyi Csikszentmihalyi and Eugene Rochberg-Halton, *The Meaning of Things* (New York: Cambridge University Press, 1981), 11.
50. Abbott 173.
51. Creative Staff Meeting 8, 9, J. Walter Thompson Collection.
52. *The Toilet Goods Association, Inc. Annual Convention—1942. Reports and Addresses* (New York: Toilet Goods Association, Inc.). Office of the Secretary, "Bulletin No. 428 The Toilet Goods Association, Inc.," July 17, 1942. Summary Report of the Activities of the Toilet Goods Association During World War II, July 7, 1950. All these items are in the archives of the History Factory, Washington, D.C.

## CHAPTER 8

1. Stuart Rogers, "How a Publicity Blitz Created the Myth of Subliminal Advertising," *Public Relations Quarterly* (Winter 1992–1993): 12–17.
2. Simone de Beauvoir, *The Second Sex,* H. M. Parshley, trans. (New York: Vintage Books, 1974, first published in 1952) 1, 311–315, 47, 55, 49. Betty Freidan, *The Feminine Mystique* (New York: Dell, 1974, first published in 1963) 97–98, 110–113, 96–97, 109, 95.
3. Beauvoir 313–315.
4. Beauvoir 361. Quotes are on 396 and 375.
5. Laura Mulvey, "Visual Pleasure and Narrative Cinema," in *Popular Television and Film,* ed. Tony Bennet, Susan Boyd-Bowman, Colin Mercer, and Janet Woollcott (London: Open University Press, 1981), 206–215. Teresa Di Lauretis, *Alice Doesn't* (Bloomington: Indiana University Press, 1984).
6. Reviews of *The Second Sex:* George N. Shuster, "Woman," *The Commonweal* (January 23, 1953): 409–410. Wilton M. Krogman, "A First Sexer Tackles 'The Second Sex'" *Chicago Sunday Tribune* (March 1, 1953): 5. Miriam Allen deFord, "A Long, Detailed Inquiry into Why Woman is Still 'The Second Sex'" *San Francisco Chronicle* (February 22, 1953): 20. Clyde Kluckhohn, "The Female of Our Species," *New York Times* (February 22, 1953): 3. Karl A. Menninger, "A SR Panel Takes Aim at "The Second Sex'" *Saturday Review* (February 28, 1953): 26. Patrick Mullahy, "Woman's Place," *The Nation* 176 (February 21, 1953): 171–172. Majorie Grene, "A Nous La Liberté!" *New Republic* 128 (March 9, 1953): 22–23. Margaret Park Redfield, "Review of *The Second Sex,*" *American Journal of Sociology* 56 (November 1953): 269–270. "Lady with a Lance," *Time* (February 23, 1953): 110–111.
7. Sara M. Evans, *Born to Liberty* (New York: Free Press, 1989), 243–261. Landon Jones, *Great Expectations* (New York: Ballantine, 1980), 10–89.
8. Freidan 7, 38. Quote on 69.
9. "1959 Consumer Magazine Report" (New York: Daniel Starch and Staff, 1959): 8–15. "Audiences Reached through Magazine Combinations—1958," based on "The Audiences of Nine Magazines, 1958," (Conducted by Alfred Politz Research, inc. Copyright 1958 by Cowles Magazines) 10–15. *A Study of Seven Publications, Their Audiences and Reading Days* (Copyright by Reader's Digest, 1956). "A Study of Four Media, Their Accumulative and Repeat Audiences, Conducted for Life by Alfred Politz Research, Inc. 1950. "A Study of Duplication," Conducted for *Life* by Alfred Politz Research, 1954. "Consumer Magazine Report," November 1955, by Daniel Starch and Staff, Chicago. Helen Woodward, *The Lady Persuaders* (New York: I. Oboloensky, 1960) 182. (These are reprints or pamphlets. Self-published for—apparently—promotional use.)
10. Linda Scott, "Markets and Audiences" *The History of the Book,* vol. 5, ed. Michael Schudson, Navid Nord, Joan Shelly Rubin (New York: Cambridge University Press, forthcoming).
11. Packard 3.
12. Sigmund Freud, *The Complete Introductory Lectures,* tr. and ed. James Strachey (New York: Norton, 1966), 348–349.
13. Allan Berube, "Marching to a Different Drummer: Lesbian and Gay GIs in World War II," in *Powers of Desire,* ed. Ann Snitow, et al. (New York: Monthly Review Press, 1983), 88–99; quote on 88. John D'Emilio, *Sexual Politics, Sexual Communities* (Chicago: University of Chicago Press, 1983).

14. Barbara Smith, "The Dance of Masks," in *Persistent Desire: A Femme-Butch Reader,* ed. Joan Nestle (Boston: Alyson Publications, 1992), 426–430, quote on 428.
15. Dorothy Allison, "Her Thighs," in *Persistent Desire,* 406–415, quote on 406.
16. Leslie Feinberg, "Butch to Butch: Love Song," in *Persistent Desire,* 80–94, quote on 83.
17. Feinberg 103.
18. Smith 429.
19. U.S. Bureau of the Census, *Statistical Abstracts of United States: 1950,* 71st ed. (Washington, D.C., 1950), 176.
20. Shirley Polykoff, *"Does She . . . or Doesn't She? And How She Did It* (Garden City, NY: Doubleday, 1975), 21–22.
21. Polykoff 21, 22, 27. Leslie Cabarga, *The Fleischer Story* (New York: DaCapo Press, 1988), 10.
22. Polykoff 2.
23. Polykoff 26, 27.
24. Polykoff 28.
25. Polykoff 29, 32.
26. Polykoff 32.
27. Polykoff 33.
28. Polykoff 33.
29. See, for instance, Robin Tolmach Lakoff and Raquel L. Scherr, *Face Value, The Politics of Beauty* (Boston: Routledge & Kegan Paul, 1984).
30. Sources on Dorian Leigh: Dorian Leigh with Laura Hobe, *The Girl Who Had Everything* (Garden City, NY: Doubleday, 1980). Michael Gross, *Model: The Ugly Business of Beautiful Women* (New York: Morrow, 1995). Andrew Tobias, *Fire and Ice: The Story of Charles Revson the Man Who Built the Revlon Empire* (New York: Morrow, 1976).
31. Tobias 122, 123. The note about Kay Daley's salary is under her picture just opposite page 184.
32. Leigh 88–89.
33. Tobias 123.
34. Tobias 124.
35. Joan Didion, "Bosses Make Lousy Lovers," *Saturday Evening Post* (January 30, 1965): 34. "Meat Loaf Anyone?" *Newsweek* (August 31, 1964): 53. Shana Alexander, "Singular Girl's Success," *Life* (March 1, 1963): 60. "What Price the Single Girl?" *Esquire* (October 1964): 108. "Down with Pippypoo," *Newsweek* (July 18, 1966): 60. "New Direction for Cosmopolitan," *Writer* (July 1965): 20. C.Welles, "Helen Gurley Brown Turns Editor," *Life* (November 19, 1965): 65. "Sex and the Editor," *Time* (March 26, 1965): 40. Helen Gurley Brown, *I'm Wild Again* (New York: Warner, 2001). Marcia Cohen, *The Sisterhood: The True Story of the Women Who Changed the World* (New York: Simon and Schuster, 1988), 98–99, 333. "What Price the Single Girl?" *Esquire* (October 1964): 108–109. "Bad Girl," *Psychology Today* 27 (March/April 1996): 22–24. "Sex and the Editor," *Time* (March 26, 1965). "Big Sister," *Time* (February 9, 1968): 60. Harris Dienstfrey, "That Cosmopolitan Girl," *Antioch Review* 61 (Fall 1983): 430–463. Florence King, "Italics in Amber," *National Review* (May 24, 1993): 71. "The Single Girl's Guru," (August 1983): 40. Helen Gurley Brown, *Sex and the Single Girl* (New York: Bernard Geis, 1962). "Helen Gurley Brown: The Original Cosmo Girl," videotape, A&E Television Networks, 1996.
36. "Bad Girl" 70, 71.
37. Dientsfrey 434. "Bad Girl" 24. "Sex and the Editor," *Time.*
38. Jessica Mitford, "Pretty, Lascivious, Undignified," *Vogue* (March 15, 1966): 92–93.
39. Woodward 182. "Big Sister" 60.
40. Beauvoir 371.
41. Janet Saltzman Chafetz and Anthony Gary Dworkin, *Female Revolt: Women's Movements in World and Historical Perspective* (Totowa, NJ: Rowman & Allanheld, 1986).

## Chapter 9

1. Michael Gross, *Model: The Ugly Business of Beautiful Women* (New York: Morrow, 1995), 225.
2. Polly Devlin, "The Penelope Tree," *Vogue* (October 1, 1967): 162–175, quote on 162. Joel Lobenthal, *Radical Rags* (New York: Abbeville Press, 1990), 181.

3. Elizabeth Fox-Genovese, *Feminism Is Not the Story of My Life* (New York: Anchor Books, 1997), 49.
4. Wini Brienes, *Young, White, and Miserable* (Boston: Beacon Press, 1992).
5. Esther Singleton, *Dolls* (New York: Payson & Clarke Ltd., 1927), 47–48. Antonia Fraser, *Dolls* (London: Octopus Books, 1973), 63, 108–109.
6. This story and much of the other information included here on Barbie is from M. G. Lord, *Forever Barbie* (New York: Avon Books, 1994). Other sources on Barbie: Ruth Handler, *Dream Doll* (Stamford, CT: Longmeadow Press, 1994). Kitturah B. Westenhouser, *The Story of Barbie* (Paducah, KY: Collector Books, 1994). Sarah Sink Eames, *Barbie Fashion,* vol. 1, 1959–1967 (Paducah, KY: Collector Books, 1990). Stefanie Deutsch, *Barbie: The First 30 Years: 1959–1989* (Paducah, KY: Collector Books, 1996). Billy Boy, *Barbie: Her Life and Times* (New York: Crown Trade Publications, 1987). Laura Jacobs, *Barbie: What a Doll!* (New York: Abbeville Press, 1994). Gwenda Blair, "Blame It on Barbie," *Self* (December 1993): 124. Mary Frances Rogers, *Barbie Culture* (Thousand Oaks, CA: Sage Publications, 1999). Yona Zeldis McDonough, *The Barbie Chronicles* (New York: Simon & Schuster, 1999).
7. Lord 38–40.
8. For example, Mrs. Harold S. Vanderbilt in the October 1964 issue of *Harper's Bazaar;* Mrs. Angier Biddle Duke in the May 1967 issue and Mrs. Nelson A. Rockefeller in the February 15, 1967, issue of *Vogue.* Marilyn Bender, *The Beautiful People* (New York: Coward-McCann, 1967), 75. Lobenthal 75. Carolyn Milbank, *New York Fashion* (New York: Abrams, 1989). "The Face of the Hour: The Strong Face," *Vogue* (October 1, 1967): 155. "The New Cushing Sisters," *Vogue* (October 1, 1962): 174–175. "Upstaging the Scene in Furs," *Harper's Bazaar* (November 1964): 186–187. "Marilyn Monroe," *Vogue* (September 1, 1962): 190.
9. Lobenthal 9.
10. Bender 193.
11. Lobenthal 58. Bender 55.
12. Lobenthal 24, 92. Millbank 225–226. Bender 186.
13. "A Letter from Gloria Guinness," *Harper's Bazaar* (August 1964): 120–121.
14. "Twiggy: Click! Click!" *Newsweek* (April 10, 1967): 62–66. Other sources on Twiggy: Twiggy, *Twiggy* (New York: Hawthorn Books, 1968) 7, 54, 92, 96, 119, 136. Frank De Caro, "From 60s Icon to 80s Actress," *Newsday* (Oct. 12 1988).
15. Lord 62–63.
16. *Twiggy* 91.
17. Twiggy: Click! Click!" 62, 65. Gross 181. Twiggy 140.
18. Diane Ackerman, *A Natural History of Love* (New York: Random House, 1994), 192.
19. Susan Douglas, *Where the Girls Are* (New York: Times Books, 1994).
20. Twiggy 69.
21. Sources on Vreeland: "Diana Vreeland, Fashion's Formidable First Lady, Set the Styles for Generations." *People* (Sept 11, 1989): 119. Cathleen McGuigan, "The Divine Madame V." *Newsweek* (September 4, 1989): 62. Julia Szabo, "The Empress Diana," *Harper's Bazaar* (December 1993): 45. Amy Fine Collins, "The Cult of Diana," *Vanity Fair* (November 1993): 174–184. Diana Vreeland and Christopher Hemphill, *Allure* (Garden City, NY: Doubleday, 1980). Dodie Kazanjian and Calvin Tomkins, *Alex* (New York: Knopf, 1993). Diana Vreeland, *D.V.* (New York: Random House, 1984). Eleanor Dwight, *Diana Vreeland* (New York: Morrow, 2002). Andre Léon Talley, "Diana Vreeland," *Vogue* (December 1989): 306.
22. Collins 183, 188, 190.
23. Collins 190.
24. Gross 217–218. Collins 212.
25. Gross 218, 225.
26. Twiggy 62–63.
27. Lobenthal 191.
28. Gross 188.
29. Lobenthal 181.
30. "The Girl, The Face, The Shrimp," *Newsweek* (May 10, 1965): 67–70.
31. Bender 151. Devlin 162–175.

32. Twiggy 8–9.
33. Gross 225.
34. Tom Wolfe, "Girl of the Year," *The Sixties,* ed. Gerald Howard (New York: Marlowe & Co., 1995).
35. Wolfe 184, 181. "Three Beauties of Our Time," *Life* (October 1, 1964): 146–147. Bender 74.
36. "Instant Barbra," *Vogue* (March 15, 1966): 69–73. Curtice Taylor, "Follow a Star," *Seventeen* (January 1965): 76.
37. Sondra Henry and Emily Taitz, *One Woman's Power* (Minneapolis, MN: Dillon Press, 1987), 124. Cohen 219. Gloria Steinem, "The Party," *Vogue* (January 15, 1967): 53. Leonard Levitt, "She: The Awesome Power of Gloria Steinem," *Esquire* 76 (October 1971): 202.
38. Bender 40.
39. "Gloria Steinem," *Newsweek (*August 16, 1971): 51–55.
40. Cohen 217, 218, 223–224. Levitt 89, 202.
41. Tom Wolfe, *Radical Chic and Mau-Mauing the Flak Catchers* (New York: Farrar, Straus and Giroux, 1970).
42. Barbara Coffey, "The Woman behind the Cover Girl," *Glamour* (May 1974): 200. Gross 234–239.
43. Diane Ackerman, *A Natural History of Love* (New York: Random House, 1994), 190.
44. Lobenthal 109, 126–127, 125.
45. Lobenthal 109.
46. See, for instance: Robin Tolmach Lakoff and Raquel L. Scherr, *Face Value, The Politics of Beauty* (Boston: Routledge & Kegan Paul, 1984), 14, 7, 146. Susan Brownmiller, *Femininity* (New York: Linden Press, 1984), 67–72. Rita Jackaway Freedman, *Beauty Bound* (Lexington, MA: Lexington Books, 1986), 196–197. Jean Kilbourne, "Beauty . . . and the Beast of Advertising," *Media and Values* (Winter 1989): 8.
47. This chart was produced by counting the images in advertisements appearing in alternating months between 1935 and 1985 (at five year intervals) in *Vogue, Glamour, Mademoiselle,* and the *Ladies' Home Journal.*
48. Dick Huebner, interview, Cover Girl Collection, Modern Advertising History Archives, National Museum of American History, Washington, D.C.
49. Lynn Giordano, interview, Cover Girl Collection, Modern Advertising History Archives, National Museum of American History, Washington, D.C.
50. Gross 254.
51. Gross 253. Talley/
52. McGuigan 62. Collins 189. Gross 254.
53. Unna Stannard, "The Mask of Beauty," in *Woman in Sexist Society,* ed. Vivian Gornick (New York: Times Mirror, 1971), 118–132. Naomi Wolf, *The Beauty Myth* (New York: Doubleday, 1992).
54. Gross 183. "The Fifty Most Beautiful People in the World," *People* (May 5, 1995): 66. Jerene Jones, "Once the Face of the 60s, Jean Shrimpton Is Now the Model of an English Innkeeper," *Time* (June 14, 1982): 117. "Dynamic Duos," *Top Model* (Winter 1995/6): 54–60, 82–84. Christine Fellingham, "The Secret Life of Models," *Glamour* (October 1994): 207.
55. Lucinda Ebersole and Richard Peabody, *Mondo Barbie* (New York: St. Martin's Press, 1993). Craig Yoe, *The Art of Barbie* (New York: Workman Pub. Co., 1994). Billy Boy, *Barbie: Her Life & Times* (New York: Crown, 1992).
56. Wolf 2.
57. Ingeborg Day, "Diana Vreeland: A Velvet Hand in an Iron Glove," *Ms.* (August 1975): 24.

## Chapter 10

1. The histories of the Second Wave used here include: Marcia Cohen, *The Sisterhood* (New York: Simon and Schuster, 1988); the story of the *Ladies' Home Journal* is on 189–194. Susan Brownmiller, *In Our Time* (New York: Delta, 1999); the *LHJ* occupation is on 83–90.
2. Cohen 193.
3. Many claim today that there was little press coverage of the Second Wave or that most coverage ridiculed the movement. My students retrieved every article on "women's lib" cited in the *Readers' Guide to Periodical Literature* from 1969 to 1973. I read all this material. I found it to be serious

and, to a surprising extent, supportive in tone. I had no way of checking the non-print record. However, my assessment of the printed material is consistent with the picture reported by Myrna Blyth's recent account in *Spin Sisters* and with what I remember of the Second Wave broadcast coverage: There was a lot of coverage and it was mostly supportive. Myrna Blyth, *Spin Sisters* (New York: St. Martin's Press, 2004). See www.freshlipstick.com for a bibliographic essay.

4. Cohen 155, 201. "Gloria Steinem," *Newsweek* (August 16, 1971): 52. "Women's Lib: The War on 'Sexism'" *Time* (March 23, 1970): 73.
5. Cohen 135.
6. Cohen 138.
7. 1970 Harris Poll (New York: Louis Harris & Associates, 1970): 446, 457, 458, 460, 464, 465. 1972 Harris Poll (New York: Louis Harris & Associates, 1972): 265. *The 1972 Virginia Slims American Women's Opinion Poll* (New York: Louis Harris & Associates, 1972), 29–30. Gloria Steinem, "Sexual Politics," *Newsweek* (July 10, 1972): 32–33.
8. Lucy Komisar, "The New Feminism, *Saturday Review* (February 21, 1970): 27; quote is on 314. "Liberating Women," *Time* (June 15, 1970): 93.
9. "Amelia Bassin Makes Women's Lib Appeal as She Accepts Adwoman of Year Award," *Advertising Age* (June 29, 1970): 81. Alice E. Courtney and Sarah Wernick Lockeretz, "A Woman's Place: An Analysis of the Roles Portrayed by Women in Magazine Advertisements," *Journal of Marketing Research* 1 (February 1971): 92–95, quote on 93.
10. Rena Bartos, *Moving Target* (New York: Free Press, 1982), 9, 14–17, 39.
11. "What to Wear When You're Doing the Talking: How to Present a Confident Image," *Glamour* (October 1978): 250–251. "For the Girl Who Hasn't Much Time to Think About Fashion," *Glamour* (February 1971): 132–133. John Molloy, *Dress for Success* (New York: Warner Books, 1976). Claudia Jessup and Genie Chipps, "Working for Yourself: Is It for You?" *Glamour* (March 1977): 164. Shari Steiner, "How to Start Doing What You Are Too Scared to Do," *Glamour* (March 1977): 200. "What You Should Know about Business Travel," *Glamour* (October 1978): 196–197. Margaret Hennig and Anne Jardim, *The Managerial Woman* (New York: Pocket Books, 1978). Betty Lehan Harragan, *Games Mother Never Taught You* (New York: Warner, 1977).
12. Liz Smith, "Gloria Steinem, Writer and Social Critic, Talks about Sex, Politics and Marriage," *Redbook* (January 1972): 69, quote on 69. Frances Fitzgerald, "War Without End," *Redbook* (March 1975): 82. "Women at Work: Why We Do the Work We Do," *Redbook* (March 1975): 88. "Survival in the Suburbs," *McCall's* (July 1976): 54. Shana Alexander, "The Feminine Eye," *McCall's* (July 1970): 8. Madeline Costigan, "The Last of the Long Hot Summers, *McCall's* (July 1976): 116–117. Ann O'Shea, "Discrimination Against Policewomen," *McCall*'s (July 1976): 52. Letty Cotton Pogrebin, "Working Woman" *Ladies' Home Journal* (November 1973): 46. Joel Stone, "The Meeting," *Redbook* (March 1975): 93.
13. Anthony West, "Who Takes Advantage of American Women? Men," *Vogue* September (1970): 49. Lorraine Davis, "What Counts," *Vogue* (June 1979): 194. Sally Beauman, "Who's Liberated?" *Vogue* (September 1970): 382.
14. "Where to Find a Women's Lib Group Wherever You Are," *Glamour* (May 1971): 78. Barbara Coffey, "Are You Obsessed with Being Thin?" *Glamour* (March 1977): 110. *Mademoiselle* (October 1978): 180. Judith Coburn, "The Intelligent Woman's Guide to Sex," *Mademoiselle* (October 1978): 110. Barbara Quint, "The Supreme Court Ruling on Pregnancy Benefits: What It Means to You and Other Women," *Glamour (*March 1977): 188. "The Women's Education Equity Act," *Glamour* (May 1974): 56. *Glamour* ran regular ERA updates in "How to Do Anything Better Guide." Example: " ERA Update," October 1978.
15. See, for instance, Marjorie H. Jenkins, "Marlo Thomas," *Ladies' Home Journal* (December 1979): 36.
16. Sandie North, "Reporting the Movement," *Atlantic* (March 1970) Special Issue on "Women Against Men": 106. Cohen 207–210.
17. Cohen 210.
18. Unna Stannard, "The Mask of Beauty," in *Woman in Sexist Society,* ed. Vivian Gornick (New York: Times Mirror, 1971), 188–189, 193.
19. Joyce Carol Oates, "Out of the Machine," *Atlantic* (July 1971): 42–45, quote on 43.

20. Stannard 201. Lillian Faderman, "The Return of Butch and Femme: A Phenomenon in Lesbian Sexuality of the 1980s and 1990s," in *American Sexual Politics* ed. John C. Fout and Maura Shaw Tantill (Chicago: University of Chicago, 1993): 93.
21. "All in the Jeans," *Time* (January 11, 1971): 35. Phyllis Batelle, "The Bra . . . Then and Now!" *Ladies' Home Journal* (October 1969): 20. Cynthia Lindsey, "Whither the Bra," *McCall's* (November 1969): 90. "The Big Let-Down," *Time* (September 1, 1969): 49–50. "Ban the Bra," *Look* (February 24, 1970): 54–57. Judith Ramsey, "The Bosom," *Ladies' Home Journal* (1969): 79.
22. "Who's Come a Long Way, Baby?" *Time* (August 31, 1970): 16–17. Cohen 232–239, 251.
23. "A Day in the Life of Kate Millett," *Mademoiselle* (February 1971): 138. "Shining Reds," *Mademoiselle* (December 1968): 113.
24. Lucy Komisar, "Liberating Women," *Time* (June 15, 1970): 93. Lucy Komisar, "The Image of Woman in Advertising," in *Woman in Sexist Society*, ed. Vivian Gornick (New York: New American Library, 1971), 304–317. Elizabeth Cagan, "The Selling of the Women's Movement," *Social Policy* (May/June 1978): 5–12.
25. A Redstocking Sister, "Consumerism and Women," in *Women in Sexist Society*, 658.
26. 1970 Louis Harris Poll, 458.
27. "Gloria Steinem" 51.
28. Leonard Levitt, "She: The Awesome Power of Gloria Steinem," *Esquire* 76 (October 1971): 214.
29. Cohen 226.
30. Levitt 87, 210. Cohen 332, 334. Nora Ephron, "Women," *Esquire* (November 1972): 10.
31. "Gloria Steinem," 51. Smith 72.
32. Smith 72.
33. Cohen 261–265, 288–304, quote on 291. Jordan Bonfante, "The Feminist Even Men Like," *Life* (May 7, 1971): 30, quote on 32.
34. Bonfante 30.
35. Cohen 324–330.
36. Cohen 336, 96.
37. Valerie Harper appeared on the May 1978 cover. The hairy-chested young man is on April 1978's cover.
38. Harriet Lyons and Rebecca Rosenblatt, "Body Hair: The Last Frontier," *Ms.* (July 1972): 64. Marcia Tucker, "Pssst! Wanna See My Tattoo . . ." *Ms.* (April 1976): 29–33. For instance, Judith Thurman, "How to Get Dressed and Still be Yourself: Breaking through the Politics of Style," *Ms.* (April 1979): 49.
39. Vivian Cadden, "Women's Lib? I've Seen It on TV," *McCalls'* (February 1972): 89, quote on 96.
40. Marabel Morgan, *The Total Woman* (Old Tappan, NJ: F. H. Revell, 1973). D. Keith Mano, "The Gimlet Eye," *National Review* (April 25, 1975): 457. Joyce Maynard, "The Liberation of the Total Woman," *New York Times Magazine* (Sept. 28, 1975): 9, quote on 48.
41. "Marabel and Charlie Morgan: Being a 'Total Woman' May Mean Love Under the Dinner Table," *People* (April 7, 1975): 44–46. "The New Housewife Blues," *Time* (March 14 1977): 62–70. Barbara Grizzuti Harrison, "The Books That Teach Wives to Be Submissive," *McCall's* (June 1975): 83. "An Old-Fashioned Girl," *Newsweek* (June 24, 1974): 75. Marabel Morgan, "Total Joy!" *Good Housekeeping* (November 1976): 111.
42. "New Housewife Blues" 65. "Old Fashioned Girl" 75. Maynard 48.
43. See note 40.
44. Maynard 61.
45. Susan Brownmiller, *Femininity* (New York: Linden Press, 1984) 160.
46. Karen S. Kendler, "All Kinds of Turn-Ons," (Letters), *New York Times Magazine* (October 18, 1975): 64. Carol Gehrhardt, "Marital Bliss" (Letters), *New York Times Magazine* (October 18, 1975): 67.
47. Gloria Steinem, "We Need a Woman President in 1976," *Look* (January 13, 1970): 53. Eugene Boe, "I Want to Come Back as a New Woman," *New Woman* (February1972): 69, quote on 71.
48. Helen Gurley Brown, "What It Will Be Like When We Elect a Woman President," *Today's Health* (July 1971): 27.
49. "New Housewife Blues," 63. George F. Will, "The Cold War Among Women," *Newsweek* (June 26, 1978): 100.

50. Sally Kempton, "Cutting Loose: A Private View of Women's Uprising," *Esquire* (July 1970): 53.
51. Susan Fraker with Elaine Sciolino, "A Kitchen Crusader," *Time* (July 25, 1977): 35. Morton Kondracke, "End of an ERA?" *New Republic* (April 30, 1977): 14–15, quote on 15. The differences in press treatment regarding "women's lib" in general and Gloria Steinem, Marabel Morgan, and Phyllis Schlafly were also interesting. Gloria Steinem's coverage, except for Levitt at *Esquire,* all reads like fan mail. Marabel Morgan is mostly made to look silly. Schlafly's coverage is pretty uniformly negative, sometimes vituperative. I was surprised that one of the most negative articles on Schlafly appeared in the *Christian Century:* James M. Wall, "The Gospel According to Schlafly," *Christian Century* (April 11, 1979): 395–396.
52. Marilyn Mercer, "ERA: What Would It Really Mean?" *McCall's* (July 1976) p.107+.
53. Ibid.
54. "Women versus Women," *Newsweek* (July 25, 1977): 34–35.
55. Kondrake 14. Nancy Seifer, *Absent from the Majority: Working Class Women in America* (The American Jewish Committee, National Project on Ethnic America, 1973), 59, 58.
56. Seifer 57.

## Chapter 11

1. M. G. Lord, *Forever Barbie* (New York: Avon Books, 1994), 7, 124–128, quote on 125.
2. Lord 125, 127.
3. Lord 125,128, 117–118
4. M. G. Lord, "I'm Ready for My Close-Up, Miss Winfrey," *Elle* (November 30, 1195): 164.
5. For just a few examples of the effort to "negotiate" what the correct feminist politics should be, see: Carol Stabile, "Postmodernism and Marx: Notes from the Abyss," *Monthly Review* (July-August 1995): 89–107. Susan Haack, *Manifesto of a Passionate Moderate* (Chicago: University of Chicago Press, 1998). Sandra Kemp and Judith Squires, *Feminisms* (New York: Oxford University Press, 1997). Alison M. Jaggar and Paula S. Rothenberg, *Feminist Frameworks* (New York: McGraw-Hill, 1984). Judith Butler and Joan W. Scott, *Feminists Theorize the Political* (New York: Routledge, 1992). Jennifer Wicke, "Celebrity Material," *South Atlantic Quarterly* 93 (4): 751–778.
6. Jeanine C. Cogan and Joanie M. Erickson, *Lesbians, Levis and Lipstick* (Binghamton, NY: Harrington Park Press, 1999). Ayan D. Byrd and Lori L. Tharps, *Hair Story* (New York: St. Martin's Press, 2001). Noliwe M. Rooks, *Hair Raising* (New Brunswick, NJ: Rutgers University Press, 1996). Della A. Yannuzzi, *Madame C. J. Walker* (Berkeley Heights, NJ: Enslow Publishers, 2000). A'Lelia Bundles, *On Her Own Ground* (New York: Scribner, 2001).
7. Naomi Wolf, *The Beauty Myth* (New York: Doubleday, 1992). Susan Faludi, *Backlash* (New York: Crown, 1991). Mary Bray Pipher, *Reviving Ophelia* (New York: Putnam, 1994). Susan Bordo, *Unbearable Weight* (Berkeley: University of California Press, 1993). Kathy Lee Peiss, *Hope in a Jar* (New York: Metropolitan Books, 1998). Lois W. Banner, *American Beauty* (Chicago: University of Chicago Press, 1983). Joan Jacobs Brumberg, *The Body Project* (New York: Random House, 1997). Ophira Edut, *Adiós, Barbie* (Seattle, WA: Seal Press, 2000). Sara Halprin, *"Look at My Ugly Face!"* (New York: Viking, 1995). Nancy Friday, *The Power of Beauty* (London: Hutchinson, 1996). Karen Lee-Thorp and Cynthia Hicks, *Why Beauty Matters* (Colorado Springs, CO: NavPress, 1997). Debra L. Gimlin, *Bodywork* (Berkeley: University of California Press, 2002). Susan Brownmiller, Femininity (New York: Linden Press, 1984). Peggy Orenstein, *Schoolgirls* (New York: Doubleday, 1994). Susie Orbach, *Fat is a Feminist Issue* (New York: Berkley, 1980).
8. Rogers Worthington, "Colleges Battle for Sexes Becoming Gender Neutral," *Chicago Tribune* (February 4, 1997): 1. E-mail communication with Bridget Jamieson, who forwarded a memo from Barbara Huffman. Saturday, September 7, 2002, 12:36 P.M.
9. Tad Friend, "Yes," *Esquire* (February 1994): 48–56. Wicke 763–765.
10. If you choose to view the book details offered on Amazon.com, then zoom in at least once on the cover; you can read a small legend disclosing that *Can't Buy Me Love* was originally published as *Deadly Persuasion.* There is no way—that I could find—to tell that these two books are the same by the information offered at Barnes & Noble.com

11. Ellen Zetzel Lambert, *The Face of Love* (Boston: Beacon Press, 1995). Karen Lehrman, *The Lipstick Proviso* (New York: Anchor Books, 1997). Christina Hoff Sommers, *Who Stole Feminism?* (New York: Simon & Schuster, 1994). Elizabeth Fox-Genovese, *Feminism Is Not the Story of My Life* (New York: Anchor Books, 1996). Susan Faludi, "I'm Not a Feminist, But I Play One on TV," *Ms.* (March/April 1993): 33.
12. Diane Barthel, *Putting on Appearances* (Philadelphia: Temple University Press, 1988).
13. Jean Kilbourne, *Killing Us Softly,* videotape (Cambridge: Cambridge Documentary Films, 1979).
14. Judith Williamson, *Decoding Advertisements* (London: Marion Boyars, 1978).
15. Rita Jackaway Freedman, *Beauty Bound* (Lexington, MA Lexington Books, 1986), 27. Barthel 51.
16. Barthel 33, 39–40. Wolf 70.
17. Linda Busby and Greg Leichty, "Feminism and Advertising in Traditional and Nontraditional Women's Magazines, 1950s–1980s," *Journalism Quarterly* 70/2 (1993): 247–264. Joanne Entwistle, "Power Dressing and the Fashioning of the Career Woman," in *Buy This Book,* ed. M. Nava, I. MacRury, A. Blake, and B. Richards (London: Routledge, 1997), 312–314.
18. Shannon Brownlee, "The Importance of Being First," *Working Woman* (November/December 1996): 22. Diane Furchtgott-Roth and Christine Stolba, *Women's Figures* (Arlington, VA: AEI, 1999). Matt Towery, *Powerchicks* (New York: Longstreet, 1998).
19. Furchtgott-Roth 37. Leonie Huddy, Francis K. Neely, Marilyn R. Lafay, "The Polls—Trends: Support for the Women's Movement," *Public Opinion Quarterly* 64 (2000): 309–350.
20. Entwhistle 314.
21. Elizabeth Cagan, "The Selling of the Women's Movement," *Social Policy* (May/June 1978): 5–12, quote on 10.
22. Brownmiller 158. Freedman 53.
23. Brownmiller 100.
24. See, e.g., Edut, *Adiós Barbie.*
25. Katie Roiphe, *The Morning After* (Boston: Little, Brown, 1993). Rene Denfeld, *The New Victorians* (New York: Warner Books, 1995). Julie Craig, "I Can't Believe It's Not Feminism," *Bitch,* no. 16 (Spring 2002): 36–43, quote on 43.
26. Jennifer Baumgardner and Amy Richards, *Manifesta* (New York: Farrar, Straus and Giroux, 2000).
27. Huddy, et al. Furchtgott-Roth 14–15.
28. Kendrick and Lazier, 206.
29. One of the first feminist works to come from economics, for instance, did not appear until 1993: Marianne A. Ferber and Julie A. Nelson, *Beyond Economic Man* (Chicago: University of Chicago Press, 1993).

## CHAPTER 12

1. Angela Fisher, *Africa Adorned* (New York: Abrams, 1984), 48–51. See also Carol Beckwith and Angela Fisher, *African Ceremonies* (New York: Abrams, 1999).
2. Enid Schildkrout, quoted in Michael D. Lemonick, "Body Art," *Time* (November 29, 1999), 71.
3. Susan Bordo, *Unbearable Weight: Feminism, Western Culture, and the Body* (Berkeley: University of California Press, 1993), 218.

# Index

Key concepts and arguments: